FREDERICK W. D

D0450739

MULTIPURPOSE TOOLS FOR BIBLE STUDY

REVISED AND EXPANDED EDITION

FORTRESS PRESS
MINNEAPOLIS

BS
511.2
.D355
1993

MULTIPURPOSE TOOLS FOR BIBLE STUDY
Revised and Expanded Edition

Copyright © 1993 Augsburg Fortress. All rights reserved. Except for brief quotations in critical articles or reviews, no part of this book may be reproduced in any manner without prior written permission from the publisher. Write to: Permissions, Augsburg Fortress, 426 S. Fifth St., Box 1209, Minneapolis, MN 55440.

Scripture quotations, unless otherwise noted, are from the New Revised Standard Version Bible, copyright © 1989 by the Division of Christian Education of the National Council of Churches of Christ in the United States of America. Used with permission.

Interior design: The HK Scriptorium, Inc.
Cover design: McCormick Creative
Cover photo: Cheryl Walsh Bellville
Special thanks to Luther Northwestern Theological Seminary, St. Paul, Minnesota, and curator Terrance L. Dinovo, for use of its Rare Books Room in the cover photography.

Library of Congress Cataloging-in-Publication Data

Danker, Frederick W.
  Multipurpose tools for Bible study / Frederick W. Danker. — Rev. and expanded ed.
    p.   cm.
  Includes bibliographical references and indexes.
  ISBN 0-8006-2598-6 (alk. paper)
  1. Bible—Criticism, interpretation, etc.   2. Bible—Bibliography.
I. Title.
BS511.2.D355   1993
220'.07—dc20   93-14303
                                                                 CIP

The paper used in this publication meets the minimum requirements of American National Standard for Information Sciences—Permanence of Paper for Printed Library Materials, ANSI Z329.49-1984.   ∞

Manufactured in the U.S.A.   AF 1-2598

97   96   95   94   93   1   2   3   4   5   6   7   8   9   10

To the best commentary on Proverbs 31:10–31

CONCORDIA COLLEGE LIBRARY
2811 NE HOLMAN ST.
PORTLAND, OR 97211-6099

CONTENTS

v

ABBREVIATIONS

WORKS CITED

This list includes only those abbreviations and short titles that are not identified in full in the immediate context and accompanying notes, For further details and discussion see the page(s) cited at the end of many of the entries.

AB   Anchor Bible (p. 288)

ABD   D. N. Freedman (ed.), *Anchor Bible Dictionary* (pp. 150–51)

AJSL   *American Journal of Semitic Languages and Literature*

ANRW   *Aufstieg und Niedergang der römischen Welt*

BA   *Biblical Archaeologist*

BAAR   W. Bauer, K. Aland, B. Aland, V. Reichmann, *Wörterbuch zum neuen Testament* (pp. 119–20)

BAG   W. Bauer, W. F. Arndt, F. W. Gingrich, *A Greek-English Lexicon of the New Testament and Other Early Christian Literature* (1957) (pp. 117–19)

BAGD   W. Bauer, W. F. Arndt, F. W. Gingrich, F. W. Danker, *A Greek-English Lexicon of the New Testament and Other Early Christian Literature*, a revision of BAG (1979) (pp. 119–20)

BAR   *Biblical Archaeology Review*

BD   F. Blass, *Grammatik des neutestamentlichen Griechisch*, 9th ed. A. Debrunner (1954) (p. 115)

BDF   F. Blass, A. Debrunner. *A Greek Grammar of the New Testament and Other Early Christian Literature*, trans. and ed. R. Funk (1961) (pp. 115–16)

BDB   F. Brown, S. R. Driver, and C. A. Briggs, *A Hebrew and English Lexicon of the Old Testament* (p. 96)

BHK   R. Kittel, *Biblia hebraica* (pp. 44–45)

BHS   *Biblia hebraica stuttgartensia* (p. 45)

BR   *Bible Review*

CCD   Confraternity of Christian Doctrine edition of the Bible (p. 190)

CE   *New Catholic Encyclopedia*

CPJ   *Corpus papyrorum judaicarum* (p. 254)

CQR   *Church Quarterly Review*

CRINT   Compendia Rerum Iudaicarum ad Novum Testamentum

CSCO   Corpus scriptorum christianorum orientalium

CTM   *Concordia Theological Monthly*

Danker, *Benefactor*   F. Danker, *Benefactor: Epigraphic Study* (p. 267)

Danker, *Century*   F. Danker, *A Century of Greco-Roman Philology* (p. 252)

DCG   J. B. Green, S. McKnight, I. Howard

Marshall, *Dictionary of Jesus and the Gospels* (p. 153)

EncRel   The Encyclopedia of Religion (p. 157)

Eus, *HE*   Eusebius of Caesarea, *Historia ecclesiastica*

Gdsp   E. J. Goodspeed,

Hatch and Redpath   E. Hatch, and H. Redpath, *A Concordance to the Septuagint* (pp. 5–6)

HAT   Handbuch zum Alten Testament (p. 295).

HDB   *Dictionary of the Bible*, ed. J. Hastings; rev. ed. F. C. Grant, and H. H. Rowley (p. 152)

HDCG   J. Hastings, et al. *A Dictionary of Christ and the Gospels* (p. 153)

HTR   *Harvard Theological Review*

ISBE   *International Standard Bible Encyclopaedia*, rev. ed. (pp. 150–51)

JE   *The Jewish Encyclopedia.* (p. 155)

JBL   *Journal of Biblical Literature*

JJS   *Journal of Jewish Studies*

JNES   *Journal of Near Eastern Studies*

JQR   *Jewish Quarterly Review*

JSS   *Journal of Semitic Studies*

KJV   King James Version of the Bible (pp. 180–81)

Koehler-Baumgartner   Ludwig Koehler, Walter Baumgartner, *Lexicon in veteris testamenti libros* (p. 97)

LSJM   H. G. Liddell, R. Scott, H. S. Jones, with R. McKenzie, *A Greek-English Lexicon* (pp. 122–23)

LXX   Septuagint Version of the Old Testament, Standard students' edition: A. Rahlfs, ed., *Septuagint* (p. 73)

M'Clintock-Strong   J. M'Clintock, J. Strong, *Cyclopaedia of Biblical, Theological, and Ecclesiastical Literature* (p. 156)

Metzger, *Text.*   B. M. Metzger, *The Text of the New Testament* (p. 22)

Mikra.   M. J. Mulder, ed., *Mikra: Text, Translation, Reading and Interpretation of the Hebrew Bible in Ancient Judaism and Early Christianity*, CRINT 2/1. Philadelphia: Fortress Press, 1988.

MM   J. H. Moulton, G. Milligan, *The Vocabulary of the Greek Testament* (p. 117)

MT   Masoretic Text

NAB   New American Bible (p. 190)

NEB   New English Bible. (pp. 192–93)

NRSV   New Revised Standard Version (pp. 182–87)

NIV   New International Version (p. 194)

NTS   *New Testament Studies*

OCD   *Oxford Classical Dictionary* (p. 159)

OGIS   *Orientis graeci inscriptiones selectae* (p. 261)

OLZ   *Orientalische Literaturzeitung*

Or   *Orientalia*

PG   J. P. Migne, ed. *Patrologiae cursus completus. Series graeca.* 162 vols. Paris, 1857–1866.

PG   J. P. Migne, ed. *Patrologiae cursus completus. Series latina.* 221 vols. Paris, 1844–1864.

RAC   *Reallexikon für Antike und Christentum* (p. 159)

REB   Revised English Bible. (p. 193)

RGG³   *Religion in Geschichte und Gegenwart*, 3d ed. (pp. 156–57)

RSV   Revised Standard Version (pp. 182–87)

RV   English Revised Version of the Bible, 1881–1883 (pp. 181–82)

SBLSCS   Society of Biblical Literature Septuagint and Cognate Studies

SIG   *Sylloge inscriptionum graecarum* (pp. 260–61)

SOTS   Society for Old Testament Studies

Str-B   H. Strack, P. Billerbeck, *Kommentar zum Neuen Testament* (p. 219)

TDNT   G. Kittel, G. Friedrich, eds., *Theological Dictionary of the New Testament* (p. 121)

TEV   Today's English Version

TLZ   *Theologische Literaturzeitung*

TRu   *Theologische Rundschau*

TWNT   *Theologisches Wörterbuch zum Neuen Testament*

UBSGNT   *United Bible Societies Greek New Testament* (p. 23)

UBS   United Bible Societies

UJE I. Landman, ed., *The Universal Jewish Encyclopedia* (p. 155)

UT C. H. Gordon, *Ugaritic Textbook* (pp. 100–101)

Vg Vulgate

VKGNT K. Aland, ed., *Vollständige Konkordanz zum griechischen Neuen Testament* (pp. 7–8)

VT *Vetus Testamentum*

Tov, *Textual Criticism* E. Tov, *Textual Criticism of the Hebrew Bible* (p. 46)

Waldman, *Recent Study* N. M. Waldmann, *The Recent Study of Hebrew: A Survey of the Recent Literature with Selected Bibliography* (p. 46)

Würthwein E. Würthwein, *The Text of the Old Testament* (p. 46)

ZAW *Zeitschrift für die alttestamentliche Wissenschaft*

ZNW *Zeitschrift für die neutestamentliche Wissenschaft*

PREFACE

Since the first edition of *Multipurpose Tools for Bible Study* (*MTBS*; St. Louis: Concordia Publishing House, 1960), a veritable explosion of data and demolition of cherished institutions of the mind have changed forever the way we assess the past and its demands on our attention. Following the example of the masoretes, I filled the margins of the second (1966) and third (1970) editions with notices of new discoveries and their challenges to scholars. But the tide was unrelenting, and it became obvious that a thorough revision was demanded, not only to incorporate new developments but to meet the challenge of a generation of students faced with inundation of the past. To all intents and purposes, therefore, the present work is a new edition.

This book grew out of classroom experience and demand for a textbook that would aid students in the selection of basic resources for biblical study and at the same time provide some guidance in the use of such tools. Beyond the classroom, the book served as a refresher course for ministers, and it provided specialists a shortcut to information beyond their own areas of research. These practical objectives remained undiminished in the preparation of the present edition.

The historical discussions are not designed to satisfy mere antiquarian curiosity. To ignore the contributions of those who have gone before is base ingratitude. Sad to say, arrogance is no stranger to our craft, and to imbue students with incivility promotes demeaning of our enterprise. The truth is that the future will declare us all myopic. To understand the lineage of a book is to appreciate better its character and function. To that end, the Index of Names functions as a multipurpose tool. Moreover, libraries frequently shelve only one copy of a given title. This means that newer titles will be in great demand. It is all the more important, therefore, that students receive guidance to aging books of quality as aids to study, especially of an assigned topic. It will also be observed that reprints of interpreters' classics continue to flood the book mart. Frequently they contain no indication of the original date of publication: an unwary purchaser may think that Matthew Henry wrote only fifty years ago instead of before the Revolutionary War; or that it makes no difference what edition of Gesenius one buys, if only the binding is new.

In most of the chapters a discussion on the use of the aids treated follows the bibliographic presentation. Professional scholars will, of course, not require such guidance, but undergraduates have repeatedly expressed appreciation for the time they have saved in learning quickly how to make the best use, for instance, of the many resources in their Hebrew Bible and their Nestle Greek New Testament.

When Queen Elizabeth was crowned in Westminster Abbey, prior to the beginning of the Communion service a copy of the Bible was presented to her with these words:

> Our Gracious Queen: To keep Your Majesty ever mindful of the Law and the Gospel of God as the rule for the whole life and government of Christian princes, we present you with this Book, the most valuable thing that the world affords. Here is wisdom; this is the royal law; these are the lively oracles of God.

Such a book the interpreter is privileged to expound. Shortcuts, slipshod methods, or recourse to second-rate merchandise are not for one who moves in such exalted company. Students may rest assured that in the pages of the present work they will encounter the best of the world's scholars and the prime fruits of their endeavors. At the same time, while meeting the needs of professional workers, I have kept the general reader in mind. Teachers and ministers are frequently asked what books they can recommend to their publics. Again, they have here direction to useful and helpful books.

Unless otherwise indicated, the translations of biblical texts and other material are my own. The abbreviations accompanying many of the titles are included primarily as a practical measure to facilitate reference in student projects. They also facilitate reference in the immediate context, in which case I did not consider it necessary to record all of them in the list of abbreviations, except when used in other chapters. The same applies to short titles within a chapter and its notes.

No special effort is made to alert readers to reprints or paperbound editions; those who handle books with care and are economy minded may wish to check current lists before purchase or call the publisher's customer-service department. In some cases students will note a discrepancy between my date for a book and one found in another work. Except in instances where I must bear responsibility for error (and I hope that I will be honored with a correction), the cause is frequently traceable to reprinting of unrevised editions. Also, after appearing in fascicles, a book ordinarily shows the date of the completed publication, but some accessioned books include the title pages of the fascicles. Sometimes works first published in two or more volumes come out in one volume. A reviewer once charged me with negligence in citing two volumes for a well-known Greek-English lexicon. He happened to have it on his shelf in a later reprint, a one-volume edition. In this book I frequently cite the first occurrence of a work, with notice of later editions, if any.

In the earlier editions of this work I included a list of commentaries on individual books of the Bible. The current proliferation of commentaries precludes such a format. I have therefore provided more detailed information in connection with description of commentary series.

As was my custom in the earlier editions, I have tried to avoid such descriptions as "liberal" and "conservative." When one or the other or a similar term occurs, it is in a quotation derived from the book under discussion. Biblical scholarship is now, as never before, in the public square, and scholarly literature must rise or fall on its merits. Moreover, one of the purposes of this book is to encourage development of independent, objective scholarly judgment without prejudicial admonitions that may deter investigation of the facts or sanctify what Eugene Nida has called "hallowed falsehood." In keeping with the same principles, I have avoided denominational terminology, except when the books themselves invite it, or praise for exceptional performance is due.

Canonical criticism, rhetorical criticism, reader-response criticism, narrative criticism, and many other varieties of literary-critical approaches are subjects for a separate comprehensive hermeneutical inquiry, a task that needs doing before biblical study becomes hopelessly divided between diachronic and synchronic approaches. Fulfillment of such an enterprise would complement the services provided in this book. Some direction to current discussions of these and related matters is provided especially in chapter 14.

I owe thanks to numerous libraries and will say so with copies of this book. For advice from many colleagues I am exceedingly grateful. Paul J. Kobelski and his colleagues at the HK Scriptorium, Denver, Colorado, not only ensured expeditious production of *MTBS,* but have left on it the imprint of their knowledge and the dedication of their craft to excellence. I salute both them and the staff at Fortress Press for welcome contributions to this enterprise. To Professor Paul R. Raabe, I am especially in debt for counsel relating to matters treated in chapters 3 and 6. To all who used earlier editions of this book, I express my appreciation. May my obligations abound in the future.

F. W. D.

CHAPTER ONE

Concordances

THE PUBLICATION in 1957 of Nelson's *Complete Concordance of the Revised Standard Version Bible* (Nashville/New York: Nelson) focused attention on biblical concordances in general as necessary tools for vital interpretation. This chapter presents a brief historical survey and answers in some small measure questions frequently asked by students: What is a good concordance? How can I use a concordance profitably?

Dr. Samuel Johnson defined a concordance as "a book which shows in how many texts of scripture any word occurs." Few will be satisfied with the purely quantitative evaluation suggested by this definition, but it does emphasize the formal aspects. Originally the word was employed in medieval Latin in the plural *concordantiae,* that is, groups of parallel passages, each group being a *concordantia*.[1]

At the outset it is important to understand that publishers occasionally display some semantic elasticity in hawking their concordance wares. The three principal terms are "analytical," "exhaustive," and "complete." An "analytical" concordance is one in which the words of the translated Bible are presented alphabetically, with passages in which each term occurs being apportioned under the respective Hebrew, Latin (in the case of certain deuterocanonical texts), or Greek words underlying the term. An "exhaustive" concordance is one that lists passages in sequence under a headword, without classifying under the various original terms, and in some way accounts for every occurrence of a word in the translation, including the word "if" and other frequently used conjunctions, relatives, and particles. A "complete" concordance is one in which every word is cited and at least one passage is indicated for a word, as is the case especially for words that occur hundreds or thousands of times. When

---

[1] On the history of this and parallel terms applied to concordances, see Karl H. Bruder, *ΤΑΜΙΕΙΟΝ ΤΩΝ ΤΗΣ ΚΑΙΝΗΣ ΔΙΑΘΗΚΗΣ ΛΕΞΕΩΝ sive Concordantiae omnium vocum Novi Testamenti Graeci,* 4th ed. (Leipzig, 1888), xii n. 7.

1

in doubt, read the preface. In the case of reprints that lack detailed editorial information, *caveat emptor,* "buyer beware."

CONCORDANCES
OF THE LATIN AND SYRIAC BIBLE

The first use of the term "concordance" in connection with an organized list is usually associated with Antony of Padua (d. 1231), who formed his *Concordantiae morales* — not strictly a biblical concordance — from the Latin Vulgate, but it was Hugo de Santo Caro (his name is found in various forms) who really broke the ground with an index to the Vulgate completed under his direction with the help of three hundred to five hundred monks in 1230.[2] In lieu of verse divisions Cardinal Hugo divided each chapter into seven equal parts marked with the letters of the alphabet. But his concordance was of little service because it merely listed references instead of giving the relevant quotations. Three English Dominicans remedied this deficiency in 1250–1252, and François Pascal Dutripon, *Concordantiae bibliorum sacrorum Vulgatae editionis* (Paris, 1838), 7th ed. (1880), marks the climax of early efforts to make the contents of the Latin Vulgate generally accessible. For modern study of the Vulgate one can use Boniface Fischer's *Novae concordantiae bibliorum sacrorum iuxta Vulgatam versionem critice editum,* 5 vols. (Stuttgart/Bad Cannstatt: Fromann-Holzboog, 1977), whose 4,519 pages were computer generated through the efforts of Dr. Wilhelm Ott at the University of Tübingen. It uses R. Weber's edition of the Vulgate (see chap. 10) and lacks only twenty-two of the most frequently used words.[3] Also a product of the electronic age is *Concordantia polyglotta: La concordance de la Bible,* 5 vols. (Turnhout: Brepols, 1980), compiled by the Benedictine monks of Maredsous, a name synonymous with concordance productivity (see below, p. 14). Their goal is to produce an exhaustive, comparative, analytical, multilingual index of

---

[2] See bibliography cited in Gottlieb Stolle, *Anleitung zur Historie der theologischen Gelahrtheit* (Jena, 1739), 826. On the history to the eighteenth century, see ibid., 827–29. For most of the material in the historical portion of this study I am indebted to the prefaces in the concordances edited by K. Bruder, J. Buxtorf-B. Baer, F. P. Dutripon, and S. Mandelkern. See also Eugène Mangenot, "Concordances de la Bible," *Dictionnaire de la Bible,* ed. Fulcran Grégoire Vigouroux (Paris, 1895ff.) 11:892–905; Heinrich Ernst Bindseil, "Ueber die Concordanzen," *Theologische Studien und Kritiken* 43/4 (1870): 673–720.

[3] The twenty-two words are *ad, de, ego, et, hic, ille, in, ipse, is, iste, meus, non, nos, noster, qui, sui, sum, suus, tu, tuus, vester, vos.* The use of these words accounts for 27 percent of the Latin Pentateuch. A number of words omitted by Dutripon are included in Fischer's work. Among them are *a, ab, abque,* and the like. Many of the latter are annotated by Dutripon after one citation with the words *deinceps omittitur* ("succeeding references are omitted"). Some of them, like *dico,* are considered "notable exceptions"; see also Dutripon's lengthy note under *deus.*

the primary biblical texts (Masoretic, Septuagint, Greek New Testament), selected Latin, French, and English translations, and all the Hebrew manuscripts of the book of Sirach. It will "display lexical correspondence among twelve versions."

Useful for the study of the Syriac text of the prophets is *Konkordanz zur Syrischen Bibel: Die Propheten,* Göttinger Orientforschungen, ser. 1, Syriaca 25, ed. Werner Stothman, with assistance of Kurt Johannes and Manfred Zumpe, 4 vols. (Wiesbaden, 1984). This concordance makes use of the Urmia Bible and the Syriac text of B. Walton, *Biblia Sacra Polyglotta* (London, 1653–57; reprint, Graz, 1963–65) and follows the listing in Carl Brockelman, *Lexicon Syriacum,* 2d ed. (Halle: Niemeyer, 1928; reprint, Hildesheim: Olms, 1966).[4] Based on the British and Foreign Bible Society's 1920 edition of the Peshitta is George Anton Kiraz's *A Computer-Generated Concordance to the Syriac New Testament,* in 6 vols. (Leiden: Brill, 1993).

CONCORDANCES OF THE HEBREW OLD TESTAMENT

Apologetic interests prompted the production of the first concordance of the Hebrew Old Testament. Isaac Nathan ben Kalonymus of Arles in Provence, France, began the work in 1438 and with some assistance completed it by 1448. He called his pioneer effort מֵאִיר נָתִיב, "enlightener of the path," though the title page of the first edition (Venice, 1524) reads יָאִיר נָתִיב, "it will light the path," taken from Job 41:24 (MT). The British Museum houses an edition published in Basel in 1556.

This work omitted proper names and indeclinable particles and failed to present the verbs in any grammatical order. Marius de Calasio, a Franciscan monk, made numerous corrections and additions for a new edition published in 1621. Julius Fürst's publication *Veteris Testamenti concordantiae* (Leipzig, 1840) marked a new departure. Subsequently, with the publication of the revised edition of Johann Buxtorf's *Concordantiae bibliorum Hebraicae et Chaldaicae,* edited by Bernhard Baer in two parts (Berlin, 1862), the way was paved for Solomon Mandelkern's monumental work, though the latter acknowledges the distinct contribution also made by Benjamin Davidson, who published Fürst's concordance in an English edition, *Concordance of the Hebrew and Chaldaic Scripture* (London, 1876). In the preface to his *Veteris Testamenti concordantiae Hebraicae atque Chaldaicae,* 2 vols. (Leipzig, 1896, 1900), 2d ed. rev. by F. Margolin (Berlin, 1925), 3d ed. corrected and

---

[4] The name "Urmia Bible" is derived from the place of origin, Lake Urmia (=Lake Rezāʾīyeh, Iran).

supplemented by Moshe Henry Goshen-Gottstein, 1 vol. (Jerusalem and Tel-Aviv: Schocken, 1959; rev. ed., 1967), Mandelkern points out the advantages of his work over previous compilations: citations according to sense, proper placement of entries misplaced under false roots, correction of grammatical confusions, and addition of a great number of words—including *hapax legomena*—omitted by Fürst and Buxtorf-Baer.[5]

In view of the high price of Mandelkern's work, the completion of Gerhard Lisowsky and Leonhard Rost, *Konkordanz zum hebräischen Alten Testament, nach dem von Paul Kahle in der Biblia Hebraica edidit R. Kittel besorgten masoretischen Text,* 2d ed. (Stuttgart: Württembergische Bibelanstalt, 1958), came as good news. This concordance with emphasis on nouns and verbs is a photographic reproduction of a manuscript prepared by Lisowsky, with brief translations of words into German, English, and classical Latin. Some common terms are selectively referenced, but the entire Old Testament vocabulary is included. Semantic considerations are emphasized and show awareness of linguistic developments that have led to reexamination of traditional grammatical categories. This concordance in a sense previews later computerized morphological analysis, permitting one, for example, to see what subject goes with a specific verb. Through such organization one can ascertain that the verb ברא in the qal has only God as its subject, whereas created things are associated with the niphal. Similarly, fruitful analyses can be made by noting the position of a given noun.

Another work, in preparation under the editorship of Samuel E. Loewenstamm in cooperation with Joshua Blau, *Thesaurus of the Language of the Bible: Complete Concordance, Hebrew Bible Dictionary, Hebrew-English Bible Dictionary,* is destined to win attention. The results of extensive and intensive research, projected to fill six volumes in all, began to issue from the Bible Concordance Press of Jerusalem in 1957. Although the work is based on previous lexicographical aids, the editors are hopeful that it will supersede the major European works by incorporating conclusions from much material only more recently exploited by scholarly study. For the convenience of English readers the entries, with the exception of verbs, have been arranged alphabetically instead of according to roots, and a summary follows each Hebrew entry, which is drawn from the Leningrad manuscript, B19a(=L). The editors

---

[5] The term "edition" is loosely used in connection with frequent reprints of Mandelkern's concordance. The second edition (Berlin, 1937) carries the notice "cura F. Margolin" and contains a Latin preface. It is evidently a reprint of the 1925 edition The seventh edition (1967) is apparently a reprint of editions by F. Margolin and M. H. Goshen-Gottstein. There are numerous other editions and reprints. Some editions are sometimes slightly abridged (e.g., one published in Leipzig, 1910). Students baffled by errors in the second edition and not equipped with the third edition may want to see Solomon L. Skoss, "Corrections to Mandelkern's Concordance היכל הקדש', Second Edition by Margolin (1925)," *JQR* n.s. 40 (1949): 173–88.

augment Mandelkern's word list, even to the extent of including אֵת as a mark of the direct accusative. Some of the articles include a section in smaller Hebrew type in which views of various scholars on technical details are outlined to encourage further investigation.

Hebraists will also be attracted to Abraham Even-Shoshan, קוֹנְקוֹרְדַנְצִיָה חֲדָשָׁה לְתוֹרָה נְבִיאִים וּכְתוּבִים *A New Concordance of the Bible,* 3 vols., the 3d in 2 parts (Jerusalem: Kiryat Sepher, 1980), also published in Jerusalem, 1989, under the title *A New Concordance of the Bible: Thesaurus of the Language of the Bible, Hebrew and Aramaic Roots, Words, Proper Names, Phrases, and Synonyms.*[6] This work is in Hebrew and lists all words, not by roots, but as one might find them in a dictionary. Students of more limited background in Hebrew can still benefit from *The Englishman's Hebrew and Chaldee Concordance of the Old Testament: Being an Attempt at a Verbal Connexion Between the Original and the English Translation,* ed. George V. Wigram, 2 vols. (London, 1843).

CONCORDANCES OF THE SEPTUAGINT

Conrad Kircher is responsible for the first printed concordance of the Septuagint, published in two volumes (Frankfurt, 1607). His work was amplified by Abraham Tromm (variously spelled), a learned minister at Groningen, who in 1718 incorporated the readings from Aquila, Theodotion, and Symmachus. But all such efforts were made obsolete by the publication of Edwin Hatch and Henry Redpath, *A Concordance to the Septuagint and the Other Greek Versions of the Old Testament (Including the Apocryphal Books),* 2 vols. and supplement (Oxford: Clarendon Press, 1892–1906), which competes very well with the products of the computer age. The reprint in two volumes (Graz, Austria: Akademische Druck- und Verlagsanstalt, 1954) has not significantly depreciated the clarity of the original publication. Each Greek word in the canonical and apocryphal books is listed with the Hebrew word(s) corresponding to it in numbered sequence. A glance at the numbers behind the quotations readily identifies the Hebrew word rendered by the Septuagint in each passage. The second volume includes a supplement that presents, among other features, a concordance to the Greek proper names and a Hebrew index to the entire concordance. Elmar Camilo dos Santos has enhanced the use of this work with his *An Expanded Hebrew Index for the Hatch-Redpath Concordance to the Septuagint* (Jerusalem: Dugith Publishers, 1973). Students owe a great debt of gratitude to the compiler of this index, for he has completed what Hatch-Redpath (H-R) left undone, namely, providing the Greek terms

---

[6] Directions for use are included in an inserted pamphlet, "Introduction to a New Concordance of the Old Testament" (Grand Rapids: Baker, 1989), by John H. Sailhamer.

for the references cited after the words in the "Hebrew Index to the Entire Concordance," in volume 2, end pages 219–72. Each page of this work therefore consists of one column of text photocopied from those pages and a corresponding column of handwritten text containing the Greek words, with lines that hook up with the lines in the photocopied text. For the quick trip use *A Handy Concordance of the Septuagint* (reprint, London: Samuel Bagster & Sons, 1970), with no references to the Apocrypha.

CONCORDANCES OF THE GREEK NEW TESTAMENT

The first concordance of the Greek New Testament, *ΣΥΜΦΩΝΙΑ Η ΣΥΛΛΕΞΙΣ ΤΗΣ ΔΙΑΘΗΚΗΣ ΤΗΣ ΚΑΙΝΗΣ* (*Symphonia sive Novi Testamenti concordantiae Graecae*), was compiled by Xystus Betuleius (Sixtus Birken) and was published at Basel in 1546.[7] Despite the fact that the work lacked verse divisions — Robert Estienne (Stephanus) is responsible for these in 1551[8] — and that the indeclinable parts of speech have only a representative listing, the praise is justified, and the foundation was laid. Robert Estienne's projected improvement of Betuleius's work was published by his son Henri in Geneva in 1594 under the title *Concordantiae Graeco-Latinae Testamenti Novi,* 2d ed. (1624).

Erasmus Schmid's ταμιεῖον τῶν τῆς καινῆς διαθήκης λέξεων, *sive Concordantiae omnium vocum Novi Testamenti* (Wittenberg, 1638), broke new ground and formed the basis for all subsequent efforts.[9] Notable of these is

---

[7] Euthalius Rhodius, a monk of the Order of St. Basil, is said to have composed a concordance of the Greek New Testament in 1300. See Bruder, *TAMIEION,* xi. Stolle (*Anleitung*) already could find no reliable information on this bit of tradition.

[8] Estienne says of his father's achievement that it was done "inter equitandum." The phrase "inter equitandum" may refer, as Bruce Metzger observes, to stops at inns, not to work done while riding (*The Text of the New Testament: Its Transmission, Corruption, and Restoration,* 2d ed. [New York: Oxford University Press, 1968], 104). In the fourteenth century Rabbi Solomon ben Ishmael divided the Hebrew Bible into chapters on the basis of a Vulgate manuscript. These divisions appeared in printed editions of the Hebrew Bible from Bomberg's First Rabbinic Bible, 1516–17. Division of chapters into verses made its appearance in 1563 for the Psalter and in 1571 for the entire Hebrew Bible.

[9] The book was republished in Gotha and Leipzig in 1717, *Novi Testamenti Iesu Christi Graeci, hoc est, originalis linguae TAMEION, aliis concordantiae.* A new preface was added by Ernst Cyprian, who called attention to Erasmus Schmid's critique of a concordance begun by Robert Stephan. The criticism primarily concerned three points: (a) confusion of similar vocables, (b) omission of many vocables, and (c) a host of false roots. From the title page one can gather that Erasmus Schmid's own work has undergone painstaking correction by Cyprian, for it reads: "Singulari studio denuo revisum atque ab innumeris mendis repurgatum." But, as Bruder noted (*TAMIEION*), the errors of the first edition are repeated, and Cyprian himself indicates in his preface that he did not feel called upon to change more than a few typographical errors, on the theory that the

Karl H. Bruder's *TAMIEION TΩN THΣ KAINHΣ ΔIAΘHKHΣ ΛEΞEΩN,* *sive Concordantiae omnium vocum Novi Testamenti Graeci* (Leipzig, 1842), 4th rev. ed. (Leipzig, 1888). This work was based on the *textus receptus.* Though Bruder's 1888 edition included the readings of Tischendorf, Tregelles, and Westcott-Hort, the results were not entirely satisfying. Therefore, William F. Moulton and Albert S. Geden sought to supply a concordance that would be up-to-date and meet the scholar's exacting demands. Using the Greek text of Westcott and Hort, published in 1881, as their standard, they compared this text with that of Tischendorf and of the English revisers. Moulton and Geden's *A Concordance to the Greek Testament,* first published in Edinburgh (T. & T. Clark, 1897), slightly revised with the assistance of John Recks (1963), and issued in a fifth edition (1978) by H. K. Moulton with a supplement of seventy-six pages, has been for many years a basic tool for New Testament interpreters. The editors have sought to secure maximum intelligibility. The quotations are somewhat longer than in most concordances. With the use of single and double asterisks the editors succeed in indicating the status of a word insofar as its occurrence in the LXX, other Greek versions of the Old Testament, and in the Apocrypha are concerned. The use of a dagger indicates that the word is not in classical or standard ancient Greek usage. A further advantage is the quotation in Hebrew characters of Old Testament parallel passages. Unfortunately, the supplement in the fifth edition cites only the particles ἀπό, εἰς, ἐκ, ἐν, ὅτι, οὖν, and σύν in full; the particles καί and δέ are ignored, and a number of other words, for example, the oblique cases of some pronouns and οὐ, are recognized only by chapter and verse.

Remedying many of the deficiencies in Bruder and Moulton-Geden is the massive production titled *Vollständige Konkordanz zum griechischen Neuen Testament: Unter Zugrundlegung aller modernen kritischen Ausgaben und des Textus Receptus (VKGNT),* compiled by H. Riesenfeld, H.-U. Rosenbaum, Chr. Hannick, B. Bonsack, with K. Junack, et al., under the direction of Kurt Aland, 2 vols. in 3 (Berlin and New York: de Gruyter, vol. 1/1 in 14 fascicles, 1975–83; 1/2, 1982; vol. 2, *Spezialübersichten,* 1978) and based on Nestle[26], with variants from the critical editions of Bover, Merk, Nestle[25], von Soden, "Textus Receptus," Tischendorf, Vogels, Westcott-Hort. As in Moulton-Geden, superscript letters classify the usage of the words. The second volume, produced with the help of computer specialists H. Bachmann and W. A. Slaby, organizes

---

dead do not desire to have the labors of others mingled with their own. A few examples of the deficiencies in Schmid will suffice: (a) omitted *hapax legomena* include ἐπικέλλω and ἐπιλείχω, (b) inconsistent listing of base verbal forms, e.g., προβλέπω, but προγράφομαι. One might add that Erasmus Schmid was quite anxious that his readers should not consider the three years he spent on his concordance a reflection on his sanity. Otto Schmoller, in the preface to his concordance published in 1868 (see n. 13), alludes to an abridged edition of Erasmus Schmid's work, ed. William Greenfield (London: Samuel Bagster). No date is given; Schmoller may have had in mind the publication of 1830.

numerical data in five ways. In addition to a statistical analysis of words in each New Testament document, the compilers offer a computation of all grammatical forms after each entry word (e.g., the word ὄχλος [accents are not generally used] is found twelve times in the dative singular); a simple numerical list of occurrences (in descending order, from ὁ [19,904 times] to ὠφελεια, the last of the words used only twice, followed by a new alphabetical order listing all words occurring only once, with the book cited for each such usage); a list of words used only once (*hapax legomena*) in the New Testament, with each book having its own alphabetical listing; and, finally, a reverse index of inflected forms found in the New Testament.[10] The massiveness of this work can be gauged from the fact that the citation of καί covers pp. 584–662. But some reviewers charged that the title was misleading, for not all readings of modern critical editions were incorporated. Aland replied in the preface to his concordance that for a variety of reasons editions by Richard Francis Weymouth (1896), Bernhard Weiss (1894–1900), Alexander Souter (1910, 1947), Stanley C. E. Legg (1935, 1940), George Dunbar Kilpatrick (1958), and some others from Samuel Prideaux Tregelles (1857–72) to Randolph V. G. Tasker (1964) did not qualify for inclusion. Besides, he noted, their inclusion would have made the work unwieldly and decreased its usefulness. It does indeed appear that the use of questionable quantitative adjectives in titles of concordances is a temptation few publishers can resist (see also below, pp. 15–16).

For a smaller and less pricey item, many will find the abridged form of *VKGNT* more to their liking. A product of Bachmann-Slaby electronic ingenuity, *Computer-Konkordanz zum Novum Testamentum graece von Nestle-Aland, 26. Auflage und zum Greek New Testament, 3rd Edition* (Berlin: de Gruyter, 1980) prints all except twenty-nine words in italics with context; those words and their applicable inflected forms are given book by book, with only chapter and verse indicated, in an appendix — καί, for example, consumes almost four columns, or a total of 9,164 occurrences (see *VKGNT*, 2:143). Statistical analysis is also available at a modest price in Robert Morgenthaler, *Statistik des neutestamentlichen Wortschatzes*, 3d ed. with supplement (Zurich: Gotthelf-Verlag, 1982).

Even larger possibilities beyond those available in Aland's *VKGNT* for study of linguistic data in the New Testament are made possible by the *Analytical Concordance of the Greek New Testament (ACGNT)*, ed. Philip S. Clapp,

---

[10] A supplement to the kind of analysis Aland offers is available in Xavier Jacques, *List of New Testament Words Sharing Common Elements: Supplement to Concordance and Dictionary* (Rome: Pontifical Biblical Institute, 1969), and in F. Neirynck, *New Testament Vocabulary: A Companion Volume to the Concordance*, Bibliotheca Ephemeridum Theologicarum Lovaniensium 65 (Leuven: University Press/Peeters, 1984). Neirynck points to the limited organization of word groups or cognate features in the work of both Aland and Jacques and provides a much more detailed set of word groupings and statistics.

Barbara Friberg, Timothy Friberg, 2 vols. (Grand Rapids: Baker, 1991). In the first portion, called *Lexical Focus,* the editors segregate each word by its distinctive forms, which are alphabetized by lemmas (citation forms). The second installment, *Grammatical Focus,* deals with morphological structures classified in seven major analytical divisions: adjective (adverb), conjunction, determiner (article), noun (and pronoun), preposition, particle, and verb. For the statistically minded it may be of interest merely to know that the entry θεός lists 1,318 occurrences in various forms. But the alert student will probe the significance of usage in the various grammatical cases. Discourse analysis is a high priority for the Fribergs.[11] They trumpeted that interest in their precursor of these two volumes in Baker's Greek New Testament Library, *Analytical Greek New Testament (AGNT),* (Grand Rapids: Baker, 1981), which uses the third edition (1975) of the United Bible Societies' *Greek New Testament.* A fourth volume, *Analytical Lexicon of New Testament Greek,* is to complete the series.[12]

Far more ambitious than the Baker series is the "Computer Bible," begun in 1971 with the publication of *A Critical Concordance to the Synoptic Gospels,* by J. Arthur Baird and David Noel Freedman, in the name of Biblical Research Associates. The same scholars note in their second volume, *An Analytical Linguistic Concordance to the Book of Isaiah* (1971), that their project aims at production of a series of open-ended studies of all portions of the Bible. By using computers they are able to index, arrange, and cross-correlate exhaustive masses of data for biblical study in key-word-in-context concordances. Analyses of content, morphology, syntax, and style are but a few of the benefits generated by this project, which in 1989 produced volume 32, *A Critical Concordance to I, II Peter (Revised).* The shockwaves of this and related works will begin to be felt in earnest when grammars based on electronically generated data hasten the obsolescence of Davidson, Gesenius, Blass-Debrunner, and all the rest.

Zest for computerized tools arrives in varying degrees, and some students

---

[11] Note the essay by John J. Hughes and Peter C. Patton, "Concordances to the Bible: A History and Perspective," in *ACGNT,* xiii–xxxii. The Fribergs' *AGNT* includes an appendix, "The Grammatical Analysis," 797–854, which is in essence a basic introduction to morphological tagging procedures. For details on the history of the use of the computer in the making of concordances, see *ACGNT,* xiv n. 4. See also *Computing in the Humanities,* ed. Peter C. Patton, Renee A. Holoien (Lexington: D. C. Heath and Company, 1981). Patton is the director of the University Computer Center, University of Minnesota. For concordance computer programs, see John J. Hughes, *Bits, Bytes & Biblical Studies* (Grand Rapids: Zondervan, 1987), 266–74; on the Friberg project, see Hughes, 565–68. For machine-readable versions of the Greek New Testament, see Hughes, 556–64.

[12] A comparable work on the Old Testament is envisaged. See Patton, *ACGNT,* xviii, on the Project "Old Testament in the Computer" (OTIK), namely, the production of a tagged Hebrew Old Testament, which will be the stepping stone to the "Instrumenta Biblica" series. Each volume in this series will be devoted to one book of the Bible. Each of these volumes in turn will be in two parts: 1. morphological features, grammatical; 2. lexical features.

of the Bible will appreciate knowledge of works that have gained respect over the years. Moreover, convenience and circumstance invite use of tools that may seem antiquated next to their electronic relatives. Therefore, one ought to have at least one or two of the old alongside the new. Even typewriters are not completely obsolete.

For a quick reconnaissance in the labyrinths of New Testament usage one can use Alfred Schmoller's *Handkonkordanz zum griechischen Neuen Testament*. First published in 1868 (Stuttgart) by Alfred Schmoller's father (Otto) in answer to the need for a vest-pocket Bruder,[13] this handy book has gone through many editions and become a sort of Greek Cruden's concordance. Additions beginning with the seventh edition (Stuttgart, 1938), based on the fiifteenth and sixteenth editions of Nestle, include signs informing the reader of Septuagint usage and the Vulgate renderings of the word in question. Because of the limiting format, the submitted data are of course minimal and of little help in dealing with textual-critical matters.[14] The same applies to Ταμεῖον ἤτοι εὑρετήριον τῶν λέξεων τῆς καινῆς διαθήκης, *Concordance to the Greek New Testament: An Abridgement from the Edition of Erasmus Schmidt Made by W. Greenfield*, published by Astir in Athens (1977), which is the handiest Greek concordance, measuring only 17.4 cm. x 11.4 cm. x 2 cm. Used with discretion, either one, along with Nestle[26], makes a most desirable traveling companion, whether to the conference hall or the seashore.

Students should also be aware of other useful supplements to standard concordances. Xavier Jacques's *List of New Testament Words Sharing Common Elements* (Rome: Pontifical Biblical Institute, 1969) groups cognate terms not found in sequence in the concordances. Two books dealing with limited areas of the biblical corpus invite the attention of more curious probers of early Christian thought. In *A Concordance to Q*, Sources for Biblical Study 7 (Missoula, Mont.: Society of Biblical Literature and Scholars Press, 1975), Richard A. Edwards highlights the gospel tradition common to Matthew and Luke but not found in Mark. The key-word-in-context (KWIC) procedure is in two stages: the first presents a center column listing alphabetically all words in Q, with context on either side; the second identifies the pericopes of Q and alphabetizes the words in each of them. In the second work, limited to a portion of the canon, J. D. Yoder, *Concordance to the Distinctive Greek Text of Codex Bezae* (Leiden: Brill; Grand Rapids: Eerdmans, 1961), encourages exploration of the so-called "Western Text."

---

[13] Otto Schmoller, *TAMIEION τῆς καινῆς διαθήκης 'ΕΓΧΕΙΡΙΔΙΟΝ, oder Handkonkordanz zum griechischen Neuen Testament* (Stuttgart: Württembergische Bibelanstalt, 1868). In his seventh edition Alfred Schmoller dates the first edition 1869.

[14] In fairness to this concordance, the elder Schmoller's *Vorwort*, p. vi, should be consulted. In the preface Schmoller explains, among other things, the critical value of citing parallel passages by location only.

The need for a concordance that would secure to English-speaking students unacquainted with the original the advantages of a Greek concordance was first met by *The Englishman's Greek Concordance of the New Testament: Being an Attempt at a Verbal Connexion Between the Greek and English Texts* (London, 1839), 9th ed. (1903), published under the direction of George V. Wigram. This book lists the Greek words as in the Greek concordances, but instead of the Greek it cites the passages of the KJV in which the word occurs. The English word rendering the original is italicized for quick reference. Thus, one handicap of concordances of Bible translations, multiple translations of single Greek words, is overcome. Serious students of the Bible without a knowledge of Greek need to learn only the Greek alphabet, and they have moderate access to the verbal treasures of the Greek New Testament. From a study of the context in which the translated words appear one can fairly infer the connotations of the original. The English-Greek and Greek-English indexes help to accelerate the process. In 1972 an edition with Strong's numbers (see below) made its appearance (Lafayette, Ind.: Associated Publishers and Authors, Inc.), followed by *The New Englishman's Greek Concordance and Lexicon,* ed. Jay P. Green, Sr. (1982). This last edition eliminates the need for an English-Greek index in this kind of work. Each headword gives Strong's number, reference to Bauer's lexicon ("AG"), the Greek word, TWNT volume and page, Thayer's lexicon page and column. Even καί is cited with a few references, and with the notation to see concordances for lists of uses.

A Critical Greek and English Concordance of the New Testament, prepared by Charles F. Hudson under the direction of Horace L. Hastings and revised and completed by Ezra Abbot (1870), 8th ed. (Boston and London, 1891), was designed to meet deficiencies encountered in Wigram's publication. According to the preface of the seventh edition, Hudson's concordance was used in their work by all the New Testament revisers, both in England and America, and its "convenience and helpfulness was most heartily acknowledged by those eminent scholars, both individually and collectively; and it undoubtedly filled a place which was occupied by no other single volume." Not only does this concordance present the significant variants found in the critical editions published by Griesbach, Lachmann, Tischendorf, and Tregelles, but at a single glance it classifies the passages in which each Greek word occurs and reveals the number of ways in which it is translated in the New Testament. In other respects Wigram's publication appears to have the edge over Hudson-Abbot. In the interests of cost and convenience of form, extended quotation, as found in Wigram's concordance, gives way to mere citation of chapter and verse in Hudson-Abbot. Wigram's work provides the additional advantage of listing in the English-Greek index all the Greek words underlying a single English rendering. Hudson-Abbot cites only page numbers, and readers must run the eye over a whole page to find the Greek word that underlies the English translation.

A modern, if not completely adequate, successor to the Greek-English concordances of the past century is Jacob Brubaker Smith, *Greek-English Concordance to the New Testament* (Scottdale, Penn.: Herald Press, 1955). This concordance lists the Greek words, 5,524 all told, and tabulates each according to its various renderings in the KJV, together with the number of times each one of these renderings occurs. An English index lists the corresponding Greek entries. This type of concordance is especially useful in comparative statistical analysis, but the electronically organized concordances help one do the job more efficiently. In any event, who could have foretold the richness of endowment in Erasmus Schmid's progeny?

CONCORDANCES OF THE ENGLISH BIBLE

Pioneer work in concordances of English versions of the New Testament is to be credited to a John Day, who about 1540 published in London (probably through Thomas Gybson) *The Concordance of the new Testament, most necessary to be had in ye hands of all soche as delyte in the communycacion of any place contayned in ye new Testament.* John Marbeck is responsible for the first concordance of the entire English Bible. Marbeck, a church musician, was sentenced to the stake for heresy in 1544. Bishop Stephen Gardiner, who was fond of his music, interceded for him. Marbeck's life was spared, and in 1550 his concordance based on the Great Bible was published in London: *A Concordance, that is to saie, a worke wherein by the ordre of the letters of the A. B. C. ye maie redely finde any worde conteigned in the whole Bible, so often as it is there expressed or mencioned.*

It was Alexander Cruden, bookseller and proclaimer of return to moral values, who made "concordance" a household word. Since the first edition, dedicated to the Queen of England in 1737, Cruden's *A Complete Concordance to the Holy Scriptures of the Old and New Testament* has gone through many improvements and revisions and remains a standby for those who continue to retain affection for the KJV. The third edition (London, 1769) is valued especially for its incorporation of the last corrections made by Cruden and is the base for all subsequent editions and abridgments.[15]

For sheer completeness James Strong, *The Exhaustive Concordance of the Bible* (New York: Hunt & Eaton; Cincinnati: Cranston & Curts, 1894 [copy-

---

[15] Cruden's work has been a gold mine for publishers, but *caveat emptor.* The publisher Broadman's, for example, advertised a *Cruden's Unabridged Concordance,* but it lacks references to the apocrypha, of which Cruden took account, even though his work was not complete in other respects. To judge from the many formats in which the name of Cruden is exploited, Midas is doing well. But the adjective in the title *Cruden's Compact Concordance* (Grand Rapids: Zondervan, 1968) is at least honest, even though the book is not especially helpful to a searching general reader.

right 1890]), is not to be surpassed for users of the KJV, whose every word is listed. Its popularity may be measured by the fact that other concordances and dictionaries cross-reference its contents by the number that accompanies each entry. These numbers take the user to the appended dictionaries, which display, with a brief gloss, the Hebrew, Aramaic, or Greek words that underlie the renderings in specific passages. One can determine from the dictionaries the different translations of a single word. A revised edition, *The New Strong's Exhaustive Concordance of the Bible with Main Concordance, Appendix to the Main Concordance, Key verse Comparison chart, Dictionary of the Hebrew Bible, Dictionary of the Greek Testament* (Nashville: Nelson, 1984) truly merits the adjective "exhaustive." Like its predecessor, it offers mere references for every occurrence of forty-seven common words, such as "a," "an," "and," etc. The "Key verse comparison chart" is a new feature. More than 1,800 Bible verses, selected for "doctrinal importance and for their familiarity to readers," and representing every book of the Bible, are cited in six columns according to renderings in KJV, NKJV, NASB, NIV, RSV, TEV.[16]

Despite some of the advantages of Strong, certain helpful features in Robert Young's *Analytical Concordance to the Bible,* revised by William B. Stevenson, have edged Strong out of many pastors' libraries. Young was a theologian, printer, and Orientalist. His first publishing effort was a translation of the 613 precepts of Maimonides. The first edition of his concordance appears to have been published in 1879.[17] Under each English word are included generally in lexical sequence the various Hebrew and Greek words that are translated by that word. In addition, the English words are broken up into various self-contained lists of references. Thus the entry "Begotten (Son), only" is differentiated from "Begotten, first." In addition, the listings of Hebrew and Greek words function as index-lexicons and are not mere vocabulary listings as in Strong. That is, under each Hebrew and Greek word, cited in transliterated and original language form, the various ways in which the word is rendered are listed along with the number of times each rendering is to be found. These are distinctive advantages over Strong. Lacking Mandelkern or a major Greek concordance or both, the student with judicious use of the indexes to Hebrew

---

[16] Because of Strong's popularity, students must be wary in wending their way through advertising blurbs. There is an abridged version, *Strong's Concordance of the Bible* (Nashville, 1980). Another edition, *Strong's Exhaustive Concordance of the Bible* (Nashville and New York, 1977), lacks the tabulation of variant translations available in the unabridged revised version.

[17] Tracing the publishing fortunes of Young's concordance is very difficult. The work became the property of a number of publishers. British and American publishers numbered the editions differently, and frequently impressions or reprints were called editions. Young's 20th edition (New York: Funk & Wagnalls, 1936) includes William Foxwell Albright's essay, "Recent Discoveries in Bible Lands" (45 pages), which was revised to 51 pages for a later edition of the concordance (1955).

and Greek words in Young can do a fairly creditable exegetical stint based on the original languages.

It is not our intention to enumerate concordances of all the English versions,[18] especially since the proliferation of Bible versions will invite new productions that will make many existing concordances obsolete. But history demands recognition of a few, and among them *Nelson's Complete Concordance of the Revised Standard Version Bible* (New York: Nelson, 1957), 2d rev. ed. (1972), merits more than mere mention.[19] Howard Aiken, of the Harvard Computation Laboratory, said of John W. Ellison, who headed its production, that he was the "first human to walk into the . . . Laboratory with a specific problem wanting to use the computer." As in many concordances, frequently used words, such as "no," "to," "us," and many others similar to these, which would have increased the bulk of the book without achieving any appreciable advantage, were omitted, but the title is, strictly speaking, misleading. For coverage beyond the traditional sixty-six books, the generalist will find help in *A Concordance to the Apocrypha/Deuterocanonical Books of the Revised Standard Version* (Grand Rapids: Eerdmans, 1983), which makes use of the data stored at the Abbey of Maredsous (see above, p. 2). This concordance is based on the 1977 edition of the RSV Apocrypha/Deuterocanonical books, and thus includes references also to 3 and 4 Maccabees and Psalm 151. For each word, except seventy-seven that are omitted, the number of occurrences is cited along with percentage of use. For example, the word "realize" occurs ten times=0.007%.

The wish for a multilingual concordance to the RSV along the lines of Young was first honored, but only in part, by Clinton Morrison in *An Analytical Concordance to the Revised Standard Version of the New Testament* (Philadelphia: Westminster, 1979), based on the second edition of the New Testament portion of the RSV. In *The Eerdmans Analytical Concordance to the Revised Standard Version of the Bible,* biblical scholarship and computer science reached a new peak. Compiled by Richard E. Whitaker and James E. Goehring (Grand Rapids, 1988), this impressive achievement contains over 400,000 entries, which were set with the help of an Ibycus computer program and self-acclaimed as an "easy-to-use aid, not just a scholarly reference tool." Each occurrence of a term (a single word or a phrase) is followed by the Hebrew, Aramaic, Greek, or Latin words that underlie it and are given numerals. It is easy, then, to determine what Hebrew or Greek word underlies usage in a specific passage. As indicated after the frequent references to 2 Esdras, the Latin applies to passages included in the Vulgate but not extant in Hebrew

---

[18] On concordances to German versions, see Wilhelm Michaelis, *Übersetzungen, Konkordanzen und Konkordante Übersetzung des Neuen Testaments* (Basel: Heinrich Majer, 1947), 185–200. The revision of the *Luther Bibel* required a new concordance: *Grosse Konkordanz zur Luther Bibel* (Stuttgart: Calwer Verlag, 1979).

[19] See the writer's review of this work in CTM 29 (1958): 223–24.

or Greek. Indexes list all the Hebrew, Greek, and Latin words that underlie the terms used in the RSV, followed by the terms or phrases used to translate each.

Among the most ethically phrased titles is *The NRSV Concordance Unabridged, Including the Apocryphal/Deuterocanonical Books,* ed. John R. Kohlenberger III (Grand Rapids, 1991). Amazingly, this work, based on the NRSV, which was released in May, 1990, became available on May 1, 1991. It is "exhaustive," insofar as it includes references for the common words "a," "and," etc., but it lacks references to the original languages. It contains a topical index, which displays, for example, fifteen passages for the use of "if." The opportunities for homiletical imagination are practically boundless. One of the many possible lines of exploration one can make through this concordance is the use of inclusive language in the NRSV. See, for example, the topical listing "brothers." Then check the concordance entry "brothers," where one can readily determine how many times "b. and sisters" is used to translate the single word in the original.

Because of the correspondence-type rendering in NASB, many students who lack Hebrew or Greek are fond of the *New American Standard Exhaustive Concordance of the Bible, Hebrew-Aramaic and Greek Dictionaries* (Nashville: Holman, 1981), edited under the direction of Robert L. Thomas. This concordance uses the Brown-Driver-Briggs lexicon (1907) and follows the numbering system used in Strong. A list of frequently recurring words not included in the concordance is listed in the preface, but unlike their treatment in Strong's concordance of the KJV they are not referenced in an appendix. The term "exhaustive" is therefore misleading.

Stephen J. Hartdegen, gen. ed., *Nelson's Complete Concordance of the New American Bible* (Collegeville, Minn.: Liturgical Press, 1977) is "complete" only to the extent that it references 18,000 key words and recites in the preface a long list of omitted words. More extravagant in claims is *The NIV Complete Concordance,* ed. E. W. Goodrick and J. R. Kohlenberger III (Grand Rapids: Zondervan, 1981), which, as acknowledged in the preface, is complete only to the extent that it cites all references for any word that it includes: about 950 words are not entered. This work was evidently a steppingstone to *The NIV Exhaustive Concordance,* ed. Goodrick and Kohlenberger III, with Donald L. Potts and James A. Swanson (Grand Rapids: Zondervan, 1990), which employs the word "exhaustive" with integrity. Instead of the dictionary format it uses the index-lexicon format after the main concordance. For example, πρόσωπον is rendered "face" twenty-four times; under the entry "face" in the main concordance one will find numbers keyed to the index. The number for πρόσωπον is 4725. All the references that show "face" followed by this number point to passages in which πρόσωπον is used.

Most certainly qualifying as a multipurpose tool is M. Darton's *Modern Concordance to the New Testament* (Garden City, N.Y.: Doubleday, 1976), which is based on the concordance designed for use with the Jerusalem Bible: *Concordance de la Bible: Nouveau Testament* (Paris: Cerf/Desclée de Brouwer, 1970). Of concordances to older works, the one by William J. Gant, *Concordance of the Bible in the Moffatt Translation* (London: Hodder & Stoughton, 1950), remains especially serviceable because of Moffatt's vigorous renderings. Others include: Newton W. Thompson and Raymond Stock, *Concordance to the Bible* (1942; 3d impression, St. Louis: Herder, 1943), based on the Douay-Rheims version, with Thompson doing the Old Testament and Stock the New Testament; and Marshall Custiss Hazard, *A Complete Concordance to the American Standard Version of the Holy Bible* (New York: Nelson, 1922). The latter falls in the category of overly boastful "complete" concordances.

Some works of a related nature organize biblical terms thematically. One of the most popular, and based on the KJV, is Charles R. Joy, *Harper's Topical Concordance,* rev. ed. (New York: Harper, 1962). Some Bible students still delight in Orville J. Nave's *Topical Bible,* first copyrighted in 1896 and 1897. It takes its place with the many "new" issues of popular works, having been revised by Edward Viening as *The New Nave's Topical Bible* (Grand Rapids: Zondervan, 1969).

USE OF CONCORDANCES

With such high-priced books on the shelf it is eminently desirable that one know how to use them. In the following suggestions we shall bypass the more remote objectives mentioned by Elijah ben Asher ha-Levi (Levita, 1469–1549), whose unpublished concordance of the Hebrew Old Testament, finished between 1515 and 1521, was designed, among other things, to serve as a rhyming dictionary and as an aid to cabalistic speculations.

One of the primary uses of a concordance is, of course, to help the user find in a moment the location of any passage, if only a leading word is recalled. If, for example, one has forgotten where St. Paul's extensive treatment of marriage occurs, one can look up the word "marry" in either Young or in, for instance, the RSV concordance. A cluster of references to 1 Corinthians 7 will be readily apparent. But to limit the concordance to this function is to sacrifice its magnificent interpretive possibilities.

Systematizer

The preface to Dutripon's concordance illustrates through the use of the word *laudare* the systematizing possibilities of a concordance. For professional theologians a concordance of the original language is a *sine qua non,* but even for them a concordance based on a version or translation can be of great assistance. Consider these themes: The Disastrous Tree, The Inevitable Tree, The Tree that Lived on Borrowed Time, The Murder Tree, The Resurrection Tree. A preacher in desperate search for a sermon series could do worse. These were all suggested by a brief glance down the RSV/NRSV concordance column marked "tree." Suppose the subject in a church study group involves the question of divorce. A concordance at the elbow can save time and possible embarrassment by directing the leader to Matthew 19, Mark 10, and 1 Corinthians 7. Still better, it might suggest a good assignment for some member of the study group to present at the next meeting. If the scene is a mountain youth camp, perhaps a study of famous mountain episodes in the Bible might prove extremely rewarding and exhilarating. A concordance is the thing to use. Perhaps a biblical character like Timothy might provide material for profitable discussion. Few concordances will let you down.

LINGUISTIC CONTRIBUTION

For workers in the original languages, the use of concordances can prove to be a departure for an excitingly new interpreter's world. Shaking off the shackles of debilitating dependence on commentaries is akin to a revival experience. In a lexicon a word is like a friend in a coffin. A concordance restores her to life. Take the word παρακαλέω as an example. The lexicon BAGD includes as primary "meanings" (a) summon, (b) appeal to, urge, exhort, encourage, (c) request, appeal to, entreat, implore, (d) comfort, encourage, cheer up. The editors refer 2 Cor. 1:4b to the passages under "d." This passage speaks of "God, who comforts us in all our affliction." But it is the concordance that loads this word in its context with real meaning. There is more here than a cosmic handholding. We see from a comparison with other passages that the word is used primarily of the will — not the emotions — and that the alleged lexical "meanings" are in fact glosses on the word. There are not really four different "meanings" to the word. The lexicographer considers the way a word is used and takes snapshots from various angles. A concordance helps one do what the lexicographer does but permits its user to look anew at the evidence. Our being comforted takes on a kind of urging, a propulsion that alerts us in trouble to the possibilities. Does tribulation stop us momentarily? We get a go-ahead signal in God's παράκλησις, which beckons us out of the mire of our demoralizing self-preoccupation. It is a comfort that makes us strong, and the Latin is not far off course. It is the same with the moral imperatives (cf. Rom. 12:1; Eph. 4:1). This is not legalistic pressure; it is a call to the wide-open spaces of gospel freedom.

If it is the task of a concordance to help one etch more clearly the features of words, then it is especially useful for chalking the line that separates synonyms. This is where one gets money back with interest out of Young, Moulton-Geden, Hatch and Redpath, and Mandelkern. Consider the words ὑπομονή, μακροθυμία. A concordance study clearly indicates that the former has to do with bearing up under difficult situations that call for endurance until the storm is weathered. The latter involves the ability to restrain the impulse of impatience when interested in securing a desired objective. Thus in 2 Tim. 4:2 the writer urges the teacher not to be disappointed at the persistent density of his pupils. On the other hand, the meaning of the parable in Luke 8 hinges on a correct understanding of the word ὑπομονή in 8:15 as endurance in the face of the apparent anomalies of a messianic reign that exposes Christians to unexpected trials and tribulations.

GRAMMATICAL USE

Concordances are useful for unveiling the nuances of grammatical constructions. A simple case in point is the μὴ κλαῖε of Luke 7:13, where the NRSV renders, "Do not weep." A glance in Moulton-Geden leads the eye to a similar prohibition in Luke 8:52. There it is quite evident that the prohibition is aimed at an act in progress, and that more accurately it should be rendered, "Stop your weeping." In 7:13, then, Luke's Jesus is undoubtedly saying to the woman, "Dry up your tears now." And with good reason, for he does not offer merely a funereal convention. He calls her to an exercise of her faith. It is as though he consoles her: "There is really no need for tears, for I am here." The question of overinterpretation can be explored in connection with a work such as Stanley E. Porter's on verbal aspect (see below, chap. 7).

THEMATIC AND TOPICAL CONTRIBUTION

The really exciting part of concordance study, though, lies in the compositional arena, where the writer's artistic and thematic competence is exhibited. Naturally, since the Bible has to do with people's thoughts about transcendent matters and beings, there will be much attention paid to theological issues and topics and the way these are given texture in the document. Like fingerprint powder, the concordance can disclose distinctive, latent whorls of the divine hand. Look up the word Ἰσραήλ. A glance in Moulton-Geden shows that the concentration lies in Matthew, Luke, Acts, Romans. The beginner in Bible study has learned to expect this in Matthew and Paul, but Luke-Acts comes as a surprise in view of its apparent interest in Gentiles. Indeed, the concordance reveals that the references to Israel in Luke-Acts outnumber those in Matthew and Romans taken together. For an understanding of the purpose and objective of the two-volume work this discovery is of compelling significance, and it reverberates with theological overtones.

The matter of tithing, involving as it does the question of the Christian's relation to the Old Testament legal prescriptions, has a ray of light beamed on it whether one looks up the word in the NRSV or checks under δεκατόω and its cognate ἀποδεκατός. The evidence suggests that nowhere in the New Testament is the Old Testament practice made a model for the Christian to follow.

For those who have a little of Sherlock Holmes in them we throw in Matt. 22:34 as a teaser. One will need Hatch and Redpath for this. Clue: The point hinges on the phrase συνήχθησαν ἐπὶ τὸ αὐτό. Make the most of your findings to relate vitally the two parts of the text, if proclamation of the text is your assignment. Of the same order is the phrase καὶ ἦν μετὰ τῶν θηρίων in Mark 1:13. This phrase could easily slip past a casual reader. But it is just such apparently insignificant items, like John's "and it was night" (John 13:30), that are thematically significant. Jerome once said: *Singuli sermones, syllabae, apices, et puncta in divinis Scripturis plena sunt sensibus* (every word or part of a word in the Bible is full of meaning). Hatch and Redpath may have the answer for this one from Mark, s.v. θηρίον. Try under the prophets, but expect an argument from someone who begins with Genesis. Mark has a number of these sly little simplicities.

CASE STUDY

The preceding examples illustrate a few of the many possible advantages accruing to diligent users of concordances. But it has been our experience that beginners in a more serious type of Bible study, when it comes to working on their own, are as bewildered as high school freshmen on their first theme. Where do I start? What do I look for? There is no rule of thumb one can follow, but an illustration of how one might proceed may be useful. Suppose my text is Luke 16:19-31. There are no special problem words. All appear quite simple. The story revolves, though, around a rich man and a poor man. Here I begin the probe. I note that this Gospel suggests a revolutionary approach to the matter of poverty and riches. Therefore, the word πτωχός would seem to merit further investigation. I take down Moulton-Geden. Under πτωχός I find Luke 4:18; 6:20; 7:22; and others. It is the poor who are the chosen recipients of the messianic benefits. But why? I go to Hatch and Redpath. There are more than one hundred references. I cannot possibly look at all of them. But the heaviest concentration is in the Psalms. A study of these passages reveals that the "poor" are the people in Israel who depend on the Lord. They are the ones who look to God for salvation (see Ps. 70:6 [MT]; 69:6 [LXX, Rahlfs]). The rich man, by contrast, is representative of Israel's self-sufficient element. This thought in turn suggests that I look up the simple word πατήρ, which appears three times in this pericope. I know that it will be impossible to consider all the passages in which such a common word occurs. Therefore I stay with Luke and let my eye wander down the list of passages in Moulton-Geden. No bells ring until I reach Luke 3:8. This reference is especially resonant because Ἀβραάμ is mentioned. I could find no better commentary than this. It is the rich man's purely formal religious association that has cost him his soul and the fellowship of God. It is equally evident that the point of the story is not a plea for slum clearance. Following these leads I concentrate on such important terms as ἐλεέω (16:24) and μετανοέω.

"But how can I possibly look up every word if, as you suggest, even a common word like πατήρ may be richly significant?" There is no need to make a panicky dash to the bookshelf marked theological tranquilizers (i.e., "Best Sermon Helps of the Year"). This is like tackling troubles. Tussle with one at a time. Move out of strength, not weakness. The first time around on a particular text, work on two or three words. File the data in your computer under some such rubric as "Searches, Concordance." The next time you meet the text brood over it a little more, and check on a few other possibilities. Detectives sometimes sift 100 false leads. But number 101 may nail the crook. The nuggets no longer lie on the surface of the biblical text. It takes a deal of panning to get a single grain. But what a thrill when the discovery is made! And it makes no difference if later on you find it buried in an old commentary. Have no regrets over what appears wasted effort. There comes from study such as this a conviction wrought by the impact of truth, a feeling of intellectual ownership that only personal contact can give. In hope that this study may prove to be stimulating especially to seminarians beginning their exegetical studies, the following summary and supplementary exhortations (recall the word παρακαλέω) are submitted:

1. When preparing the exegesis of a particular passage, begin your use of the concordance with the less-common words. Then think in terms of possible thematic or theological implications, always remembering, of course, that it is the writer's thought, not some later theologian's idea that you are endeavoring to discover and understand. Try to establish associations with what you have previously extracted and learned from Scripture. This procedure will alert you to the significant in the insignificant.
2. Look up the word in the author you are working with. Branch out into other authors, beginning with those that have the fewest references. Pass up those passages that evidently have little or nothing to contribute to clarity. Despite Jerome's warning, you must run some hazards.
3. Proceed to check the word in Hatch and Redpath. Find either the heaviest or the lightest area of concentration, and begin there. If you still have time

and find that the Septuagint renders several Hebrew words with one Greek word, give yourself a real treat and follow the same process in Mandelkern.

4. Keep in mind that the New Testament relies heavily on Psalms, Isaiah, and Jeremiah. Key concepts can usually be traced to these particular Old Testament writings. Wade directly into these sections if the listings are heavy elsewhere.

5. Note cognates and track them down. Learn to know the whole word family. Again, don't let the staggering possibilities keep you from doing something. Even God used up a week to make the world. Try one word-family at a time. Work on another the next time you treat the text.

It was Chrysostom who said: Οὐχ ἁπλῶς ταῦτα διερευνᾶσθαι σπουδάζομεν, φιλοτιμίας ἕνεκεν περιττῆς, ἀλλ' ἵνα μετὰ ἀκριβείας ὑμῖν ἅπαντα ἑρμηνεύοντες παιδεύσωμεν ὑμᾶς μηδὲ βραχεῖαν λέξιν, μηδὲ συλλαβὴν μίαν παρατρέχειν τῶν ἐν ταῖς θείαις Γραφαῖς κειμένων. Οὐ γὰρ ῥήματα ἐστιν ἁπλῶς, ἀλλὰ τοῦ Πνεύματος τοῦ ἁγίου ῥήματα, καὶ διὰ τοῦτο πολύν ἐστι [sic] τὸν θησαυρὸν εὑρεῖν καὶ ἐν μιᾷ συλλαβῇ.[20]

"It was another divine, John Donne by name, who also said: "Search the Scriptures, not as though thou wouldst make a concordance but an application.""

---

[20] Migne, *PG* 53:119. "It is not in the interest of extravagant ambition that we trouble ourselves with this detailed exposition, but we hope through such painstaking interpretation to train you in the importance of not passing up even one slight word or syllable in the sacred Scriptures. For they are not ordinary utterances, but the very expression of the Holy Spirit, and for this reason it is possible to find great treasure even in a single syllable." Compare Chrysostom's statement in connection with the salutation of Aquila and Priscilla in Rom. 16:3: (τοῦτο λέγω) . . . ἵνα μάθητε, ὅτι τῶν θείων Γραφῶν οὐδὲν περιττόν, οὐδὲν παρεργόν ἐστι, κἂν μία κεραια ᾖ, ἀλλὰ καὶ φιλὴ πρόσρησις πολὺ πέλαγος ἡμῖν ἀνοίγει νοημάτων, *PG* 51:187. Freely rendered "nothing in the sacred Scriptures is superfluous or insignificant whether it be the single dotting of an 'i' or crossing of a 't.' Even a slight verbal alteration [as in the case of 'Abram' to 'Abraham'] opens up for one a vast ocean of ideas."

CHAPTER TWO

The Greek
New Testament

T O MANY STUDENTS of the Greek New Testament the word "Nestle" is code for standard text. This chapter will indeed have a good deal to say about this form of the New Testament, but at the same time it is necessary to take note of the larger context of dedication to finding ways out of bewilderment in the face of conflicting textual data. Since the use of a "synopsis" is so intimately linked with primary study of the Greek New Testament, attention is also paid to that type of tool.

Since its first edition in 1898 some form of Eberhard Nestle's progeny known as *Novum Testamentum Graece* has become standard equipment for students of the New Testament. The 25th edition (1963), edited by his son Erwin Nestle and Kurt Aland, who succeeded Nestle as editor, erased some blemishes of its predecessors and included readings from new papyri.[1] With the publication of the 26th edition (1979; hereafter Nestle[26]), the Nestle text took on a completely new look.

The elder Nestle had developed a composite text based on the editions of Konstantine Tischendorf, Brooke Foss Westcott and Fenton John Anthony Hort, and Bernhard Weiss (replacing one by Richard Francis Weymouth). Out of the three editions Nestle constructed a majority text, incorporating the agreement of two editions in the case of a divergent reading by any one of the three. When all three differed, Nestle offered a mediating solution.[2]

---

[1] In "Neue neutestamentliche Papyri," *NTS* 3 (1957): 261–86; 9 (1963): 303–16; 10 (1963): 62–79, Kurt Aland prepared the way for his series Arbeiten zur Neutestamentlichen Textforschung—a product of the Institute for New Testament Textual Research in Münster—of which the first volume was *Kurzgefasste Liste der griechischen Handschriften des Neuen Testaments* (Berlin: de Gruyter, 1963). Bruce M. Metzger, *The Text of the New Testament: Its Transmission, Corruption, and Restoration* (New York/Oxford: Oxford University Press, 1964); 3d enlarged ed. (New York: Oxford University Press, 1992) is a nonspecialist's best introduction to New Testament texts and versions. The main text of Metzger's third edition remains unaltered, but a new appendix, "Additional Notes," replaces the one made for the second edition (1968).

[2] See the introductions in Nestle[26] and in the *UBSGNT*.

Developments in textual criticism mandated the production of a text based on more scientific principles. At the same time Bible translators throughout the world were pleading with various Bible societies to prepare a text especially adapted to their requirements. Eugene A. Nida of the American Bible Society, ceaselessly enthusiastic in linguistic enterprise, gave the idea its needed impetus by organizing and administering an international project sponsored by the United Bible Societies. Included on the editorial committee were Kurt Aland, Matthew Black, Bruce Manning Metzger, and Allen Wikgren, with Arthur Vööbus participating during the first part of the work.[3]

In 1966 *The Greek New Testament* of the United Bible Societies (*UBSGNT*) appeared and displayed the special feature that was to become its distinguishing mark: a four-level (A, B, C, D) rating system for readings. In addition to some textual changes, a second edition offered revisions for the evaluation of readings, and the third (1975) introduced more than five hundred changes.

The text of the 26th edition of Nestle is for the most part identical in wording with that of the United Bible Societies' third edition, but its apparatus contains more information about variants.[4] Students will do well to have both editions close at hand. In addition, they will find in Bruce M. Metzger's *A Textual Commentary on the Greek Testament* (London/New York: United Bible Societies, 1971) an extraordinary opportunity to see how scholars arrive at conclusions about various readings.[5]

---

[3] Nida's attention to linguistic developments and their importance for biblical study have been too little noted in the exegetical craft. No one should attempt biblical translation or critique of such without having read his *Toward a Science of Translating* (Leiden, 1964) or his joint effort with Charles R. Taber, *The Theory and Practice of Translation* (Leiden, 1969), both with ample bibliographies.

[4] For a critique of Nestle[26] and an evaluation of developments since the beginning of the twentieth century, see Eldon J. Epp, "The Twentieth Century Interlude in the New Testament Criticism," *JBL* 93 (1974): 386–414. For information on other editions, see K. and B. Aland, *The Text of the New Testament: An Introduction to the Critical Editions and to the Theory and Practice of Modern Textual Criticism,* trans. Erroll F. Rhodes (Grand Rapids: Eerdmans, 1986), and Bruce M. Metzger, *The Text of the New Testament* (see above, note 1). For a critique of the Alands' work, see E. J. Epp, "New Testament Textual Criticism Past, Present, and Future: Reflections on the Alands' Text of the New Testament," *HTR* 82 (1989): 213–29. For a detailed study of the changes made in Nestle[26], see David Holly, *Comparative Studies in Recent Greek New Testaments: Nestle-Aland's 25th and 26th Editions* (Rome: Pontifical Biblical Institute, 1983). Among the changes listed, many of them book by book, are punctuation (some of it affecting accents), lexical elements, orthography, and substitution or subtraction of words. There is also a list of errors. Anyone engaging in critical comment on the Greek text of the New Testament must consult this work.

[5] As a product of cooperating Bible societies, this text is designed to meet the special needs of translators; it does not supplant the more detailed Nestle-Aland editions. From it the American Bible Society translation, *Good News for Modern Man,* Today's English Version (TEV) (New York: American Bible Society, 1966), was made under the direction of Robert G. Bratcher. For other editions, as well as the ambitious International Greek New Testament Project, see Bruce M. Metzger, *Text,* 119–46, 280–84; and bibliography in *The Greek New Testament,* ed. Kurt Aland,

The interpretive possibilities of Nestle[26] are nothing short of miraculous, but experience with seminary students would indicate that many are unaware of the vast resources at their disposal. Initial exegetical courses do indeed acquaint seminarians with the textual tradition embraced in the apparatus and attempt to help them find their way through the maze of variant readings, but little more than a casual acquaintance with all the signs and symbols and notations employed can be struck up in a course that must go on to the larger aspects of hermeneutics or introductory matters (isagogics).

This chapter therefore confines discussion to those functions of the critical apparatus at the bottom of the Nestle page and especially of the marginal notations that might otherwise be completely overlooked or neglected. It endeavors through ample illustration to show what a student, with nothing but the Nestle text and the Old Testament, can do by way of vital exposition. It aims further to aid in the development of an awareness of the critical problems that are suggested by the Nestle content. Certainly it is a great gain if, for example, in the course of sermon preparation, the hints here given encourage the expositor to an investigation that might otherwise not have been undertaken. The investigation itself will, of course, require detailed reference to standard exegetical tools and therefore properly lies outside the scope of this chapter, whose primary objective is an introduction to Nestle. Since a cluttering of these pages with Greek footnotes would not materially advance this objective, it is assumed that each reference will be checked in the Nestle text.

THE APPARATUS

To explore the critical apparatus in a Nestle edition is itself an adventure in biblical learning. Here can be found much of the stuff that makes the professional commentator appear so learned, and it is available for only a few cents

Matthew Black, Bruce M. Metzger, Allen Wikgren; 3d ed. (New York, London, Edinburgh, Amsterdam, Stuttgart, 1975), lv–lxii. A massive bibliography of New Testament textual criticism is available in Harry A. Sturz, *The Byzantine Text-Type and New Testament Textual Criticism* (Nashville: Nelson, 1984). Apart from Metzger's own works, much information on textual-critical matters can be gained from *New Testament Textual Criticism: Its Significance for Exegesis: Essays in Honor of Bruce M. Metzger*, ed. Eldon Jay Epp and Gordon D. Fee (Oxford: Oxford University Press, 1981), 231–74; included are indexes to the bibliography so that a researcher can find all the authors who, for example, discuss the "Caesarean text" or "Family E." This collection of twenty-nine essays by many who are distinguished in their own right as textual critics also contains a contribution by Kurt Aland, "Der Neue 'Standard Text' in seinem Verhältnis zu den frühen Papyri und Majuskeln," 257–75. Aland concludes that Nestle[26] brings us close to the earliest text-form that made its way out to the church of the first and second centuries. For various formats of the Nestle and the *UBSGNT* text, including facing texts in a variety of languages, see the catalogues of the American Bible Society.

per page. There are, first of all, those curious items that suggest fresh insights into the attitudes and approaches of early Christians to the New Testament documents.

CURIOS

A striking example of the free hand applied to the Gospels is found in the critical note on Mark 16:14. The sign ⊤·, with its counterpart in the main text marking the item for consideration in the apparatus, suggests an interpolation. The dot inside it marks it as the second interpolation in this verse. It is found in W, the Freer MS in Washington (fourth to fifth century; see Nestle, p. 692 [W 032]). The syntax is not too clear, but one can translate as follows:

> And they excused themselves, saying, "This age of lawlessness and unbelief is under the domination of Satan, who through the agency of the unclean spirits does not permit the true power of God to be apprehended. Therefore reveal now your righteousness," they said to Christ. And Christ said: "The bounds of the years of Satan's power are fulfilled, but other terrible things are drawing near. And in behalf of those who sinned I was delivered into death that they might be converted to the truth and might no longer sin, to the end that they might inherit the spiritual and incorruptible glory of righteousness in heaven."

The scribe evidently felt no compunctions about sanitizing the reputations of the apostles.

At Acts 24:24 the Harclean Syriac (see p. 57* of the Nestle text) reads in the margin, "who desired to see Paul and hear his word; wishing therefore to please her. . . ." Clearly this scribe was not particularly impressed with Felix's potential for conversion.

Someone with antiquarian interests, perhaps reflecting a recent trip to the Holy Land, is careful to insert the names of the two public enemies Joathas and Maggatras at Luke 23:32. Unfortunately the scribe does not identify the repentant bandit. An Old Latin witness at Mark 15:27 displays a slight variation in the names.

The bracketing of 'Ιησοῦν in Matt. 27:16 and 17 may well arouse curiosity: was the name very early omitted out of reverence for Jesus, or was it added because of typological interest?

We are grateful for the research of the P[75] copyist who assures us that the rich man's name was Νευης (Finees, according to Priscillian) at Luke 16:19,[6] but the attempt at identification seems to destroy a significant insight in the original text—God's personal interest in those who depend on divine mercy and God's rejection of the proud and complacent. This man is any person

---

[6] On *Neues*, see Metzger, *Text*, 188–89 n. 3; 205.

who is barreled alive in a cask of self, dying without a name. God knows him not (cf. Luke 13:27). Although the theology of the text is obscured, the documentation of an early approach to the literary form is valuable: the intrusion of the proper name Νευης makes it at least doubtful that we are dealing here with a parable in the narrower sense of the word, as the copyist of D believed (see the ⊤ at 16:19), rather than with what may be termed theological story.

The Magnificat (Luke 1:46-55) has never been widely ascribed to anyone but Mary, but one must face the fact that there is very early testimony, possibly second century, for the ascription of this memorable song to Elizabeth (Luke 1:46).

TRANSLATOR'S AID

Few students realize how useful the apparatus can be to help one out of an embarrassing translation situation. The critical apparatus quite often suggests clarification of the text or helps solve some particularly intricate syntax. At 2 Cor. 8:24 the syntax loses its apparent obscurity when one looks at ἐνδείξασθε, the variant for the participle preferred by the Nestle editor. The student is reminded here of a familiar New Testament phenomenon related to the Semitic love for the participle to express imperatival relations. The aorist participle in Acts 25:13 might easily evoke an awkward translation, but the copyists represented in the apparatus assure us that this was not a *long-distance* salutation. Yet in their anxiety to rid the text of a troublesome "subsequent" aorist participle, these copyists miss the point: Agrippa and Bernice not only send greetings to Festus but, astute politicians that they are, communicate them in person. Literally, "they came down to Caesarea in salutation of Festus."[7]

The difficulty in the phrase ἐπὶ Τίτου at 2 Cor. 7:14 is immediately removed by looking at the scribal gloss πρὸς Τίτον. It is the boast that Paul made before Titus, in the latter's presence, face to face with him.

Also, lest the novice develop careless grammatical habits, there is always the pedantic copyist with a neat correction in standard or classical Greek, as at 1 Thess. 3:8.

DOGMATIC ARENA

The apparatus also permits us to catch a glimpse of theologians engaged in heated debate. We see daring alterations of hallowed texts emerging out of earnest concern for truth.

---

[7] A parallel phenomenon occurs in Rom. 5:11, where the variant καυχώμεθα explains the participle καυχώμενοι.

The tampering at Luke 2:33 is well known. The virginal conception is preserved by inserting "Joseph" in place of ὁ πατὴρ αὐτοῦ (see also 2:41, 43, 49 [cf. Matt. 1:16]). A cognate concern for the doctrine of Jesus' virginal conception is evident in the interesting variant in John 1:13. In place of the plural (οἱ . . . ἐγεννήθησαν) the singular (*qui . . . natus est*) is in *b*, Irenaeus (Latin), and Tertullian, with the qualification that Tertullian omits the *qui*.

In a similar vein is the omission by a few minuscules of οὐδὲ υἱός in Mark 13:32 to preserve our Lord's omniscience.

An interesting omission occurs at Mark 7:4. Some of the great uncials do not include καὶ κλινῶν, but the word has catholic support. If the word was originally a part of Mark's autograph, its omission would tend to confirm belief in a widespread practice of immersion at the time of baptism. A copyist would observe that the immersion of dining couches was difficult if not impossible. In any event, Mark 7:4 is not the most convincing argument in favor of sprinkling.

Philemon 5 presents an instructive illustration of altered word order. Instead of ἀγάπην καὶ τὴν πίστιν, D, a few minuscules, and the Peshitta read πίστιν καὶ τὴν ἀγάπην. The copyist or copyists originally responsible for this alteration display commendable awareness of Pauline thought in placing faith ahead of works, but a little of the edge is taken off what must certainly have been Paul's original statement. It is Paul's intention to emphasize Philemon's past displays of *agape;* the present situation calls for maximum effort, and therefore Paul is grateful to hear of the faith that Philemon has to spark still more *agape.* Thus, the original reading does not place faith alongside love as two separate entities but relates them vitally in such a way that faith stands midway between Philemon's past and the future that is now expected of him. On the hinge of faith Philemon's past and future swing. Later copyists missed the point, but the fact that they missed it helps us to note it.

Misapplied knowledge can be hazardous, especially when it invites rebuttal from the mean spirited. Antisegregationists and opponents of racial intolerance would do well therefore to take a second look at Acts 17:26 before introducing it as biblical exhibit A disproving white supremacy. An antiprejudice punch is there, but probably not in the doubtful variant αἵματος, which was popularized by the KJV, and to which NRSV invites attention through the marginal note: "other ancient authorities read: *From one blood.*" Bigotry is better smitten by more potent passages.

The question whether the Bible affirms that the resurrection of the body is a signal prerogative of the Holy Spirit depends on whether the διά in Rom. 8:11 is followed by an accusative or a genitive.

The variant Ἰησοῦς, Jude 5, suggests an early connection of Joshua (Jesus) with the Exodus and raises the question of the lengths to which the early church went in its christological interpretation of the Old Testament.

Of primary significance for many Christians is the text of John 1:18. The reading of Papyrus Bodmer II (P⁶⁶), which unequivocally asserts the divinity of Jesus Christ, outbids other textual evidence for the ascendancy in the 26th edition of Nestle.[8]

Interpreter's Paradise

Often the apparatus is helpful in interpreting the material accepted in the text. The Latin addition to Luke 23:48 leads one to the correct interpretation of the passion events as God's most decisive action evoking repentance and faith. This is not to say that all who returned to their homes were repentant, but as the Latin addition suggests ("Woe . . . for the desolation of Jerusalem has drawn near"), it was not Jesus who was on trial but those who condemned him.

The possibility of reading the words κἀμὲ οἴδατε καὶ οἴδατε πόθεν εἰμι in John 7:28 as a question (see *UBSGNT* margin) would appear to add considerable clarity to a difficult passage. At any rate, if the declarative statement is read, as in the text of both *UBSGNT* and Nestle, the expositor should be able to give adequate reasons for an apparent ambiguity in the Greek.

The jolt at John 3:25 is not really felt until one looks at the apparatus and realizes that from childhood one has been reading "with the Jews." The various conjectures that suggest Jesus in place of the singular Ἰουδαίου indicate the difficulty. The context seems to require Jesus as the second party in the dispute.

One might miss the evangelist's point entirely in John 6:15, were it not for the variant φεύγει, read by the first hand in Sinaiticus in place of ἀνεχώρησεν.

On the other hand, scribal suggestions are not always premium grade. Yet even an erroneous interpretation can alert one to the hazards of reading something alien into the text. The scribe responsible for the addition of τῶν ψιχίων in Luke 16:21 probably recollected part of Matt. 15:27, as the Nestle margin observes, and was also aware of parallel phrasing in Luke 15:16, with the result that the rich man appeared to be even more insensitive than the narrative originally indicated. There is no firm indication in the story that the rich man's heart was shut to Lazarus's need. On the other hand, the variant helps document an early distortion of the narrative.

A Note of Harmony

Interesting questions involving harmonization of biblical material are often suggested by the apparatus. Especially notorious are the harmonistic variants in the genealogies of Matthew 1 and Luke 3.

---

[8] On this, see Charles Kingsley Barrett's observations in "Papyrus Bodmer II: A Preliminary Report," *Expository Times* 68 (1957): 175.

The variants in Sinaiticus and other manuscripts in Mark 14:68 and 72 (cf. 14:30) suggest concern in the minds of scribes for greater harmony with the record of the single cockcrow recorded in the other evangelists. The record of two cockcrows, on the other hand, may reflect an early attempt to make the actual events conform with a literal understanding of Jesus' prediction in Mark 14:30. Some of the scribes responsible for the transmission of Matt. 26:34 cut the knot with their ἀλεκτοροφωνίας, thereby preserving harmony with the accepted Markan text.

The apparatus to Acts indicates singular deviations of MS D. Especially interesting is the alteration in Acts 10:40. The phrase ἐν τῇ τρίτῃ ἡμέρᾳ is altered to read μετὰ τὴν τρίτην ἡμέραν, in conformity with Matt. 12:40 and 27:63. Similarly, Matt. 16:21; 17:23; and Luke 9:22 are brought in harmony. On the other hand there is a remarkable absence of variants in MS D at Matt. 20:19; Luke 18:33; and 24:7.

THE MARGINS

From the bottom of the Nestle page we move upward to the margins. These are virtually inexhaustible mines of information. The average student is unaware of their potentialities, and many a preacher has wearied himself in vain while the answer to the problems in a text lay a few centimeters to the right or left.

The Outer Margins

Concordance

Often a glance at the margins will save a trip to the lexicon or spare the taking of a massive concordance like Moulton-Geden or Aland off the shelf. Take, for example, 1 Cor. 7:31 and its obvious paronomasia. What is the force of καταχρώμενοι? The margin refers to 9:18. (Lack of a book reference in Nestle indicates the document in hand.) In this latter passage Paul says, "What, then, is my reward? This, that in preaching the gospel I might offer it without charge, and not insist on my full rights in the gospel." The word he uses here in the last part of the sentence is exactly this word καταχράομαι. Paul does not use up his authority in the gospel. In the former passage, then, he is saying that we should use the world, but not as people who cannot wait to *use it up*. We should use it, but not stake out a claim on it! For this cosmic pattern is out-dated. (Question: Of what validity here is the argument that the Koine tends to use compound verbs without making fine distinctions from the simplex forms. See below, chap. 7.)

The term παράδεισος in Luke 23:43 finds a parallel in 2 Cor. 12:4. The exclamation mark in Nestle's margin implies that at this latter passage all the relevant references will be found. A glance in the margin at 2 Cor. 12:4 leads to Rev. 2:7, where significant Old Testament passages are cited, such as Gen. 2:9 and 3:22, 24. The point is clear without even a look at the initial chapters of Genesis. Paradise is symbolic of the choicest association one can enjoy with the Creator. Here on the cross Jesus effects a redemption that restores what Adam lost (see Luke 3:38). Jesus eats with publicans and sinners. Here on the cross he communicates God's offer of intimate association to the repentant robber. Forgiveness spells fellowship with God. This word to the robber is one of Jesus' most sublime claims to Deity.

Undoubtedly the Pastorals would be consulted first if one were looking for the New Testament data on ecclesiastical offices. Experience in dealing with the marginal references immediately suggests that at Acts 20:28 the Nestle editor has a concordance of all passages dealing with the term ἐπίσκοπος.

The margin is intensely illuminating at John 2:4. Does Jesus mean to say with the phrase ἡ ὥρα μου that he will determine the appropriate time to relieve the bridegroom's embarrassment, or is there a deeper significance? A look at John 13:1, to which the reference in the margin at 7:30 points, suggests that Jesus' true messianic function is synonymous with his passion. It is in this larger context that the miracle at Cana is to be viewed.

Don't throw away Nestle[25]! At 1 Pet. 1:1-2, for example, it carries a reference to Exod. 24:3-8, which the 26th edition does not include. The Septuagint will be of help here. It provides the linguistic clues for understanding these verses as a summary of basic themes in 1 Peter.

Historical Information

As in the apparatus so in the margin one may find much useful supplementary information. A significant insight into Paul's missionary method (assuming that the speech at the Areopagus substantially represents his missionary approach) is gained with the realization that the phrase τοῦ γὰρ καὶ γένος ἐσμέν (Acts 17:28) is a citation from the *Phaenomena* of Aratus. Similar citations from gentile authors may be observed at 1 Cor. 15:33 and Titus 1:12.

A parallel approach to apocryphal literature, especially apocalyptic, is apparent from the marginal references in the Epistle of Jude. The *Book of Enoch,* popular at the beginning of the Christian era, is abstracted and cited with evident approval. The possibility of dependence on another work, the *Assumptio Mosis,* is hinted at in Jude 9. See also 1 Pet. 1:12 and 3:19.

Of even greater value is the reconstruction of the historical situation to which the various New Testament documents owe their origin. No exposition worth a second look dare be divorced from the historical roots. Of a more general isagogical nature are the handy references next to the superscriptions of many individual books. At the beginning of St. Luke's Gospel the reader finds all the references in the New Testament to one named Luke. The same applies to Mark's Gospel. There are no references at the beginning of Matthew. The references at Jude 1 suggest that the letter is probably written in the name of Jesus' brother mentioned in Matt. 13:55 (at the head of the pericope in which this passage is found the editor makes reference to Mark 6:1-6a, which includes the name).

From the references at the superscription of 1 Corinthians it is easy to reconstruct the context of Paul's initial mission efforts in Corinth (Acts 18:1-11). 1 Thessalonians 3:1-8 and Paul's entire relationship with the Thessalonians gains new point if the references to Acts 17 and 18 are checked. At Acts 18:5, in turn, the exclamation behind 15:27 in the margin alerts the reader to all references to Timothy. These historical references must, of course, be used with caution, for the Nestle editor aims merely to make accessible as much relevant data as possible. For example, the references in the Pastorals to historical situations recorded in Acts should be evaluated in the light of the problems associated with the authenticity of the Pastorals. The references to a Gaius at 3 John are not to be construed as an editorial identification. On the other hand, judicious use of the margin will alert the student to many points buried in learned books on introduction.

Synoptic Criticism

Synoptic study means to recognize the fact that when a set of documents displays common characteristics, it is probable that there was some interdependence. Below we shall have more to say about books that record such phenomena, but at this point it is important to examine the possibilities that Nestle[26] offers for at least elementary synoptic study when a bulky synopsis is not available or is inconvenient to use. The Nestle margin in the Gospels, especially in the Synoptics, is veritably a miniature Aland *Synopsis*.[9] Identity of the source for a given pericope or portion thereof is greatly simplified by a glance at the margin. At Luke 5, for example, vv. 1-11 are noted in italics. A colon indicates that the citations that follow (Matt. 4:18-22; Mark 1:16-20; John 21:1-11) relate in some way to the text at hand; the abbreviation "cf." suggests that the parallels are not so clear as, for example, those cited for the narrative units that immediately precede 5:1-11. A comparison of the passages cited for the latter passages suggests that Luke has relied heavily on a special source (L) for the story of a record catch of fish. A study of the placement of pericopes preceding this account and paralleled in the other Synoptists, including especially the story of Jesus' rejection at Nazareth (Luke 4:16-30),

---

[9] For published synopses, see below (pp. 41–43).

indicates that Luke adjusts Mark's outline in the interests of his own particular aims and objectives.

Between Mark 1:15 and 16 Luke has placed, first of all, the story of Jesus' rejection at Nazareth (4:16-30). Mark introduces this event after Jesus' ministry is well under way, at Mark 6:1-6a according to the Nestle margin. Luke's purpose is quite apparent. He is alerting his readers to the nature of the conflict that he is about to describe. The story also gives him an opportunity to introduce the gentile motif that is so close to his heart (4:25-27). The second alteration (noted at 4:31 and 33) is the transfer of Mark 1:21-22 and 1:23-28 to a point before the calling of the first disciples. Mark's emphasis appears to be placed on Jesus' person. He is the Son of God, who shows his power by casting out the demons, and the disciples are to testify thereto. Luke, on the other hand, emphasizes Jesus' program. The juxtaposition of this incident with that of the rejection at Nazareth gives him the opportunity to show not only the demonic nature of the opposition that develops against Jesus but also how Jesus understands his mission, namely, as an assault on Satan's stronghold. It is in this light that Jesus' healing ministry is to be understood. Hence, the incident involving Peter's mother-in-law is preserved here, especially because of the general reference in Mark to Jesus' power over the demons (Mark 1:34). Admirable is the skill with which Luke uses the story of a catch of fish. Jesus overcomes the devices of the devil by taking people like Simon into his program. This association with sinners, one that plays so large a role in this Gospel, communicates God's forgiving presence. And in forgiveness God's victory over Satan is begun. Luke 23:43 with its gigantic μετά is the finest commentary on this theme. Thus, a study of the Synoptic parallels suggests that in Luke's account the emphasis is not on the disciples' ultimate activity, "catching human beings," but on the privilege that such activity accents.

The reference to Luke 7:1-10 at Matt. 8:5-13 is extremely instructive. Luke has placed the healing of the leper (5:12-16) before Jesus' sermon. Matthew places this story after the sermon because together with that of the centurion it emphasizes the fulfillment of messianic expectation (see Matt. 11:5). The inclusion in Matt. 8:11 and 12 of material that seems originally to have been attached more closely to the context in which it is found in Luke 13 would tend to support this view. Luke's emphasis is rather on the proper response that Jesus' word ought to find: faith! Hence he prefers the story of the centurion after the sermon.

The reference to Matt. 24:42 at Mark 13:35 suggests how the evangelists used the materials as they were shaped in the varied work of the church—in its proclamation, polemics, instruction, and worship. A host of variants such as that in MS *k* (Mark 13:37), "but what I have said to one, I have said to all of you," points in this direction. It is quite apparent that the early church was greatly concerned to preserve the full significance of Jesus' words and thought in its own vital involvement in the destiny of the reign of God.

The identification of material probably taken from Q is simplified through the use of the Nestle margins.[10] For example, from the absence of any reference to Mark and from the presence of a reference to Luke at Matt. 6:25-34 one may deduce that the passage is generally considered Q material, following the rule that Q is principally material common to Matthew and Luke but not found in Mark. Caution: At Matt. 5:1, for example, there is a reference to Luke 6:20-49. One may readily infer that the Sermon on the Mount is largely Q material. But what about Matt. 6:1-6, to mention but one passage in this section? This material is found in none of the other Synoptists. In the narrower definition of Q it is not strictly Q material, but, for want of a better designation, M (peculiarly Matthew) material. But the hazard is not really too great, as we shall later see in the discussion of Eusebius's canons. Alertness to the differences in presentation of Q material can be instructive, as for example in the case of the Beatitudes, Luke 6:20-23 (par. Matt. 5:2-12). It will be noted that Luke's version emphasizes the circumstances involving the kingdom candidates, whereas Matthew's version stresses their inward qualifications.

A study of Luke 23:37 teaches one the finer points of Nestle investigation. There is no immediate reference in the margin to the words εἰ σὺ εἶ ὁ βασιλεὺς τῶν Ἰουδαίων, σῶσον σεαυτόν, but going back to the beginning of the paragraph signaled by the reference 35-38, we find the Synoptic parallels. We follow up the Matthew account and find that the closest parallel to our passage is in Matt. 27:40. Here Nestle has a reference to Matt. 4:3, with an exclamation point. Matthew 4:3 happens to contain the words of the devil, εἰ υἱὸς εἶ τοῦ θεοῦ (see Luke 4:3). We begin to grasp the point. The passion is presented by both evangelists as a conflict with Satan in which the concept of divine sonship is at stake. The devil suggests that sonship excludes the idea of suffering and thereby the task of saving others. Save yourself! The demonic temptation is thus seen in its most concentrated and climactic dimension.

Cross Illumination

The margins are especially helpful in locating specific parallels on a number of topics. Heeding Nestle's exclamation points can save teachers, students, or ministers valuable time and earn them points for quick recognition.

If the subject is views of woman's role in the early church and if a passage such as 1 Tim. 2:11 is known or found through use of a concordance, one can light upon other significant passages at 1 Cor. 14:34.

---

[10] One of the best introductions to the subject of Q, M, and L can be found in Frederick C. Grant, *The Gospels: Their Origin and Their Growth* (New York: Harper, 1957), chaps. 4, 5, pp. 40–63; for a specialized theory about the origin of Luke's Gospel involving use of Q, see Burnett Hillman Streeter, *The Four Gospels: A Study of Origins, Treating of the Manuscript Tradition, Sources, Authorship, & Dates,* 1st ed. (1924); 4th impression, rev. (London: Macmillan, 1956).

Some idea of the esteem enjoyed by biblical writings in Christian circles is documented at 2 Tim. 3:16 with references to 2 Pet. 1:19-21 and Rom. 15:4. If it is a catalog of Christian virtues one needs, the references at Gal. 5:22 will be helpful. In connection with the tradition of Jesus' descent into the nether world, the margin at 1 Pet. 3:19 suggests relevant pseudepigraphic as well as biblical parallels.

Yet the Nestle margins invite one to even more subtle cross-illumination. The problem of the man without a wedding garment has long been a perplexing exegetical problem. Is this part of the story really an integral part of the original parable? The reference to Rev. 19:8 at Matt. 22:11 appears to suggest the answer. In the Revelation passage the white garment is identified with the righteous deeds of the saints. Translating this information to Matthew's passage, we hypothesize that the man without the wedding garment is one who attempts to enter without the deeds that correspond to kingdom expectations. This interpretation, of course, does not help us much, if faith, not deeds, is the prior requirement for entry into the kingdom. But we shall not give up our hypothesis as yet. Instead we examine the context and note that in the later expanded context of the church's mission the despisers of the king's invitation really image those who rely on their own performance or on liturgical associations. The man without a wedding garment, then, is representative of those who claim to be identified with the objectives and purposes of God but lack real commitment. Though in effect they reject the invitation, through their liturgical claims they have the audacity to appear at the feast, but it is as one without a wedding garment. The fruits of the truly repentant life are missing. Thus the parable's life-situation (*Sitz im Leben*) seems clear. Christian Israel has its problems with those in their midst who, like the rich man in the story of Lazarus, rest on their Abrahamic laurels. But they will be discovered as guests who crash the party without a wedding garment.

The marginal reference to Luke 2:49 at Luke 23:46 helps tie the entire Gospel together in terms of Jesus' obedient activity, and it all hinges on the word πατήρ. Jesus must be in his Father's house. Now, as it were, He is "going home." The task is fulfilled. What the temple symbolized is now reality. A similar type of reference at Luke 2:14 links the text with Palm Sunday and puts the Christmas message in the perspective of the events in Holy Week.

To the mind of the Nestle editor a probable solution to the meaning of Jude 6 is hinted at by the reference to Gen. 6:1-4, which suggests the attempt of hostile spirits to defile the godly community. Compare a similar suggestion for the obscure allusion in 1 Cor. 11:10.[11]

One can considerably reduce the difficulty concerning Paul's argument in Galatians 3 by following up the reference to Rom. 4:15 at Gal. 3:19. Moreover,

---

[11] The student may find it interesting to compare the question mark at this passage in Nestle[25] with its absence in Nestle[26].

the references to passages in Romans 7 at Rom. 4:15 suggest that the primary function of the Law is not to curb sins but rather to have sin express itself, so that through sins one's sinful nature might find exposure of its awful reality.

At Mark 9:7 there is mention of 2 Pet. 1:17. A look at the latter passage in its context shows that the transfiguration was understood eschatologically in the apostolic community. That is, the Christian hope is rooted in past realities. From this interpretive point of vantage the statement (Mark 9:1) immediately preceding the story of the transfiguration, that some "shall not taste death until they see the reign of God coming in power," gains in point. The reference to 2 Pet. 2:22 at Matt. 7:6 suggests an entirely new and challenging interpretation of Matthew's passage. The point appears to be that there is no advantage in admonishing people who desire no moral improvement. Locating their motes will only irritate them, and they will resent what they suspect is your own hypocrisy.

Things New and Old

The rich treasury of Old Testament and pseudepigraphic passages accessible in the Nestle margins offers inspiring possibilities. Eminently instructive is the survey of these passages at the end of Nestle (pp. 739–75).

At Luke 7:12 and 15, we have references to 2 Kings 4:32-37 and 1 Kings 17:23, respectively. These passages not only suggest that the evangelist is here following a primitive account of the acts and words of Jesus, to which he seems to make reference in Luke 1:1-4, but also show that in his person Jesus fulfills the Old Testament, in this case by being the greater Elijah–Elisha. In a similar vein at John 2:4 the citation from Gen. 41:55 suggests Jesus as a second Joseph, who comes to rescue a needy people. The messianic significance of the parable in Matt. 13:31-32 is inescapable in the light of Dan. 4:9, 18; Ezek. 17:23; 31:6; and Ps. 103:12 (LXX), all of which speak of the rush of Gentiles for salvation in the messianic era.

At Matt. 27:5 a reference is made to 2 Sam. 17:23. The parallel is striking. Judas is to Christ as Ahithophel was to David in his counsel to Absalom. Of interest in this connection is the echo of 2 Sam. 17:3 in John 11:50, but the margin offers no clue. The student must here and elsewhere therefore go beyond the listed references. Much of the point of Matt. 22:34-40, for example, rests on the allusion in v. 34 to Ps. 2:2 (LXX), but Nestle gives no indication of a probable connection.

THE INNER MARGINS

The outer margins are, to be sure, the most fruitful, but the inner margins can also be the source of valuable exegetical insights.

Paragraph Divisions

Details on the inner margins are given in Nestle's introduction, p. 69. As the editors indicate, small italicized numbers are to be noted. These reproduce the paragraph divisions or κεφάλαια found in many manuscripts. In the Gospels they appear to antedate Eusebius and are sometimes referred to as the Ammonian sections, but their actual origin is shrouded in antique mists.[12] Synoptic interests dominate in the notation of the Gospel material. Both the existence of parallels and their absence may be noted by these little numbers. For example, at Matt. 13:3 the 24 reminds the reader of parallels to the parable of the sower, whereas the 12 at John 12:3 suggests that Mary is not specifically mentioned in the Synoptic parallels. But consistency is not a primary virtue of these κεφάλαια, and there is no suggestion, for example, of the complexity of the problem posed by the parallels to the Matthaean version of the Sermon on the Mount.

Sometimes a useful insight is suggested by these marginal numbers. The presence of the 34 at Mark 11:25, for example, alerts the reader to the fact that this verse incorporates an idea that was probably not originally connected integrally with the preceding account. The conjunction of material, we theorize, is probably to be traced to Mark's creative pen. A comparison with Matthew's use of the thought (6:14-15, aided by the outer margin) suggests that Mark as well as Matthew wishes to emphasize that in prayer people are beggars before God and that their beggary begins before the throne of forgiving mercy. The origin of a great faith is, then, to be found in the recognition of sin and its cure. At Luke 8:1-3, however, the originator of this system has missed the point completely, by failing to highlight the role of the women in Jesus' ministry. But at Luke 11:27, alerted by the numeral 40, we hear the voice of the woman who praises Jesus.

The Gospels provide the most interesting material for examination of the κεφάλαια, but a study of the epistles, such as the structure of 1 Corinthians, at the hand of the old Greek paragraph divisions can prove rewarding. For example, the traditional paragraphing at 5:1 is at odds with the ancient division, which saw in 4:21 the introduction to St. Paul's expression of indignation beginning at 5:1.

It is regrettable that the editors of Nestle[26] did not include the system of division found in Vaticanus (MS B).[13] Earlier editions of Nestle indicate this system of division with upright figures, larger than those used for the κεφάλαια.

---

[12] For exhaustive discussion of the κεφάλαια, see Hermann von Soden, *Die Schriften des Neuen Testaments* (Göttingen, 1911), 1/1:402–75. Detailed lists, including the τίτλοι, are given. See also Caspar Gregory, *Textkritik des Neuen Testaments* (Leipzig, 1909), 858–80.

[13] See Von Soden, *Die Schriften,* 432–42 (Gospels); 460 (Catholic Epistles, except 2 Peter, 2 and 3 John); 471–72 (Pauline Epistles).

In view of the fact that despite its superiority this system was unable to dislodge the old Greek paragraph divisions used in the Gospels, it is probably of later origin. In the case of the remaining writings the question of priority is more complex.

The practical advantages of this system of division can be explored in connection with Matt. 5:17-48. Students may find it interesting to compare the paragraphing of Nestle[26] and the capitalization of initial words in an earlier edition at vv. 21, 27, 31, 33, 38, and 43. In any case, such examination will provide a double check on significant structural phenomena. Having opted for omission of the ancient chapter divisions in Vaticanus, the editors of Nestle[26] do not offer the student a valuable datum that is available in earlier editions at Mark 8:10, for example, where the numeral 33 should be examined closely in relation to the indication of a new paragraph at v. 11. Does Mark prefer a topical or a chronological arrangement at this point?

Also omitted in the inner margin of Nestle[26] are the small heavy boldface numbers that in earlier editions (see, e.g., the small 3 at Acts 2:5) indicated a second division made by a later hand in the text of Vaticanus.[14] In many respects both the old Greek paragraph divisions and the parallel systems will be found superior to the chapter divisions standardized since Stephen Langton.[15]

EUSEBIAN CANON

A final word respecting the usefulness of Nestle[26] is reserved for the canons of Eusebius. These devices for harmonizing the four Gospels are a marvel of ingenuity. Eusebius's own directions for their use as well as his acknowledgment of indebtedness to Ammonius of Alexandria are outlined in a letter to Carpian. Eusebius of Caesarea writes to this effect:

> Ammonius the Alexandrian in an extraordinary display of industry and diligence has indeed left us a harmony of the Gospels by placing alongside Matthew's Gospel the parallel sections from the other evangelists, but with the result that the train of thought of the other three Gospels is necessarily destroyed as far as consecutive reading is concerned. Therefore, in order that you might be able to identify in each Gospel those sections which are faithfully paralleled elsewhere and yet have the entire structure and train of thought preserved intact, I have taken my cue from my predecessor, but have used a different approach, in that I have drawn

[14] Ibid., 444–45 (Acts); 461 (Catholic Epistles); and 472 (Paul).

[15] On the modern chapter and verse divisions, see Von Soden, *Die Schriften*, 475–85; Caspar Gregory, *Textkritik*, 880–95 (especially the citation of Ezra Abbot's material on verse divisions, pp. 883–95); Bruce M. Metzger, *Manuscripts of the Greek Bible: An Introduction to Greek Palaeography* (New York: Oxford University Press, 1981), 41–42. For the Old Testament, see below, chap. 3, pp. 56–57.

up for you the accompanying tables, ten in number. Of these the first comprises the numbers in which all four say substantially the same things: Matthew, Mark, Luke, and John. The second in which three: Matthew, Mark, Luke. The third in which three, Matthew, Luke, John. The fourth in which three: Matthew, Mark, John. The fifth in which two: Matthew and Luke. The sixth in which two: Matthew and Mark. The seventh in which two: Matthew and John. The eighth in which two: Luke and Mark. The ninth in which two: Luke and John. The tenth in which each one has included material peculiar to himself alone. So much, then, for the basic pattern.

Now this is the manner in which the tables function. In each of the four Gospels all the individual sections are numbered in sequence, beginning with one, then two, then three, and so on clear through each one of the books. Alongside each of these numbers a notation is made in red, to indicate in which one of the ten tables a given number is to be found. So for example, if the notation in red is a one, then it is clear that Table I is to be consulted. If a two, then the number of the section is to be found in Table II, and so on through the ten tables. Now suppose that you have opened up one of the four Gospels at random. You select some paragraph that strikes your fancy and wish to know not only which evangelists contain the parallels but the exact locations in which the inspired parallels are to be found. To do this you need only note the number identifying your pericope, and then look for it in the table specified by the red notation (under the corresponding evangelist). You will know immediately from the headings at the top of the table the number and the identity of the evangelists who contain parallels. Then if you note the numbers in the other evangelists that run parallel to the number you have already noted and look for them in the individual Gospels, you will experience no difficulty in locating the parallel items.[16]

Eusebius's directions can be applied to the figures in the Nestle margin with but a slight alteration. Instead of a red notation the present Nestle text provides the number of the particular table in roman numerals directly under the pericope sequence number in arabic numerals. In earlier editions a comma divided the two. There is no possibility of confusion with the *kephalaia,* which, as indicated above, are noted in italics.

It was previously noted that the Nestle text, through the outer margins, supplies readers with what is essentially a harmony of the Gospels. But to avoid cluttering the margin the editors confine themselves in the main to identification of principal units. The Eusebian canons are quite useful therefore in hunting parallels to individual verses buried deep inside these longer passages. For example, at Matt. 24:1 one of the parallels for the pericope is Mark 13:1-37.

---

[16] Migne, *PG* 22:1275-92. Full details can be found in Von Soden, *Die Schriften,* 388-402; see Gregory, *Textkritik,* 861-72; also Dr. Eberhard Nestle's article, "Die Eusebianische Evangelien-Synopse," *Neue Kirchliche Zeitschrift* 19 (1908): 40-51, 93-114, 219-32; Metzger, *Manuscripts,* 42. See Nestle[26], 73*-78*, for the canons of Eusebius, directions for their decipherment, and the Greek text of the letter to Carpian.

But if one is interested in finding quickly the Markan reference for the thought in Matt. 24:36, the Eusebian canon is the aid to use. The reference "260,VI" means that I must look for number 260 under the column marked Matthew in Canon VI. Next to the number 260 in that column, I find 152 in Mark's column. I proceed to trace this number through Mark's sequence until I come to it at Mark 13:32. Again, at Matt. 26:41 the notation "297,IV" readily refers me to Mark 14:38 as well as a parallel idea in John 6:63. And at John 1:18 the Eusebian canon is the only marker directing me to Luke 10:22. A singular phenomenon occurs at John 12:2: two canons are indicated (98,I and IV).

Little known is the textual-critical function of these canons. Mark 15:28 is located in the apparatus, but the Eusebian notation suggests that Eusebius's manuscripts had this verse (see Luke 23:17). The apparatus does not state it, but the presence of the Eusebian notation at Luke 22:43 suggests that Eusebius read also this significant verse. On the other hand, the absence of a notation at Mark 9:46, for example, would seem to indicate that Eusebius did not read the verse.

Study of a particular text at the hand of the Eusebian notations can be singularly illuminating. Mark 14:48, 49 is a fair example. The position of "185,VI" indicates that the present verse division is different from that followed by Eusebius. The logic in Eusebius's division is readily apparent. The entire verse 48, up to and including με, is for the most part paralleled in all the other evangelists (Canon I), but the words ἵνα πληρωθῶσιν αἱ γραφαί are found in only one other evangelist (Canon VI), in this case Matt. 26:56. Luke instead has αὕτη ἐστὶν ὑμῶν ἡ ὥρα καὶ ἡ ἐξουσία τοῦ σκότους (22:53). In agreement with the Synoptists he sees in the events a fulfillment of God's purpose but wishes to highlight the demonic dimensions of things to come.

A further testimony to Eusebius's sharp insight is the notation at Mark 12:40 ("136,VIII"), instead of at 12:41, as the ancient paragraph systems have it. The reader is immediately grateful for this significant contrast between certain Pharisees who devour widows' houses and this widow, who gives God all that such Pharisees have not already taken.

Special attention should be paid to Canon X whenever it is noted in the margin. The fact that a particular verse or group of verses is found in only one evangelist may have great bearing on the interpretation. And for anyone who questions the priority of Mark, a study of Canon X for Mark may turn out to be a wholesome critical leaven. The identification of material peculiar to Matthew (M) or Luke (L) is also considerably simplified by noting Canon X.

A little practice in the use of the Eusebian canons is required, but the initial effort followed by constant judicious use will more than repay the student in valuable insights that often escape the most astute commentator.

Whether it is the Eusebian canons, the ancient paragraph divisions, the outer margin, or the apparatus that one happens to use at a given moment, no student can fail to feel indebtedness to the editors and to the publishers of the Nestle text for the amazing amount of information they have been able to compact into this little book.

OTHER EDITIONS

It is appropriate here to call attention to a number of other editions of the Greek New Testament that must be consulted for advanced work on the New Testament text. The Bauer Greek lexicon (see chap. 7) refers frequently to some of the following:

1. Konstantin von Tischendorf, *Novum Testamentum Graece,* editio octava critica maior, I (Leipzig, 1869); II (1872), and Prolegomena by Caspar René Gregory, III (1884–94), not to be confused with the editio minor by Oskar von Gebhardt, 5th impression (Leipzig, 1891).
2. Brooke Foss Westcott and Fenton John Anthony Hort, *The New Testament in the Original Greek,* vol. 1, the Greek text; vol. 2, *Introduction and Appendix* (Cambridge, UK, 1881).
3. Richard Francis Weymouth, *The Resultant Greek Testament* (London, 1886).
4. Bernhard Weiss, *Das Neue Testament,* 3 parts (Leipzig: J. C. Hinrichs'sche Buchhandlung, 1894–1900), the substitute for Weymouth in Nestle's third (1901) and later editions.
5. Alexander Souter, 1910; the revised edition of 1947 incorporates further manuscript evidence, especially papyri. The text is substantially the *Textus Receptus*.[17]
6. José Maria Bover, *Novi Testamenti Biblia Graeca et Latina* (1943), 5th ed. (Madrid, 1968). This is an eclectic text and approaches the Western or Caesarean text type; see Metzger, *Text,* 143–44.
7. Augustinus Merk, *Novum Testamentum Graece et Latine,* 9th ed. (Rome: Pontifical Biblical Institute, 1964); except for some alterations in orthography and punctuation, Merk's Latin text reproduces the Sixto-Clementine edition of 1592.
8. Hermann Freiherr von Soden, *Die Schriften des Neuen Testaments in ihrer ältesten erreichbaren Textgestalt, hergestellt auf Grund ihrer Textgeschichte,* pt. 1, vols. 1–3, *Untersuchungen* (Berlin, 1902–1910; reprint, Göttingen, 1911); pt. 2, *Text mit Apparat,* with addition to pt. 1 (Göttingen, 1913), well known for von Soden's division of witnesses to the text into three main groups: K (Koine), associated with Lucian of Antioch and characteristic of the Byzantine Church (Westcott and Hort's Syrian text); H (Hesychian), traced to Hesychius of Egypt (what Westcott

---

[17] Metzger, *Text,* 138–39.

and Hort termed the Neutral and the Alexandrian text); I (Jerusalem), associated with Eusebius and Pamphilus of Caesarea in Palestine.

9. Heinrich Joseph Vogels, *Novum Testamentum Graece et Latine,* 4th ed. (Freiburg im Breisgau: Herder, 1955).

10. British and Foreign Bible Society. A new edition of Eberhard Nestle's 4th edition (1903) was produced by George Dunbar Kilpatrick with Erwin Nestle and others, including Copticist Paul Eric Kahle, to mark the 150th anniversary of the British and Foreign Bible Society (London, 1958).

11. International Greek New Testament Project (IGNTP. *The New Testament in Greek III: The Gospel According to St. Luke. Part One. Chapters 1–12,* ed. by the American and British Committee of the IGNTP (Oxford: Clarendon Press, 1984); *Part Two. Chapters 13–24* (1987).[18]

For a thoroughgoing "koine" experience one must at least look into *Η ΚΑΙΝΗ ΔΙΑΘΗΚΗ: Τὸ πρωτότυπον κείμενον μὲ νεοελληνικὴν μετάφρασιν,* published by the United Bible Societies (Athens, 1967). This is a diglot edition containing in the main the *Textus Receptus,* but with some attention to readings in Nestle. At the front of this book is a letter of appreciation from the headquarters of the Greek Orthodox Church. Students may find it interesting to read this piece of official ecclesiastical correspondence alongside the Second Epistle of John. In Eastern Orthodoxy some things remain much the same.

SYNOPSES

A synopsis or work that permits simultaneous review of parallel accounts is the most valuable tool, after a concordance and a critical edition of the original text, for analysis of texts in the Gospels or other groups of writings, for example, the Pauline corpus. As noted above, Eusebius improved on the efforts of Ammonius of Alexandria to assist readers of a Gospel in noting parallel passages in other Gospels.

A synopsis of the Gospels is not a harmonizing work, in the sense of a conflation that destroys the integrity of an individual Gospel. A notable early example of the latter is Tatian's *Diatessaron* (ca. 175).[19]

Modern synopses of the Gospels permit one to see in parallel columns one

---

[18] S. C. E. Legg produced the first volume for the IGNTP on Mark (1935) and a second on Matthew (1940). He delivered his manuscript on Luke in 1948 and then resigned as editor. The committee could not publish the latter because the first two volumes had met with severe criticism and "it had become clear that the task was beyond the powers of any one man."

[19] Thanks to Bishop Theodoret's questionable zeal in the fifth century we have no complete text of Tatian's work. For details, see "Diatessaron," *Oxford Dictionary of the Christian Church,* with bibliography; B. M. Metzger, *Text,* 89–92. On "harmonies" and "synopses" in general, see F. Danker, "Synopsis," *ISBE,* 4:685-86.

or more related accounts or to note those pericopes that are singular to each Gospel. These are among the initial steps in evaluating literary and other data. As a multipurpose tool, the best is Kurt Aland, *Synopsis quattuor evangeliorum: Locis parallelis evangeliorum apocryphorum et patrum adhibitis,* 13th ed. (Stuttgart: Deutsche Bibelstiftung, 1985; 1988). One can read each Gospel in sequence — bold type is used for *lectio continua* — or as interrupted by intercalation of parallels. This edition is essential for users of the latest edition of the Bauer lexicon (see BAGD, chap. 7 below), for it expedites location of references to the *Gospel of Thomas,* numerous apocryphal documents, and patristic writings. Aland's *Synopsis* is available in various formats, including a diglot containing the Greek text and an English translation, but these other editions do not contain all the features of the one noted above, especially original patristic texts.[20]

For many decades the name Huck was synonymous with synopsis. His *Synopse der drei ersten Evangelien* first appeared in 1892. A ninth edition, revised by Hans Lietzmann with Hans-Georg Opitz (Tübingen: J. C. B. Mohr, 1936), and an edition with English titles of pericopes by Frank Leslie Cross, took account of new developments.[21] Modeled after Huck-Lietzmann, but based on the RSV, is *Gospel Parallels: A Synopsis of the First Three Gospels,* 3d ed. rev. Burton H. Throckmorton, Jr. (Camden, N.J.: Nelson, 1967). This work retains advantages over Hedley F. D. Sparks, *A Synopsis of the Gospels: The Synoptic Gospels with the Johannine Parallels* (Philadelphia: Fortress Press, 1964), which uses the older RV (see below, pp. 181–82).

Not until 1981 did "Huck" regain some of its former prestige in *Synopse der drei ersten Evangelien mit Beigabe der johanneischen Parallelstellen: Synopsis of the First Three Gospels with the addition of the Johannine Parallels,* 13th ed. (Tübingen: J. C. B. Mohr, 1981). The ample critical apparatus suggests the breadth of the manuscript evidence on which the newly reconstructed text of this edition is based. The same text was prepared by Heinrich Greeven for publication outside Germany, but without translation: *Synopsis of the First Three Gospels with the Addition of the Johannine Parallels,* 13th ed. "fundamentally revised."

In reaction to what he considered overemphasis on the priority of Mark, Bernhard Orchard based his *Synopsis of the Four Gospels, in Greek* (Edinburgh: T. & T. Clark, 1983) on the two-Gospel hypothesis, according to which Luke used Matthew and then Mark abridged both (the "Griesbach hypothesis"). A corresponding format with only an English translation of

---

[20] Editions and formats change with such rapidity that the student is advised to write to the American Bible Society and request its advertisement of "Scholarly Publications."

[21] The edition by Cross was prepared in conjunction with the German edition and was published in Tübingen in the same year, 1936. There are various reprints.

Orchard's reconstructed text appeared in 1982 (Macon, Ga.: Mercer University Press).

Drawing largely on the text of the Jerusalem Bible (see below, chap. 10), P. Benoit and M.-E. Boismard include noncanonical parallels in their edition, *Synopse des quatre évangiles en français avec parallèles des apocryphes et des Pères*, 3 vols. (Paris: Cerf, 1965–77). See also M.-E. Boismard and A. Lamouille, *Synopsis Graeca Quattuor Evangeliorum* (Leuven/Paris: Peeters, 1986).

In *New Gospel Parallels*, vol. 1: *The Synoptic Gospels;* vol. 2: *John and the Other Gospels* (Philadelphia: Fortress Press, 1985), R. W. Funk promotes the emphasis on literary appreciation of the Gospels that has been developing in biblical academia. His work is designed to assist in narrative analysis of the Gospels by featuring paradigmatic and syntagmatic dimensions.

By departing in *The Horizontal Line Synopsis of the Gospels* (Dillsboro, N.C.: Western North Carolina Press, 1975; rev. ed., Pasadena: William Carey Library, 1984) from the familiar columnar arrangement, Reuben J. Swanson permits students to see at a glance the points of similarity or dissimilarity in the Gospel accounts. Each of the Gospels has its turn at the lead role in the four parts of this work, with the parallel material set between lines of text and underlined. Swanson began the publication of a Greek-text edition with *The Gospel of Matthew* (Dillsboro, N.C.: Western North Carolina Press, 1982).[22]

Analogous to the preceding works on the Gospels is *Pauline Parallels*, 2d ed. (Philadelphia: Fortress Press, 1984), by Fred O. Francis and J. Paul Sampley, who endeavor to display similarity of letter structure, form, and theme or image within the Pauline corpus.

---

[22] On this see Frans Neirynck, *The Minor Agreements in a Horizontal-Line Synopsis*, Studiorum Novi Testamenti Auxilia 15 (Leuven, 1991). Laden with a variety of instructive comment, and without much loss of usefulness even after nearly a century, is Sir John C. Hawkins, *Horae Synopticae: Contributions to the Study of the Synoptic Problem*, 2nd ed. (Oxford: Clarendon Press, 1909). For a different perspective and critique of Hawkins, see William R. Farmer, *The Synoptic Problem: A Critical Analysis* (Dillsboro, N.C.: Western North Carolina Press, 1976), esp. 104–111. For a review of the latter, see F. W. Beare, *JBL* 84 (1965): 295–97. Although students will do well to do their own coloring, based on suggestions, for example, in Frederick C. Grant, *The Four Gospels: A Study of Origins* (New York: Harper, 1957), 40–50, they can find hues for thought in Allan Barr, *A Diagram of Synoptic Relationships* (Edinburgh: T. & T. Clark, 1938), which vivifies synoptic data in four colors on a single chart. Xavier Léon-Dufour, *Concordance of the Synoptic Gospels in Seven Colors*, trans. Robert J. O'Connell (Paris: Desclée, 1956), takes a related approach, but cites the evidence in three separate charts, one for each of the synoptists. Of genealogical significance is W. G. Rushbrooke, who pioneered in polychrome with *Synopticon: An Exposition of the Common Matter of the Synoptic Gospels* (London, 1880). For a computerized data base, see Lloyd Gaston, *Horae Synopticae Electronicae: Word Statistics of the Synoptic Gospels*, Sources for Biblical Study 3 (Missoula, Mont.: Society of Biblical Literature, 1973).

CHAPTER THREE

The Hebrew Old Testament

"WE HAVE GONE a long way," laments a scholar, "since Ezra Stiles, President of Yale University, himself taught the freshmen and other classes Hebrew and Greek, and in 1781 delivered his Commencement Address in Hebrew." It is regrettable that Hebrew is gradually fading out of the academic picture. Seminaries are decreasing their requirements in Semitics, and its study is now being left more and more to the elective inclinations of the student. To the remnant in Israel, however, this chapter of our discussion is dedicated in the hope that it may encourage some to return to Zion and exhilarate others as they stand on the ramparts and catch the vision of fresh and exciting interpretive possibilities in their Hebrew texts.

Frequent reference will be made in these pages to *Biblia Hebraica Stuttgartensia* (*BHS*) the successor to the third edition of *Biblia Hebraica*, whose acronym is *BHK*, the K standing for Rudolph Kittel (1853–1929). Kittel aimed at doing for the Old Testament what other scholars had done in developing critical editions of the New Testament text. After Kittel's death Paul Kahle assumed editorial responsibility for the Masoretic Text, with Albrecht Alt and Otto Eissfeldt as associates, and their work brought the labors of Rudolf Kittel to a riper stage. Published by the Privilegierte Württembergische Bibelanstalt of Stuttgart (1937), *BHK* went beyond the thirteenth- and fourteenth-century manuscripts represented in Jacob ben Chayyim's edition, published in Venice, 1524–25, by Daniel Bomberg. Jacob ben Chayyim's text had been virtually the Old Testament *Textus Receptus* and was used in Kittel's first two editions. His hope was to present a text that lay somewhere between the original form and the masoretic tradition. The third edition of *BHK* was based on Codex Leningradensis (A.D. 1008), alleged to be a copy of manuscripts written by Aaron ben Moshe ben Asher.[1]

---

[1] See Paul Kahle, *BH,* xxix–xxxvii. In "The Hebrew Ben Asher Bible Manuscripts," *VT* 1 (1951): 164–67, Kahle meets Jacob L. Teicher's objection (*JJS* 2 (1950): 17–25) that the Leningrad manuscript is not a copy of a ben Asher manuscript. See Kahle's earlier essay (1933), "Der

Since its major revision in the third edition, *BHK* underwent many corrections and improvements. The seventh edition added not only a translation of the prolegomena into English but also a third critical apparatus to the books of Isaiah and Habakkuk in order to accommodate a modest selection of Qumran readings bound separately earlier in *Variae lectiones,* ed. Otto Eissfeldt (Stuttgart, 1951).

Unfortunately some of the deficiencies of *BHK,* especially in the apparatus, outweighed even the virtue of its exceptional typography. So thorough was its replacement, *Biblia Hebraica Stuttgartensia,* brought out in fascicles (Stuttgart, 1967–77), that the editors, Karl Elliger and Wilhelm Rudolph, reminded scholars to use the acronym *BHS* for their edition and *BHK* for the "Kittel" publication. In *BHS* the Deutsche Bibelstiftung produced a work in which the technical achievement is obscured only by the quality of the aesthetic effect. The text reproduces the latest hand of Codex Leningradensis (MS L), with the Masora parva (Mp, see below) in the margin. In place of *BHS*'s two-fold critical apparatus, one for mere variants and less important information and the other for significant textual modifications, *BHS* has one apparatus for textual matters and one for citation of the index numbers of the Masora magna (Mm, see below). The critical apparatus deplorably indulges in some of the improprieties, especially literary emendations and conjectural readings, for which *BHK* was criticized. It also places Chronicles at the end of the Ketubim instead of at the head of the Hagiographa, where L has it.

We are grateful to the British and Foreign Bible Society for preparing a new edition to replace Meir ha-Levi Letteris's edition, which has been reprinted by the society since 1866. Norman Henry Snaith, editor of *Old Testament in Hebrew* (London, 1958), keeps close to the text of the third to the ninth edition of *BHK* in an attempt to reproduce as much as possible the ben Asher text. A defect of Kittel's third edition, it has been asserted, is its too great dependence on one manuscript. Snaith's work is developed on a broader manuscript base, with focus on Spanish manuscripts that, according to Snaith, exhibit a reliable ben Asher textual tradition. Ben Asher's name is also associated with the ambitious "Hebrew University Bible Project," which is dedicated to the reproduction of the famous Aleppo Codex.[2] Other critical editions of

---

alttestamentliche Bibeltext," in his *Opera minora: Festgabe zum 21. Januar 1956* (Leiden, 1956), 68–78. A new edition of MS L was undertaken in the Hebrew Old Testament Text Project; see *Preliminary and Interim Report of the Hebrew Old Testament Text Project,* ed. D. Barthélemy (Jerusalem, 1974–).

2 This project began with the publication of Isaiah in two volumes (1975, 1981), but because of self-assigned complexities, not the least of which is a fourfold apparatus, it will take many years to complete; see Martin Jan Mulder, in *Mikra: Text, Translation, Reading and Interpretation of the Hebrew Bible in Ancient Judaism and Early Christianity* (Assen Maastricht: Van Gorcum; Philadelphia: Fortress Press, 1988), 87–88, 115. The fortunes of the Aleppo Codex (ca. A.D. 920) and its importance in the preparation of a more reliable critical edition of the Hebrew

historical interest include those of Christian D. Ginsburg, *The Old Testament, Diligently Revised According to the Massorah and the Early Editions, with the Various Readings from Manuscripts and the Ancient Versions,* 4 vols. (London: British and Foreign Bible Society, 1926), and of Seligmann Baer and Franz Delitzsch (Leipzig, 1869–95). Ginsburg's edition is a massive collection of masoretic material and minute variations, but its critical value is considerably depreciated by methodological defects. Baer and Delitzsch published the Old Testament in installments, omitting Exodus, Leviticus, Numbers, and Deuteronomy. Paul Kahle severely criticizes their attempt to produce a text that never really had historical existence.[3]

Although representing only a portion of the Old Testament, the Samaritan Pentateuch cannot remain unnoticed. In *Der hebräische Pentateuch der Samaritaner,* 5 vols. (Giessen, 1914–18), A. von Gall mainly relies on medieval manuscripts for his edition of the Samaritan text, whereas the Paris Polyglot (1632) and Walton's London Polyglot (1675) included one from the seventh century.

THE MASORETES

The present consonantal text of the Hebrew Scriptures is an outgrowth of a concern in Judaism for an authoritative text. The new role of the Torah after the destruction of the temple and the peculiar exegetical methods advocated by Rabbi Akiba and his school encouraged uniformity and elimination of all variant textual traditions. In fixing the text they attempted to go behind the popular text forms to the more ancient tradition.[4]

Bible are discussed in vol. 4 (1964) of *Textus: Annual of the Hebrew University Bible Project,* begun in 1960 in Jerusalem with Chaim Rabin as editor, succeeded by Shemaryahu Talmon.

[3] *Masoreten des Ostens: Die ältesten punktierten Handschriften des Alten Testaments und der Targume,* Beiträge zur Wissenschaft vom Alten Testaments 15 (Leipzig: J. C. Hinrichs'sche Buchhandlung, 1913), xiii. See also *Mikra,* 126–28, on the Baer-Delitzsch and Ginsburg editions.

[4] For general orientation on this and other matters treated in this chapter, see Emanuel Tov, *Textual Criticism of the Hebrew Bible* (Minneapolis: Fortress Press, 1992); Nahum M. Waldman, *The Recent Study of Hebrew: A Survey of the Recent Literature with Selected Bibliography* (Winona Lake, Ind.: Eisenbrauns, 1989); Martin Jan Mulder, in *Mikra,* 87–135, including a helpful bibliography; and Ernst Würthwein, *Der Text des Alten Testaments: Eine Einführung in die Biblia Hebraica,* 5th ed. (Stuttgart: Württembergische Bibelanstalt, 1988). The first edition of this latter work appeared in 1952 and was translated by P. Ackroyd, *The Text of the Old Testament: An Introduction to Kittel-Kahle's Biblia Hebraica* (Oxford, 1957). The translation by Erroll F. Rhodes, *The Text of the Old Testament: An Introduction to the Biblia Hebraica* (Grand Rapids: Eerdmans, 1979; reprinted with "Addenda," 1992), hereafter "Würthwein," is based on Würthwein's fourth revised edition (1973). One of the handiest guides to the sigla in *BHS* is R. I. Vasholz, "Data for the Sigla of the BHS" (Winona Lake, Ind.: Eisenbrauns, 1983), an eight-page columnar chart, which organizes the data in *BHS* with the following headings: symbol, date of origin, language,

The scholars responsible for this attempt at textual conservation were first known as the *sopherim,* that is, the scribes, namely, writers or secretaries.[5] According to the rabbinic literature, Ezra holds the place of honor in this notable guild. Through careful copying of the text and oral transmission of traditional text-forms and pronunciation of words these scholars paved the way for the experts on tradition, known as the masoretes, a term whose spelling, with one "s" or two, has elicited a warmth of debate matched almost by controversy about the origins of masoretic tradition. Near the beginning of the sixth century A.D. the history of Judaism as well as its literary activity experienced profound changes. This was the period when the Talmud reached completion. It was a time of theological consolidation. All that the scribes and rabbis had done on the sacred text was now carefully collected. Since the scholars responsible for this conservation effort were concerned not so much for originality as for maintenance of a tradition, they are known as the masoretes, a title derived from a late Hebrew word translated "tradition."

In keeping with the nature of the subject there is a lively dispute among scholars concerning the exact formation of the Hebrew word underlying this translation. Some insist that the object of the masoretes' research, namely, the

---

date of manuscript, and additional notes. William R. Scott discusses the critical apparatus, Masorah, unusual letters, and other markings in *A Simplified Guide to BHS,* 1st ed. 1987; 2d ed. (Berkeley: Bibal Press, 1990), with "An English Key to the Latin Words and Abbreviations and the Symbols of Biblia Hebraica Stuttgartensia," by H. P. Rüger. For more detail, see Reinhard Wonneberger, *Understanding BHS: A Manual for the Users of Biblia Hebraica Stuttgartensia,* Subsidia Biblica 8, trans. Dwight R. Daniels (Rome: Pontifical Biblical Institute, 1990). The publishers of *BHS* include a 3-page index to the terminology of the Masorah in Genesis, Isaiah, and Psalms. For earlier excellent discussions consult Aage Bentzen, *Introduction to the Old Testament,* 3d ed. (Copenhagen: G. E. C. Gad, 1957), 1: 42–65; Robert H. Pfeiffer, *Introduction to the Old Testament,* rev. ed. (New York: Harper, 1948), 71–101; D. R. Ap-Thomas, *A Primer of Old Testament Text Criticism* (London, 1947; rev. ed., Oxford: Basil Blackwell, 1964), published as Facet Book, Biblical Series, 14 (Philadelphia: Fortress Press, 1966); and other introductions to the Old Testament. Apart from the sources themselves, the resort of every true scholar, the standard and fountainhead for much of the information in later publications is Christian David Ginsburg, *Introduction to the Masoretico-Critical Edition of the Hebrew Bible* (London, 1897), reprinted with prolegomenon by Harry M. Orlinsky (New York: KTAV, 1966). Bleddyn J. Roberts, *The Old Testament Text and Versions: The Hebrew Text in Transmission and the History of the Ancient Versions* (Cardiff: University of Wales Press, 1951), updates Ginsburg's discussion.

[5] Late Talmudic etymology, which the careful student will learn to suspect and conscientiously check against more technical studies, asserts that the original sense of the root ספר, from which the word סופרים is derived, is "to count." "The early [scholars] were called soferim because they used to count all the letters of the Torah" (Seder Nashim, Kiddushin, i, 30a, *Kiddushin,* trans. Harry Freedman, in *The Babylonian Talmud,* ed. Isidore Epstein [London: Soncino, 1936], 22:144). The purpose of such counting was not to satisfy curiosity but to safeguard the exactness of the text. On the correctness of the etymology, see Roberts, *The Old Testament Text,* 31, and n. 2. See also M. Gertner, "The Masorah and the Levites: An Essay in the History of a Concept," *VT* 10 (1960): 241–72. On the alternative English spelling, see *Mikra,* 105–6.

tradition, is properly called מָסוֹרָה. Others with equal vehemence maintain that the older and better-attested form is מָסוֹרָה.

In Ezek. 20:37 the word מָסֹרֶה is found and appears to be derived from the verb אָסַר, "to bind," but the apparatus in *BHS* suggests substituting מִסְפָּר with the LXX and one manuscript of the Old Latin. In any event, the postbiblical root מסר, "to hand down," certainly underlies the late Hebrew word מָסוֹרָה or מָסוֹרָה. The preference in these pages for the former should not be construed as dismissal of the debate on this question in B. J. Roberts's concise treatment.[6]

The principal feature distinguishing the masoretes from their scribal predecessors is, as indicated, their codification of what the scribal tradition had already transmitted. They added nothing—they only conserved. But it would be erroneous to conclude that there was a closely knit guild of scholars called masoretes who worked in a single continuing tradition. Actually scholars were at work endeavoring to codify what the scribes in various parts of dispersed Judaism had left them. Roughly, however, the masoretes may be divided into two groups, the East and the West, the Babylonian and the Palestinian. The latter group ultimately surpassed its rival and presented Judaism its recognized textual form, the Masoretic Text, commonly abbreviated MT.[7]

The writing labors of the masoretes involved codification in two principal areas. The first of these is the text itself. In the interest of conserving the traditional reading of the text without disturbing its sacred consonants, they invented an elaborate pointing system. Concern for faithful reproduction of what lay before them in their textual tradition is reflected in some of the textual peculiarities, such as the suspension of certain letters, which will be treated in the following pages. The second area is the territory outside the text proper. It is here that the codified tradition, or Masorah, is to be found.

THE MASORAH

The Masorah consists of annotations that literally hedge in the text.[8] They are usually classified as follows: (1) The initial Masorah, surrounding the first

---

[6] Pp. 4–42, esp. p. 41 n. 4.

[7] For detailed bibliographies on the MT, see Otto Eissfeldt, *The Old Testament: An Introduction,* trans. from 3d German ed. (Tübingen, 1964) by Peter R. Ackroyd (New York: Harper & Row, 1965), 678–93, 781–82; Roberts, *Old Testament Text,* 286–99; Waldman, *Recent Study,* chap. 3; Tov, *Textual Criticism,* passim.

[8] On the subject of the Masorah, see Ginsburg, *Introduction,* passim. *The Massoreth Ha-Massoreth of Elias Levita, Being an Exposition of the Massoretic Notes on the Hebrew Bible,* ed. with a trans. by Christian D. Ginsburg (London, 1867), explains the origin and import of the Masorah and comments on its signs and abbreviations; see also Waldman, *Recent Study,* 136–52, with bibliographic details. Sid Z. Leiman, ed., prepares a feast in *The Canon and Masorah*

word of a book. (2) The marginal Masorah. This is of two types. The small, usually termed *masorah parva* (Mp), is ordinarily located on the side margins, though it may also be interlinear; the larger *masorah magna* (Mm), is usually on the lower margin, though it is also found on the top or side margins of the leaves of other manuscripts. (3) The Masorah following the text, *masorah finalis*. This is a classification in alphabetic order of the masoretic tradition and is located at the end of masoretic manuscripts. It is not to be confused with the final Masorah terminating individual books.

One of the most elaborate Masorah collections is Christian D. Ginsburg's *The Massorah,* in four huge volumes (London, 1880–1905; reprint, New York: KTAV, 1975). The first two volumes present the Hebrew text of the Masorah; volume 3 is a supplement, and volume 4 presents an English translation of the material through the letter *yodh.* The work is incomplete. Although Paul Kahle, annoyed chiefly by the uncritical massing of material without concern for manuscript evaluation, had some harsh words for this work,[9] it is nevertheless a major production and with its volume 4 does help novices make their way through the painstaking notations of dedicated scribes. For advanced work on the Masorah the student will of course check carefully the material presented by Ginsburg and, if possible, consult Gérard E. Weil, *Massorah Gedolah iuxta codicem Leningradensem B19a,* 1 (Rome: Pontifical Biblical Institute; Stuttgart: Württembergische Bibelanstalt, 1971). Of more modest size is *Das Buch Ochlah W'ochlah (Massora),* by Solomon Frensdorff (Hannover, 1864), an ancient masoretic work so entitled from its first two entries, אָכְלָה (1 Sam. 1:9) and וְאָכְלָה (Gen. 27:19). Various phenomena noted in the Masorah are here found neatly grouped together under numbered paragraphs, together with an index of Scripture passages. Thus, on page 99 of this book, under para. 106, it is stated that לֹו is found twice when it should be read as a לֹא (with an *aleph*). The passages are then cited, 1 Sam. 2:16 and 20:2. Both notations appear in the margins of *BHS*.

Printed texts of the Hebrew Bible have at various times incorporated the Masorah in varying degrees of completeness. The second edition of Daniel Bomberg's Rabbinic Bible, edited by Jacob ben Chayyim (Venice, 1524–25), was the first to print large portions of the Masorah. The Sixth Rabbinic Bible, edited by Johann Buxtorf (Basel, 1618), is one of the more accessible republications of Chayyim's work. A companion volume, *Tiberias sive commentarius masorethicus triplex, historicus, didacticus, criticus,* first published in 1620 (Basel) by the elder Buxtorf, was revised by his son and, according to the title page, carefully reedited by his grandson Johann Jacob (Basel, 1665). As the

---

of the Hebrew Bible: An Introductory Reader, Library of Biblical Studies, ed. Harry Orlinsky (New York: KTAV, 1974): selected articles by numerous scholars on topics relating to the history of the Old Testament and the pre-Tiberian and post-Tiberian evidence for the Masorah.

[9] *Masoreten des Ostens,* xiv–xvi.

title indicates, the work includes a history of the Masorah, a key to its contents, and a critique of readings found in various copies of the Masorah. C. D. Ginsburg's edition, as observed earlier, includes much masoretic material. The edition of the Hebrew Bible produced by Baer and Delitzsch (Leipzig, 1869–95) is much scantier by comparison. Kittel's third edition of *Biblia Hebraica* aimed to make accessible to the average student a fairly representative survey of masoretic data, as found in the Leningrad MS, but only the Mp edited by Paul Kahle was printed (see *BHK,* v, viii–ix). A completely reedited text of the Mp was done for *BHS* in conjunction with Weil's edition of the *masorah magna,* which was published separately. The first apparatus in *BHS,* readily recognized by the recurring abbreviation "Mm," directs the reader of the Mp to a numbered section in Weil's edition of the Mm, where the masoretes' detailed data on the specific item are presented.

When using the Masorah, one must give attention to the various sources of the tradition. There is no such thing as *the* Masorah. Many manuscripts include no Masorah whatever; others vary in the number, the position, and the contents of the Masorah. Numerical inconsistencies, incomplete or even contradictory codifications, are to be expected in a comparison of two or more Masorah traditions in different manuscripts.[10]

It is true that many of the notations in the margins of *BHS* deal with minutiae, but buried in these marginal notes coming from a long tradition are countless items of interest, and with only a little labor the average student may not only develop a finer appreciation of the zeal that propelled these singular students of the Word but also pick up valuable philological and lexicographical data.

As in the case of Nestle's *Novum Testamentum Graece,* it has been our experience that few users of the printed masoretic text are familiar with the meanings of the many signs and notations employed. Some may even say "good luck," when looking at the Latin-locked "Index siglorum et abbreviationum masorae parvae" in *BHS* (pp. l–lv). This is a glossary that provides Latin equivalents for abbreviations and other sigla in the Mp. On the other hand, press on and use the Hebrew as a converter for the Roman tongue, for this list, along with the "Sigla et compendia apparatuum" (pp. xliv–l) is the key to the mysteries of the marginalia in *BHS.* With slight effort the door will open. Special attention should be given to Weil's own directions for using the Mp (pp. xiii–xviii). Since many of the dotted letters in the margins are Hebrew numerals, it will repay the student to memorize the basic numerical equivalents given in any grammar. Once this Hebrew method of numerical notation is

---

[10] See Ginsburg, *Introduction,* 425–68, on the conflicting data in the Masorah. On early concern for preparation of a critical edition of the *masorah magna,* see Paul Ernst Kahle's classic work on the textual history of the Old Testament, *The Cairo Geniza,* 2d ed. (Oxford: Basil Blackwell, 1959), 134.

understood, the facts in the margins will be meaningful and many of them appreciated at a glance.

The reader may have perceived with some disappointment and chagrin that most writers on introductory matters to the MT give only a slight orientation on the marginal notations. One or two examples are usually presented, but these are, in the nature of the case, quite simple and hardly representative of the gamut of masoretic notation. The following paragraphs, therefore, present a detailed explanation of all the masoretic notations in the margin of *BHS* for Gen. 1:1-6, in the hope that students may have a broader appreciation of what they may expect to find in these marginalia and may know how to proceed in evaluating the data presented.

CIRCELLUS

Genesis 1:1-6

The first thing to note is a small circle (°) called a *circellus* (see the "Prolegomena," *BHS,* xvii–xviii. Almost every line of text contains one or more of these *circelli*. These *circelli* (hereafter cited in roman font) signal the marginal notations.

In Gen. 1:1 the first circellus is above the expression בְּרֵאשִׁית. The first letter in the Masorah is ה, the dot indicating that this is a numeral, in this case 5, since ה is the fifth letter in the alphabet. The ג is the numeral 3 followed by the abbreviation ר"פ (see p. lv=initium versus). Of the five occurrences of this form, three are at the beginning of a verse. Then it is stated that the form is used two of these times in the middle of a verse (ו ב מ"פ). The period separates this set of data from the next set. The superscript numerals 1 and 2 refer to the Mm, and its pertinent sections are cited in the first apparatus. "Mm 1" will reveal that the five occurrences are Gen. 1:1; Jer. 26:1; 27:1; 28:1; 49:34. The next circellus appears between the two words בָּרָא אֱלֹהִים. This means that this syntactical combination is discussed in the margin, where the Masorah states that this combination appears three times in the Pentateuch (תור). The reason for this notation becomes clear when it is recalled that the more frequent form is the name יְהוָה in conjunction with some form of the verb בָּרָא.

The next three circelli again mark a combination (see p. xvii). The first abbreviation is the numeral יג signifying that the combination את השמים ואת הארץ occurs thirteen times. But this observation is followed by the notation ול בליש. Here the ו is adversative and the ל is the abbreviation for לית signifying "does not occur elsewhere" (see p. xvi). The uniqueness of the entire expression is specified by what follows: בליש; the ב here is a preposition followed by the abbreviation ליש, which means "in the form (as cited in the text)."

Apart from the information in Weil's *Massora Gedolah,* a glance at a concordance will quickly reveal a number of passages. Choose one and compare
the pointing of the Hebrew with the pointing in Gen. 1:1.

In 1:2 the first circellus calls attention to the form וְהָאָרֶץ, which appears
eight times "at the beginning of a verse." According to the notation on the phrase
תֹהוּ וָבֹהוּ, this combination occurs only one other time, namely, Jer. 4:23. The
notation on וְחֹשֶׁךְ in 1:2 is of grammatical interest. The scribes note that the
form וְחֹשֶׁךְ employed here appears only once elsewhere. The reason for this
notation is clear when a related form וְחֹשֶׁךְ (וְחֹשֵׁךְ) is seen in Prov. 10:19 and
11:24. The latter is the participle of חָשַׁךְ. The Mm notes that Job 38:19 is
the only other passage in which the form וְחֹשֶׁךְ is used. Notations like this
helped the masoretes maintain their extraordinarily high level of accuracy. The
combination עַל־פְּנֵי תְהוֹם appears only twice (see Prov. 8:27). The combination וְרוּחַ אֱלֹהִים appears only one other time in precisely the form cited in
Gen. 1:2: as the upper apparatus notes, see 2 Chr. 24:20. The Masorah parva
goes on to note that in Samuel the combination is common, except for five
instances in which the tetragrammaton occurs. The term מְרַחֶפֶת is a *hapax
legomenon.* The notation next to the third line of Hebrew text alerts the scribe
not to drop the phrase specified on the assumption that it is a duplication.
This is the one place that it appears in this form. According to the Mp, in
1:3, the phrase וַיֹּאמֶר אֱלֹהִים occurs twenty-five times. We may infer that copyists
are being alerted not to be misled by the more usual use of the tetragrammaton
with the verb of saying. The combination יְהִי אוֹר appears only in Gen. 1:3.
In 1:4 the masoretes note that this hiphil form וַיַּבְדֵּל occurs only three times.
In the fifth line the Masorah states that the form לָאוֹר is used seven times.
The form וְלַחֹשֶׁךְ appears only here, the Mm noting that the form in Job 28:3 is
prefaced by a *lamedh.* The phrase יוֹם אֶחָד is used ten times in the Pentateuch,
and two of those times at the end of a verse. The phrase וַיֹּאמֶר אֱלֹהִים in 1:6
is annotated as noted above, but with the additional note that the accentua-
tion (תע,, see p. lii; with *munach* and *zaqeph qaton*) differs here and in two
other places in this section (עינ; see 1:20 and 26) from the twenty-six other
occurrences of the phrase. Genesis 1:20 and 26 contain the other two instances.
The probable reason for the latter notation, as Ginsburg points out, is to
safeguard the reading against conformation to the other seven instances in
which the *munach* is followed by *rebhia*: Gen. 1:9, 11, 14, 24, 29; 9:12; 17:19.[11]

Throughout the Hebrew Bible the meticulous concerns of the masoretes
are evident. The Masorah has codified many of these phenomena, and most
books on Old Testament introduction discuss, in varying detail, the more significant classifications. Robert H. Pfeiffer, who plows at length with Ginsburg's
work, has one of the more lucid and comprehensive discussions in this area
(*Introduction,* 79–97).

---

[11] Ginsburg, *The Massorah,* 4:105, para. 858.

SUSPENDED LETTERS

The lengths to which the masoretes went in their passionate concern for the preservation of a textual tradition is clear, for example, from the unusual position of certain letters (Ginsburg, *Introduction,* 334–47). The Masorah at Ps. 80:14 states that the peculiarity (the raised letter, in this instance *ayin*) in the writing of the text is one of four to be noted in the Hebrew Bible. The others are Job 38:13, 15 and Judg. 18:30. The first three offer a raised or suspended *ayin,* the last a suspended *nun.* According to the Talmud, the suspended *ayin* indicates the middle letter of the Psalter. Quite possibly a tradition concerning a variant is here documented. In the Job passages the latter appears almost certainly to be the case, since the omission of the *ayin* forms the word רָשִׁים ("poor"). A slight transposition and substitution of *aleph* for *ayin* would also form רָאשִׁים ("chiefs"). The latter would fit very well in the context, but has no manuscript support to my knowledge.

INVERTED NUN

Of a similar nature is the inverted *nun* (found nine times in manuscripts of the Hebrew text: Num. 10:35, 36; Ps. 106:21-26, 40 (Ginsburg, *Introduction,* 341–45). Pfeiffer mentions a tenth occurrence noted by a masorete at Gen. 11:32 (not in *BHS*).[12] According to Ginsburg, the inversions denote transpositions of the text. But, as Roberts notes, the witness of the rabbis is not consistent, and one Jehudah ha-Nasi refused to admit any dislocations in the Sacred Scriptures, insisting that the marks (which are to be confined, he says, to the two cases in Numbers 10) were designed to show that the two verses in the Pentateuch form a separate book. His father, Simon ben Gamaliel, on the other hand, espoused the less traditional view.[13]

PUNCTA EXTRAORDINARIA

In fifteen passages the Masoretic Text contains dots placed over certain words and letters. These dots are called *puncta extraordinaria.* They mark passages which the masoretes, according to Ginsburg (*Introduction,* 318–34), considered textually, grammatically, or exegetically questionable. Numbers 3:39 provides a typical example in the word וְאַהֲרֹן, which the Masorah notes is one of fifteen terms with such dots and that ten of them occur in the Pentateuch. The editor

---

[12] Pfeiffer, *Introduction,* 83.
[13] Roberts, *Old Testament Text,* 34.

of *BHS* obligingly suggests the reason. The scribes had evidently encountered manuscripts that did not include Aaron's name. They did the best they could with the text, but marked it with these dots. The masoretes then preserved this bit of textual tradition, even though they may not have been aware of the reasons underlying the diacritical marking. The other passages are Gen. 16:5; 18:9; 19:33; 33:4; 37:12; Num. 9:10; 21:30; 29:15; Deut. 29:28; 2 Sam. 19:20; Isa. 44:9; Ezek. 41:20; 46:22; Ps. 27:13.

SEBIR

In about 350 places, according to Ginsburg (*Introduction,* 187–96), the manuscripts of the Old Testament reflect suspicions as to the correctness of a given reading. The word or form that would normally be expected is introduced in the margin by סְבִיר (from the Aramaic סְבַר, "think, suppose").

In the margin at Gen. 19:23 the masoretes note that יָצָא is viewed with suspicion on three occasions, and in its place the form יצאה is read. The critical apparatus refers to Gen. 15:17, where הַשֶּׁמֶשׁ appears as feminine instead of masculine as in the transmitted text of 19:23. At Gen. 49:13 no masoretic reference to a textual problem is made, but *BHS,* as the abbreviation "Seb" in the critical apparatus indicates, alerts the student to the fact that in this passage עַל equals עַד. Some translations reflect awareness of the notation: The KJV, "unto Sidon" follows the *Sebir* reading; NRSV "at S"; RV follows the traditional text, "upon Zidon," margin "by."

KETHIBH AND QERE

The masoretes were extremely loath to undertake emendations of the text, but called attention to probable corruptions by suggesting in their notes what they considered the correct reading. These readings are accompanied by a ק or קרׄ, that is, *qere,* that which is to be called or read in place of what is written.[14] The latter is termed the *kethibh.* Thus in the margin at Josh. 8:11 we read ביניו with a ק beneath it. This means that in place of בֵּינָו the form בֵּינָיו is to be read. The vowel pointings for the *qere* form are given under the *kethibh.*

Certain words are known as *perpetual qere*s. Thus הוא is read הִיא throughout the Pentateuch. The tetragrammaton יְהֹוָה is usually to be read אֲדֹנָי. Likewise the perpetual *qere* for the *kethibh* יְרֻשָׁלֵם is יְרוּשָׁלַם; for יִשָּׂשְׂכָר, the perpetual *qere* is יִשָּׂכָר.

---

[14] See Ginsburg, *Introduction,* 183–86; Harry M. Orlinsky, "The Origin of the Kethib-Qere System: A New Approach," in *Congress Volume: Oxford 1959,* Supplements to Vetus Testamentum 7 (Leiden: Brill, 1960), 184–92.

TIQQUNE SOPHERIM AND ITTURE SOPHERIM

Alhough most of the masoretic tradition documents a conservative approach, there appears here and there to be evidence of textual alteration. These alterations are of two kinds. The first consist of תקוני ספרם or "corrections of the scribes," designed chiefly to safeguard the divine majesty. Thus in Gen. 18:22 the student will note in the apparatus the abbreviation "Tiq soph." The original reading, as alleged by tradition, was not: "And Abraham remained standing before the Lord," but "The Lord remained standing before Abraham." Since the word "to stand before another" can also mean "to serve" (see Gen. 41:46; 1 Kings 1:2), it was felt that the term was unworthy of God and the text was altered accordingly. So in Num. 11:15 Moses is made to refer to his own wretchedness rather than to that of Yahweh.[15]

In a few cases the traditional text appears to suggest that somewhere along the line scribes nodded at their work. These oversights, or what are termed "omissions of the scribes," עטורי ספרים, are treated as follows. When it appears that the traditional text is defective in a word, the masoretes introduce into the text the vowel points of the word they think is missing. But they do not dare to emend the consonantal text. In the margin they then cite the omitted word and state that it is to be "read, though not written," קרי ולא כתיב. Thus in 2 Sam. 8:3 the last part of the verse consists of a *shewa* and a *qamets*. The margin states that פרת is to be read with the pointing suggested in the text. In 2 Sam. 16:23 a *chireqh* is noted under a *maqqeph*. The margin states that איש is to be read.

When it appears that the traditional text includes material that inadvertently intruded itself, the masoretes note that the expression in question is indeed written but is not to be read. The vowel points are therefore omitted in the biblical text but the consonants retained. A patent instance is the dittography of the consonantal ידרך in Jer. 51:3. (See also Ezek. 48:16.)

STATISTICS

Other indications of the painstaking labors of the scribes and masoretes appear here and there in the Masorah. The margin at Lev. 8:8 states that this verse

---

[15] Würthwein, 18–19. W. E. Barnes, who treats all the *tiqqune sopherim* in "Ancient Corrections in the Text of the Old Testament (Tikkun Sopherim)," *JTS* 1 (1900): 387–414, concludes that the masoretes have preserved not attempted corrections but homiletical and exegetical comments. Other *tiqqunin* are: Num. 12:12; 1 Sam. 3:13; 2 Sam. 16:12; 20:1; Jer. 2:11; Ezek. 8:17; Hos. 4:7; Hab. 1:12; Zech. 2:12; Mal. 1:12; Ps. 106:20; Job 7:20; 32:3; Lam. 3:20. Most of these are discussed in *BHS*. See also Ginsburg, *Introduction*, 347–63; but especially Carmel McCarthy, *The Tiqqune Sopherim and Other Theological Corrections in the Masoretic Text of the Old Testament*, Orbis Biblicus et Orientalis 36 (Freiburg, Switzerland: Universitätsverlag; Göttingen: Vandenhoeck & Ruprecht, 1981).

is the middle verse of the Pentateuch. According to the note at Lev. 10:16 דרש is the middle word in the Pentateuch, and at 11:42 we are assured that the ו in גָּחוֹן is its middle letter.[16] The apparatus assists in the identification by noting that in this latter case many manuscripts write the ו extra large. In a similar vein the ע in שְׁמַע (Deut. 6:4) is written as one of the *litterae maiusculae*.

Statistics will also be found at the end of each book. At the end of the Pentateuch the following information is given in *BHS*. The total number of verses in the book of Deuteronomy is 955. The verses in the Torah number 5,845, the words 97,856, and the letters 400,945.

DIVISIONS OF THE HEBREW TEXT

Since the MT is replete with notations relative to the division of the text, a brief survey of the history of the divisions of the Hebrew Bible may be welcome.

The chapter divisions in the MT are an inheritance from the Latin Vulgate. Stephen Langton, Archbishop of Canterbury (d. 1228), is credited with the division about 1204 or 1205. The first to note the chapter numbers in the margin of the Hebrew text was Solomon ben Ishmael, ca. 1330. The Complutensian Polyglot (1517) was the first printed edition of the entire Hebrew Bible to follow this procedure. In Benito Arias Montano's edition (1569–72), chapter numbers were put into the text.[17]

The divisions into verses are much older and, according to Pfeiffer, probably originated in the practice of translating portions of Scripture into Aramaic as they were read from the Hebrew text. These verse divisions varied considerably for centuries, until finally, in the tenth century, the text was edited in the current verse division by Aaron ben Moshe ben Asher. The two dots (*soph pasuq*) marking the end of a verse seem to have come into use after the year 500.[18] Rabbi Isaac Nathan ben Kalonymus employed these verse divisions in his concordance, completed about 1447 and printed in Venice (1523). The verse enumeration first appears in Bomberg's edition of the Hebrew Bible (1547). In this edition every fifth verse is indicated by a Hebrew letter used numerically. The small Hebrew Psalter published by Froben (Basel, 1563) is the first printed text of some portion of the Hebrew Bible to contain arabic

---

[16] *The Babylonian Talmud,* loc. cit., 144–45, comments: "Thus, they [the scholars] said, the *waw* in gahon [Lev. 11:42] marks half the letters of the Torah; *darosh darash* [Lev. 10:16] half the words; *we-hithggalah* [Lev. 13:33], half the verses. *The boar out of the wood (mi-ya'ar) doth ravage it* [Ps. 80:14]: the *'ayin* of *ya'ar* marks half of the Psalms. *But he, being full of compassion, forgiveth their iniquity* [Ps. 78:38], half of the verses." This passage is an excellent testimony to the variations in the scribal tradition. *BHS* signals half the verses of the Torah at Lev. 8:8 (but note the comment in the apparatus at 13:33) and half the verses of the Psalms at Ps. 78:36.

[17] On chapter divisions in the Old Testament, see Ginsburg, *Introduction,* 25–31.

[18] Pfeiffer, *Introduction,* 80.

numerals with each verse (Ginsburg, *Introduction,* 107). The reason for some of the divergent verse enumeration in printed texts of the MT and modern English versions may be seen in this edition of the Psalter. According to the Masorah, the titles of the Psalms are integral parts of the text and, depending on length and content, may be counted as a first or even as a first and second verse. Froben, on the other hand, did not follow the masoretic custom. This is the reason why in Psalm 60, for example, he counts only twelve verses to the MT's fourteen. To the Spanish Orientalist Benito Arias Montano's *Antwerp Polyglot (Biblia Regia)*, published by Christophe Plantin, 8 vols. (Antwerp, 1569–72), falls the distinction of being the first edition of the complete Hebrew Bible to mark the verses with arabic numerals. The addition of the sign of the cross at each numeral limited the sale of the book.[19] The earliest division of the Hebrew text into larger sections is pre-Talmudic. These sections are called פרשיות, that is, *Parashoth,* and are to be distinguished from the later liturgical sections to be discussed shortly. The earlier divisions were of two kinds, the פְּתוּחָה, or "open" paragraph, and the סתומה, or "closed" paragraph. The open *Parashoth* were so termed because they were begun on a new line, leaving an open space of an incomplete line, or a whole line (if the preceding verse ended at the end of a line), before the beginning of the paragraph. The closed *Parashoth* began with only a single blank space between the new paragraph and the preceding. The ancient spacing is no longer followed, but the divisions are preserved by the use of the letters פ for open paragraphs and ס for closed paragraphs. The Pentateuch is composed of 669 of these *Parashoth.* A careful study of these divisions suggests that in most cases the scribes had a keen appreciation of the literary structure and rarely, as in Exod. 6:28, did violence to the thought.

A second division into larger sections was made for synagogal use. According to the Babylonian Talmud (*Megillah* 29b and 31b), the Pentateuch was read in Palestine over a three-year period in weekly sections called *Sedarim* (from סדר, "order," "arrangement").[20] The Babylonian one-year cycle was divided into 54 (or 53) weekly sections, called *Parashoth.* In BHS the *qamets* over *samech* indicates the beginning of a *Seder.* The beginning of a *Parashah* is noted by the word פרש in the margin. The numerals at the end of a *Parashah* (see, e.g., Gen. 6:8 ק ט ו) total the number of verses in the section. In some instances the larger divisions coincide with the smaller divisions. When this happens the manuscripts and some printed editions use ססס for coincidence with "open" *Parashoth,* צצצ for coincidence with closed *Parashoth.*

---

[19] On the subject of verse division in the Old Testament, see Ginsburg, *Introduction,* 68–108.
[20] On the *Sedarim,* see Ginsburg, *Introduction,* 32–65.

THE CRITICAL APPARATUS IN BHS

The critical apparatus in Kittel's editions of *Biblia Hebraica* endured severe criticism, and *BHS* has also received its share; but the widespread use of the text, not least of all in the preparation of modern Bible versions, requires knowledge of its methodology.[21]

In the preceding discussion of the masoretic notations, attention was called to the upper apparatus in the lower margin. The second apparatus includes textual-critical notes. Letters of the Latin alphabet corresponding to raised characters interspersed in the text signal these textual problems.

The MT and the NRSV

As a commentary on controversial readings reflected in the versions, especially in the NRSV, the apparatus in *BHS* is decidedly helpful. Thus an analysis of the evidence presented in the apparatus covering Judg. 18:30 conveys a more accurate picture of the situation described by the NRSV in its own comment on the passage. The question is, should "Moses" or "Manasseh" be read? The editors note that the MT reads מְנַשֶּׁה and that most of the manuscripts and editions of the Hebrew text do likewise, but they conclude that מֹשֶׁה is to be read with a few manuscripts, the Septuagint, and the Vulgate (cp. the Syriac Hexapla). Perhaps copyists loyal to the name of Moses attempted to preserve Moses' name from horrible associations with idolatrous practices.

Some of the thinking underlying NRSV's conjecture in Isa. 41:27, "I first have declared it to Zion," can be seen from the critical apparatus in *BHS*. The editors make a number of proposals for clarifying a puzzling passage. In general, the Hebrew emendation behind the conjectural renderings in the NRSV can readily be ascertained from the apparatus in *BHS*. Thus in connection with Isa. 44:7 it is suggested that the passage be clarified by substituting the words מִי הִשְׁמִיעַ מֵעוֹלָם אוֹתִיּוֹת for וְאֹתִיּוֹת עַם־עוֹלָם מְשׂוּמִי, not without apparent paleographical justification.

---

[21] For criticism of *BHK* by perhaps the most severe critic, see Harry M. Orlinsky, "Studies in the St. Mark's Isaiah Scroll, IV," *JQR* n.s. 43 (1953): 329–40; "Notes on the Present State of the Textual Criticism of the Judean Biblical Cave Scrolls," in *A Stubborn Faith: Papers on Old Testament and Related Subjects Presented to Honor William Andrew Irwin,* ed. Edward C. Hobbs (Dallas: Southern Methodist University Press, 1956): 117–31; "Whither Biblical Research?" *JBL* 90 (1971): 1–14, esp. 6–7; his reviews of Ernst Würthwein's introduction to *BHK* in *JBL* 78 (1959): 176–78, and esp. *JSS* 4 (1959): 149–51, where Orlinsky calls Charles C. Torrey, Joseph Ziegler, and Peter Katz to his support. For other reviews of *BH* with special reference to the treatment of the Greek readings, see Peter Katz, *Theologische Literaturzeitung* 63 (1938): cols. 32–34. See James A. Sanders, "Text and Canon: Concepts and Method," *JBL* 98 (1979): 5–29, on the weaknesses of *BHS* and the theoretical assumptions on which the textual criticism is based.

In those instances in which the NRSV does not indicate the reason for a rendering divergent from the KJV, the apparatus in *BHS* will usually reflect the considerations that prompted the translators to depart from the MT. Thus the NRSV renders 1 Kings 13:12: "Their father said to them, 'Which way did he go?' And his sons *showed him* [italics ours] the way that the man of God who came from Judah had gone." The KJV, it will be noted, reads: "For his sons *had seen* [italics ours] what way the man of God went, which came from Judah." The apparatus in *BHS* readily reveals that the hiphil form וַיַּרְאֻהוּ, read by numerous versions, was preferred by the committee of translators.

Again, in Ps. 8:1 (8:2 MT) the RSV follows the LXX (*BHS*, ὅτι ἐπήρθη) in part, and does not note a departure from the traditional text. The MT reads the difficult imperative form תְּנָה. The LXX appears to have followed a passive form תֻּנָּה (not listed by *BHS*), which suggests a more fluent sense. On the other hand, the NRSV and the NAB read נָתַתָּה, as suggested in *BHS*.

According to the AV, Nahum 3:8 states that Nineveh has a wall that extends from the sea. But the NRSV indicates that the sea is Nineveh's wall. Clearly the NRSV follows a different Hebrew reading without alerting the reader to the fact. The apparatus in *BHS* supplies that reading, and it is clear that with a slight change in pointing (מַיִם for מִיָּם) the NRSV has attempted to preserve what appears to be a designed parallelism in Nahum's text. Use of the apparatus in a critical edition of the MT in conjunction with Bible versions can be a fascinating venture in multipurpose-tool use, but any departure from the Masoretic Text should be done with great respect for those careful transmitters of tradition, the masoretes.

PROBLEMS OF HARMONY

Problems in harmony of the biblical text are also reflected in the critical apparatus. Thus, in the apparatus at 1 Chron. 18:4 we are alerted to 2 Sam. 8:4, where the statistics are different. In connection with 1 Chron. 21:12 the editor notes that 2 Sam. 24:13 reads seven years of famine instead of the three years expressed in the chronicler's text. The NRSV reads three years in both texts, with the LXX casting the deciding vote for it in 2 Samuel. The NAB adopts the LXX reading for the latter without offering its customary textual annotation in the "Textual Notes" appended to the 1970 edition. The RV opted for the Hebrew in both texts; so also Beck's translation (see below, chap. 10). No completely satisfactory explanation of this discrepancy in the transmitted texts has as yet been given.

In the event the Masorah is overlooked, the apparatus in *BHS* will alert the student to the *kethibh* and *qere* readings. Thus in Deut. 28:27 the editor suggests that the *kethibh* be retained. It appears that later copyists attempted to avoid the implication of sexual aberrations connected with עפל and substituted a less noxious word, תחורים, "hemorrhoids."[22]

One could with little effort produce many more examples and illustrations of the type of material available in a critical edition of the Hebrew Bible. But enough avenues of exploration are here outlined to help make the study of the Hebrew text of the Sacred Scriptures a rewarding pilgrimage. The history of the transmission of that text is long and fascinating. Preserved in all these minutiae is a dedicated concern for the perpetuation of a spiritual heritage, a profound sense of obligation to future generations, and a deeply seated conviction that nowhere else in the world's literature are there words so worthy of the best that humans can offer of time and intellect.

[22] See Pfeiffer, *Introduction*, 85.

CHAPTER FOUR

The Greek
Old Testament

"**H**AVE YOU A SEPTUAGINT?**" Ferdinand Hitzig, eminent biblical critic and Hebraist, used to say to his class. "If not, sell all you have, and buy one." Current biblical studies reflect the accuracy of his judgment and suggest that there is ample reward for those who wish to enjoy seeing new things come out of the old.[1]

THE LETTER OF ARISTEAS

The *Letter of Aristeas,* written to one Philocrates, presents the oldest, as well as most romantic, account of the origin of Septuagint.[2] According to the letter,

---

[1] For a start on the immense Septuagint bibliography, see Bleddyn J. Roberts, *The Old Testament Text and Versions: The Hebrew Text in Transmission and the History of the Ancient Versions* (Cardiff: University of Wales Press, 1951), 299–307; John W. Wevers, "Septuaginta-Forschungen: I. Ausgaben und Texte," *TRu* n.s. 22 (1954): 85–91; Sidney Jellicoe, *The Septuagint and Modern Study* (Oxford: Clarendon Press, 1968); Sebastian P. Brock, Charles T. Fritsch, and Sidney Jellicoe, *A Classified Bibliography of the Septuagint,* Arbeiten zur Literatur und Geschichte des hellenistischen Judentums 6 (Leiden, 1973), with literature cited from about 1860–1969. In *Studies in the Septuagint: Origins, Recensions, and Interpretations* (New York: KTAV, 1974) Jellicoe gathers choice essays by various scholars; see also Melvin K. H. Peters, "Septuagint," *ABD* 5:1102–1104; Nahum M. Waldman, *The Recent Study of Hebrew* (Winona Lake, Ind.: Eisenbrauns, 1989), 89–91; E. Tov's excellent update of research, in *ANRW* II.20.1 (1987), 121–89; also idem, *Textual Criticism of the Hebrew Bible* (Minneapolis: Fortress Press, 1992), 134–47; Harry M. Orlinsky, in *The Cambridge History of Judaism,* vol. 2: *The Hellenistic Age,* ed. W. D. Davies and Louis Finkelstein (Cambridge, UK: Cambridge University Press, 1989), 534–62. For a brief summary of textual characteristics of the Septuagint, see E. Tov, in *Mikra,* 161–88. For continuing update check the reports of the Congress of the International Organization for Septuagint and Cognate Studies, SBLSCS, ed. Claude E. Cox.

[2] The letter is printed, together with a detailed introduction, in the appendix to Henry Barclay Swete, *An Introduction to the Old Testament in Greek* (Cambridge, UK: Cambridge University Press, 1900 [and later editions]). *Aristeae ad Philocratem Epistula cum ceteris de origine versionis LXX interpretum testimoniis,* ed. Paul Wendland; Bibliotheca scriptorum graecorum et romanorum

Aristeas is a person of considerable station in the court of Ptolemy Philadelphus (285–247 B.C.). Ptolemy was sympathetic to Jews. One day he asked his librarian Demetrius (in the presence of Aristeas, of course) about the progress of the royal library. Demetrius assured the king that more than 200,000 volumes had been catalogued and that he soon hoped to have a half-million. He pointed out that there was a big gap in the legal section and that a copy of the Jewish Law would be a welcome addition. But since Hebrew letters were as difficult to read as hieroglyphics, a translation was urgently needed. The king determined to write at once to the high priest in Jerusalem. At this point Aristeas, after first buttering up the royal bodyguard, suggested that it might be in somewhat poor taste to approach the high priest on this matter when so many of his compatriots were slaves in Egypt. With a silent prayer that Ptolemy might see the light he waited for the king's reply. Ptolemy's social consciousness cast the deciding vote, and at a considerable depletion of the royal treasury, plus a bonus to his bodyguard for seconding such a sensible proposal (the text is somewhat obscure at this point), he ordered the emancipation of more than 100,000 slaves.

Demetrius suggested that the king write to the high priest and ask him to send six elders from each of the twelve tribes in Israel. In this way the translation would represent the consensus of all Israel and be completely authoritative. The king accompanied his request with lavish presents for the temple. The embassy arrived in due time with Aristeas in convenient attendance. After a long discourse on Jewish diet the high priest Eleazar bade farewell to the seventy-two men he had selected for the task.

On their arrival the king could scarcely wait to see the sacred books, and when they were opened he did obeisance about seven times. For a solid week the king wined and dined his guests and interlarded the festivities with a game of seventy-two questions for seven nights running. At this point Aristeas is suddenly appalled by the fact that the unusual character of the narrative might subject Philocrates' historical credulity to considerable strain. Forthwith he

---

Teubneriana (Leipzig: Teubner, 1900) supplies additional witnesses and detailed indexes. Henry George Meecham, *The Letter of Aristeas: A Linguistic Study with Special Reference to the Greek Bible,* in Publications of the University of Manchester 241 (Manchester: University of Manchester, 1935) uses the Greek text edited by Thackeray. Meecham's own copious annotations and study of the vocabulary and grammar are very informative. *Aristeas to Philocrates (Letter of Aristeas),* ed. and trans. Moses Hadas; Jewish Apocryphal Literature, Dropsie College Edition (New York, 1951) reproduces Thackeray's Greek text and adds lengthy introduction, helpful bibliography (pp. 84–90), and English translation, commentary, and critical notes. Among many translations, see especially the one by Herbert T. Andrews in *Apocrypha and Pseudepigrapha of the Old Testament,* ed. Robert H. Charles (Oxford: Clarendon Press, 1913), 2:83–122. When examining scholarly evaluations of Aristeas's letter (or book, Hadas, *Aristeas,* 56) note carefully the particular scholar's opinion concerning the origin of the LXX and of the Hebrew text. Some start with the Hebrew text and permit their view of it to regulate estimates placed upon the other document.

reassures him of his delicate concern for historical data, despite the fact that some readers might ungraciously question the veracity of these marvelous accounts.

Having offered this touching testimony to historical sensitivity, Aristeas recounts how the king, duly impressed with the intellectual qualifications of the translators but somewhat disillusioned about the intelligence of his own courtiers, after a three-day interval dispatched the translators to the island of Pharos. There he lodged them in a building where they might enjoy peace and quiet. They set to the task of translation, and after repeated comparison of notes and collation of their various renderings, within seventy-two days they presented the king with a version which expressed their unanimous accord. Demetrius then summoned all the Jews to the island to hear the reading of the translation. The customary curse was pronounced on anyone who might display the temerity to tamper with the contents. The king in turn was impressed with the version, and the elders were sent on their ways with a caliph's ransom. In a final stab at historical rectitude, Aristeas concludes: "And so, Philocrates, you have the account, exactly as I promised you. For it is my opinion that you enjoy such things as these much more than the books of the mythologists." With a promise of more of the same Aristeas takes leave of his trusting reader.

Written about 125 B.C. the *Letter of Aristeas* is useful despite its patent inventions. For one thing, it aids in tracing the name traditionally ascribed to our Greek translation of the Old Testament. Just how the change from seventy-two to seventy came about is shrouded in mystery, but the Latin term, strictly speaking, is not accurate. Second, the letter advances no claims of inspiration for the version. As a corrective therefore of later romantic embellishments the letter is invaluable. Philo, for example, asserts that a comparison of the Greek version with the original will show that the former is of divine origin.[3]

Justin Martyr (*Apology* 31.2) does not invite confidence in his knowledge of septuagintal origins by having Ptolemy send to King Herod for the translators. Irenaeus (in Eusebius, *Ecclesiastical History* 5.8) says Ptolemy had the men isolated and each translated the whole, and when they came together all were in agreement. Evidently this historian also anticipated reader resistance and hastens to add that this should not be considered surprising, seeing that God inspired Ezra to rewrite the Scriptures after they had been lost during the Babylonian Captivity. Epiphanius, whose hobby was the collection of

---

[3] In his version of the translators' undertaking Philo writes: Καθάπερ ἐνθουσιῶντες προεφήτευόν οὐκ ἄλλα ἄλλοι, τὰ δ'αὐτὰ πάντες ὀνόματα καὶ ῥήματα ὥσπερ ὑποβολέως ἑκάστοις ἀοράτως ἐνηχοῦτος, "they seemed to be in ecstasy, and all rendered the same text, word for word, as though each one were listening to an unseen prompter" (*De vita Mosis* 2.37 [140]). The entire account is worth reading for purposes of comparison.

ancient heresies and sundry other ecclesiastical gossip, blandly assures us that the interpreters were shut up two by two and labored under lock and key. In the evening they were taken in thirty-six different boats to dine with Ptolemy. They slept in thirty-six different bedrooms. But when the thirty-six copies of each book of the Bible were examined, behold, they agreed perfectly. Even the lacunae and additions to the LXX are marvelously explained.[4]

Finally, the *Letter of Aristeas* corrects any notion that in the third century B.C. or later a monumental concerted effort was put forth to produce a Greek version of the whole Old Testament. The letter specifically mentions the Law. A warning is in order, then, not to speak too glibly about *the* Septuagint.

THE SEPTUAGINT AND OTHER GREEK VERSIONS

From the prologue to Ecclesiasticus we can safely conclude that a Greek version now termed the Septuagint was substantially complete by the end of the second century B.C. Scholars are generally agreed that the Pentateuch was completed in the first half of the third century B.C.; the Prophets, including the Latter and the Former Prophets, ca. 200 B.C.; the Hagiographa, near the turn of the era.[5]

---

[4] Migne, *PG* 43:249–55. The less credible details of the Letter of Aristeas have caused some scholars to classify it as typical Jewish apologetics written in self-defense as propaganda for Greek consumption. For a study that runs counter to much scholarly opinion and argues that it was written to meet the needs of Jewish readers, see Victor A. Tcherikover, "The Ideology of the Letter of Aristeas," *HTR* 51 (1958): 59–85.

[5] See Roberts, *The Old Testament Text*, 116. But scholars continue to debate several theories of the origin of the LXX. For a general overview of the problem and convenient summary of arguments forwarded by various scholars and schools of scholars, see Roberts, 104–15. See Harold Henry Rowley, "The Proto-Septuagint Question," *JQR* n.s. 32 (1943): 497–99, for critical comparison and fairly objective evaluation of the major opposing views, specifically Harry M. Orlinsky's vigorous defense of Lagardian principles in LXX studies (*On the Present State of Proto-Septuagint Studies,* in American Oriental Society Offprint Series 13 (New Haven, Conn.: Yale University Press, 1941) against attack by Paul Ernst Kahle (see, e.g., his *The Cairo Geniza,* 2d ed. [Oxford, 1959], 209–64) and his student Alexander Sperber (see below p. 67 n. 10, and the personal bibliography rehearsed in the two articles). Later studies by Orlinsky continued to uphold the recensional hypothesis; see, e.g., his "The Septuagint—Its Use in Textual Criticism," *The Biblical Archaeologist* 9 (1946): 21–34; "Current Progress and Problems in Septuagint Research," in *The Study of the Bible Today and Tomorrow,* ed. Harold R. Willoughby (Chicago: University of Chicago Press, 1947), 144–61; and "Recent Developments in the Study of the Text of the Bible: Qumran and the Present State of Old Testament Text Studies: The Septuagint Text," *JBL* 78 (1959): 26–33, esp. 33. The exacting arguments of Orlinsky, who has been called the "leading authority on the LXX in America," have the support of many modern scholars. See, e.g., Peter Katz, "Septuagintal Studies in the Mid-Century: Their Links with the Past and Their Present Tendencies," in *The Background of the New Testament and Its Eschatology: In Honor of Charles Harold Dodd,*

At first the Septuagint was designed to aid Jews in the Dispersion. Later on, when the Christians adopted the translation and used it with an apparent disregard for verbal correspondence with the Hebrew text, so that the variations in the text were in direct proportion to the number of copies in circulation, the Jews took measures to correct the Greek tradition and bring it more in line with their own established canon of the Scriptures.

AQUILA

One of the earliest identifiable attempts to align the LXX with the Hebrew text was made by Aquila in the second century A.D. Except for a few fragments in Origen's *Hexapla,* for a long time Aquila's version was known only through occasional patristic and rabbinic quotations. Now, thanks to the Old Cairo Genizah (storeroom or hiding place), whose contents were taken from concealment near the end of the nineteenth century, our knowledge of Aquila's extremely literal translation of the Old Testament has steadily grown in detail and accuracy.[6] According to Jerome (commentary on Isa. 8:14 [Migne, *PL* 24:119]), Aquila was the student of Akiba. This Akiba was vitally concerned about the minutiae of the Hebrew text and was able to transform the smallest prepositions into mountainous theological propositions. To aid in the controversies with the Christians, Aquila published his extremely literal Greek version of the Hebrew Bible. An anti-Christian bias is apparent in such renderings as ἠλειμμένος instead of Χριστός in Dan. 9:26 and νεᾶνις for ἡ παρθένος in Isa. 7:14.

THEODOTION

About the same time, a scholar of obscure lineage, Theodotion, undertook a revision of the Septuagint, based on manuscripts of the Hebrew Old Testament that seem to have been more closely allied to the MT than those used

---

ed. William David Davies and David Daube (Cambridge, UK: Cambridge University Press, 1956), 176–208; and Frank Moore Cross, Jr., *The Ancient Library of Qumran and Modern Biblical Studies: The Haskell Lectures, 1956–57,* rev. ed., Anchor Book A272 (Garden City, N.Y.: Doubleday, 1961), 170–72 n. 13, who makes a special point of criticizing Kahle's contentions.

[6] On Aquila, see Kyösti Hyvärinen, *Die Übersetzung von Aquila* (Uppsala: Gleerup, 1977); Roberts, *The Old Testament Text,* 120–23; and essays such as Hans Pete Rüger, "Vier Aquila-Glossen in einem hebräischen Proverbien-Fragment aus der Kairo-Geniza," *ZNW 50 (1959):* 275–77. Joseph Reider prepared an index-concordance to Aquila, which was deposited in 1913 in the Library of Dropsie College, then completed and revised a half century later by Nigel Turner, *An Index to Aquila,* Supplements to Vetus Testamentum 12 (Leiden: Brill, 1966). On the Old Cairo Genizah and its contents, consult Kahle, *The Cairo Genizah,* 1–13.

by the translators of the Septuagint. For this reason Theodotion's Book of Job is one-sixth longer than the Septuagint version, and his rendering of Daniel is preferred in many editions of the Septuagint. Whether he belongs to church or to synagogue is still debated. That Theodotionic renderings were popular in Christian circles and much esteemed by the seer of Patmos complicates evaluation of Theodotion's own contribution.

SYMMACHUS

Not much is known of Symmachus's version of the Old Testament in Greek. Only a few fragments have survived in Origen's fragmentary *Hexapla*. But we can gather that his version aimed at stylistic excellence and articulation of Jewish belief to Jews as well as non-Jews. As a result of his rabbinic exegetical training Symmachus softened or even eliminated many of the anthropomorphisms of the Old Testament.

ORIGEN'S HEXAPLA

The outstanding Septuagint scholar of antiquity is Origen, b. A.D. 185 or 186 in Alexandria. Origen found the textual tradition of the Greek text of the Old Testament a mass of confusion. Taking the standardized Hebrew Bible as his basis, he proceeded in an attempt to bring the manuscript tradition into harmony. The result was his *Hexapla,* or "six-in-one." Beginning the work in 240 while the head of the school of Caesarea, he aligned six texts in parallel columns. The first column contained the Hebrew text. It was the text accepted by the Jews themselves and is closely allied to that used by the masoretes. The second column contained a transcription of the Hebrew text in Greek characters. The chief value of the remains of this column is the contribution they make to study of the pronunciation in vogue at Origen's time as compared with the vocalization suggested by the masoretes. The third and fourth columns included the versions prepared by Aquila and Symmachus. In the fifth column Origen edited the Septuagint text. Forgetting that the Hebrew text behind the Septuagint undoubtedly differed from his contemporary Hebrew text, he made efforts to bring the manuscript tradition in line with the standard Hebrew text. Divergent renderings were set aside, Hebrew texts not included in the Greek version were introduced and supplemented with Theodotion's renderings, and Greek texts without a corresponding Hebrew text were plainly marked.

For his edition of the text Origen used the Aristarchian signs, named after Aristarchus (ca. 220–150 B.C.), an early editor of Homer, Hesiod, Pindar, and other Greek authors. Additions to the Greek text were marked with an asterisk (※); desirable deletions from the Greek text—those which had no Hebrew counterpart—were marked with an obelus (—, ÷, ÷) Passages so marked with an ※ or an ÷ at the beginning were terminated with a metobelus (/· , ·/· , or ⦂).[7] A sample of Origen's work may be seen in Job 32. When the Greek text did not follow the Hebrew text, he rearranged the passages. In the Greek text of Proverbs he was content to note the dislocation with diacritical marks. Theodotion's version went into the sixth column. Other versions, called Quinta, Sexta, and Septima, have also been identified.

It was inevitable, perhaps, that the bulk of Origen's *Hexapla* should have been lost.[8] The most complete collection of the remains is still Frederick Field's two-volume work *Origenis hexaplorum quae supersunt . . . fragmenta* (Oxford, 1875), but newly discovered fragments, such as that of Psalm 22 in all six columns, mentioned by Kenyon,[9] as well as other considerations, demand a revision of this valuable work. Yet, thanks to Pamphilus and Eusebius, who issued separately the fifth column containing the Septuagint text, Origen's labors filtered down to succeeding generations. At first his diacritical marks were retained, but gradually they were sloughed off and together with them the portions of the Greek text that had no corresponding Hebrew.

OTHER RECENSIONS

According to Jerome, there were other recensions. In addition to that of Origen and Pamphilus he mentions the recensions made by Hesychius and Lucian. The former cannot be clearly identified. Whether the Hesychian text was an independent version, as Alexander Sperber suggests,[10] or a recension of existing

---

[7] The signs are discussed at length in Swete's *Introduction,* 69–72, and with less accuracy by Epiphanius, *De mensuris et ponderibus,* in Migne, *PG* 43:237–41. See also B. M. Metzger, *Manuscripts of the Greek Bible: An Introduction to Greek Palaeography* (Oxford, 1981), 38. The first part of Metzger's book deals with palaeography in general, including information on the making of ancient books, the various ways in which the divine name was written, and much more. The second part consist of forty-five plates and description of manuscripts, both Old Testament and New Testament, arranged chronologically. Bibliographies accompany all the exhibits. This is a book for scholar and novice alike.

[8] The general appearance of the *Hexapla* may be seen from Swete's treatment of a Milan fragment containing Ps. 45:1-3 (46:1-3 MT) in his *Introduction,* 62–63.

[9] Sir Frederic George Kenyon, *Our Bible and the Ancient Manuscripts,* 5th ed. rev. Arthur White Adams (New York: Harper & Row, 1958) 106.

[10] "The Problems of the Septuagint Recensions," *JBL* 44 (1935): 73–92. In opposition to the Lagardian school Sperber prefers to speak of translations rather than recensions in referring to later texts, asserting thereby that later manuscripts represent entirely different texts rather than variant readings of a single Greek text. In a later essay, "Probleme einer Edition der Septuaginta," in *Studien zur Geschichte und Kultur des Nahen und Fernen Ostens: Paul Kahle zum 60. Geburtstag überreicht von Freunden und Schülern aus dem Kreise des Orientalischen Seminars der Universität Bonn,* ed. Wilhelm Heffening and Willibald Kirfel (Leiden, 1935), 39–46, he acknowledges

texts, is shrouded in uncertainty. Quotations found in Egyptian fathers, including Cyril of Alexandria (d. 444), may well represent a Hesychian tradition.

The recension made by Lucian of Samosata, a presbyter from Antioch who died a martyr's death in 311 or 312, is better known. Field, from a study of the marginal notes in the hexaplaric version, and Paul de Lagarde, by a comparison of manuscripts, independently established its existence. The recension seems to feature grammatical emphases and stylistic effect.

MANUSCRIPTS AND PRINTED EDITIONS OF THE SEPTUAGINT

From this survey of ancient Greek versions it should be apparent that the recovery of a pure Septuagint text is next to impossible. Jerome informs us that

> Alexandria and Egypt praise Hesychius as the author of their Septuagint. Constantinople as far as Antioch accepts that of Lucian the martyr. The provinces between these areas read the Palestinian codices edited by Origen and published by Eusebius and Pamphilus. The whole world is at odds with itself over this threefold tradition.[11]

The texts we meet therefore are always, to some degree, mixed texts, and it is the self-imposed task of Septuagint scholars to isolate the regional texts with a view to breaking the barrier that separates a more fluid tradition from the later attempts to provide a more uniform or standard text.

MANUSCRIPTS

The text of the Greek translation of the Old Testament ordinarily found in printed editions represents in the main the text of one or more of the three great uncials, Codex Sinaiticus (S or ℵ), Codex Alexandrinus (A), and Codex Vaticanus (B). Codex S was discovered by Tischendorf in 1844 and includes Genesis 23 and 24; Numbers 5–7; 1 Chronicles 9:27–19:17; 2 Esdras (i.e., Ezra-Nehemiah) 9:9–23:31; Esther; Tobit; Judith; 1 Maccabees; 4 Macca-

---

his loyalties and argues theoretically that it is now futile to hope to restore even the three recensions referred to by St. Jerome, let alone some single Greek translation underlying later textual forms. "Überall nur Mischtexte, und nirgendwo hat sich eine Rezension rein erhalten," he concludes (p. 46).

[11] "Alexandria et Aegyptus in Septuaginta suis Hesychium laudat auctorem. Constantinopolis usque ad Antiochiam Luciani martyris exemplaria probat. Mediae inter has provinciae Palaestinos codices legunt, quos ab Origene elaboratos Eusebius et Pamphilius vulgaverunt: totusque orbis hac inter se trifaria varietate compugnat" (*Contra Rufinum* 2.26, in Migne, *PL* 23:471).

bees; Isaiah; Jeremiah; Lamentations 1:1—2:20; Joel; Obadiah; Jonah; Nahum to Malachi; Psalms; Proverbs; Ecclesiastes; Song of Songs; Ecclesiasticus; Job. The manuscript is usually dated in the fourth century and evidences either an Egyptian or Caesarean text.

Codex Alexandrinus was written in the first half of the fifth century A.D. Except for a few lacunae, the majority of which are in the New Testament, it contains the entire Bible, including the Apocrypha. In the Old Testament the following portions are missing: Gen. 14:14-17; 15:1-5, 16-19; 16:6-9; 1 Kgdms. 12:18—14:9; Ps. 49:20–79:11 (50:20—80:11 MT).

Both Codex S and Codex A are early witnesses to the Septuagint text, but the queen of the uncials is Codex Vaticanus (B), which continues to demand extra attention in editions of the Greek Old Testament. Coming from the fourth century some time after A.D. 367, the manuscript includes all of the Bible, except Gen. 1:1—46:28; 2 Kgdms. 2:5-7, 10-13; Ps. 105:27–137:6 (106:27—138:6 MT), and in the New Testament Heb. 9:14 to the end. The Prayer of Manasses and the books of Maccabees were not included in this manuscript.

The frontiers of Septuagint tradition have been pushed still farther back by papyrus finds. The Chester Beatty Papyri discovered about 1930 contain portions of seven manuscripts of the Old Testament and, next to the Dead Sea Scrolls, are among the most spectacular finds since Sinaiticus. These were edited by Sir Frederic Kenyon in *The Chester Beatty Biblical Papyri,* Fasc. 1–7, 1933–37. Since Vaticanus and Sinaiticus lack all but a few verses of Genesis, excluding medieval additions, the inclusion of Gen.9:1—44:22 in these papyri is a most welcome resource.[12]

In August 1952, Bedouin south of Khirbet Qumran found the remains of a Greek text of the Minor Prophets written on leather, containing fragments of Micah, Jonah, Nahum, Habakkuk, Zephaniah, and Zechariah. Their discovery kindled further interest in the textual history of the Septuagint. In the opinion of Colin Roberts, which was rendered at the request of Paul Kahle, the scroll is to be dated between 50 B.C. and A.D. 50.[13] Dominique Barthélemy, among the first to discuss the discovery in some detail, had proposed a date near the end of the first century. Barthélemy concludes that the version presented by these fragments is a recension rather than an independent text.[14]

Emanuel Tov, with Robert A. Kraft and P. J. Parsons, has fulfilled scholars' expectations with the full and official publication of a work that will have far-reaching effects on textual criticism of the LXX, *The Greek Minor Prophets Scroll from Naḥal Ḥever (8ḤevXIIgr): The Seiyâl Collection I* (Discoveries

[12] For details on these and other papyri and manuscripts, especially minuscules, see Sidney Jellicoe, *The Septuagint and Modern Study* (Oxford, 1968), chap. 7, and extensive bibliography, pp. 386–90; see also Kenyon-Adams, *Our Bible,* 114–27.

[13] Paul Kahle, "Der gegenwärtige Stand der Erforschung der in Palästina neugefundenen hebräischen Handschriften," *TLZ* 79 (1954): cols. 81–94. See Kenyon-Adams, *Our Bible,* 112.

[14] "Redécouverte d'un chainon manquant de l'histoire de la Septante," *RB* 60 (1953): 18–29.

in the Judean Desert 8 (Oxford: Clarendon, 1990). The generalist will be grateful for Ralph W. Klein's *Textual Criticism of the Old Testament: The Septuagint After Qumran,* Guides to Biblical Scholarship (Philadelphia: Fortress Press, 1974). Together with much judicious advice on assessment of readings, it offers a helpful glossary of technical terminology.

PRINTED EDITIONS

The *Complutensian Polyglot,* edited and printed in Spain (1514 to 1517) under the auspices of Cardinal Archbishop Ximenes of Toledo, included the first printed text of the complete Greek Old Testament. The name of the polyglot is derived from the place where it appeared, Complutum (Latin for Alcalá). Owing perhaps to suspicions of the Inquisition, actual publication of the work was delayed until 1521/22. The edition includes three columns, the first containing the Hebrew text with Targum Onkelos, the second the Vulgate, and the third column the LXX. Because of certain readings not found in known manuscripts, the Greek text of this edition is especially valued.[15]

Another notable edition is the Sixtine, published in Rome, 1587, under the direction of Pope Sixtus V. Though Codex B served as the basis for this edition, the editors did not slavishly adhere to it. The lacunae of this codex were filled from other manuscripts. The reprint of this edition by the Clarendon Press in 1875 formed one of the texts on which Hatch and Redpath based their concordance. The Greek column in the Old Testament portion of the Stier-Theile *Polyglot,* 6 vols. (Bielefeld, 1846–55) is also derived from it.

After paying brief respects to the Aldine edition (Venice, 1518–19), which embraced far less significant manuscript data than the *Sixtine,* one can pass on to John Ernest Grabe's four-volume work known as the Oxford edition. Whereas the *Sixtine* made Codex Vaticanus its base of operations, Grabe reproduced substantially Codex Alexandrinus, carefully indicating any departures from its text with the signs used by Origen in his *Hexapla.*

In 1859 the Society for the Promotion of Christian Knowledge (SPCK) published Frederick Field, *Vetus Testamentum Graece iuxta LXX interpretes* (Oxford), which aimed at a reproduction of Grabe's text, but failed to include the critical devices by which one could extract the text of Alexandrinus from this edition. The result is an arbitrary and mixed text. The relegation in Field's edition of the noncanonical books to a section known as ἀπόκρυφα finds no support in the manuscript tradition.

---

[15] On this work see Randolph Tasker, "The Complutensian Polyglot," *CQR* 94 (1953): 197–210. On early printed texts, see Swete's *Introduction,* rev. ed. (1914), 171–94.

MODERN CRITICAL EDITIONS

The first comprehensive effort to provide a really critical treatment of the entire Septuagint was undertaken by Robert Holmes, professor of poetry at Oxford and, from 1804, Dean of Winchester. He lived to complete only the first volume, containing the Pentateuch, with a preface and appendix. James Parsons completed the work, *Vetus Testamentum Graecum cum variis lectionibus,* 5 vols. (Oxford, 1798–1827), which saw the use of 297 separate codices, of which twenty are uncial. The text is that of the *Sixtine.* In his *Essays in Biblical Greek* (Oxford, 1889), Edwin Hatch takes the editors severely to task for entrusting "no small part of the task of collation to careless or incompetent hands" and making it necessary to collate the material afresh (pp. 131–32), but as Swete more graciously notes (*Introduction,* 187), the "work is an almost unequalled monument of industry and learning, and will perhaps never be superseded as a storehouse of materials."

The mention of Swete suggests his more notable project, *The Old Testament in Greek,* first published at Cambridge in three volumes, 1887–94. Swete reproduced the text of B and filled the lacunae from A and S.[16] A companion to this popular edition is *The Old Testament in Greek According to the Text of Codex Vaticanus, Supplemented from Other Uncial Manuscripts, with a Critical Apparatus Containing the Variants of the Chief Ancient Authorities for the Text of the Septuagint,* ed. Alan E. Brooke, Norman McLean, and Henry St. John Thackeray (1906–). As the prefatory note to Genesis in volume 1, part 1, states, no attempt has been made to "provide a reconstructed, or 'true,' text." The editors follow the text of B and fill its lacunae from the Alexandrian and other uncials in the order of their relative value.[17]

Not to be outdone, the Germans have underwritten a Septuagint monument parallel to the Cambridge Septuagint. The project, still in progress, goes back to the work of Paul de Lagarde.[18] In 1882 Lagarde announced his plans to produce a new edition of the Greek Old Testament. His intent was to attempt a reconstruction of Lucian's recension, with a view to moving closer to a prehexaplaric Septuagint and ultimately to a pure Septuagint text. The attempt was doomed to failure, partially because of the limitation imposed by the

---

[16] For critique of the scientific accuracy of this work and for its limitations in textual criticism, see Max L. Margolis, "The K Text of Joshua," *AJSL* 28 (1911–12): 1–55; and Joseph Ziegler, "Studien zur Verwertung der Septuaginta im Zwölfprophetenbuch," *ZAW* 60 (1944): 126–28.

[17] On the "Large" Cambridge Septuagint edition, see Jellicoe, *The Septuagint and Modern Study,* 269–97.

[18] On the Göttingen edition, see Jellicoe, *The Septuagint and Modern Study,* 297–310. For details on Lagarde's work, see Alfred Rahlfs, *Septuaginta-Studien* (Göttingen, 1911), 3:23–30, of which all 3 volumes are now available in a second edition in 1 volume (Göttingen, 1965). Peter Katz (Walters), *The Text of the Septuagint: Its Corruptions and Their Emendations,* ed. D. W. Gooding (Cambridge, UK, 1973).

psalmist's threescore and ten years but mainly because of inherent impossibility. Lagarde, nevertheless, was determined, and his productivity warrants somewhat the gigantic scale on which he dreamed. On May 26, 1881, he concluded his collations in Rome. On August 9, 1883, he saw the publication of his book *Librorum Veteris Testamenti canonicorum pars prior* (Göttingen), containing the Octateuch and the historical books as far as Esther, 560 pages in large octavo format. During the last eighteen months preceding the actual publication date of his chief work Lagarde kept up his lectures; served as dean of the Göttingen philosophical faculty; made trips to Turin and Florence to investigate the Latin and Coptic texts of the Old Testament wisdom books; published several articles; presented the first part of his Persian studies to the Scientific Academy of Göttingen on May 5, 1883; and in his spare time published four books involving Latin, Coptic, Hebrew, Spanish, and Arabic.

Not all shared the larger dream, for in 1891 Paul de Lagarde wrote bitterly in the introductory paragraphs of his *Septuaginta-Studien.*

> For years it has been my intention to restore the three official recensions of the Septuagint attested to us by Jerome, to see to their printing in parallel columns, and to draw further conclusions from a comparison of these three texts. By working this way I wished to hold subjectivity and error in check. Disgust prevents me from explaining how and through whom the execution of this plan has been made impossible. Not even the first half of Lucian's [recension] have I been able to set forth as I would have been capable of editing it, had I been granted, at least as in the case of Mommsen, the freedom of movement which is more necessary for me than for any other scholar. Now finally, to prevent others from any longer considering me a fool because of my promises, I am resolved to divulge nothing about my own plans. Since my shamefully managed, betrayed, and homeless life is coming to a close in grief and sorrow, I want to do in the meantime that which I certainly can accomplish.[19]

The Göttingen Septuagint, *Septuaginta, Vetus Testamentum Graecum auctoritate Societatis Litterarum Gottingensis editum* (Stuttgart, Göttingen), continues along some of the paths worn by Lagarde. The first volume of a projected sixteen-volume work was Alfred Rahlfs's edition of Genesis (1926). A pilot volume on Ruth appeared in 1922. After discovering that the recovery of a pure Septuagint text was a sheer impossibility, the editors of the Göttingen Septuagint set themselves the task of classifying manuscripts into families and recensions. The Cambridge editors reproduce B with corrections of obvious errors and in the apparatus present selected manuscript data carefully grouped for purposes of comparison. In any given instance readers may decide for themselves which reading is preferable. The Göttingen editors also submit a

---

[19] *Septuaginta-Studien,* pt. 1, from Abhandlungen der königlichen Gesellschaft der Wissenschaften zu Göttingen 37 (Göttingen, 1891), 3. See also *Paul de Lagarde: Erinnerungen aus seinem Leben,* compiled by Anna de Lagarde (Göttingen, 1894).

text which is primarily that of B, but it is the result of critical attempts to select "at each point the reading . . . which appears best in the light of the manuscript tradition as a whole, and with due reference to the Hebrew text."[20] Hence the text of the Göttingen Septuagint is an "eclectic," or mixed, text. On the other hand, the detailed apparatus enables the reader to get behind the editorial decisions. Some appreciation of the scope of the work may be gained by noting the number of pages devoted to writings associated with the name of Jeremiah. Joseph Ziegler, *Ieremias, Baruch, Threni, Epistula Ieremiae,* 15 (Göttingen, 1957), devotes 148 pages to introductory matters regarding the textual tradition in a book totaling 504 pages.

With the publication of Alfred Rahlfs's two-volume student edition of the Septuagint (*Septuaginta, id est, Vetus Testamentum Graece iuxta LXX interpretes*) by the Stuttgart Bible Society in 1935, a limited amount of textual-critical data became available at a modest price. The popularity of the work is evident from the number of printings through which it has gone. It has also appeared in a one-volume format (1979). The text is eclectic (see, e.g., text and variant, Gen. 6:2), based in the main on the uncials B, A, and S, with a critical apparatus presenting variants from these and other manuscripts. The brief history of the Septuagint text in German, English, and Latin is a model summary, and I am indebted to it for much of the information included in these pages. Although the eclectic character of the text makes it questionable whether the title "Septuagint" is valid for Rahlfs's edition, students may be sure that they have access in these two volumes to many standard Septuagint readings. For one who lacks a critical edition of the Septuagint, this is easily a best buy. Users of the Bauer lexicon of the New Testament (see chap. 7) will find it a convenient resource for tracking down most of its references to the Septuagint, but for sustained research the Cambridge and Göttingen editions are essential.

OTHER SEPTUAGINTAL RESOURCES

LEXICAL

Many of the resources for Septuagint study have already been cited. Hatch and Redpath's concordance should be underscored as the most efficient port of entry into the treasures of the Septuagint. Peter Katz and Joseph Ziegler spearheaded the task of indexing afresh the hexaplaric authors.[21] Swete's *Introduction* still wears well on introductory matters. Richard R. Ottley's *A Handbook to the Septuagint* (London, 1920) includes a helpful glossary.

---

[20] Ernst Würthwein, *The Text of the Old Testament: An Introduction to the Biblia Hebraica,* trans. Erroll F. Rhodes (Grand Rapids: Eerdmans, 1979; reprinted, 1992, with "Addenda"), 73.
[21] P. Katz and J. Ziegler, "Ein Aquila-Index in Vorbereitung," *VT* 8 (1958): 264–85

Johann F. Schleusner's *Novus thesaurus philologico-criticus: sive lexicon in LXX, et reliquos interpretes Graecos ac scriptores apocryphos Veteris Testamenti,* 5 vols. (Leipzig, 1820–21), has been reprinted photomechanically, but his work is merely an amplification of J. Christian Biel's *Novus thesaurus philologicus sive lexicon in LXX,* ed. E. H. Mutzenbecher; 3 vols. (The Hague, 1779), and displays throughout the unlexical procedure of Biel. For statistical analysis one must use F. Rehkopf, *Septuaginta-Vokabular* (Göttingen: Vandenhoeck & Ruprecht, 1989), which exhibits in columnar form the complete vocabulary of the LXX as exhibited in the Hatch-Redpath concordance. In addition to furnishing statistics on usage, the layout permits ready identification of the Hebrew or Aramaic equivalents, and calls attention to occurrences in the New Testament.

Along with others, Takamitsu Muraoka looked to the future, "Towards a Septuagint Lexicon," in *VI Congress of the International Organization for Septuagint and Cognate Studies,* ed. Claude E. Cox; SBLSCS 23 (Atlanta: Scholars Press, 1987), 255–76, with emphasis on the Minor Prophets. In 1992 some of the dreams became reality in the first part of *A Greek-English Lexicon of the Septuagint,* covering the letters A–I (Stuttgart: Deutsche Bibelgesellschaft, 1992). The compilation was done by J. Lust, E. Eynikel, and K. Hauspie in collaboration with G. Chamberlain and draws on the files of CATSS (Computer Assisted Tools for Septuagint Studies, ed. R. A. Kraft and E. Tov). A statistical feature improves on Xavier Jacques, *Index des mots apparentés dans la Septante,* Subsidia biblica (Rome, 1972); English: *List of Septuagint Words Sharing Common Elements* (Rome, 1972). Somewhat along the lines of the *Shorter Lexicon of the Greek New Testament* (see below, chap. 7), the work by Lust et al. is a modest stepping stone to a large-scale lexicon. Especially helpful in the introduction is the review of previous lexical work.

GRAMMATICAL

Mirabile dictu, no complete grammar of the Septuagint is yet available. Only a few have even entertained the challenge, of whom Henry St. John Thackeray especially stands out for his *A Grammar of the Old Testament in Greek According to the Septuagint* (Cambridge, UK: Cambridge University Press, 1909), which unfortunately covers only orthography, phonology, and morphology, but makes use of the papyri. Somewhat less valued is Robert Helbing's *Grammatik der Septuaginta: Laut- und Wortlehre* (Göttingen: Vandenhoeck & Ruprecht, 1907), but his work on syntax, *Die Kasussyntax der Verba bei den Septuaginta: Ein Beitrag zur Hebraismenfrage und zur Syntax der κοινή* (Göttingen, 1928) is given better marks. Conybeare and Stock, *Selections from the Septuagint* (Boston: Ginn and Company, 1905), includes an introduction, a discussion of grammar, and selections of readings from the Septuagint for the beginner in Septuagint studies. Swete's "The Septuagint as a Version," chap. 5 in his *Introduction,* is also intended for the beginner.

The rationale behind Greek structure for Hebrew expression in the Greek versions has long been a source of perplexity. One of the more determined investigators of the problem is Martin Johannessohn, three of whose instructive articles are frequently cited in BAGD: "Der Gebrauch der Kasus und der Präpositionen in der Septuaginta" (Diss., Berlin, 1910); "Das biblische καὶ ἐγένετο und seine Geschichte," *Zeitschrift für vergleichende Sprachforschung* 53 (1925): 161–212; "Das biblische καὶ ἰδού in der Erzählung samt seiner hebräischen Vorlage," *Zeitschrift für vergleichende Sprachforschung* 66 (1939): 145–95. We are also grateful for a collection of seventeen essays by Ilmari Soisalon-Soininen published during the years 1965–86 on renderings of a variety of Hebrew constructions; the selection was made and edited in his honor by two students, Anneli Aejmelaeus and Raija Sollamo, and is titled *Studien zur Septuaginta-Syntax: Zu seinem 70. Geburtstag am 4 Juni 1987* Annalas Academiae Scientiarum Fennicae, Ser. B, 237 (Helsinki: Suomalainen Tiedeakatemia, 1987).

A work edited by D. Fraenkel, U. Quast, and J. W. Wevers, *Studien zur Septuaginta — Robert Hanhart zu Ehren: Aus Anlass seines 65. Geburtstages,* Mitteilungen des Septuaginta-Unternehmens 20 (Göttingen: Vandenhoeck & Ruprecht, 1990), contains specialized studies relating to grammar and sources of readings in various text traditions.

TEXTUAL-CRITICAL

Before attempting reconstruction of the Hebrew text, one must read Emanuel Tov, *The Text-Critical Use of the Septuagint in Biblical Research* (Jerusalem: Simor Ltd., 1981), and his *Textual Criticism of the Hebrew Bible* (Minneapolis: Fortress Press, 1992). See also Peter Katz, *The Text of the Septuagint: Its Corruptions and Their Emendation,* ed. D. W. Gooding (Cambridge, UK: Cambridge University Press, 1973).

Tov, with R. A. Kraft and P. J. Parsons, has fulfilled scholars' expectations with the full and official publication of a work that will have far-reaching effects on textual criticism of the LXX, *The Greek Minor Prophets Scroll from Naḥal Ḥever (8ḤevXIIgr): The Seiyâl Collection I,* Discoveries in the Judean Desert 8 (Oxford, 1990).

THE FUTURE

Robert A. Kraft, who misses no opportunity to pull scholars into the electronic age through reports in the *Religious Studies Review,* has now, together with

Emanuel Tov, and with the assistance of John R. Abercrombie and William Adler, ushered in a new era in Septuagint studies with the production of the first volume, *Ruth,* in the series Computer Assisted Tools for Septuagint Studies (CATSS); SBLSCS 20 (Atlanta: Scholars Press, 1986).

TRANSLATIONS

The Septuagint Version of the Old Testament with an English Translation and with Various Readings and Critical Notes (London and New York: Samuel Bagster and Sons, n.d. [ca. 1956]), includes the translation of the LXX according to Codex Vaticanus, prepared by Sir Lancelot Charles Lee-Brenton and published in London in 1844. It is more reliable than the overadvertised reissue of *The Septuagint Bible: The Oldest Version of the Old Testament,* trans. Charles Thomson; ed. rev. and enlarged by Charles Arthur Muses (Indian Hills, Colo., 1954).[22]

---

[22] The extravagant advertising claims made by the publisher of this edition are scathingly reviewed in *Biblica* 37 (1956): 497–500. For a sketch of the life of Charles Thomson (1729–1824), see John H. P. Reumann, "Philadelphia's Patriot Scholar," in his *The Romance of Bible Scripts and Scholars: Chapters in the History of Bible Transmissions and Translation* (Englewood Cliffs, N.J.: Prentice Hall, 1965); see also his comments on Muses's edition, pp. 142–43; for references to reviews and responses by Muses, see ibid. p. 227, endnote 27.

CHAPTER FIVE

The Use
of the Septuagint

"**O**F WHAT USE is the Septuagint to me in my Biblical studies?" The question echoes in the halls of biblical inquiry. "I have my Rahlfs; what do I do with it?"

There is enough in the LXX to appeal to almost anyone. Lovers of sound textual criticism will find here a deep sea of alluring opportunity. Students of theology will be intrigued by the subtle alterations of the text effected by the Alexandrians. Old Testament interpreters will appreciate the light shed by this version on obscure words and syntax. Philologists will note the evolution of meanings. As for New Testament expositors, lavish are their endowments; they will have new visions, dream new dreams.

It is well that users of the LXX thoroughly familiarize themselves at the outset with the varying systems of reference in the printed texts of the LXX occasioned by departure from the chapter and verse divisions found in the MT and vernacular versions. These variations are traceable, in part, to the vagaries of printers before the divisions of the biblical text had been more or less standardized and, in part, to deviations of the LXX text from that of the MT.

The major differences between the divisions of the LXX and the MT are to be found in the Psalms and Jeremiah. Since Psalms 9 and 10 of the MT are printed as one psalm in editions of the LXX, the enumeration from Psalm 10 to Psalm 146 in the LXX is one chapter short of the MT. A division of Psalm 147 (MT) into Psalms 146 and 147 in the LXX restores the MT chapter division.

The dislocations in Jeremiah are more complicated, but with a little patience one can easily master them. It must be remembered that the MT divides Jeremiah into fifty-two chapters. The LXX introduces its translation of chaps. 46–51, with liberal rearrangement of the contents, at 25:13 and continues with its enumeration as if no transposition had taken place. Jeremiah 25:13b, 15-38 (MT) is picked up again (chap. 32 LXX) after chaps. 46–51 (MT) have been translated, but the editors of the LXX, in order to maintain the versification of the MT, must begin a new chapter and omit the numbers 1 to 12. The words ὅσα ἐπροφήτευσεν Ιερεμιας ἐπὶ πάντα τὰ ἔθνη, which form a part of 25:13 (MT), were dropped in the LXX's translation of that verse but are recovered here and marked off as v. 13. Since 25:14 (MT) is not translated, the verse number is omitted in order that the enumeration of both texts in 25:15 and succeeding verses might correspond. From that point on through chap. 51 the LXX's chapter enumeration is seven figures higher than that of the MT. Chapter 52 in the LXX coincides with that of the MT, since only chaps. 46–51 had suffered a shift. Rahlfs marks all departures from the MT's division of the text with 𝔐. Except in works such as Bauer's lexicon where versions other than the LXX are the exception, it is customary, when citing the LXX, to give in parentheses the MT's enumeration wherever it varies from the Greek version.

TEXTUAL CRITICISM

We are now prepared to survey some of the values of the LXX. The first of these is in the area of textual criticism. The textual-critical value of the LXX is apparent from a cursory study of readings and marginal notes in the KJV and NRSV, many of which draw attention to passages in which Greek versions have influenced the revisers to depart from the MT in an endeavor to arrive at a closer approximation of the original Hebrew.

Genesis 4:8 presents a well-known example. The KJV reads: "And Cain talked with Abel his brother; and it came to pass, when they were in the field, that Cain rose up against Abel his brother and slew him." The NRSV relieves the awkwardness in the first part of the sentence with its rendering: "Cain said to his brother Abel, 'Let us go out to the field.'" This interpretation follows the LXX's Διέλθωμεν εἰς τὸ πεδίον, which undergirds the witness of the Samaritan Pentateuch, the Peshitta, and the Vulgate.

Translators of the KJV did the best they could with the MT in Judg. 13:19, but the proleptic introduction of the angel in the italics so familiar to readers of the KJV is not convincing. The NRSV, more alertly following the LXX's τῷ κυρίῳ τῷ θαυμαστὰ ποιοῦντι κυρίῳ renders: "So Manoah took the kid with the grain offering, and offered it on the rock to the Lord, to him who works wonders."

In 1 Sam. 9:25, 26 (MT) the repetitious sequence invites improvement via the LXX. The translators apparently read a slight transposition of the MT consonants in the form וַיְדַבֵּר and translated וַיִּרְבְּדוּ with the preposition לְ in place of עַם, with the resultant καὶ διέστρωσαν τῷ Σαουλ, "they spread a couch for Saul."

The LXX again provides the clue that solves the mystery of the MT's reading in 2 Sam. 4:6. The KJV's "*as though* they would have fetched wheat" already signals what many consider a textual corruption. The LXX, on the other hand, states how the assassins Rechab and Baanah were able to enter the house unseen and slay Ishbosheth. While the doorkeeper was cleaning wheat, she dozed and was then sleeping.

The italics in the rendering of Ps. 49:11 (KJV) betray the desperation of the translators. The LXX (Ps. 48:12) gives what appears to be a more coherent text: καὶ οἱ τάφοι αὐτῶν οἰκίαι αὐτῶν εἰς τὸν αἰῶνα. The psalmist's point is that the only permanent dwelling places for the wicked are their graves! The NRSV seconds the thought.

The novice in biblical criticism is not hereby encouraged to begin emending the MT at every point where it diverges from the Septuagint. Textual criticism is a science that requires a detailed knowledge and precise methodology mastered by only a few experts. But acquaintance with critical editions of both Hebrew and Greek texts of the Old Testament, as well as a basic knowledge of textual-critical principles, will assist students in evaluating conclusions reached by others. At the very least, they will know more of what lies behind significant variations in Bible versions.

THE SEPTUAGINT AND MODERN VERSIONS

The Septuagint will also prove to be a most valuable aid in identifying the probable reasons supporting the variations noted in modern translations.

In Exod. 3:19 the center column found in many editions of the KJV reads "or, *but by strong hand.*" The LXX rendering, ἐὰν μὴ μετὰ χειρὸς κραταιᾶς, clearly exhibits the basis for this alternate reading, which the NRSV prefers to the "no, not by a mighty hand" of the MT. The reading preserved in the LXX heightens the dramatic tension.

Often the LXX will be found lurking behind rare instances in which the KJV departs from the MT. In Gen. 41:56 we read πάντας τοὺς σιτοβολῶνας, "all the storehouses," in place of the obscure "all which was in them." Beside Ps. 22:16 (22:17 MT; 21:17 LXX) the KJV's center column does not even note a departure from the MT. In place of the MT's unintelligible "like a lion" the KJV (followed by the RSV) has the LXX's ὤρυξαν χεῖράς μου καὶ πόδας, "they pierced my hands and my feet." The NRSV renders "my hands and feet have shriveled," without reference to any source and only with the notation: "Meaning of Heb. uncertain."

In 1 Sam. 6:19 Moffatt's translation reads: "The sons of Jechoniah, however, did not rejoice along with the men of Beth-shemesh when they saw the ark of the Eternal." No hint is given as to the reason for a departure from the renderings found in the KJV and the RSV. A look at the LXX reveals that Moffatt preferred the Greek version to the Hebrew of the MT in this passage, and the NRSV followed suit.

The NRSV includes the phrase "and the Egyptians oppressed them" in 1 Sam. 12:8, thus giving the reason for the petition of the fathers. The Old Testament student who has the dreary misfortune of being without a LXX or lacks a knowledge of the Greek can at best offer from Kittel's critical apparatus a probable reconstruction of the Hebrew clause underlying the NRSV's rendering. The user of the LXX knows beyond question the additional words that the revisers were translating: καὶ ἐταπείνωσεν αὐτοὺς Αἴγυπτος.[1]

This, then, is a good rule to remember: Whenever the translation with which you are working diverges from a text in another translation or from the Hebrew text, first consult the Septuagint.

THEOLOGICAL CONCERNS

One of the primary reasons for the suggested caution against overenthusiastic emendation on the basis of the LXX is the complex of evident theological presuppositions that often color the translation.[2]

A tendency to preserve inviolate God's transcendence and providence appears well documented in the Book of Job and elsewhere in the Greek Old Testament. The ancient Hebrews did not hesitate to approach the Almighty in a frank and forthright manner. Familiar is Abraham's haggling with Yahweh. Job's complaints fall into a similar category. The Greek translator of Job, though, feels qualms about putting such sentiments in Hellenistic dress. On the other hand, Hellenes know how to accept the fell blows of circumstance and they shy away from hubris. Moffatt's inimitable rendering of Job 10:13 highlights what the Greek translator had concealed: "And all the while this was thy dark design!—plotting this, well I know it, against me!" This is a Prometheus talking. Contrast the limpness of the LXX: "Since you have these things in yourself, I know that you can do all things, and that nothing is beyond your control." In Job 13:3 the LXX cools Job's ardor to challenge the Almighty by having him meekly add, "if he wills." The dilution of Job's audacity in Job 32:2 is in the same vein. Job's friends accuse him, not because he tried to be *more* righteous than God (MT) but because he "showed himself off righteous *before* God." The LXX translators evidently doubt that Job could have displayed the type of hubris that seemed to stare at them in the MT.

A number of scholars have searched the LXX for anti-anthropomorphisms

---

[1] The contribution of Qumran materials to the evaluation of readings found in the LXX will be considered below, chap. 15.

[2] A fine summary treatment of this subject is made by John W. Wevers in his "Septuaginta-Forschungen: II. Die Septuaginta als Übersetzungsurkunde," *TRu* n.s. 22 (1954): 171–90. I have also profited from Gillis Gerleman, *Studies in the Septuagint: I. Book of Job,* Lunds Universitets Arsskrift, New Series, Sec. 1, 43/2 (Lund: Gleerup, 1946).

and anti-anthropopathisms.[3] Exodus 24:10 frequently emerges as an instance of this alleged antipathy. The MT states that the leaders of the Israelites "saw the God of Israel." The LXX reads καὶ εἶδον τὸν τόπον οὗ εἰστήκει ἐκεῖ ὁ θεὸς τοῦ Ισραηλ, "they saw the place where the God of Israel stood." Harry M. Orlinsky, who has taken up cudgels in defense of the translators and has trained his reinforcements for action against critics who charge the translators of the LXX with willful distortion of the Hebrew text, deserves respectful audience when he reminds that many of the passages cited as evidence do not support such a contention.[4] But, as Wevers once observed, stylistic considerations cannot account for all such divergences.[5] It seems anti-anthropomorphic bias proposed the alteration of the MT's "his hand pierced the fleeing serpent" (Job 26:13 NRSV). The LXX renders "and by a command he put to death the apostate serpent." Similar reasoning may be responsible for the alteration of the phrase "sons of God" to οἱ ἄγγελοι τοῦ θεοῦ (Job 1:6; 2:1) or ἄγγελοί μου (Job 38:7).

By avoiding or softening statements that might prejudice God's providence the LXX further preserves the Creator's majesty. In Job 24:12 the hero complains that God pays no attention to the oppression of the helpless. The Greek translator has softened this considerably by turning the declarative statement of 24:12 into a question that is then answered by 24:13. "Why has God not taken notice of these (poor people)?" The answer in substance: Because they ignored the way of the Lord.

"If I sin, what harm is that to thee, O thou Spy upon mankind?" is Moffatt's unvarnished rendering of Job 7:20. The LXX circumspectly paraphrases: "If I have sinned, what can I do to you, who understands the human mind?"

According to the MT in Job 12:6, God is oblivious of the wicked. The LXX tips the scales in favor of divine justice with: "the wicked provoke the Lord, as though they would never face trial."

The tendency in Alexandrian Judaism to emphasize God's transcendent character is accompanied by other theological patterns contemporary with the translators. The more clearly defined belief in the corruption of human nature by sin finds expression in various contexts. In Ecclesiastes (1:14 et al.)

---

[3] See especially the entries cited by Wevers under the names of Gard, Gehman, and Gerleman in his "Septuaginta-Forschungen: I. Ausgaben und Texte," *TRu* n.s. 22 (1954): 86f.

[4] See Orlinsky's rigorously methodological discussions in "The Treatment of Anthropomorphisms and Anthropopathisms in the Septuagint of Isaiah," *Hebrew Union College Annual* 27 (1956): 193–200; and a series of articles titled "Studies in the Septuagint of the Book of Job": "Chapter I. An Analytical Survey of Previous Studies," ibid. 28 (1957): 53–74; "Chapter II. The Character of the Septuagint Translation of the Book of Job," ibid. 29 (1958): 229–71; "Chapter III. On the Matter of Anthropomorphisms, Anthropopathisms, and Euphemisms," ibid. 30 (1959): 153–67; "Chapter IV. The Present State of the Greek Text of Job," ibid. 33 (1962): 119–51; and "Chapter V. The Hebrew *Vorlage* of the Septuagint of Job. The Text and the Script," ibid. 35 (1964): 57–78.

[5] See our n. 2 above, p. 80.

the rendering προαίρεσις πνεύματος ("self-expression of the spirit") is given for the Hebrew רְעוּת רוּחַ, "a striving after (or "a feeding on") wind." Προαίρεσις, a favorite word of the moral philosophers, denotes express purpose or volition. The translator of Qoheleth bemoans not so much the disappointing character of human effort as the vanity and self-will of the inner person.

The theory of rewards and punishments held by postexilic Judaism is imported into the Greek text of Job 15:11. In place of the MT's "Are the consolations of God too small for you, or the word that deals gently with you?" (NRSV), the LXX renders: "For only a few of your sins have you been scourged; even though you have spoken high and mightily." In Job 42:7 not only is the anthropopathic element subdued but the concept of sin is heightened. The MT reads: "My wrath is kindled against you and against your two friends" (NRSV). The LXX reads: "You have sinned, and your two friends."

A contemporary concern is reflected in the nationalistic feeling expressed in Isa. 43:15, where Israel is assured a messianic king. The design is to keep messianic hope alive. In the same vein Zion is termed a μητρόπολις (Isa. 1:26). And the note sounded in Isa. 31:9 is unmistakable: "Blessed is the one who has seed in Zion and household friends in Jerusalem." Unless harmonistic attempts have been made by the Greek translator in Isa. 11:16, the alteration of "Assyria" (MT) to "Egypt" must be traced to the translator's zeal to assure his fellow Jews in Egypt that they can expect deliverance.

The surge of converts into Judaism in pre-Christian decades also receives divine encouragement from the Greek translators. The words in Isa. 54:15, ἰδοὺ προσήλυτοι προσελεύσονταί σοι δι᾽ ἐμοῦ καὶ ἐπὶ σὲ καταφεύξονται ("Look, converts shall come to you through me, and they shall take refuge with you"), bear no resemblance to the MT. In Amos 9:12 Gentiles take precedence over Israelites as end-time beneficiaries, and the Book of Acts (15:17) sanctions the alteration.

Nor is a rationalistic approach absent from the version. In the description of Goliath and his armor we find the LXX trimming the giant's height to four cubits and a span (1 Kgdms. 17:4); and the 600-shekel weight takes in the whole spear (17:7), not simply the spearhead as in the MT. In 3 Kgdms. 18:38 the devastating power of the fire is somewhat lessened. The fire does indeed devour the water, but it "licks up" the stones and the earth.[6]

EXEGETICAL PROBLEMS

Interpreters of the Old Testament are often grateful for the assistance rendered by the LXX in solving exegetical problems. It will be noted that the KJV in

---

[6] The possibility, of course, always exists that a variant Hebrew text, rather than theological predilection, may underlie a LXX rendering that is at variance with the MT. Qumran materials may aid textual critics as a control. See below, chap. 14.

its text and center column offers two possible interpretations of Deut. 20:19; neither is satisfactory. The problem concerns the Israelites' disposition toward enemy property. The LXX has captured the sense. The Israelites are not to treat the trees in enemy country as combatants worthy of capital punishment. The NRSV follows this exegesis.

Without the help of the LXX the reference to the potter's wheel in Exod. 1:16 would be quite unintelligible, but the Greek version with its periphrasis καὶ ὦσιν πρὸς τῷ τίκτειν suggests that the word הָאָבְנָיִם ("potter's wheels") is used in an extended sense of "birth stools," which perhaps resembled a potter's wheel (see the lexicons).

Some help for the explanation of the enigmatic מָן הוּא in Exod. 16:15 is gained from the LXX's Τί ἐστιν τοῦτο. Genesis 30:11 presents a parallel problem. The masoretes suggest that in place of the unusual formation בְּגָד, the phrase בָּא גָד, "good fortune comes" (*qere*), be read. But the LXX reveals the purity of the traditional consonantal text by rendering Ἐν τύχῃ. Merely a change of pointing, בְּגָד, is required.

In 1 Sam. 13:21 the KJV reads: "They had a file for the mattocks," which contributes little to a reader's comprehension. Moffatt threw up his hands, left three dots at the end of 13:20, and skipped 13:21. He should have consulted the LXX, which helps clarify the matter by suggesting that the Philistines were charging inflated prices for sharpening the Israelites' farming implements. The RSV was on the right track with the transliteration "pim" in reference to a medium of exchange, which the NRSV translated with the help of the LXX's τρεῖς σίκλοι (three shekels).

INTERPRETING THE NEW TESTAMENT

Philological contributions of the LXX to an understanding of the New Testament have been the subject of detailed treatments,[7] but increasing emphasis on the close relations between the two major parts of the Bible has flung the LXX into a fresh orbit from which it casts new beams of light on old passages. Readers acquainted with the Nestle text are aware of the imposing bulk of dependence on the Old Testament displayed in the New. The Nestle editors,

---

[7] See Edwin Hatch, *Essays in Biblical Greek* (Oxford, 1889); Charles H. Dodd, *The Bible and the Greeks* (London: Hodder & Stoughton, 1935); and Everett P. Harrison, "The Importance of the Septuagint for Biblical Studies: Part II. The Influence of the Septuagint on the New Testament Vocabulary," *Bibliotheca Sacra* 113, 449 (January, 1956): 37–45. A note of caution is in order, for students must be on guard against the easy assumption that the LXX had an enormous impact on the vocabulary of the Greek New Testament; for refutations of Hatch on this score, see G. H. R. Horsley, *New Documents Illustrating Early Christianity*. Vol. 5, *Linguistic Essays* (Macquarie University, N.S.W., Australia: Ancient History Documentary Research Centre, 1989), 28.

though, have by no means cited all references and allusions; the prospect of finding fresh points of contact is a part of the exciting adventure of New Testament study.

CITATIONS

Citations from the LXX form the bulk of Old Testament references in the New Testament, for the LXX was the principal text of Scripture in the hellenized areas of the early Christian church. Occasionally two or more passages from various parts of the Old Testament are compounded as a single reference. The LXX is helpful in identifying such passages. Thus the first part of Matt. 11:10, ἰδοὺ ἐγὼ ἀποστέλλω τὸν ἄγγελόν μου πρὸ προσώπου σου, comes verbatim from the LXX (Exod. 23:20). The second part, ὃς κατασκευάσει τὴν ὁδόν σου ἔμπροσθέν σου, reproduces in free form a portion of Mal. 3:1. Matthew evidently ties up the fortunes of Israel's past history as presented in the Exodus along with her future destiny as seen by the prophet Malachi and alleges that Israel's entire history has meaning primarily in terms of John the Baptist's activity as related to Jesus' messianic mission. Significant is the alteration in the second quotation of μου to σου to conform to the pronoun in the quotation from Exodus. Jesus is the embodiment of Israel. In connection with him, God now acts in such a way that the followers of Jesus share in the fortunes of Israel.

A similar significant alteration appears in the quotation of Isa. 40:3 in Mark 1:3 and Luke 3:4. The LXX reads εὐθείας ποιεῖτε τὰς τρίβους τοῦ θεοῦ ἡμῶν, but the evangelists cite it as εὐθείας ποιεῖτε τὰς τρίβους αὐτοῦ, replacing τοῦ θεοῦ ἡμῶν with αὐτοῦ. God's saving activity reaches a climax in the person and work of Jesus Christ. The preparation for God is in reality the preparation for Jesus the Messiah.

ALLUSIONS

More often the point of contact is a passing allusion. The phrase μὴ φοβεῖσθε appears so frequently in the New Testament that its true force is apt to be lost. The LXX, with a context like that surrounding Isa. 35:4, where the phrase appears, sharpens one's appreciation. The prophet's presentation is made a springboard for a high Christology by the New Testament writers. The eyes of the blind, the limbs of the lame, the tongue of the mute—all will experience the saving hand of God, says the prophet. God makes an appearance, the evangelists would seem to say in such passages as Matt. 28:10; Mark 5:36; 6:50; Luke 1:13; 2:10.

A study of John 6:1-13 suggests that the writer of the fourth Gospel was steeped in the LXX. The phrase ἦν δὲ χόρτος πολύς (6:10) appears at first view redundant, but a check of the LXX via Hatch and Redpath indicates that Ps. 146:8 (147:8 MT) may have suggested the evangelist's wording. The LXX reads τῷ [θεῷ] ἐξανατέλλοντι ἐν ὄρεσι χόρτον. The fact that other allusions to the Greek version appear to be present in this section helps confirm the probability of a septuagintal reminiscence in 6:6. John 6:3 specifically states that Jesus went up into a mountain. It is possible that the word ἀρκοῦσιν in 6:7 is prompted by Num. 11:22; and the word ἐνεπλήσθησαν in 6:12 may well be a striking echo of Ps. 104:40 LXX. Moreover, in John's sequel to the feeding of the 5,000 Jesus displays his mastery over the sea by walking on it and accompanies this demonstration with a reassuring word to the disciples. As in Psalms 146 and 147 LXX, omnipotence and love are here brought into telling juxtaposition. The evangelist's botanical observation, then, has definite theological and messianic overtones. The hazard of an artificial reconstruction of an ancient author's mental processes must, of course, be taken into account in any such analysis, but the by-products are no small gain.

If Ps. 34:23 (35:23 MT) finds an echo in John 20:28, ὁ κύριός μου καὶ ὁ θεός μου, the force of Thomas's reaction to the Lord's treatment of his doubts heightens. In Psalm 34 the psalmist cries out to the Lord for help in his miseries and persecutions. His cry culminates in the words ἐξεγέρθητι, κύριε, καὶ πρόσχες τῇ κρίσει μου, ὁ θεός μου καὶ ὁ κύριός μου, εἰς τὴν δίκην μου (v. 23). The Lord is the source of the poet's salvation. And that is exactly what Thomas is made to enunciate here. Whereas previously Thomas had failed to perceive the theological significance of Jesus' death, now the full splendor of it dawns on him. Through the use of these words from Psalm 34 LXX the evangelist is able to give subtle dramatic expression to the meaning of Jesus' death. The writer's emphasis is placed not first of all on the deity of Jesus Christ but on the fact that in Jesus and his crucifixion believers encounter the Lord's salvation.

TYPOLOGY

Searching for typological strains is an attractive enterprise for biblical interpreters. Subjectivity is a grave danger, but the LXX can offer some controls. Words from Judg. 13:5 certainly appear to underlie the phrase αὐτὸς γὰρ σώσει τὸν λαὸν αὐτοῦ in Matt. 1:21. According to the writer of the first Gospel, Jesus is a second Samson, who comes to play the role of a "judge" or deliverer. The Samson motif seems to emerge also in Matt. 27:29. The soldiers mocked (ἐνέπαιξαν) Jesus, even as Samson's captors made Israel's national hero the butt of ridicule (ἐνέπαιζον, Judg. 16:25). Samson is placed between two pillars, Jesus between two criminals; and the blows dealt their prospective enemies in the hour of their death are more devastating than in their lifetimes. Thousands of Philistines lie dead beneath the stones of the pleasure house; conversely Jesus' death spells release from the captivity of death for many of the saints who had fallen asleep (Matt. 27:51, 52). That the evangelists treat the Lord's passion not as a defeat but as a victorious achievement receives support from such and other probable allusions to the LXX. In all this it is important to note that the writers of the Gospels brought to their task a canonical sense of Israel's experiences. The Old Testament was to them as Homer was to the Hellenes, and association of ideas and events played an important role. In the same way, it was difficult for pious Israelites to think of future salvation without evoking deliverance from pharaoh. What came natural to them we must evoke through laborious enterprise. Probable association is, of course, the best that we can achieve.

In Luke 9:51 we encounter the ambivalent ἀνάλημψις. The verb cognate is found in the account of Elijah's ascension (4 Kgdms. 2:9-11). Take account of Luke's numerous associations of Jesus with the Elijah-Elisha cycle, and it is easy to understand that here Jesus is very probably associated with Elijah. His ascent into heaven is a return to his heavenly parent, but the road to the celestial palace leads past Caiaphas's dwelling. All this does not mean that Luke views Jesus as a second Elijah. Remember, parallel lines never meet.

EXEGESIS

The LXX offers exegetical help of a different nature in putting into proper focus the Pharisee's problem in Luke 18:9-14. Psalm 34:13 (35:13 MT) notes that the purpose of fasting is to assist in humbling the soul and stimulating appropriate prayer. In the prayer that "turns back into the bosom"—the phrase is obscure—we may see a parallel to the utterance of the publican whose words, coming as they did from a head bowed in humility, fell, as it were, into his bosom.

Hatch and Redpath alert to seven occurrences of the word πίπτειν within the space of five verses in Ezekiel 13. The passage in its context is the best commentary on Matt. 7:24-27. Some in the upper spiritual echelons in Israel misused good intentions in Pharisaism for purposes of moral whitewashing. They sought refuge in their interpretation and hedging of the Torah. But the fortress was to collapse. Jesus' reiterated "You have heard, but I say unto you" gains significance.

HOMILETICS

Snake-handling cults have no monopoly on Mark 16:18. Homileticians who know their Septuagint will see the contemporary edifying value of the promise in this passage, when they reexamine Isa. 65:25 via Hatch and Redpath under ὄφις. The transitory character of the "signs" is not the main thing.

Couched in material terms we see fulfilled Isaiah's vision of the messianic age, in which God acts triumphantly to destroy wickedness. The serpent motif of Genesis 3 is well known. Not so familiar is the context of Isa. 11:8, where the universal proclamation of God's marvelous works is associated with reptile allusions.

APOCRYPHA

Although more detailed discussion must be reserved for chap. 9, some reference to the Apocrypha is required at this point. The subject is discussed for the general reader by Bruce M. Metzger, *An Introduction to the Apocrypha* (New York: Oxford University Press, 1957). His warning against the widespread assumption that the New Testament does not make use of the Apocrypha invites reinforcement. In all ancient manuscripts that contain portions of the LXX one finds the so-called apocryphal writings interspersed with the canonical writings recognized by Palestinian Jews. That the writers of the New Testament made constant use of Greek translations of the Old Testament and Greek translations of other religious writings not included in the Jewish canon as we know it today is clear not only from the patent allusion to the *Book of Enoch* in the Epistle of Jude but also from a study of the many passages cited in the margin of Nestle's *Novum Testamentum Graece*. On the other hand, it must be pointed out that none of the Apocrypha are cited by name in the New Testament.

An arresting example of possible dependence on the Book of Ecclesiasticus (*Siracides,* Rahlfs) occurs in Luke 12:16-21, the parable of the rich fool whose bountiful harvest caught him by surprise. The LXX parallel reads:

> There is a man who is rich through his diligence and self-denial
> And this is the reward allotted to him:
> When he says, "I have found rest,
> And now I shall enjoy my goods!"
> He does not know when his time will come;
> He will leave them to others and die (11:18, 19).[8]

In at least one instance the Epistle of James is illumined by Jesus ben Sirach. James 1:5 reads in the KJV: "If any of you lack wisdom, let him ask of God, that giveth to all men liberally and upbraideth not; and it shall be given him." In place of "upbraideth not," the RSV reads "without reproaching." Neither version is very helpful. "But," as Metzger observes, "a comparison with the exhortation in Ecclus. 18:15, 'My son, do not mix reproach with your good deeds, or cause grief by your words when you present a gift,' suggests at once

---

[8] Metzger, *Introduction to the Apocrypha,* 168.

that according to James God's gifts are made in such a manner as never to embarrass the recipient for his asking."[9] Metzger's awareness of this passage in the LXX appears to have influenced the substitution of the phrase "and ungrudgingly" in the NRSV.

Aspects of distorted mentality that helped motivate the crucifixion of Jesus are clearly depicted in the Wisdom of Solomon 2:12-20. As a commentary on Luke 23:35, for example, it is difficult to surpass:

> Let us lie in wait for the righteous, for he is an annoyance to us. He objects to our actions; he charges us with circumventions of the Law and chides us for violating the precepts of our training. He claims to have a knowledge of God and calls himself the Lord's child. He takes it on himself to reprove our very thoughts. It is distressing even to look at him; for his life is so unlike that of others, and his ways are of another world. We are counterfeit in his sight, and he avoids our paths like the plague. He pronounces a favorable judgment on the end of the righteous, and boasts that God is his father. Let us see whether his words are true, and let us test him in the extremity. For if the righteous man is God's son, God will help him and will rescue him out of the hands of his enemies. Let us subject him to insult and torture to determine the quality of his goodness, and let us make proof of his forbearance. Let us consign him to a shameful death, for according to his own words, God will surely take note of him.

It is tempting to add further examples of the interpretive possibilities of the LXX. Specialists recognize its values, but enough suggestions have been offered to challenge a renewed search of its treasures by students and pastors also. As an aid to Bible study the LXX has few rivals. Like the woman described in Proverbs 31, its value is beyond rubies. Blessed are those preachers who have espoused it, for the congregations shall come to hear them regularly.

---

[9] Ibid., 165.

CHAPTER SIX

Hebrew Old Testament Grammars and Lexicons

G EORGE CARVER once was asked how he managed to discover so many things. He replied, "Anything will give up its secrets — if you love it enough." Grammarians and lexicographers have conspired to assist the humblest interpreter in extracting the sacred treasure. The tools they have placed at the disposal of Bible students are the envy of all who must work in less favorably endowed areas of philological study.

It is the task of the lexicographer to classify verbal phenomena and guide the reader of a given language in determining what meaning a particular word is intended to convey in specific literary contexts. The resources of archaeology and comparative philology are all brought into play in an attempt to recover the concepts plus nuances conveyed to those for whom these languages were once a mother tongue. The task of the grammarian is to deduce the general laws and principles according to which people in a given cultural milieu communicate with one another and express their ideas.

Exegetes come to these experts to receive assistance in the interpretation of particular phenomena in the texts they are scrutinizing. Quite often they find that the authorities themselves assume the role of exegete. Lexicons and grammars to the Hebrew Old Testament and the Greek New Testament are often unusually comprehensive because of the peculiar demands and intrinsic importance of the data. Not infrequently every occurrence of a particular word or idiom is discussed. This means that general principles must give way to specific exposition. Indeed, exegetes may on the basis of additional and corroborative evidence uncovered by their own researches draw different conclusions from those reached by the lexicographer or grammarian on a specific philological point. They may record their judgments in a professional journal, in a monograph, or in a commentary. Succeeding lexicographers and grammarians may take note of such conclusions and may even set up new classifications and fresh categories, as their works become even more copious treasuries of the exegetical coin circulating in the interpreter's realm.

In the last analysis the exegete is both lexicographer and grammarian, and any grammarian or lexicographer worth a stipend must accept the role of an exegete. The conversation must always go on, and because the silence never comes, new lexicons and grammars will always be in demand, as well as interpreters, including pastors and students, who will evaluate critically their conclusions.[1]

It is our pleasant task in this and the following chapter to document a part of that conversation as we trace the history of linguistic science in the disciplines of Old Testament Hebrew and New Testament Greek. In chap. 8 we shall endeavor to entice interest in the philological vistas that await the diligent user of grammatical and lexical tools.[2]

THE JEWISH PERIOD, A.D. 900–1500

The history of Hebrew grammar and lexicography embraces two main eras, the Jewish and the Christian. The period of the Jewish grammarians extends roughly from the ninth to the sixteenth century. The connecting link between

---

[1] The loan-word "lexicon" is an inheritance of the centuries when Latin was the standard means of scholarly communication. For some reason or other the word *lexicon* was preferred to *dictionarium*. Because of the historic associations "lexicon" is generally reserved today for word-books that treat specific literary areas, with special reference to ancient languages. The word "dictionary" is applied mainly to wordbooks covering an entire language, such as *The Oxford Dictionary* or *Webster's New International Dictionary*. The term "vocabulary" is applied technically to selected word lists.

[2] The source of sources for the history of Hebrew philology is Moritz Steinschneider's *Bibliographisches Handbuch über die theoretische und praktische Literatur für hebräische Sprachkunde* (Leipzig, 1859). Bernard Pick, "The Study of the Hebrew Language Among Jews and Christians," *Bibliotheca Sacra* 41, 163 (July, 1884): 450–77, covering the period 900–1500; ibid., 42, 166 (July, 1885): 470–495, covering the period 1500–1700, includes much valuable information. Detailed bibliographies may also be found in the excellent articles by Morris Lehrer, "Hebraists, Christian," in *The Universal Jewish Encyclopedia*, vol. 5 (New York: The Universal Jewish Encyclopedia, Inc., 1941), and Solomon L. Skoss, "Lexicography, Hebrew," ibid., vol. 7. Wilhelm Bacher, "Dictionaries, Hebrew," in *The Jewish Encyclopedia*, vol. 4 (New York and London: Funk & Wagnalls, 1907), and "Grammar, Hebrew," ibid., vol. 6, draws heavily from Steinschneider. See also W. S. LaSor, *A Basic Semitic Bibliography (Annotated)* (Wheaton, Ill.: Van Kampen Press, 1950). For detailed inventory, see J. H. Hospers, *A Basic Bibliography for the Study of the Semitic Languages*, vol. 2 (Leiden: Brill, 1973); Nahum M. Waldman, *The Recent Study of Hebrew: A Survey of the Literature with Selected Bibliography* (Cincinnati: Hebrew Union College Press, 1989), which updates the literature since World War II; Joseph A. Fitzmyer and Stephen A. Kaufman, et al., *An Aramaic Bibliography.* Pt. I. *Old, Official, and Biblical Aramaic,* Publications of the Comprehensive Aramaic Lexicon Project (Baltimore: Johns Hopkins University Press, 1992). To remain somewhat in touch with the tide of publications, a student can make a point of checking regularly at least a few serials mentioned in the list of abbreviations by Waldman, *The Recent Study,* xv–xx. For starters, try *BAR, JNES, OLZ, Or, VT, ZAW,* and add to the inventory the *Book List* of The Society for Old Testament Study, *Elenchus Bibliographicus Biblicus,* and the annual bulletin published in *Syria.*

the masoretes and the grammarians is Aaron ben Asher, who flourished in Tiberias in the tenth century.

The masoretes had indeed observed peculiarities in the Hebrew text, but had made no systematic attempt to analyze these phenomena. A fresh departure was evident in the work of Saadia ben Joseph (882–942), the *gaon,* or head, of the academy at Sura, who laid the foundations which transformed Hebrew letters into a science independent of the masoretes. Praised by Abraham ibn Ezra as "the first of authorities in every field," Saadia distinguished himself not only as a philosopher but as a philologist of the first rank. His *Agron* (from the word אָגַר, to collect), the earliest known Hebrew dictionary, was designed to help poets with their versification. His Hebrew grammar, written in twelve books and titled *Kutub al-Lughah* (i.e., *Book of Language*), is extant only in fragments.[3] His elder contemporary Judah ibn Kuraish is noted for a letter (*Risalah*) sent to the Jews in Fez who had dispensed with the reading of the Aramaic Targum. This work marks the first emphasis on comparative Semitic philology for the study of Hebrew. In his letter Judah ibn Kuraish pleads for a return to the ancient customs and submits three alphabetical lists in which he relates the biblical vocabulary to Aramaic, Talmudic, and Arabic usage. The work was of such significance that it was edited as late as 1857 by Jean L. Bargès and Baer ben Alexander Goldberg under the title *Epistola de studii Targum . . . utilitate* (Paris).

The first complete Hebrew lexicon of the Hebrew Bible was compiled by the Spaniard Menahem ben Saruk (910–ca. 970) and is known as *Mahbereth,* ed. H. Filipowski (London, 1854). Menahem wrote his explanations in Hebrew and introduced them with a grammatical treatise in which he reduced all roots to one or two letters. Judah ben David Hayyuj (ca. 940–ca. 1010) corrected the error and established the triliteral law of Hebrew verb roots, namely, that all are to consist of three consonants. He is also largely responsible for the conjugations used in modern grammars.

Jonah ibn Janah, born ca. 990 at Cordova, made use of Hayyuj's triliteral theory, and his *Book of Roots,* written in Arabic, is a milestone in Hebrew lexicography. His enterprising use of the Talmud and Arabic in mapping lexical terrain is prophetic of an Albert Schultens.

---

[3] For further details on Saadia's work, see Solomon L. Skoss, *Saadia Gaon, The Earliest Hebrew Grammarian* (Philadelphia: Dropsie College Press, 1955). The usual date cited for the birth of Saadia is 892. I am grateful to Dr. Robert Gordis of the Jewish Theological Seminary of America for confirmatory data on the earlier date that he adopts in *The Universal Jewish Encyclopedia.* He makes reference to Henry Malter's standard biography, *Saadia Gaon: His Life and Works* (Philadelphia: Jewish Publication Society of America, 1921), 421–28, where the author summarizes evidence for the earlier date, gleaned from a twelfth-century manuscript fragment containing a list of the works of Saadia and a biographical sketch composed by Saadia's sons Sheerit Alluf and Dosa. Jacob Mann, "II. A Fihrist of Saʿadya's Works," *JQR* n.s. 11 (1921): 423–24, sets forth the evidence in greater detail.

Jewish philologists had been in the habit of imitating their Arabian kin and wrote their grammatical works in Arabic. Abraham ibn Ezra (ca. 1092–1167) was the first to present grammatical materials on the Old Testament in Hebrew. He is also one of the few reliable sources on earlier Hebrew grammatical studies. His work was eclipsed by the prince of Jewish grammarians, David ben Joseph Kimḥi (1160–1235), whose *Sefer Miklol* (grammar) and *Sefer ha-Shorashim* ("Book of Roots," a lexicon), originally two parts of a single work, helped to prepare the way for historical and critical study of the Hebrew language. The name of his brother, Moses ben Joseph Kimḥi, is remembered chiefly because of his introduction of the word פָּקַד in place of פָּעַל as a paradigm of the regular verb.

Elijah ben Asher ha-Levi (1469–1549) marks the close of an era and the beginning of a new, when Hebrew letters became Christian property. This voluminous writer, noted for his grammatical and lexical work, stirred up a controversy that raged for three centuries when he suggested in his *Massoreth Hammassoreth* that the vowel points in the Hebrew text of the Old Testament were not really integral elements of the autographs but were introduced by the masoretes in the fifth century after Christ.

THE CHRISTIAN ERA

Ever since the work of Johannes Reuchlin, Japheth has been dwelling in the tents of Shem. The parent of Hebrew letters among Christians was born at Pforzheim, February 22, 1455, and died at Bad Liebenzell, June 30, 1522. His pleas were responsible for the rescinding of an edict that had ordered the destruction of all Jewish writings. His chief work, *De rudimentis hebraicis,* 3 vols. (Pforzheim, 1506), supplanted the first Christian Hebrew grammar, *De modo legendi et intelligendi Hebraeum* (Strassburg, 1504), written by Konrad Pellicanus (1478–1556). Reuchlin's *rudimenta* consist principally of lexical material but include a section on grammar. Conscious of the epoch-making character of the work, Reuchlin closed it with Horace's word, *Exegi monumentum aere perennius* ("I have created a memorial more enduring than bronze").

Sebastian Münster (1489–1552), one of Reuchlin's outstanding students, is remembered chiefly for his popularization of the term "Chaldean" for Aramaic, which remained in use even in Gesenius's earlier editions. His philological achievements were eclipsed by Johann Buxtorf (1564–1629), who applied his vast acquaintance with rabbinical writings to the study of Hebrew grammar and lexicography and helped establish Hebrew alongside Greek and Latin as an indispensable cultural acquisition at the end of the seventeenth century. The brilliance of his achievements is somewhat dimmed by his insistence on the divine authority of the vowel points and accents. It was his influence that was largely responsible for the dogmatic pronouncement on this matter in the *Formula Consensus Helvetica* of 1675, aimed especially at Louis Cappel.[4]

COMPARATIVE PHILOLOGY

The relation of Hebrew linguistic study to cognate languages, first recognized by Judah ibn Kuraish, was stimulated by the printing of the polyglot Bibles and by Roman missionary interest. Valentin Schindler, in his *Lexicon pentaglotton Hebraicum, Chaldaicum, Syriacum, Talmudico-Rabbinicum, et Arabicum* (Frankfurt am Main, 1612), first made use of the cognate languages in lexicography. He was followed by Johann Heinrich Hottinger, *Etymologicum orientale; sive lexicon harmonicum ἑπτάγλωττον* (Frankfurt, 1661), and by Edmund Castell, whose *Lexicon heptaglotton, Hebraicum, Chaldaicum, Syriacum, Samaritanum, Aethiopicum, Arabicum, et Persicum* (London, 1669) revealed a broad knowledge of Hebrew and Aramaic. Modern Semitic studies owes the greatest debt to Albert Schultens (1686–1750), *Institutiones ad fundamenta linguae Hebraeae* (Leiden, 1737), and Nikolaus Wilhelm Schröder (1721–98), *Institutiones ad fundamenta linguae Hebraeae in usum studiosae juventutis* (Groningen, 1766), who laid the foundations for comparative grammatical methodology.

Heinrich Friedrich Wilhelm Gesenius

The name of Wilhelm Gesenius marks a new era in Semitic studies. A son of his age, he was to Hebrew letters what Julius August Ludwig Wegscheider was to theology. Standing on the shoulders of the Dutch orientalists, he liberated Hebrew letters from what he considered the fetters of dogmatic theology. With the help of comparative philology he pursued a strictly scientific and critical approach to linguistic data. The Latin phrase *Dies docet diem* ("One day instructs another"), which has become a Gesenius trademark, well describes his passionate concern for factual accuracy; and his description of the scientist, in his preface to the 11th edition of his grammar, is really a self-portrait:

---

[4] For the original wording of the Formula, see *Collectio confessionum in ecclesiis reformatis publicatarum,* ed. Hermann Agathon Niemeyer (Leipzig, 1840), 731. Johann Buxtorf's position is detailed in the words written by his son, Johann Buxtorf II, titled *Tractatus de punctorum, vocalium et accentuum, in libris Veteris Testamenti Hebraicis, origine, antiquitate, et authoritate: Oppositus arcano punctationis revelato, Ludovici Cappelli* (Basel, 1648).

Unwearied personal observation and an impartial examination of the researches of others; the grateful admission and adoption of every real advance and illustration of science; but also a manly foresight and caution, which does not with eager levity adopt every novelty thrown out in haste and from the love of innovation; all these must go hand in hand, wherever scientific truth is to be successfully promoted.[5]

Gesenius's Grammar

The illustrious German Hebraist was born at Nordhausen, February 3, 1786, and served as professor at Halle from 1810 until his death, October 23, 1842. The first edition of his *Hebräische Grammatik,* covering a slight 202 pages, was published in Halle in 1813. A more comprehensive work titled *Ausführliches grammatisch-kritisches Lehrgebäude der hebräischen Sprache mit Vergleichung der verwandten Dialekte* followed in 1817, but the publication of 1813 set the pattern for subsequent editions of the work now known as Gesenius's grammar. Emil Roediger edited the 14th (Leipzig, 1845) through the 21st editions (Leipzig, 1872). Emil Kautzsch assumed the editorial burden in the 22d edition (Leipzig, 1878) and continued with a thoroughly revised 23d edition (1881). With further improvements particularly on syntax, a stepchild of Hebrew grammar, the 26th edition (1896) guided Arthur E. Cowley in his revision (Oxford, 1898) of G. W. Collins's unpublished translation of the 25th edition (1889). Reprints since 1946 correct the 2d English edition (Oxford: Clarendon Press, 1910), based on the 28th German edition (1909). A 15th impression (1980) offers a revision of the index of passages by J. B. Job. Gotthelf Bergsträsser undertook a 29th edition of Gesenius-Kautzsch in *Einleitung, Schrift- und Lautlehre,* Part I (Leipzig, 1918), and *Verbum,* Part II (1926–29), the portions of Bergsträsser's uncompleted but nonetheless reprinted *Hebräische Grammatik, mit Benutzung der von E. Kautzsch bearbeiteten 28. Auflage von Wilhelm Gesenius' hebräischer Grammatik* (Hildesheim: Georg Olms Verlagsbuchhandlung, 1962). L. G. Running's *Hebräisches Wortregister zur hebräischen Grammatik von G. Bergstraesser* (Hildesheim: Georg Olms Verlagsbuchhandlung, 1968) helps lead one to the pearls in this treasure chest. At the same time one must keep in mind that more recent study of Northwest Semitic languages requires modification of perspectives here and there.

---

[5] The translation is from the preface in various editions of Edward Robinson's translation of Gesenius's Latin lexicon (1833). For critical evaluation and appreciation of Gesenius's accomplishments, see Edward Frederick Miller, *The Influence of Gesenius on Hebrew Lexicography,* Contributions to Oriental History and Philology 11 (New York: Columbia University Press, 1927), esp. "Bibliography," 103–5.

Gesenius's Lexicon

Gesenius's Hebrew lexicon appeared in its first dress as *Hebräisch-deutsches Handwörterbuch über die Schriften des Alten Testaments,* 2 vols. (Leipzig, 1810–12). His *Thesaurus philologicus-criticus linguae Hebraeae et Chaldaeae Veteris Testamenti* (1829–42), of which the last two of a total of seven fascicles (1853–58) were completed after Gesenius's death by Roediger, builds on this work and represents the ripest product of his lexicographical labors. For almost a century it remained the standard work of Hebrew lexicography and is still a mine of information. A briefer version of the *Handwörterbuch* designed especially for students was published under the title *Neues hebräisch-deutsches Handwörterbuch über das Alte Testament mit Einschluss des biblischen Chaldaismus* [*sic*] (1815). The place of publication, as for all its German successors, was Leipzig. This abbreviated edition, which did not long remain so brief, became the popular edition and the basis for all succeeding editions bearing the name of Gesenius, with the exception of the thesaurus. The second and revised edition bore the title *Hebräisches und chaldäisches Handwörterbuch über das Alte Testament* (1823). A third edition (1828) incorporated many improvements, especially in the particles, and served as the basis for his *Lexicon manuale Hebraicum et Chaldaicum in Veteris Testamenti libros* (1833), 2d ed. rev. Andreas G. Hoffmann (1847). The latter was designed to meet the needs of non-German-speaking students and scholars and introduced many new developments in comparative philology. It is here that the phrase *Dies docet diem* first appears. The fourth edition of the *Handwörterbuch* (1834), the last from Gesenius's hand, conforms to this Latin edition.

Franz E. Chr. Dietrich assumed the editorial burden of the 5th (1857), 6th (1863), and 7th (1868) editions of Gesenius's lexicon. Ferdinand Mühlau and Wilhelm Volck (d. 1904) continued with the 8th through the 11th (1890), until Gesenius's mantle fell finally on Frants Buhl, who with the help of associates edited the 12th (1895) and 13th (1899) editions substantially according to the principles of Wilhelm Gesenius, hence the title *Wilhelm Gesenius' Hebräisches und aramäisches Handwörterbuch.* Buhl blazed a more independent trail in the 14th edition (1905). The 17th, his last edition (1921), is a reprint of the improved 16th edition of 1915. Buhl's editions are especially valuable for their abundant references to philological discussions and for the textual emendations proposed in them. A new edition, the 18th, with the title *Hebräisches und aramäisches Handwörterbuch über das Alte Testament,* edited by Rudolf Meyer and Herbert Donner, under the direction of Udo Rüterswörden, began to appear in Berlin (Springer Verlag) in 1987.

Josiah W. Gibbs's translation of the abbreviated *Neues hebräisch-deutsches Handwörterbuch* of 1815 appeared in Andover, Mass., in 1824. The translation of the Latin work of 1833 was published by Edward Robinson under the title *A Hebrew and English Lexicon of the Old Testament, Including the Biblical Chaldee: From the Latin of William Gesenius* (Boston and New York, 1836); in 1854 the last revision of this translation was made. A translation by Samuel Prideaux Tregelles, *Gesenius' Hebrew and Chaldee Lexicon to the Old Testament Scriptures, Translated with Additions and Corrections from the Author's Thesaurus and Other Works* (London, 1847), was designed to combat "rationalistic and neologistic tendencies."[6]

The English text published in Oxford in 1907 and edited by Francis Brown, Samuel Rolles Driver, and Charles A. Briggs, *A Hebrew and English Lexicon of the Old Testament* (BDB), represents an attempt to bridge the gap between Robinson's last revision and the vaulting philological gains at the end of the nineteenth century. Based on Edward Robinson's translation of Gesenius's lexicon, the work introduces much comparative philological material, but it lacks the valuable bibliographical material added in Frants Buhl's 14th and subsequent editions and is therefore quite out-of-date. In other respects BDB is often more complete than Buhl. The sections on grammar, especially the particles, receive superb treatment from Driver; explanations of proper names are also included. A corrected impression appeared in 1952. Like all lexicons prepared in the days before the newer developments in linguistics began to make their mark this work suffers from confusion of gloss and meaning, as well as from some false etymologies, and users are not dismissed from careful appraisal of the data.

Other Lexicons

Carl Siegfried and Bernhard Stade's *Hebräisches Wörterbuch zum Alten Testament* (Leipzig, 1893) marked a reaction to the comparative philological method that had led to the most extraordinary associations between Hebrew and Arabic formations. Comparisons with kindred tongues were omitted, etymology became secondary, while the vocabulary and idioms were given as completely as possible. The authors refrained from "general" meanings as dreams of modern philologists and declined the attempt to trace the development of meanings on the ground that modern investigators are too far removed from the times that gave rise to the linguistic phenomena.

Friedrich Eduard König, like his British colleagues, reaffirmed the lexical advantages of comparative philology. His *Hebräisches und aramäisches Wörterbuch zum Alten Testament,* 1st ed. (Leipzig: J. C. Hinrichs, 1910), 4th and 5th ed. (Leipzig, 1931), and 6th and 7th ed. (Leipzig, 1936; reprint, Wiesbaden, 1969), like BDB, is strong on etymology and includes explanations

---

[6] A reprint of Tregelles's translation was issued in Grand Rapids (1947).

of proper names. Users of the third and succeeding editions of Kittel's *Biblia Hebraica* will appreciate König's elucidation of the masoretic notations.

The *Lexicon Hebraicum et Aramaicum Veteris Testamenti,* ed. Franz Zorell (d. 1947) and Louis Semkowski (Rome: Pontifical Biblical Institute, 1940–54), is beyond question a noteworthy achievement, and to be blessed for, among other things, Zorell's treatment of ben Sira's Hebrew diction. The Aramaic treatment originally planned for this lexicon was shifted to a more comprehensive consideration of Aramaic usage, *Lexicon linguae aramaicae Veteris Testamenti documentis antiquis illustratum,* ed. E. Vogt (Rome: Pontifical Biblical Institute, 1971). After this change in plan Zorell's work bore the title *Lexicon Hebraicum Veteris Testamenti,* and the finishing touches were completed in 1984. Vogt's illustration of biblical usage at the hand of nonbiblical texts, for example, the story of Ahikar and the *Genesis Apocryphon,* parallels Bauer's use of noncanonical material to clarify New Testament diction. Conversion of Vogt's work into English will overcome some of the limitation of outreach for its predecessors because of the Latin format.

The most frequented harbor is Ludwig Koehler and Walter Baumgartner's comprehensive lexicon of biblical Hebrew and Aramaic, *Lexicon in Veteris Testamenti libros* (Leiden: Brill, 1953), reprint and supplement (Leiden: Brill, 1958), for both German- and English-speaking students, which is based on the third edition of Kittel's *Biblia Hebraica.* The order of words is strictly alphabetical, not by root families as in BDB. In the face of Siegfried's and Stade's objections they trace the development of word meanings but pursue a middle course on comparative philological materials. A comparison with Buhl's 17th edition of Gesenius will show the broader lexical scope, including the addition of Ugaritic cognates; all earlier lexical works of major significance antedate Ras Shamra. After Koehler's death (1956), the English translation is dropped in the greatly revised 3d edition, *Hebräisches und Aramäisches Lexikon zum Alten Testament,* edited by Baumgartner with the assistance of Benedikt Hartmann and Eduard Yechezkel Kutscher (pt. 1; Leiden: Brill, 1967). After Baumgartner's death in 1970, Hartmann took charge (pt. 2, 1974), followed by Johann Jakob Stamm (pt. 3, 1983; pt. 4, 1990). A fifth part, *Aramäisches,* is in preparation. New data and sharpened linguistic science made the wholesale emendations popular in former decades unnecessary. W. L. Holladay made use of this 3d edition as it became available to him and used the earlier German editions for the balance of the alphabet and for the Aramaic section in *A Concise Hebrew and Aramaic Lexicon of the Old Testament* (Grand Rapids: Eerdmans, 1971).

For quick reference one can use G. Fohrer, ed., with H. W. Hoffman, F. Huber, S. Vollmer, and G. Wanke, *Hebräisch und aramäisches Wörterbuch zum Alten Testament,* 1st ed (1971; 2d corrected ed. [Berlin/New York: de Gruyter, 1989]). And if one prefers lexicography in French, under 500 pages, and with a minimum of linguistic baggage, the book to use is P. Reymond, *Dictionnaire d'Hébreu et d'Araméen, Bibliques* (Paris: Cerf, 1991).

Special lexicons for rabbinic and related literature are discussed in chap. 12, but an esteemed comprehensive lexicon of the Hebrew language deserves concluding recognition: Eliezer ben-Yehuda, *Thesaurus totius hebraitatis et veteris et recentioris,* 16 vols. (Berlin, Schöneberg: Langenscheidt, 1908–; New York and London: Thomas Yoseloff, 1960). This lexicon, in Hebrew, but with glosses in German, French, and English, does in a way for Hebrew what any contemporary unabridged dictionary does for another language. The biblical student has the opportunity to trace a term diachronically and perhaps note nuances that will illuminate what the standard lexicons may keep in the shadows.

Two works that organize lexical material especially for theological use have won attention. Ambitious in scope is *Theological Dictionary of the Old Testament (TDOT),* ed. G. Johannes Botterweck and Helmer Ringgren; trans. John T. Willis, vol. 1 (Grand Rapids: Eerdmans, 1974; rev. ed., 1977). Geoffrey Bromiley and David Green were involved in the translation of the third volume. David Green took over with volume 4. By design, little attention is paid to Qumran documents or to the Pseudepigrapha. In the case of the Pseudepigrapha the editors considered it too difficult to arrange their material under Hebrew words. Rabbinic material is slighted because of the problem of dating. The major goal is "to present the fundamental concepts intended by the respective words and terms, the traditions in which they occur, and the different nuances of meaning they have in each tradition." The original is *Theologisches Wörterbuch zum Alten Testament (TWAT),* editors same as above, Botterweck and Ringgren. The first fascicle appeared in 1970 (Stuttgart: Kohlhammer), with the first volume completed in 1973. Some idea of the scope can be gained from the fact that after two decades fascicles 6–7 appeared (1992) through שָׁאַף. In contrast to *TWNT (Theologisches Wörterbuch zum Neuen Testament),* this work shows more sensitivity to semantic fields and also heeds strictures concerning illegitimate totality transfer and related linguistic aberrations.[7]

More practically oriented than the former is *Theological Wordbook of the Old Testament (TWOT),* ed. R. Laird Harris; associate eds. Gleason L. Archer and Bruce K. Waltke; 2 vols. (Chicago: Moody Press, 1980). In contrast to

---

[7] See James Barr, *The Semantics of Biblical Language* (London: Oxford University Press, 1961; reprint, with a postscript of eighty-two pages, which includes discussion of M. Dahood's views on Ugaritic, Winona Lake, Ind.: Eisenbrauns, 1987); see also Barr's *Comparative Philology and the Text of the Old Testament* (Oxford: Clarendon Press, 1968); for a summary of Barr's cautionary words, see Waldman, *The Recent Study,* 50–57. Other books that share *TWNT*'s problem include: Léon-Dufour, *Dictionnaire du Nouveau Testament;* Nigel Turner, *Christian Words;* and William Barclay, *New Testament Words.* From time to time they equate concepts with words. The basic fallacy is that a theological concept is found in a single word.

the *TWNT* and *TWAT* this work has the busy pastor in mind and is "less exhaustive" than the two major works just mentioned. "A belief in the Bible's truth" is essential, the editors point out, for right understanding of the theological terms of the Old Testament. The set is keyed to Strong's concordance.

OTHER GRAMMARS

While Gesenius was establishing himself as Mr. Hebraist, one of his more unsympathetic opponents, Georg Heinrich August Ewald (1803–75), applied to the task of Hebrew grammar an extraordinary capacity for comprehensive judgment. Ewald was a student of Johann Gottfried Eichhorn (1752–1827) and became a doctor of philosophy at the age of nineteen. In his twenty-fourth year he published his *Kritische Grammatik der hebräischen Sprache* (Leipzig, 1827), later edited under the title *Ausführliches Lehrbuch der hebräischen Sprache des Alten Bundes,* 8th ed. (Göttingen, 1870). The portion on syntax was translated by James Kennedy (Edinburgh, 1879). William Henry Green, *A Grammar of the Hebrew Language* (New York, 1861; rev. ed., 1889), is one of a number of later grammatical works that betray Ewald's pervasive influence.

During this same period Justus Olshausen in *Lehrbuch der hebräischen Sprache* (Brunswick, 1861) endeavored to explain present Hebrew usage from preliterary Semitic forms. The author did not live to complete the syntax of what Driver termed a "masterly work." Friedrich Böttcher pursued a somewhat different approach in his *Ausführliches Lehrbuch der hebräischen Sprache,* 2 vols. (Leipzig, 1866), exploring linguistic phenomena in terms of the language itself. The work comprises accidence only, and is a monument to industry but inconvenient for general use.

Bernhard Stade, *Lehrbuch der hebräischen Grammatik* (Leipzig, 1879), in some respects more comprehensive than Gesenius-Kautzsch but not so elaborate as the work of Olshausen or König, follows a purely scientific approach. Friedrich Eduard König, *Historisch-kritisches Lehrgebäude der hebräischen Sprache,* 3 vols. (Leipzig, 1881–89), largely combines the methods of his predecessors in an attempt to bring grammatical discussion back to a more fluid state.

In this survey we have been content to mention only some of the more significant publications. In his article "Hebrew Grammar," *The Jewish Encyclopedia,* vol. 6, Wilhelm Bacher lists more than 400 titles for the period 1500–1900. Of those published since his review, there should be mentioned Hans Bauer and Pontus Leander's *Historische Grammatik der hebräischen Sprache des Alten Testaments* (Halle an der Saale: Niemeyer, 1918–22; reprint, Hildesheim: Olms, 1962), and Paul Joüon's *Grammaire de l'hébreu biblique,* 2d corrected ed. (Rome: Pontifical Biblical Institute, 1947), now available in

English in two volumes, *A Grammar of Biblical Hebrew,* trans. and rev. by T. Muraoka, Subsidia Biblica 14/1-2 (Rome, 1991). Bauer and Leander, only the first of whose volumes appeared, endeavored to write a detailed, systematic, scientific grammar for advanced students; Joüon's *Grammaire,* with its fine treatment of syntax, aims at reaching those who desire to advance beyond the beginner's stage but are not prepared to halt at all minutiae.

Georg Beer's *Hebräische Grammatik* (Berlin and Leipzig: G. J. Göschen, 1915–16) underwent a revision by Rudolf Meyer, 2 vols. (Berlin: de Gruyter, 1952–55). This new edition, which traces the historical development of the Hebrew language prior to fixation in its present Old Testament form by the Tiberian masoretes, is one of the first to incorporate both Qumran and Ugaritic materials. After providing a complementary *Hebräisches Textbuch* (Berlin: de Gruyter, 1960), Meyer continued to rework the grammar, of which a new edition appeared in four volumes under his name, in the *Sammlung Göschen* (Berlin: de Gruyter, 1966–72).

A comprehensive survey of the many publications that chart the rising level of studies in comparative Semitic philology does not properly lie within the scope of this study, but the increasing importance of such linguistic research for the understanding of the Hebrew text makes it imperative that the biblical student become acquainted with a number of the more significant works. Cyrus Herzl Gordon, *Ugaritic Manual: Newly Revised Grammar, Texts in Transliteration, Cuneiform Selections, Paradigms — Glossary — Indices,* Analecta Orientalia 35 (Rome: Pontifical Biblical Institute, 1955), is, with the exception of pt. 2,[8] a typical aggregation with revision of studies published earlier under other titles. A concordance, prepared by Gordon's student George Douglas Young and once planned as an appendix to the manual, appeared later as *Concordance of Ugaritic,* Analecta Orientalia 36 (Rome: Pontifical Biblical Institute, 1956). See also R. Whitaker, *A Concordance of the Ugaritic Literature* (Cambridge: Harvard University Press, 1972).[9] Gordon's *Manual,*

---

[8] "Texts in Transliteration," composed of materials originally published from 1929 to 1947, mainly in the French periodical *Syria,* and reproduced without change from Gordon's *Ugaritic Handbook: Revised Grammar, Paradigms, Texts in Transliteration, Comprehensive Glossary,* Analecta Orientalia 25 (Rome: Pontifical Biblical Institute, 1947). The texts are also found in English translation in Gordon, *Ugaritic Literature: A Comprehensive Translation of the Poetic and Prose Texts,* Scripta Pontificii Instituti Biblici 98 (Rome, 1949). See also J. C. L. Gibson and G. R. Driver, *Canaanite Myths and Legends* (Edinburgh: T. & T. Clark, 1978), an updated revision of Driver's earlier work (1956).

[9] Whitaker's concordance is based on A. Herdner, *Corpus des tablettes en cunéiformes alphabétiques* (Paris: Imprimerie Nationale Geuthner, 1963); Charles Virolleaud, *Le Palais royal d'Ugarit II* (Paris, 1963), *Le Palais royal d'Ugarit V* (Paris, 1965); Jean Nongayrol, Emmanuel Laroche, C. Virolleaud, Claude A. Schaeffer, *Ugaritica* (Paris, 1968); André Parrot, et al., *Ugaritica VI* (Paris, 1969); Cyrus H. Gordon, *Ugaritic Textbook* (Rome, 1965). Whitaker, using a program that he developed in concert with David W. Packard, with assembly done on an IBM 360/91,

whose latter part revises the former, appeared under a new title, *Ugaritic Textbook,* Analecta Orientalia 38 (Rome: Pontifical Biblical Institute, 1965), with extensive revisions and new source material.[10] For introductory exposure to Ugaritic, use Stanislas Segert, *A Basic Grammar of the Ugaritic Language with Selected Texts and Glossary* (Berkeley: University of California Press, 1984).

Two studies by Zellig S. Harris, *Grammar of the Phoenician Language,* American Oriental Series 8 (New Haven: American Oriental Society, 1936), and *Development of the Canaanite Dialects: An Investigation in Linguistic History* (New Haven: American Oriental Society, 1939) helped antiquate the standard study by P. Schröder, *Die phönizische Sprache* (1869), which had superseded Gesenius's work of 1837.[11] His works plus the philological salmagundi, *Dictionnaire des Inscriptions Sémitiques de l'Ouest* (Leiden: Brill, 1965), by Charles-F. Jean and Jacob Hoftijzer, sparked interest in the study of Northwest Semitic;[12] and S. Segert, *A Grammar of Phoenician and Punic* (Munich: Beck, 1976) ensured the burning of the flame. The publication of Richard. S. Tomback's *A Comparative Semitic Lexicon of the Phoenician and Punic Languages* (Missoula: Mont.: Scholars Press, 1978) will probably entice even more laborers into an area that is ripening for linguistic harvest. Those who find the work less onerous in French will welcome A. van den Branden, *Grammaire phénicienne,* Bibliothèque de l'Université Saint-Esprit 2 (Beirut: Librairie du Liban, 1969), which throughout uses the old Phoenician script. For a more general comparative approach to diction one must use David Cohen, *Dictionnaire des racines sémitiques ou attestées dans les langues sémitiques* (in fascicles, Paris/The Hague: Mouton, 1970–). For a general comparative approach to grammar, consult Carl Brockelmann, *Grundriss der vergleichenden Grammatik der semitischen Sprache,* 2 vols. (Berlin: Reuther and

---

employed the key-word-in-context technique. He prudently omits some very fragmentary texts and encloses in brackets words taken from proposed reconstruction of a text.

[10] As balance for Gordon, consult Joseph Aistleitner, *Wörterbuch der Ugaritischen Sprache,* ed. Otto Eissfeldt, Berichte über die Verhandlungen der sächsischen Akademie der Wissenschaften zu Leipzig, Philologisch-historische Klasse, 106/3 (Berlin: Akademie-Verlag, 1963). For a helpful bibliography and glossary, consult G. del Olmo Lete, *Mitos y Leyendas de Canaan segun la tradición de Ugarit* (Madrid: Christiandad, 1981). Mitchell Dahood is noted for his application of Ugaritic to explication of biblical terminology and emendation of biblical texts, but some of his views have not been generally shared. For some of his early conclusions, see "The Value of Ugaritic for Textual Criticism," *Biblica* 40 (1959): 160–70; also *Ugaritic–Hebrew Philology: Marginal Notes on Recent Publications,* Biblica et Orientalia 17 (Rome: Pontifical Biblical Institute, 1965).

[11] On early studies of Phoenician, see W. F. Albright, *The Bible and the Ancient Near East: Essays in Honor of William Foxwell Albright,* ed. G. Ernest Wright (Garden City, N.Y.: Doubleday, 1961), 328–62, esp. 329–30.

[12] K. Jongeling, H. L. Murre-Van den Berg, and L. Van Rompay, *Studies in Hebrew and Aramaic Syntax Presented to Professor J. Hoftijzer on the Occasion of His Sixty-fifth Birthday,* Studies in Semitic Languages and Linguistics 17 (Leiden: Brill, 1991).

Reichard, 1908, 1913). Of uneven quality is Sabatino Moscati, *An Introduction to the Comparative Grammar of the Semitic Languages: Phonology and Morphology* (Wiesbaden: Harrassowitz, 1964). A classic by G. Bergsträsser, *Einführung in der semitischen Sprache* (Munich: Hueber, 1928), is now available in English with supplementary material, including Ugaritic and bibliography: *Introduction to the Semitic Languages: Text Specimens and Grammatical Sketches,* trans. P. T. Daniels (Winona Lake, Ind.: Eisenbrauns, 1983).

Biblical students have one of the best presentations of the structure of Aramaic in Hans Bauer and Pontus Leander, *Grammatik des Biblisch-Aramäischen* (Halle an der Saale: Niemeyer, 1927; reprint, Hildesheim: Olms, 1962). In *Altaramäische Grammatik mit Bibliographie, Chrestomathie und Glossar* (Leipzig: VEB Verlag Enzyklopädie, 1975) S. Segert covers three major periods of Aramaic (925 B.C.–A.D. 200), including biblical Aramaic. A grammar of 7th and 6th century Old Aramaic from the workshop of V. Hug is promised as no. 4 in the series Heidelberger Studien zum Alten Orient. For the short trip, one can use Bauer and Leander's abbreviated version of their *Grammatik,* namely, *Kurzgefasste biblisch-aramäische Grammatik mit Texten und Glossar* (Halle an der Saale: Niemeyer, 1929; reprint, Hildesheim: Olms, 1966), or Alger F. Johns, *A Short Grammar of Biblical Aramaic* (Berrien Springs, Mich.: Andrews University Press, 1966; rev. ed., 1972). Somewhat more advanced than John's work, but simpler than Bauer-Leander, is Franz Rosenthal, *A Grammar of Biblical Aramaic,* Porta linguarum orientalium n.s. 5 (Wiesbaden: Harrassowitz, 1961; 2d ed., 1963). An index to the biblical citations is available in G. H. Wilson, *Journal of Semitic Studies* 24 (1979): 21–24. The standard source for Hebrew, Phoenician-Punic, and Aramaic inscriptions is Herbert Donner and Wolfgang Röllig, *Kanaanäische und Aramäische Inschriften,* 3 vols. (Wiesbaden: Harrassowitz, 1962–64; 3rd ed., 1971). Other inscriptional resources include John C. L. Gibson, *Textbook of Syrian Semitic Inscriptions,* 3 vols. (Oxford: Clarendon Press, 1971–82); and G. I. Davies, *Ancient Hebrew Inscriptions: Corpus and Concordance* (Cambridge: Cambridge University Press, 1991).

Akkadian Study

For the study of Akkadian, a comprehensive term used by the Babylonians and Assyrians to denote their language in its various dialects, students have at their command a choice of beginner's aids in Richard I. Caplice, *Introduction to Akkadian* (Rome: Pontifical Biblical Institute, 1983); and Arthur Ungnad, *Grammatik des Akkadischen,* 4th ed. (Munich: Beck, 1964), a thorough revision by Lubor Matouš of a durable *vade mecum.*[13] Also worth consideration

---

[13] The first edition (Munich: Beck, 1906) was titled *Babylonisch-assyrische Grammatik: Mit Übungsbuch (in Transkription),* 2d ed. (1926); 3d ed. completed by Marian San Nicolò (1949); the 4th ed. lacks the *Übungsbuch.* On the limitations of Angelo Lancellotti, *Grammatica della*

is K. K. Riemschneider, *Lehrbuch des Akkadischen,* 3d ed. (Leipzig: VEB Verlag Enzyklopädie, 1978), available in an English translation, based on the 2d German edition, by J. F. X. Sheehan, *An Akkadian Grammar* (Milwaukee: Marquette University, 1978). Advanced students will turn to Wolfram Freiherr von Soden, *Grundriss der akkadischen Grammatik,* Analecta Orientalia 33 (Rome: Pontifical Biblical Institute, 1952; see also detailed studies cited, pp. xxii–xiv), and supplement, available separately as no. 47 in the same series or bound with the preceding (Rome: Pontifical Biblical Institute, 1969). Rykle [Riekele] Borger takes students in masterful fashion into the classic texts, such as the Laws of Hammurabi and the Gilgamesh Epic, in *Babylonisch-Assyrische Lesestücke,* Analecta Orientalia 54, 2d rev. ed. (Rome: Pontifical Biblical Institute, 1979). To assist them further he has provided an updated standard list of cuneiform signs and their uses in *Assyrisch-babylonische Zeichenliste: Ergänzungshefte zur 1. Auflage,* Alter Orient und Altes Testament 33a (Neukirchen-Vluyn: Neukirchener Verlag, 1981). The need for a standard Akkadian lexicon at last is being met with the fruits of painstaking investigation in *The Assyrian Dictionary of The Oriental Institute of The University of Chicago,* to be cited CAD, under the general editorship of Adolph Leo Oppenheim (Chicago: University of Chicago Press, 1956–).[14] See also *Reallexicon der Assyriologie,* ed. Erich Ebeling and Bruno Meissner (Berlin and Leipzig: de Gruyter, 1928–). The first fascicle of Wolfram Freiherr von Soden, *Akkadisches Handwörterbuch: Unter Benutzung des lexikalischen Nachlasses von Bruno Meissner (1868–1947) bearbeitet* (Wiesbaden: Harrassowitz, 1959), began still another ambitious analysis of Akkadian dialects, completed in 3 vols. (1965–81).[15] To assist specialists in filling lacunae in cuneiform documents Karl Hecker has produced *Rückläufiges Wörterbuch des Akkadischen,* Arbeitsuchungen zur Keilschriftkunde 1 (Wiesbaden: Harrassowitz, 1990).

Arabic

The standard reference work in the study of Arabic is William Wright, *A Grammar of the Arabic Language: Translated from the German of Caspari and Edited with Numerous Additions and Corrections,* 3d ed. rev. William Robertson Smith and Michael Jan de Goeje, 2 vols. (Cambridge: Cambridge

---

lingua accadica, Analecta Hierosolymitana (Jerusalem, Jordan, 1962), see review by H. Freydank in *Orientalia* n.s. 33 (1964): 125–27.

[14] Publication by The Oriental Institute of the University of Chicago and J. J. Augustin Verlagsbuchhandlung of Glückstadt, Germany, began with vol. 6 (1956). The plan included publication of a separate volume for each letter of the Akkadian alphabet and completion of the monumental work with volumes collecting the supplements bringing earlier parts up-to-date as the project proceeded, with provision for an English-Akkadian and a Sumerian-Akkadian index.

[15] For increased appreciation of problems plaguing lexicographers in advanced Akkadian philology, see Walther von Soden, "Das Akkadische Handwörterbuch: Probleme und Schwierigkeiten," *Orientalia* n.s. 28 (1959): 26–33; Julius Lewy, "Grammatical and Lexicographical Studies," ibid., 29 (1960): 20–45.

University Press, 1896, 1898). Carl Brockelmann, *Arabische Grammatik: Paradigmen, Literatur, Übungsstücke und Glossar,* 13th ed., Porta linguarum orientalium 4 (Leipzig, 1953), continues a work prepared by Albert Socin for use by less-advanced students. J. C. Biella goes down rarely trodden paths to provide a *Dictionary of Old South Arabic, Sabaean Dialect* Harvard Semitic Studies 25 (Chico, Calif.: Scholars Press, 1982). The standard Arabic lexicon is Edward William Lane (1801–76), *An Arabic-English Lexicon,* ed. Stanley Lane-Poole, book 1 in eight parts (London, 1863–93; reprint, New York: Frederick Ungar Publishing Company, 1955–56). Since the second part of this lexicon, which was to include words that occur rarely and are not commonly known, has never appeared, research in the Arabic vocabulary must often continue in Reinhart P. A. Dozy (1820–83), *Supplément aux Dictionnaires Arabes,* 2 vols. (Leiden, 1881).

FOR BEGINNERS ONLY

Beginners in Hebrew grammar have found Andrew Bruce Davidson's *An Introductory Hebrew Grammar* (Edinburgh, 1884; 25th ed. rev. John Mauchline [Edinburgh: T. & T. Clark, 1962]) useful for grasping the inner consistency and logic of the language. The book is conveniently arranged for self-instruction. A companion volume, *Hebrew Syntax,* first appeared in 1894. The third edition (Edinburgh, 1901) has been reprinted frequently. Jacob Weingreen, *A Practical Grammar for Classical Hebrew* (Oxford: Clarendon Press, 1939; 2d ed. with alterations, 1959), is a helpful work by a Dublin professor who relies on the schematic characteristic of Hebrew grammar and employs minimal vocabulary, while concentrating the student's attention on grammatical phenomena. Principles prevail over memorization in John Joseph Owens's revision of Kyle Monroe Yates, *The Essentials of Biblical Hebrew,* rev. ed. (New York: Harper, 1954), an excellent aid for the self-taught, especially when used in combination with Weingreen's work. The exercises in Moshe Greenberg, *Introduction to Hebrew* (Englewood Cliffs, N.J.: Prentice-Hall, 1965), presuppose a teacher who will urge the study of biblical Hebrew in terms of a living language.

The cottage industry in beginner's Hebrew grammar ought to show a slowdown now that so many other inviting textbooks are on the increase. Among them is Page H. Kelley, *Biblical Hebrew: An Introductory Grammar* (Grand Rapids: Eerdmans, 1992). Even a person legally blind can use this book without frustration. The author, who enjoyed the tutelage of John J. Owens, Thomas O. Lambdin, and John Emerton, keeps the budding Hebraist close to the Tanakh through biblical based examples and exercises. In *Handbook of Biblical Hebrew: An Inductive Approach Based on the Hebrew Text of Esther,* vol. 1: *Lessons;* vol. 2: *Grammar,* with a separate pamphlet containing the Hebrew text of Esther (Grand Rapids: Eerdmans, 1979) William

Sanford LaSor uses the text of the Book of Esther as base for an inductive description of Hebrew grammar in eighty lessons. Those who learn well inductively can also profit from A. V. Hunter, *Biblical Hebrew Workbook: An Inductive Study for Beginners* (Lanham, N.Y.: University Press of America, 1988), or E. L. Carlson, *Elementary Hebrew* (Grand Rapids, 1987), which uses Genesis 1–14 as the textual base for grammatical study. Bonnie Pedrotti Kittel, Vicki Hoffner, and Rebecca Abts Wright add some pungency to the learning process in *Biblical Hebrew: A Text and Workbook,* Yale Language Series (New Haven: Yale University Press, 1989); the approach is inductive, with optional audiocassette available.

A Beginner's Handbook to Biblical Hebrew (New York and Nashville: Abingdon, 1958), by John H. Marks and Virgil M. Rogers, endeavors to steer clear of both bewildering details and obscurant oversimplification; grammatical principles are correlated with the study of Genesis. Highly favored by instructors are T. O. Lambdin, *Introduction to Biblical Hebrew* (New York: Scribner's, 1971), and Choon Leong Seow, *A Grammar for Biblical Hebrew* (Nashville: Abingdon, 1987). In user-friendly fashion H. G. M. Williamson offers an *Annotated Key to Lambdin's Introduction,* JSOT Manuals 3 (Sheffield: Sheffield Academic Press, © 1987); and J. M. Hamilton and Jeffrey S. Rogers do the same for Seow's work with *A Grammar for Biblical Hebrew: Handbook, Answer Keys, and Study Guide* (Nashville: Abingdon, 1989). With such helpful tools Hebrew is guaranteed to survive outside Israel.

Those who are not allergic to German will find that August Bertsch, *Kurz-gefasste hebräische Sprachlehre* (Stuttgart: Kohlhammer, 1956; 2d ed., 1961), offers a clear and reliable introduction to methods for mastery of the MT. Based on *BHK,* the grammar has been designed for use by both college and seminary students.

Bruce K. Waltke and M. O'Connor have filled a long-felt need with an *Introduction to Biblical Hebrew Syntax* (Winona Lake, Ind.: Eisenbrauns, 1990), which serves both as an excellent textbook and work of reference for someone who does not need all the minutiae of Gesenius.[16]

For academic outsiders who wish to look at the skeletal features of the Hebrew, or for those who need Hebrew without pain, John Joseph Owens offers *Analytical Key to the Old Testament,* 4 vols. (IV: *Malachi-Isaiah* [1989]; I: *Genesis-Joshua* [Grand Rapids: Baker, 1990]). This work is "intended to assist the person who knows some Hebrew but has not retained interpretive or grammatical discernment." Owens uses *BHS* as his textual base and keys the content to BDB. He takes the reader through the biblical books verse by verse and cites every word or phrase, identifies it grammatically, gives the root verb (as applicable), and cites the page in BDB where the explanation begins, when applicable cites Gesenius-Kautzsch, and then glosses the term in English.

---

[16] See Waldman, *The Recent Study,* 67–71, for discussion of treatments of syntax.

Time and again, rabbis and ministers have members who plead with them to have a class in basic Hebrew so that they can make use of tools that will provide them with basic information about the original text that underlies a translation. In about ten lessons one can lead them through the alphabet and provide the basic information (including masoretic pointing and grammatical categories) that will put them on the road of independent study, should they wish to go beyond elementary determination of semantic equivalence. Not too much harm will be inflicted by some weaknesses in this set. Alongside Owens's work one can use Jay Green's *The Interlinear Hebrew/Greek English Bible,* 4 vols. (Wilmington: Associated Publishers and Authors, 1976–). Also an easer of burdens is Bruce Einspahr, compiler of *Index to Brown, Driver & Briggs Hebrew Lexicon* (Chicago: Moody Press, 1976). This book goes through the Bible verse by verse and cites the Hebrew term, glosses it, and then gives page and section of BDB. Concerning the latter, Einspahr states that in using BDB one must note changes that have taken place in view of traditional documentary hypotheses. It also antedates Ugaritic research and relies too much on word meanings of the RV. Words are listed by root. This is helpful in a way, for all cognates are brought together, but it is bewildering for the beginner in Hebrew study. Einspahr's index helps the student by identifying the root and the "appropriate contextual nuances of the word" being studied.

For bare-bones glosses, book by book, along the lines of Sakae Kubo's *A Reader's Greek-English Lexicon of the New Testament* (see chap. 7) use *A Reader's Hebrew-English Lexicon of the Old Testament,* by Terry A. Armstrong, Douglas L. Busby, Cyril F. Carr, 3 vols. (Grand Rapids: Zondervan, 1980–86).

According to Francis I. Andersen and A. Dean Forbes, *The Vocabulary of the Old Testament* (Rome: Pontifical Biblical Institute, 1989), "the student of the Bible often wants to know what vocabulary occurs where. If the word is rare, the answer is easy to find in a concordance or index. If the word occurs frequently, the student has to do more work to sort out the facts." This book endeavors therefore to fill the kinds of needs met by R. Morgenthaler's *Statistik des neutestamentlichen Wortschatzes;* Aland's, *Vollständige Konkordanz,* 2: *Spezialübersichten;* and Neirynck-Segbroeck, *New Testament Vocabulary.* The basic text is ms L (see above, chap. 3). Cross references link information to BDB, Mandelkern, and A. Even-Shoshan.

For the learning of basic vocabulary, one can use Larry A. Mitchell's *A Student's Vocabulary for Biblical Hebrew and Aramaic* (Grand Rapids: Zondervan, 1984), which lists every word occurring ten times or more, except proper names, of which only those occurring fifty times or more are cited. Every word occurring in biblical Aramaic is cited.

Those who find it difficult to fit Hebrew into their schedule will have less cause for excuse now that Todd S. Beall, William A. Banks, and Colin Smith have completed publication of a verse-by-verse *Old Testament Parsing Guide* (Chicago: Moody Press, 1990). The first volume, Genesis to Esther (Chicago: Moody Press, 1986), was done by Beall and Banks. The second volume covers Job to Malachi. Based on *BHS,* this guide covers only verbs. For the New Testament counterpart, see below, chap. 7 (N. Han).

BATTLE OF THE TENSES

Ever since Samuel Rolles Driver, *A Treatise on the Use of the Tenses in Hebrew and Some Other Syntactical Questions* (Oxford, 1874; 3d ed., 1892), in which the Hebraist maintained that the tenses of Hebrew verbs were employed to express types of action rather than time, the subject of tenses and syntax has been treated more adequately and satisfactorily. The views of Driver are shared by James Washington Watts in his extensive treatment of conjunctive and consecutive *waw* in *A Survey of Syntax in the Hebrew Old Testament* (Nashville: Broadman Press, 1951; rev. ed., Grand Rapids: Eerdmans, 1964).[17] Frank Ringgold Blake, in *A Resurvey of Hebrew Tenses* (Rome: Pontifical Biblical Institute, 1951), attacks the views championed by Driver, but Carl Brockelmann, in *Hebräische Syntax* (Neukirchen, Kreis Moers: Erziehungsvereins, 1956), reaffirms with variations his British colleague's emphasis that the Hebrew tense system is not concerned primarily with time relations. Within a few decades such thinking ripened, for example, in two works that reflect greater awareness of advances in modern linguistics. A. Niccacci's *The Syntax of the Verb in Classical Hebrew Prose,* JSOT Supplement Series 86, trans. W. G. E. Watson (Sheffield: Sheffield Academic Press, 1990) recognizes the importance of contextuality for determination of meaning, and M. Eshkult, *Studies in Verbal Aspect and Narrative Technique in Biblical Hebrew Prose,* Studia Semitica Upsaliensis 12 (Stockholm: Almqvist & Wiksell, 1990), moves in a similar linguistic orbit in exploration of state and action in the verbal system.

A marvelous aid for a quick check of the "meaning" of a word is the handy pocket lexicon edited by Georg Fohrer, et al., *Hebräisches und Aramäisches Wörterbuch zum alten Testament* (Berlin: de Gruyter, 1971). An English version of this was prepared by W. A. Johnstone (London: S.C.M, 1973). This lexicon gives the meaning of a verb under each of the categories in which it is found: *qal, pual,* etc.

---

[17] Watts prepared the introductory treatment of Hebrew verbs in an earlier edition of Kyle M. Yates, *The Essentials of Biblical Hebrew* (New York: Harper, 1938), 121–29. In this work Yates amplified his *Beginner's Grammar of the Hebrew Old Testament* (New York: George H. Doran Company, 1927).

Epilogue

In addition to lexical aids already mentioned, the student is reminded of the detailed vocabulary studies of Hebrew words underlying New Testament usage in *Theologisches Wörterbuch zum Neuen Testament* (see below, p. 121). Nelson Glueck's *Das Wort ḥesed im alttestamentlichen Sprachgebrauche als menschliche und göttliche gemeinschaftsgemässe Verhaltungsweise* (Giessen, 1927; trans. Alfred Gottschalk, Cincinnati: Hebrew Union College Press, 1967), is an excellent example of detailed Old Testament philological study.[18] But two decades of development in linguistic awareness makes a difference, as can be seen, for example, in C. W. Mitchell's *The Meaning of BRK "To Bless" in the Old Testament*, SBL Dissertation Series 95 (Atlanta: Scholars Press, 1987).

What David ben Abraham al-Fāsī the Karaite said of the writer of commentaries, in thoughts relayed by Gesenius, applies also to popular expositors of the Hebrew Word. They "should not be rash in interpretations," declared this grammarian of the tenth century, "but master first the grammatical rules, inflections, the causes for change of accents, and the syntax of the language, as well as its correct use in speech. This would stimulate thinking, enhance knowledge, do away with indolence, awaken the soul, and inspire one to the search of knowledge."[19] No one can avoid this summons by pleading lack of tools.

---

[18] See also *TDOT*, s.v. *ḥesed*. F. I. Andersen, "Yahweh, the Kind and Sensitive God," in *God Who Is Rich in Mercy*, ed. P. T. O'Brien and D. G. Peterson (Homebush West, Australia: Anzea Publishers, 1986), offers a critique of Glueck's views.

[19] *The Hebrew-Arabic Dictionary of the Bible Known at Kitāh Jamiʿ al-Alfāz (Agrōn) of David ben Abraham al-Fāsi the Karaite (Tenth Cent.): Edited from Manuscripts in the State Public Library in Leningrad and in the Bodleian Library in Oxford*, ed. Solomon Leon Skoss, Yale Oriental Series Researches 20 (New Haven and London: Yale University Press, 1936), 1:lxxviii. Skoss completed his edition of this classic reference work in a second volume in the same series and section, vol. 21 (1945). The Karaite might well have included the historical perspective so well observed by William L. Moran in his article "The Hebrew Language in its Northwest Semitic Background," in *The Bible and the Ancient Near East*, 54–72. Hebrew tenses and other phenomena are freshly examined in the light of Northwest Semitic usage. For further information on the enterprising work being done by Jewish researchers of historical and linguistic data, see *A History and Guide to Judaic Encyclopedias and Lexicons*, ed. Shimeon Brisman, vol. 2 of Jewish Research Literature = Bibliographica Judaica 11 (Cincinnati: Hebrew Union College Press, 1987).

CHAPTER SEVEN

Greek New Testament Grammars and Lexicons

T HE HISTORY OF New Testament grammatical and lexical studies reveals less bulk than that of the Old Testament, but what it lacks in impressive size is notably outweighed by its own distinctive appeal. Like the history of Hebrew letters, New Testament Greek study has its great divide, owing to the work of one Gustav Adolf Deissmann, whose researches in the papyri compel us to speak of pre- and post-Deissmann periods in New Testament philology.[1]

PRE-DEISSMANN LEXICOGRAPHY

The Renaissance opened wide the doors to the classics but did not foster special studies in the area of New Testament Greek grammar and lexicography. The *Complutensian Polyglot,* I, made an effort to fill the lexical gap with a Greek-Latin glossary of seventy-five unnumbered pages, which included the words of the New Testament, Ecclesiasticus, and the Wisdom of Solomon, but the list is unreliable and rudimentary in character. A further step was taken by Joachim Steenhauwer (Lithocomus), *Lexicon Novi Testamenti et ex parte Veteris* (Cologne, 1552), which was the first work devoted wholly to the definition of biblical words. Matthias Flacius Illyricus, a Lutheran theologian,

---

[1] Harald and Blenda Riesenfeld, *Repertorium lexicographicum Graecum: A Catalogue of Indexes and Dictionaries to Greek Authors* (Stockholm: Almqvist & Wiksell, 1954), 28–35, lists concordances and lexicons of the New Testament and of the Old Testament Greek versions. Adolf Deissmann's fine discussion of the history of Greek lexicography, with special reference to the challenge for New Testament studies, in *Licht vom Osten,* 4th ed. (Tübingen: J. C. B. Mohr [Siebeck], 1923), 341–48=*Light from the Ancient East,* trans. Lionel R. M. Strachan, rev. according to the 4th German ed. (New York, 1927), 401–9, includes bibliographies on Greek lexicography. (The reference to *Theologische Rundschau* should read 1912 not 1911. German ed., p. 347 n. 5; English ed., p. 407 n. 5.) The summary article by F. Wilbur Gingrich, "Lexicons: II. Lexicons of the Greek New Testament," *Twentieth Century Encyclopedia of Religious Knowledge,* ed. Lefferts A. Loetscher (Grand Rapids: Baker, 1955), 2:657–59, cites further literature on the subject.

advanced the cause of biblical lexicography with the *pars prima* of his *Clavis Sanctae Scripturae* (Basel, 1567), a work on both Testaments. But the honor of producing the first lexicon limited to the Greek New Testament goes to Eilhard Lubin, whose *Clavis Novi Testamenti, seu breve omnium dictionum, quibus conscriptum est lexicon* was published in Rostock in 1614.

In contrast to these pioneering efforts, Georg Pasor's *Lexicon Graeco-Latinum in Novum Domini nostri Jesu Christi Testamentum,* published in 1619 at Herborn, in Nassau, looms large as the first New Testament lexicon of scientific pretensions.[2] In this work Pasor listed words alphabetically according to word roots, as Brown, Driver, and Briggs do in their Hebrew lexicon. One advantage of this etymological procedure is that the student is able to appreciate at a glance the common ancestry underlying the words derived from a single root. A disadvantage is the need for first determining the root and then locating the form in a long list of closely printed words. Pasor attempted to remedy this deficiency in his edition of 1686 by marking each cognate with an asterisk. Through the use of the index of Greek words, continued from preceding editions, the reader can find each New Testament word with a fair degree of facility. Ludovicus Lucius, *Dictionarium Novi Testamenti* (Basel, 1640), introduced the practice of listing all words in strict alphabetic order.

Johann C. Schöttgen (1687–1751), *Novum lexicon Graeco-Latinum in Novum Testamentum* (Leipzig, 1746), did not materially promote New Testament lexicography. Johann Friedrich Schleusner (1759–1831), *Lexicon Graeco-Latinum in Novum Testamentum* (Leipzig, 1792), supplied for demand,[3] but definitions are here needlessly multiplied, and we wait until the publication of Christian Abraham Wahl's work for the beginning of modern scientific lexicography. Wahl's *Clavis Novi Testamenti philologica usibus scholarum et juvenum theologiae studiosorum accommodata* (Leipzig, 1822) displayed the effects of Johann Friedrich Fischer's course of thirty-three lectures in criticism of New Testament lexicons, *Prolusiones de vitiis lexicorum Novi Testamenti* (Leipzig, 1791), and was translated by Edward Robinson, with some additions, in Andover, Mass., 1825. Robinson's own *A Greek and English Lexicon of the New Testament* appeared in 1836 (Boston: Crocker and Brewster), was published the following year in London and Edinburgh, and was largely re-written as a new edition (New York: Harper, 1850).

Christian Gottlob Wilke's *Clavis Novi Testamenti philologica* (Dresden and Leipzig, 1839; 2d ed., 2 vols., 1851) was a major lexicographical event. Karl Ludwig Wilibald Grimm used it as the basis for his *Lexicon Graeco-Latinum in libros Novi Testamenti* (Leipzig, 1862, et al.), the first New Testament

---

[2] The 6th ed. (1654) was the earliest available. Other facts of publication for the edition of 1619 are derived from Adolf Deissmann's *Licht vom Osten,* 4th ed. (p. 346; English trans., p. 406).

[3] The 3-volume London edition of 1829, which incorporates the fourth Leipzig edition, includes a list of about forty New Testament lexicons published between 1552 and 1818 (pp. xix, xx).

lexicon to incorporate variant readings. In 1886 Joseph Henry Thayer published his translation of Wilke-Grimm's second edition (1879), in which he clearly reflected the influence of the comparative philology school, with its proportionately greater emphasis on etymology as compared with more recent approaches. A corrected edition appeared in New York, 1889, and made Thayer a standard name in the English-speaking theological world until 1957. Nevertheless, discontent found repeated expression during this long period of valued service. And justly so, for even while the first lines of type were being set the seeds of Thayer's obsolescence had already been sown. But before we proceed to document this productive new era in New Testament lexicography we must come abreast of developments in the ancillary discipline, New Testament Greek grammar.

PRE-DEISSMANN GRAMMAR

The first to undertake a systematic description of the peculiarities of New Testament diction was Salomo Glassius (1593–1656), a distinguished pupil of Johann Gerhard, in *Philologia sacra* (Jena, 1623–36), but his insistence on Hebrew as the point of origin for clarification of New Testament phenomena diminished the value of his work. Much more significant were the efforts of Kaspar Wyss and Georg Pasor. The former, professor of Greek in Zurich until his death in 1659, displayed commendable sobriety in the matter of Hebraisms and cited much valuable illustrative detail in *Dialectologia sacra* (Zurich, 1650). Georg Pasor, whose lexicon has already been discussed, broke new ground with *Grammatica graeca sacra Novi Testamenti domini nostri Jesu Christi* (Groningen, 1655). Son Matthias Pasor, professor of theology at Groningen, had allowed his father's manuscript to lie unpublished for eighteen years because grammatical study was held in low repute, but finally he published it in 1655, convinced that grammar was the *clavis scientiarum omnisque solidae eruditionis basis ac fundamentum.* He was cheered on, notes Robertson in the preface to his large grammar, by Melanchthon's judgment: *Theologia vera est grammatica quaedam divinae vocis* ("True theology uses the grammar of divine speech"). The book was frequently republished.

Johann Georg Benedikt Winer

For more than a century after Pasor, New Testament grammatical studies remained fettered in Hebrew associations. In 1822 Georg Benedikt Winer (1789–1858) signaled freedom with his *Grammatik des neutestamentlichen Sprachidioms als sichere Grundlage der neutestamentlichen Exegese bearbeitet* (Leipzig, 1822). The work went through six editions in Winer's lifetime and was amplified by Gottlieb Lünemann in the seventh edition (Leipzig, 1867). An eighth edition was undertaken by Wilhelm Schmiedel but never completed. Even Alexander Buttmann, who published his own *Grammatik des neutestamentlichen Sprachgebrauches* (Berlin, 1859), acknowledged the breadth and scope of Winer's work, and its publication in English dress beginning as early as 1825 is a further testimony to its epoch-making character.

Winer's work was essentially a crusade against what he termed arbitrary approaches to the phenomena of Greek New Testament grammar and was motivated by a profound respect for the sacred Word, which he felt had been tortured long enough by uncritical linguistic assaults. Winer applied the results of critical philological methodology as developed and practiced by Gottfried Hermann and his school in the analysis of classical Greek and went to war against the prevailing insistence upon reading the New Testament through lenses properly polished for scanning pointed lines of Hebrew, against the pointless confusion of cases and tenses which was the result of such moody but modish and high-handed exegesis. If the grammarians were correct, how did the New Testament writers ever manage to communicate, he queried. Winer's own insistence on the study of New Testament Greek in terms of its own native genius was well approved by subsequent developments.

The sands of Egypt shifting and a young man named Gustav Adolf Deissmann, restlessly writing his *Bibelstudien: Beiträge, zumeist aus den Papyri und Inschriften, zur Geschichte der Sprache, des Schrifttums und der Religion des hellenistischen Judentums und des Urchristentums* (Marburg, 1895) and his *Neue Bibelstudien: Sprachgeschichtliche Beiträge, zumeist aus den Papyri und Inschriften, zur Erklärung des Neuen Testaments* (Marburg, 1897), conspired to break open a new era. Within but a few years Alexander Grieve made both works more readily accessible to English-speaking students in his *Bible Studies: Contributions Chiefly from Papyri and Inscriptions to the History of the Language, the Literature, and the Religion of Hellenistic Judaism and Primitive Christianity* (Edinburgh: T. & T. Clark, 1901; 2d ed., 1909). The implications of his climactic work, *Licht vom Osten,* were reinforced by Lionel R. M. Strachan's translation, *Light from the Ancient East.*[4] To rephrase Theodor Mommsen, the twentieth century would become known to those aware of the revolutionary significance of Deissmann's contribution, and despite the gainsayers in certain enclaves of alleged Wissenschaft, as an "Age of the Papyri and Inscriptions." On the Richter scale of ultimate impact on Greco-Roman and biblical studies Deissmann's work would register ten. Not only lexicons and grammars but also commentaries would require rewriting. And the aftershock would be felt when anthropological and sociological awareness began

---

[4] Strachan's first ed. of *Light from the Ancient Past* (Edinburgh, 1910) is based on Deissmann's "second and third edition" (Tübingen, 1909); his 2d ed. (New York, 1927) was based on the greatly rev. German 4th ed. (Tübingen: J. C. B. Mohr [Siebeck], 1923).

to take inventory of discoveries at Karanis, Oxyrhynchus, Tebtunis, and other sites of life that throbbed with a strong Hellenic pulse.

As early as 1780, Jean Baptiste Gaspard Ansse de Villoison recognized that knowledge of the later Greek was necessary for the understanding of many manuscripts emanating from the Middle Ages, and in 1841 Heinrich Wilhelm Josias Thiersch pointed out the value of the papyri for the study of the LXX in a dissertation of durable importance, *De Pentateuchi versione Alexandrina*. But the first to make serious use of papyri in study of the Greek language were G. N. Hatzidakis (*Einleitung in die neugriechische Grammatik*, 1892), who exposed some emendations as unnecessary,[5] and Karl Dieterich (*Untersuchungen zur Geschichte der griechischen Sprache von der hellenistischen Zeit bis zum 10. Jarhrh. nach Chr.*, Byzant. Archiv 1 [Leipzig, 1898]), who found missing links between Attic and later Greek.

POST-DEISSMANN GRAMMAR

It was the English-speaking world that first would see the new discoveries systematically employed in the study of New Testament grammar. *Prolegomena, vol. 1 of James Hope Moulton's A Grammar of New Testament Greek,* was published in Edinburgh (T. & T. Clark) in 1906. The second volume, *Accidence and Word-Formation with an Appendix on Semitisms in the New Testament,* met delay because of its author's death at sea, from exposure after a German submarine attack, in April, 1917. From 1919 to 1929 Wilbert Francis Howard, a pupil of Moulton, saw the three parts of vol. 2 through the press. Howard died in 1952, and a third volume, *Syntax,* by Nigel Turner, finally appeared in 1963, followed in 1976 by the fourth, titled *Style.*[6]

James Moulton's work grew out of publisher T. & T. Clark's aim to translate and edit G. B. Winer's *Grammatik.* The elder William Fiddian Moulton published his translation in 1870; a second edition appeared in 1877, and a third in 1882. A fourth edition, which was to incorporate considerable revision, scarcely found its way past the beginning stage. James Hope Moulton's first edition does indeed state that the grammar is "based on W. F. Moulton's edition of G. B. Winer's Grammar," but the acknowledgment is withdrawn from subsequent editions because of the admittedly new format and revised approach. That Moulton's translation of his *Prolegomena,* 3d ed. (1908),

---

[5] Albert Thumb, *Die griechische Sprache im Zeitalter des Hellenismus: Beiträge zur Geschichte und Beurteilung der Koine* (Strassburg, 1901), 11.

[6] G. H. R. Horsley, *New Documents Illustrating Early Christianity,* vol. 5: *Linguistic Essays* (Macquarie University, N. S. W., Australia: Ancient History Documentary Research Centre, 1989), 5:49–65, has withering words for the philological decline exhibited in the syntax volume of Moulton's grammar.

appeared as *Einleitung in die Sprache des Neuen Testaments* in the Indo-germanische Bibliothek 9 (Heidelberg: Carl Winter, 1911), attests its originality and quality. His *An Introduction to the Study of New Testament Greek* and *A First Reader in New Testament Greek,* 5th ed. rev. Henry George Meecham, 2 vols. in 1 (New York: Macmillan, 1955), written on a smaller scale, continues to be a reliable and instructive aid for beginning students.

ARCHIBALD THOMAS ROBERTSON

A distinguished scholar of Munich, Germany, stated in 1909 that American classical scholarship was singularly deficient in scientific contributions. A few years later German scholars filtered those words through A. T. Robertson's *A Grammar of the Greek New Testament in the Light of Historical Research.* Work on this grammar had spanned a quarter century. It began originally as an effort to get out a revised Winer. But Winer's obsolescence was increasing with every sheet of papyrus turned up by Egyptian spades. A completely new approach was necessary. Professor Schmiedel had, as noted, undertaken such a task, but death denied him its completion. Only James Hope Moulton was left in the race.

At first Robertson might well have imagined that publishers and poverty had formed a conspiracy against him, but with dogged devotion he completed his massive task in the early part of 1912. The authorization of a faculty publishing fund by the trustees of Southern Baptist Theological Seminary and the generous assistance of friends and well-wishers helped reduce the financial pressure. On June 12, 1914, the "Big Grammar," as it was affectionately termed, was published by Hodder and Stoughton in cooperation with George H. Doran and went through four editions in nine years. A fifth, published by Harper & Brothers, appeared in New York and London in 1931. Papyrologists preserve every letter of an ancient receipt, and someone dedicated to economic trivia in the twentieth century may appreciate knowing that the price of Robertson's first edition was $5.00 for nearly one thousand pages of handsomely printed text.

Robertson relied heavily on Albert Thumb[7] and Georgios Hatzidakis in medieval Greek and on Berthold Delbrück and Karl Brugmann in comparative philology. It is in the latter area that some of Robertson's positions are most vulnerable and betray the marks of time. His syntactical doctrine rests on a firm belief in the persistence of root meanings; whether the original writers

---

[7] Thumb did some of the clearest thinking at the beginning of the twentieth century on what constitutes the Koine. Among other critical observations, he takes classicists to task for correcting ancient authors without awareness of what corrections the papyri and inscriptions might offer the correctors (*Die griechische Sprache,* 11).

and readers of the New Testament felt so strongly some of the alleged distinctions is debatable. On the other hand, his awareness of the revolutionary semantic developments presaged by Deissmann's revelations of data in the papyri starkly contrast with the reluctance of some leading scholars of his time, and of some even after his time, to recognize the dawn of a new linguistic age. The treatment of conditional sentences is especially insightful and seems to indicate an ear for the nuances of the Greek mentality rather than a surrender to musty grammatical dogma. Such statements, on the other hand, as these — that Satan might have spoken Aramaic (p. 1009) and that Peter "clearly spoke in Greek on the Day of Pentecost" (p. 28) — reveal a tendency to ignore factors significant in the development of the New Testament as a literary product. The "Big Grammar" needs a loving hand to restore its youth, but even without such fondling it will remain one of the most comprehensive grammars on the New Testament ever published and, as Edgar J. Goodspeed put it, a "stately edition." G. H. R. Horsley states: "His grasp of developments in NT philology is masterly, not to say magisterial; and the judiciousness of his assessment of the contributions of various individuals still rings true half a century later." Horsley then takes Turner to task for engaging in a *damnatio memoriae* of Robertson.[8]

German Grammars

In the same breath with Moulton and Robertson the name of Friedrich Blass deserves commemoration. His *Grammatik des neutestamentlichen Griechisch,* first published in 1896, and revised from the 4th ed. (1913) on by Albert Debrunner (1884–1958), remains in its successive editions the standard critical grammar of New Testament Greek. Careful perusal of these editions suggests how slowly some German scholars emerged out of their "classical" dormers to recognize the reality of throbbing Greek language patterns beyond those established by Plato and Demosthenes. The last edition prepared by Debrunner is the 9th (Göttingen: Vandenhoeck & Ruprecht, 1954). Since German publishers frequently count reprintings as editions, little account need be taken of Blass-Debrunner until the 14th edition, a revision by Friedrich Rehkopf (Göttingen, 1976). This edition, BDR, includes, among other additions and alterations, work done by David Tabachovitz, who supplied a supplement for

---

[8] The source for much of the material on A. T. Robertson and the adventures of his grammar is Everett Gill's immensely fascinating account, *A. T. Robertson: A Biography* (New York: Macmillan, 1943). The references to Robertson's grammar are to the 4th ed. (New York: Hodder & Stoughton, 1923), which is not a revision of the main text. Alterations and additions were included in appendixes. For some of Horsley's views on the achievement of Robertson, see *New Documents,* 5:59–60.

the 12th edition. The 15th and 16th editions include a few additions and corrections, and the 17th is a reprint of the 16th.

Robert W. Funk has done a superb job in making the Blass-Debrunner grammatical tradition available to the English-speaking world. As privileged recipient of notes that Debrunner had prepared for a new German edition, Funk embarked on a revision of the 9th–10th German edition. His translation, *A Greek Grammar of the New Testament and Other Early Christian Literature* (Chicago: University of Chicago Press, 1961), BDF, includes not only Debrunner's proposed revisions but also the benefits of his own research. Debrunner's last edition included an appendix. An especially laudable feature of BDF is the blending of this material into the main text. Inasmuch as Professor Rehkopf apparently failed to make much use of BDF in the preparation of BDR, German students, for whom BDR's organization is clearer than that of its predecessors, must consult the English edition for revisions, adaptations, and supplementary notes.

One of the innovations of Blass was the citation of textual variants according to the manuscripts rather than according to printed editions, as Winer and Buttmann had done. Blass made liberal use of the LXX and frequently cited the apostolic fathers. Done on a somewhat smaller scale, but still valuable, especially for its citation of analogous material from the New Testament world, is Ludwig Radermacher's *Neutestamentliche Grammatik: Das Griechisch des Neuen Testaments im Zusammenhang mit der Volksprache* (Tübingen: J. C. B. Mohr [Siebeck], 1911), published in a second edition in 1925. The treatment of syntax is superior to that of accidence in this publication. For lexical and grammatical work on the papyri, see below, chap. 13.

POST-DEISSMANN LEXICOGRAPHY

The impact of Deissmann's work was soon felt also in the realm of lexicography. Erwin Preuschen had the opportunity to pioneer in this province, but his *Vollständiges griechisch-deutsches Handwörterbuch zu den Schriften des Neuen Testaments und der übrigen urchristlichen Literatur* (Giessen: Töpelmann, 1910) assimilated little of the new material. Indeed, it proved such a disappointment, in spite of its introduction of references to the apostolic fathers, that a revision was virtually a necessity to rescue the publication from oblivion.[9] Walter Bauer of Göttingen assumed the task after Preuschen's death in 1920, and his second edition of the pioneer's attempt appeared in Giessen

---

[9] See Adolf Deissmann, "Die Sprache der griechischen Bibel," *TRu* 15 (1912): 356–57, and reviews which Deissmann cites there. The entire article, pp. 339–64, should be read for its bibliography and discussion of publications in New Testament philology at the beginning of the twentieth century.

in 1928. A completely revised and reset edition was published in Berlin in 1937; thenceforth the lexicon came to be known as Walter Bauer's *Griechisch-deutsches Wörterbuch zu den Schriften des Neuen Testaments und der übrigen urchristlichen Literatur.* We will have more to say below about Bauer's legacy.

Other foreign-language publications appearing during this period and covering the complete vocabulary of the Greek New Testament include Heinrich Ebeling's *Griechisch-deutsches Wörterbuch zum Neuen Testament* (Hannover and Leipzig: Hahn, 1913) and Franz Zorell's *Lexicon Graecum Novi Testamenti* (Paris: P. Lethielleux, 1911 copyright 1904; 3d ed., 1961). The latter, produced by a capable Jesuit scholar, who was the first New Testament lexicographer to really hear Deissmann's trumpet sound, presents the definitions in traditional Latin. The third edition reprints the second with a bibliographic supplement.

For several decades after the publication of Thayer's lexicon no large-scale English-language production incorporating the papyri had been undertaken. James Hope Moulton and George Milligan, stimulated by Deissmann's work, had indeed published Part I (1914) and Part II (1915) of their *The Vocabulary of the Greek Testament, illustrated from the Papyri and Other Non-literary Sources,* abbreviated MM, later completed in eight parts (London: Hodder & Stoughton, 1929) and available as one volume since 1930. Their work helped open up even more the curtains that Deissmann had drawn aside to expose an exciting new world for New Testament explorers. Yet their aim was not to provide a lexicon of New Testament Greek. Rather they offer a select vocabulary of New Testament words illustrated from papyri.

George Abbott-Smith remedied the lexical deficiency somewhat with his *A Manual Greek Lexicon of the New Testament* (Edinburgh: T. & T. Clark, 1921; 2d ed., 1923; 3d ed., 1937). The book is handy as a supplement for quick reference and introduces features not included in Bauer, such as frequent etymologies (e.g., ἀπερίτμητος <περιτέμνω), usage in the LXX with underlying Hebrew word, and citation of synonyms. But the work is by no means comprehensive, and the need for a new Thayer corresponding to Bauer's distinguished effort was keenly felt.

BAUER IN ENGLISH

The Lutheran Academy of Scholarship, spearheaded by its chairman, Martin H. Scharlemann, paved the way for consideration of the translation of Walter Bauer's 4th edition (Berlin, 1949–52) with necessary corrections, adaptations, and additions. William F. Arndt (1880–1957) of Concordia Seminary, St. Louis, Mo., and F. Wilbur Gingrich of Albright College, Reading, Pa., were engaged for the joint editorial task. Professor Gingrich had been in contact with Bauer as early as 1937 and tried at intervals to interest the

University of Chicago Press in translating the German work, but without success. Finally, about 1944, the Press began to entertain the project, but financial considerations loomed large and destroyed the hope of beginning the translation in 1948.[10]

With the entry of The Lutheran Church — Missouri Synod on the scene, gloom gave way to scholars' joy. After receiving assurances of a substantial subsidy from this body, the University of Chicago Press agreed to undertake the publishing of the projected lexicon, and by September of 1949 the two editors had moved into the offices graciously provided for them at the University of Chicago dictionary headquarters. Not only did the two scholars benefit from the erudition of the chief lexicographer of the University of Chicago Press, Mitford M. Mathews, whose *A Dictionary of Americanisms on Historical Principles,* 2 vols. (Chicago: University of Chicago Press, 1951), 1 vol. edition (1956), is a writer's resort, but they also had the advantage of the superlative resources of the University of Chicago libraries.

The actual work of translation began in the fall of 1950, after Gingrich's return from a visit to Göttingen, where he conferred with Bauer. The work progressed, but not without perilous moments. Not the least of these was the delay occasioned by the sinking in 1952 of the *Flying Enterprise,* which consigned some proofsheets of fascicle four of Bauer's lexicon to Davy Jones's library. Finally, on April 4, 1952, almost two years after the arrival of fascicle three, fascicles four and five reached the desk of the two editors and rescued them from what could well have been a disastrous delay. The manuscript, about twenty-four thousand handwritten slips of paper, was finally finished in January, 1955. In the spring of the same year the Cambridge University Press, which had been engaged to cooperate in the venture, began setting type. In June of 1956 the editors read their last proofs. The book was published in Cambridge, UK, January 25, 1957, and in Chicago, January 29, 1957, under the title *A Greek-English Lexicon of the New Testament and Other Early Christian Literature.* The acronym for this edition is BAG. Detailed acknowledgment of indebtedness to Walter Bauer's fourth revised and augmented edition of 1952 appears on the title page.

Not much had escaped the German dean of lexicography, despite failing eyesight, but BAG contained significant improvements and additions. Not the least of these is the inclusion with corrections and supplement of a translation (pp. ix–xxv) of Walter Bauer's introduction to the 1928 edition of his lexicon, later published in a revised form as *Zur Einführung in das Wörterbuch zum Neuen Testament,* Coniectanea Neotestamentica 15 (Lund and Copenhagen, 1955). This introduction is one of the most admirable essays ever written on the Koine and should be required reading in beginners' New

---

[10] For details, consult BAGD, vi–vii.

Testament Greek courses that presuppose a knowledge of classical Greek. Few will fail to find it a thrilling reading adventure.

It was not possible for all the improvements and additions made in BAG to find their way into Bauer's 5th edition. (Berlin, 1958), his last major effort before his death, November 17, 1960, at age 84. Therefore, until a further revision appeared, German students were under scientific obligation to make use of BAG in addition to Bauer's 5th edition.

Determined that the Bauer lexical tradition not lose touch with modern developments, Scharlemann, who had instigated the production of BAG, asked Frederick William Danker, shortly after the publication of BAG, to serve as co-editor with Gingrich in its revision at the hand of Bauer's 5th edition. The final product of almost two decades of reading of primary and secondary literature, besides the inclusion of Bauer's new material gathered principally from Hellenistic authors who were not emphasized in his earlier editions, appeared in 1979. Its acronym is BAGD.[11]

Keeping the acronyms distinguished is important, for BAGD includes 20 percent more information than BAG, including, apart from Bauer's new material, words never before entered in any New Testament lexicon, other parsed forms, references to new discoveries including especially the Bodmer papyri and Qumran documents, previously unnoticed parallels, as well as numerous references to secondary literature, especially periodicals. Many words have undergone significant revision in treatment, and a considerable number have been enriched with additional references to classical and early Christian literature.

Bauer's skill in handling the smaller words, such as prepositions and conjunctions, the lexicographer's persistent bane, received attractive décor in the typography and format of BAG and BAGD. On the other hand, designers at de Gruyter, in Berlin, defied hallowed German conventions for scientific works and outdid their Cambridge and Chicago colleagues in making Kurt and Barbara Aland's production of Bauer's 6th edition easy on the eyes. Because of the extraordinary contributions of Viktor Reichmann, this edition has been given the acronym BAAR (some prefer BRAA).[12]

---

[11] The title reads: *A Greek-English Lexicon of the New Testament and Other Early Christian Literature: A translation and adaptation of the fourth revised and augmented edition of WALTER BAUER'S Griechisch-Deutsches Wörterbuch zu den Schriften des Neuen Testaments und der übrigen urchristlichen Literatur by William F. Arndt and F. Wilbur Gingrich,* 2d ed. rev. and augmented by F. Wilbur Gingrich and Frederick W. Danker from Bauer's 5th ed. (Chicago: University of Chicago Press, 1979).

[12] For a detailed review of BAAR, see Rykle Borger, "Zum Stande der neutestamentlichen Lexicographie," *Göttingische Gelehrte Anzeigen* 241 (1989): 103–46. Borger uses the acronym BRAA, in favor of Dr. Reichmann's vast input. The review is itself a basic introduction to the use of the lexicon.

Users of BAAR will note that its very title signals a change in emphasis: *Griechisch-deutsches Wörterbuch zu den Schriften des Neuen Testaments und der frühchristlichen Literatur* (Berlin and New York: de Gruyter, 1988). The alteration was necessary because of the broader database, including especially New Testament Apocrypha, many of which were included in less complete citation in previous editions of Bauer. In addition, BAAR takes more serious note of the philological value of intertestamental pseudepigrapha and such apologists as Justin, Tatian, Athenagoras, and Melito of Sardis, but includes very little new material from classical or other non-Jewish/Christian writings. To the surprise of many users of this latest edition, much of Bauer's vast inventory of secondary literature has been gutted. Moreover, the editors of BAAR failed to recognize that numerous additions and adaptations were made in BAG and BAGD, and even errors that were corrected in BAGD continue to find refuge in BAAR.[13] As in the case of the New Testament grammar BDF, German students will therefore need its companion volume BAGD as corrective to BAAR, whereas users of BAGD will need BAAR for its fuller citation of the pseudepigrapha and variant forms, chiefly in papyri, of the New Testament text and other Christian documents from the first to the third century. Until the appearance of the revision of BAGD, due before the year 2000, Bauer in its present German and English dress unquestionably presents the pastor and the student with the very latest, most comprehensive, and undeniably efficient aid to New Testament Bible study.[14]

CREMER TO KITTEL

One might, yet not without censure, omit mention of Hermann Cremer, *Biblisch-theologisches Wörterbuch der neutestamentlichen Gräcität* (Gotha, 1866), which has gone through many German editions and an English translation, *The Biblico-Theological Lexicon of New Testament Greek,* 3d Eng. ed., trans. from the German of the 2d ed., with additional matter and corrections by the author (Edinburgh, 1880), and a revision of the German text

[13] The preface in BAAR is also in error in stating that the broadly disseminated edition of "Arndt–Gingrich" (presumably AG is meant; for BRAA shows no knowledge of the many changes made in BAGD) "stellt in der Tat nur 'a translation' dar, wie es seit einiger Zeit zu Recht auf dem Titelblatt heisst" ("offers, in fact, only 'a translation,' as is correctly indicated for some time on the title page") (p. v).

[14] For much of the history of BAG I am indebted to Dr. F. Wilbur Gingrich, who also generously supplied unpublished information. His preview of the publication is presented in "A New Lexicon of the Greek New Testament," *CTM* 26 (1955): 33–37. A full review of the publishing details is given by both editors in *The Lutheran Scholar* 14 (1957): 531–33. Of the many book reviews, Martin J. Higgins's critique in *CBQ* 20 (1958): 562–70, is one of the most thorough and extensive. But see Borger (n. 12, above), who provides some very helpful information and corrections for users of BAGD.

by Julius Kögel, 11th ed. (Gotha, 1923). But to bypass *Theologisches Wörterbuch zum Neuen Testament* (*TWNT*), the successor to Cremer-Kögel, would be tantamount to passing up St. Peter's on a trip to Rome. This work was begun in November, 1928, under the editorial direction of Gerhard Kittel, son of the original editor of *Biblia Hebraica*. Kittel mobilized the leading biblical scholars in Germany and beginning on April 1, 1932, fascicles came off the presses of W. Kohlhammer Verlag, Stuttgart, at irregular intervals until the completion of *TWNT* in 1979. Professor Kittel died on July 11, 1948, and the name Gerhard Friedrich appears as editor on the title page of the fifth volume. Thanks to Geoffrey W. Bromiley, the first volume appeared in English in 1964, and the acronym *TDNT* took account of the translated title, *Theological Dictionary of the New Testament*. Eight other volumes came out of Grand Rapids with amazing speed, climaxed by the index volume in 1976. This last includes a history of the dictionary. Bromiley made no effort to revise obsolete or ill-considered philological judgments, and very little of Kittel is lost in the undertaking. Archibald M. Hunter once said in a different context, what we have here is "inner" rather than "external" lexicography, a theological wordbook rather than an "alphabetized dogmatics." As the title specifies, the work is not a lexicon but a vocabulary of those New Testament words that in the minds of the editors are theologically significant. Thus ἁμαρτάνω and cognates receive a lengthy treatment, but a word like γναφεύς is not even listed. The usual procedure is to present the word in its non-Jewish/Christian Greek background and then to discuss its role in the Old Testament, both in the Hebrew and in the Septuagint texts. Philo, Josephus, the pseudepigraphic and rabbinic literature may be treated; then the word's varied fortunes in the New Testament undergo tracing, with perhaps a division of the subject according to Synoptic, Johannine, Petrine, and Pauline usage. A subsection on the apostolic fathers is sometimes included to ensure complete coverage. Students who use this work with awareness of developments in philological inquiry since the beginning of the twentieth century[15] will profit from this massive

---

[15] In *The Semantics of Biblical Language* (London: Oxford University Press, 1961), James Barr questions the philological approach of *TWNT,* which was drawn up on the theory that a given word contained a theological freight that was discernible in each use of the word (totality transfer). The fact is that not all the referents, for example, for the word ἀλήθεια are implicit in every use of the word. Editor Friedrich accepted the rebuke, and vols. 5 (1954) through 10 (1978) reflect more acquaintance with philological realities. David Hill heeded some of Barr's admonition but tilted in the direction of *TWNT* in *Greek Words with Hebrew Meanings: Studies in the Semantics of Soteriological Terms* (Cambridge: Cambridge University Press, 1967). G. H. R. Horsley (see n. 6) issues warnings similar to those by Barr in *New Documents,* vol. 5, passim; see, e.g., his critique (pp. 67–83) of Nigel Turner, *Christian Words* (Nashville: Nelson, 1982); C. Brown, ed., *The New International Dictionary of New Testament Theology,* 3 vols. (Grand Rapids, 1975); and C. Spicq, *Notes de lexicographie néo-testamentaire,* 2 vols. and suppl., Orbis Biblicus et Orientalis 22/1–3 (Göttingen: Vandenhoeck & Ruprecht, 1978–82), all of which, Horsley points out, manifest outmoded philology and go counter to Deissmann and Thumb. On the other hand,

collection of philological data. For the quick trip one can use the one-volume abridgement.[16]

Vying to meet needs not addressed by *TWNT/TDNT* is the *Exegetisches Wörterbuch zum Neuen Testament,* ed. Horst Balz and Gerhard Schneider, 3 vols. (Stuttgart: Kohlhammer, 1978–83), also available in English: *Exegetical Dictionary of the New Testament (EDNT),* 3 vols. (Grand Rapids: Eerdmans, 1990–93). This set does not endeavor to supplant either *TDNT* or the Bauer lexicon. Although it bears some resemblance to *TDNT* in its theological interest, it endeavors to bring a sharper linguistic awareness to the discussion, and unlike *TDNT* it deals with the entire vocabulary of the Greek New Testament. Unlike Bauer's lexicon, which is primarily concerned with classification of usage and basic definition, with maximum coverage of the linguistic data in a broadly ranging literary corpus, *EDNT* engages in expanded interpretation of terms in selected contexts, but with vocabulary limited to the New Testament. In short, *EDNT* lives up to its promise to be an exegetical dictionary.

SALMAGUNDI

We have been content in the preceding paragraphs to point out the mountain peaks above the plains and valleys of specialized New Testament philology, but other names and places deserve mention. Heading the list is Henry George Liddell and Robert Scott, *A Greek-English Lexicon,* new ed. Henry Stuart Jones and Roderick McKenzie, 2 vols. (Oxford: Clarendon Press, 1925–40).[17] An addition titled *Greek-English Lexicon: A Supplement,* ed. by E. A. Barber, et al. (Oxford, 1968) added 153 pages of information, some of it in the form of new entries, and much of it atoning for deficiencies in citation of papyri and epigraphs. This additional material includes the "Addenda and Corrigenda," consisting of pages 2043–2111 at the back of volume 2 since 1940. We use the acronym LSJM, adding the M because Prof. McKenzie, like Viktor Reichmann for BAAR, was extraordinarily responsible for the contents of the revision of the main work. Contrary to popular opinion LSJM is not a lexicon to the classics only. It covers a broad range of Greek literature down to A.D. 600 and includes references to the Septuagint and the New Testament. Additional material, new definitions, and corrective interpretations by Robert

---

it must be noted that especially Spicq provides a great deal of philological data, much of it otherwise inaccessible to most students, that can be used without adopting some of his conclusions.

[16] The abridged edition. was done by Bromiley, *Theological Dictionary of the New Testament Abridged in One Volume* (Grand Rapids: Eerdmans, 1985).

[17] The 1st ed. of the Liddell-Scott lexicon appeared in 1843 and an 8th ed. in 1897. A 9th ed. was prepared 1911–24 and published in 10 parts (1925–40), edited by Sir Henry Stuart Jones, with massive input from McKenzie. It appeared in two volumes and later in a one-volume edition.

Renehan give depth to *Greek Lexicographical Notes: A Critical Supplement to the Greek-English Lexicon of Liddell-Scott-Jones,* 2 vols. (Göttingen: Vandenhoeck & Ruprecht, 1975, 1982). The values of LSJM for New Testament studies will be discussed in the next chapter. At the same time one must not forget that Homer is the teacher of Hellas, and Bruno Snell will forever be remembered for initiating *Lexikon des frühgriechischen Epos,* in association with Hans Joachim Mette and Hartmut Erbse. Some idea of the time it will take to complete the project can be derived from the fact that the first fascicle of vol. 1 appeared in 1955, but the volume was not published in complete form until 1978 (Göttingen: Vandenhoeck & Ruprecht).[18] In French, the work to consult is Anatole Bailly, *Dictionnaire grec français,* rev. ed. L. Séchan and P. Chantraine (Paris: Hachette, 1950).

Taking a look farther down the road of Greek usage is Evangelinus A. Sophocles. His labor of love, *Greek Lexicon of the Roman and Byzantine Periods (from B.C. 146 to A.D. 1100),* corrected printing of 2d impression, 2 vols. (New York: Scribners, 1887; reprinted, New York: Frederick Ungar Publishing Co., 1957), remains, despite shortcomings — something that future generations will say of most contemporary production — a useful index to Koine usage and contains data not to be had in LSJM and Bauer.

In *A Patristic Greek Lexicon,* of which the first fascicle appeared in Oxford in 1961, and the last in 1968, editor Geoffrey W. H. Lampe offers the biblical scholar entry to the rich resources of patristic comment on Scripture, from the second to the ninth century. After digesting, for example, the article on αἴνιγμα, the reader of 1 Cor. 13:12 in many modern versions that suggest a poor reflecting device, as in the translation "darkly," will be induced to second thoughts. The lexicon is useful also for reading the Greek text of such intertestamental books as the *Testaments of the Twelve Patriarchs* and the *Psalms of Solomon.*

The first lexicon of the New Testament dedicated to thoroughgoing expression of modern linguistic theory is *Greek-English Lexicon of the New Testament Based on Semantic Domains,* ed. Johannes P. Louw and Eugene A. Nida, 2 vols. (New York: United Bible Societies, 1988). This lexicon focuses on the related meanings of different words, with a view to assisting translators in finding appropriate translational equivalents. A major drawback in traditional alphabetized lexicons is the misleading signals that are sent out to the user in the form of glosses masquerading as meanings. The Louw-Nida lexicon does not discourage the use of traditional alphabetized dictionaries, but it does challenge unpondered use of the latter. In *Lexical Semantics of the Greek New*

---

[18] The plan for *LfgrE* was patterned after the proposal made in 1858 by Karl Halm of Munich for a *Thesaurus Linguae Latinae,* initially subscribed by the Bavarian King, Maximilian II, who gave 10,000 florins for the project. But wars intervened and by 1889 the 10,000 florins of 1858 rose to an estimate of 360,000 marks.

Testament (Atlanta: Scholars Press, 1992), Nida and Louw expand on the principles and procedures used in the preparation of their lexicon. This 155-page work serves as an ideal textbook for an initial course in hermeneutics.[19] Change comes with difficulty, and the Louw-Nida lexicon will continue to meet pockets of resistance in academic circles where the future is blurred by complacent acceptance of the past, but the twenty-first century will most certainly bring out a crop of alphabetized lexicons that will owe much to this pioneering effort. Like Deissmann, who tried to wake up Germany, Eugene Nida has for decades sounded a wake-up call to New Testament interpreters, some of whom seem to be unaware of such seminal works by Nida as *Toward a Science of Translating: With Special Reference to Principles and Procedures Involved in Bible Translating* (Leiden: Brill, 1964), which "explored some of the basic factors constituting a scientific approach to translation." In *The Theory and Practice of Translation* (Leiden: Brill, 1969), coauthor Charles R. Taber offers practical guidance for application of the theory expressed in the earlier work.

For etymological study, one has a choice of P. Chantraine, *Dictionnaire étymologique de la language grecque: Histoire des mots,* 4 vols. (Paris: Klincksieck, 1968–80)[20] and H. Frisk, *Griechisches etymologisches Wörterbuch,* 3 vols. (Heidelberg: C. Winter, 1960–72). The third volume of the latter contains "additions, corrections, indices, and a Nachwort."

In the area of New Testament syntax Ernest De Witt Burton, *Syntax of the Moods and Tenses in New Testament Greek* (Chicago: University of Chicago Press, 1888; 3d ed., 1898), clamors for attention. The treatment suffers somewhat from comparison with later grammatical discussions, but it still holds the field as a lucid presentation of an often elusive subject.[21] *An Idiom Book of New Testament Greek,* by Charles Francis Digby Moule (Cambridge:

---

[19] For further background on the theoretical considerations underlying the Louw-Nida lexicon, see the collection of essays in *Lexicography and Translation, with Special Reference to Bible Translation,* ed. J. P. Louw (Cape Town: Bible Society of South Africa, 1985). See also Louw's *Semantics of New Testament Greek* (Philadelphia: Fortress Press, 1982). In the same encampment with Nida is Eugene van Ness Goetchius, who laid groundwork for use of new linguistic developments in beginners' grammars. His *The Language of the New Testament* (New York: Scribners, 1965), in fifty lessons, in some quarters still remains ahead of its time. Goetchius stresses the structure of the Greek language, with a minimum of emphasis on vocabulary.

[20] Chantraine completed most of vol. 4 before his death in 1974. Colleagues completed the rest. A comparable work by Émile Boisacq may be ancient but is not antiquated: *Dictionnaire Étymologique de la Langue Grecque, étudiée dans les rapports avec ses autres langues indoeuropéennes* (Heidelberg: C. Winter; Paris: Libraire C. Klincksieck, 1916). More recently, A. J. Van Windekens, *Dictionnaire étymologique complémentaire de la langue grecque: Nouvelles contributions à l'Interprétation historique et comparée du vocabulaire* (Leuven: Peters, 1986).

[21] The reprint (Edinburgh, 1955), distributed by Kregel Publications, Grand Rapids, Mich., is oddly less up-to-date than Johannes de Zwaan's Dutch translation, *Syntaxis der Wijzen en Tijden in het Grieksche Nieuwe Testament: E. W. Burton's Syntax of New Testament Moods and Tenses voor het Nederlandsch taaleigen bewerkt* (Haarlem: H. D. Tjeenk Willink & Zoon, 1906), which incorporates papyrological data. See Deissmann, "Die Sprache," 354.

Cambridge University Press, 1953; 2d ed., with corrections and numerous additions, 1959), is designed for such as find themselves overwhelmed by detailed grammatical discussions.[22] Students who are reasonably well acquainted with the language will be able with the aid of this little book to form independent judgments on exegetical problems provoked by syntax. Those who are looking for an even less detailed but nevertheless helpful treatment will find it in Henry Preston Vaughan Nunn, *A Short Syntax of New Testament Greek* (Cambridge, 1912; 5th ed., 1938, and reprints).

Fruitful approaches to questions of syntax may also be made through an intermediate treatment, such as *A New Short Grammar of the Greek Testament* (New York and London, 1931; many eds.), by Archibald T. Robertson and William Hersey Davis. This work is an outgrowth of Robertson's *A Short Grammar of the Greek New Testament* (New York: George H. Doran, 1908) and is designed as a steppingstone to the larger grammar for students who have mastered the elements. Robertson wrote parts 1, 3, and 4; Davis, part 2. *An Exegetical Grammar of the Greek New Testament* (New York, 1941), written by William Douglas Chamberlain, moves a bit beyond Davis and dispels some of the mystery surrounding grammatical terminology, despite his adoption of the eight-case arrangement popularized by his teacher Robertson. "Maximum exposure to examples in the New Testament," is the claim made by James A. Brooks and Carlton L. Winbery for their *Syntax of New Testament Greek* (Lanham, Md.: University Press of America, 1979), through which they endeavor to hold students' attention beyond the stage of rudimentary grammar. For a study of Semitic influences in New Testament Greek, see Klaus Beyer's *Semitische Syntax im Neuen Testament,* begun with *Satzlehre, Teil I* (Göttingen: Vandenhoeck & Ruprecht, 1962) in the series Studien zur Umwelt des Neuen Testaments, edited by Karl Georg Kuhn.

Edwin Hatch's *Essays in Biblical Greek* (Oxford, 1889) presents much valuable lexical data from the LXX and suggests challenging interpretations of New Testament key words; but the method pursued does not inspire complete confidence, and the New Testament vocabulary is too unrealistically shackled to the usage of the Septuagint. In reaction to this study, H. A. A. Kennedy wrote *Sources of New Testament Greek, or The Influence of the LXX on the Vocabulary of the New Testament* (Edinburgh, 1895).[23] More reliable is Charles Harold Dodd's *The Bible and the Greeks* (London, 1935), which discusses the Hebrew, Septuagint, and New Testament vocabulary for the words

---

[22] For trivia buffs: the title page of the first printing reads *Idiom Book;* the jacket reads *Idiom-Book,* the form found in many bibliographies.

[23] James W. Voelz, "The Language of the New Testament," in *ANRW* 2: *Principat,* 25/2 (1984), 893–977, documents the debates that have gone on since Deissmann about the influence of the LXX and the extent of Hebraisms in the New Testament; see also Horsley, *New Documents,* 5:5–40. On Kennedy, see Horsley, 28; for a brief evaluation of Voelz's article, see Horsley, 38.

"law," "righteousness," "mercy," "truth," "atonement," and the names of God. The second part of the book deals with the Hermetic literature. Ernest De Witt Burton's *New Testament Word Studies,* ed. Harold R. Willoughby (Chicago: University of Chicago Press, 1927), also contains stimulating discussions, notably on the terms "flesh" and "spirit." When using these older works it is necessary, of course, to keep in mind the linguistic developments that have taken place since their production.

A model study by John Henry Paul Reumann, "The Use of OIKONOMIA and Related Terms in Greek Sources to About A.D. 100, As a Background for Patristic Application" (Diss., University of Pennsylvania, 1957), maps a fertile terrain for social study of significant aspects of the Greco-Roman world, both polytheistic and Christian.

Richard Chenevix Trench, *Synonyms of the New Testament,* 9th ed. (London, 1880), is antiquated but still valuable, if only for its citations of classical and patristic authors, which have suffered materially in reprints of this work. For a quick trip in lexical matters, use the abridged version of BAGD, namely F. Wilbur Gingrich's *Shorter Lexicon of the Greek New Testament* (Chicago: University of Chicago Press, 1965; revised by F. Danker (1983). This abridgement corrects some items in BAGD and includes some information not found in BAGD.[24] For basic glosses, but not for meaning in the true sense of the word, use *A Concise Greek-English Dictionary of the New Testament,* prepared for use with the United Bible Societies' edition of the Greek New Testament. Fritz Rienecker's (d. 1965) *Sprachlicher Schlüssel zum Griechischen Neuen Testament* (Giessen: Brunnen-Verlag, 1957; 11th ed., 1963), based on Nestle's 21st edition has been updated to some extent by Cleon L. Rogers, Jr., under the title *A Linguistic Key to the New Testament* (Grand Rapids: Zondervan, 1976–80). Rogers used the German edition of 1970 and the UBS Greek text. This tidy little work takes the student through the New Testament verse by verse, with brief definitions and rudimentary grammatical analysis. It is one of the handiest tools for a busy minister whose conscience may be disturbed by an unused Greek New Testament. Max Zerwick's *Analysis philologica Novi Testamenti Graeci* (Rome: Pontifical Biblical Institute, 1953; rev. ed., 1960), written in Latin and modeled along similar lines, reached a broad public in the translation of Mary Grosvenor, *A Grammatical Analysis*

---

[24] Not to be forgotten is Alexander Souter's *A Pocket Lexicon to the Greek New Testament* (Oxford, 1916), which remains a compact marvel with its brief but expressive and discriminating definitions. Because of its use of the papyri it is vastly superior to the popular *Greek-English Lexicon to the New Testament,* first published by William J. Hickie (New York, 1893) and since then periodically reprinted and incorporated in the Westcott-Hort edition of the New Testament text. The *Shorter Lexicon* is somewhat larger than Souter in scope, with biblical references and listing of more difficult inflectional forms. Friedrich Rehkopf has brought out a similar work in Germany, but it does not make use of the corrections of the Bauer lexicon noted in the *Shorter Lexicon.*

of the Greek New Testament, 2 vols. (Rome: Pontifical Biblical Institute, 1974–79; 1 vol., rev. ed. 1981; 3d ed., 1988). This inviting work includes material not in Rienecker. Frequent reference is also made in it to Zerwick's *Biblical Greek Illustrated by Examples,* trans. Joseph Smith, with adaptation, from the 4th Latin ed. (Rome: Pontifical Biblical Institute, 1963).

The use of all types of books devoted to word study should undergo the philological correctives and insightful directions that a study like *Biblical Words and Their Meaning: An Introduction to Lexical Semantics* (Grand Rapids: Zondervan, 1983), by Moisés Silva, or *Semantics of New Testament Greek* (Philadelphia, 1982), by J. P. Louw, can offer. Anyone who questions the need of learning the original languages of Scripture should read Silva's *God, Language and Scripture: Reading the Bible in the Light of General Linguistics* (Grand Rapids: Zondervan, 1990), a thin book, but high in protein.

Beginners in New Testament Greek will appreciate Bruce M. Metzger's *Lexical Aids for Students of New Testament Greek* (Princeton: by the author, 1946; new ed., 1969), designed to help students learn the vocabulary through verbal associations. In this little book the word lists are cited in the order of numerical occurrence and include etymological aids. To avoid some of the rote memorization necessitated by Metzger's format, Robert E. Van Voorst, *Building Your New Testament Greek Vocabulary* (Grand Rapids: Eerdmans, 1990), combines frequency and cognate features in one format. For example, all the words relating to δόξα are cited under that entry along with their frequencies. If one is on the alert to purchase some of Nigel Turner's conclusions at discount because of his opposition to Deissmann and Thumb, the British scholar's *Grammatical Insights into the New Testament* (Edinburgh: T. & T. Clark, 1965) will reward the searcher with interesting discussion of passages that have long perplexed commentators. Some of the philological strictures applying to Turner's work can be directed also to David Hill's *Greek Words and Hebrew Meanings: Studies in the Semantics of Soteriological Terms* (Cambridge: Cambridge University Press, 1967), although the latter displays more sobriety concerning totality transfer or concept-in-the-word philology.

For the study of papyri, where restoration of words is a constant challenge, reverse indexes are indispensable. Mechanical in format is the list compiled by Ernst Locker under the direction of Paul Kretschmer, *Rückläufiges Wörterbuch der griechischen Sprache* (Göttingen: Vandenhoeck & Ruprecht, 1944). In *A Reverse Index of Greek Nouns and Adjectives: Arranged by Terminations with Brief Historical Introductions* (Chicago: University of Chicago Press, 1944), Carl Darling Buck and Walter Petersen display as much interest in the history of Greek noun and adjective formation as in the reading of papyri. They record by author the first known appearance of the words cited.

For a thoroughly analytic approach to the vocabulary of the Greek New Testament, one can use J. H. Greenlee's *A New Testament Greek Morpheme Lexicon* (Grand Rapids: Zondervan, 1983). This book lists each word from

BAGD and displays its components. For example, ἀναξιώς is analyzed as ἀ—ἄγω—ως.

Beginners will welcome D. F. Hudson, *Teach Yourself New Testament Greek* (New York: David McKay, 1979). A key is provided at the back of the book, which leaves Greek words unaccented. J. W. Wenham's *The Elements of New Testament Greek* (Cambridge: Cambridge University Press, 1965) is unusually true to title. The author, a seasoned teacher who began revising the 8th ed. (Cambridge: Cambridge University Press, 1946) of Nunn's *Elements,* preserved its title while producing a completely new book, even to the abolition of most accents. Wenham's *Key to Elements of New Testament Greek* (1965) assures users that they will not be stranded while pondering assignments. Building on the premise that the best way to learn a language is to work with the way the language is used, Eric G. Jay associates facts of grammar with data from the Gospel of Mark in *New Testament Greek: An Introductory Grammar* (London: S.P.C.K., 1958). It is accompanied by *A Key to the Rev'd Dr. E. G. Jay's New Testament Greek Grammar* (1961). A similar approach is taken by W. S. LaSor, *Handbook of New Testament Greek: An Inductive Approach Based on the Greek Text of Acts,* 2 vols. (Grand Rapids: Eerdmans, 1973). Frank T. Gignac's *An Introductory New Testament Greek Course* (Chicago: Loyola University Press, 1973) includes an appendix on bilingual interference as a factor in some forms that depart from accepted Greek practice. Instructors have found Molly Whittaker, *New Testament Greek: An Introduction,* rev. ed. (London: S.C.M., 1980), a way to arouse students' interest in Greek. Finding growing acceptance is James Voelz, *Fundamental Greek Grammar* (1985; 2d ed., "updated and revised," St. Louis: Concordia Publishing House, 1993), which takes into account the kind of research done by Stanley E. Porter (see below), but does not lock the user into a single perspective. Voelz also takes account of weakness in basic knowledge of English grammar. W. H. Mare endeavors to meet the need for an approach that takes account of performance levels: *Mastering New Testament Greek: A Beginner's Grammar, Including Lesson Plans for Intermediate and Advanced Greek Students* (Grand Rapids: Baker, 1979).

After taking students through fifty-three lessons, Sakae Kubo has them do actual reading of New Testament passages, in the course of which they review the grammar. His *A Reader's Greek-English Lexicon of the New Testament and a Beginner's Guide for the Translation of New Testament Greek* (Edinbugh: T. & T. Clark, 1975) has a number of features that will help beginners who have reached the reading stage locate quickly the words with which they are unfamiliar. This is accomplished by presenting the "special" vocabulary (used less than fifty times) in a book-by-book, verse-by-verse sequence. Personally, I would, on the basis of experience with a child under three years of age who could not read English, prefer to spend the first few lessons without a grammar, using John 1:1-14, 19-23. The child, no Einstein, learned the letters of John 1:1-3 quickly and as parts of actual words, which he readily enunciated. He then had no difficulty learning how to decipher words in English. After a similar type of exposure, a college or seminary student who has the advantage of being equipped with the English-language reading skills not possessed by a young child ought to be able to move with ease into the sequence of lessons in Kubo's or any other grammar. James Allen Hewett, *New Testament Greek: A Beginning and Intermediate Grammar* (Peabody, Mass.: Hendrickson, 1986) is especially useful for students who have put in a year of Greek study and wish to refurbish and synthesize their previous knowledge.

How to fit Greek into a tight schedule—for example, when multicultural courses and other "practical" needs intrude on traditional claims—challenges the craft. James M. Efird presents the rudiments in twenty-eight lessons, but not for self-instruction, in *A Grammar for New Testament Greek* (Nashville: Abingdon, 1990). Each grammar promises a better trip than its predecessors. Solon would have questioned the wisdom of a title like *Greek without Grief,* a grammar designed by Warren F. Dicharry (Chicago: Loyola University Press, 1989), but he would have endorsed the high aim: to equip a student for continuation in the study of Greek after the formal course. "Learn joyfully," proclaims John H. Dobson, *Learn New Testament Greek* (Grand Rapids: Baker, 1989), and the book seems worth trying, for after lesson 18 a Greek New Testament is required.

Among those that have serviced tens of thousands of readers of the New Testament are H. E. Dana and J. R. Mantey, *A Manual Grammar of the Greek New Testament* (New York: Macmillan, 1927); J. Gresham Machen, *New Testament Greek for Beginners* (New York: Macmillan, 1923); and J. H. Moulton, *An Introduction to the Study of New Testament Greek,* ed. H. G. Meecham, 5th ed. (New York: Macmillan, 1955). Like Davidson's Hebrew *Grammar,* these have the durability of Euclid's geometry. To guard against loss of interest on the part of those who complete an elementary New Testament Greek course, J. Harold Greenlee prepared *A Concise Exegetical Grammar of New Testament Greek,* 1st ed. (1953; 5th rev. ed., (Grand Rapids: Eerdmans, 1986), with a new index to over seven hundred biblical passages to which reference is made. Greenlee's aim is to develop a grasp of the grammatical principles as they apply to the exegetical task.

Trouble with accents? Donald A. Carson thinks that Greek taught without introduction to Greek accents will retard students seeking mastery of the language. His book *Greek Accents: A Student's Manual* (Grand Rapids: Baker, 1985) leads one through the rules of accent by demonstrating their application in the principal classes of grammatical forms. The book concludes with a key to the exercises, which amount to rehearsal of the elements of grammar.

T. Owings, *A Cumulative Index to New Testament Greek Grammars* (Grand Rapids: Baker, 1983) opens doors to some of the resources in a number of grammars by providing an index to the biblical passages that are covered in each of the following works on grammar: Dana and Mantey, Moule, Robertson and Davis, Zerwick, Blass-Debrunner-Funk, Moulton-Howard-Turner, and Robertson.

In 1852 Samuel Bagster and Sons Ltd. published *Analytical Greek Lexicon.* It has been often reprinted, but without any indication of its age or origin. The ethics of such blatant disregard for history is questionable, for unsophisticated users think that they are securing in a sparkling binding the latest philological thinking. A revised edition by H. K. Moulton appeared in 1977. Nathan E. Han's *A Parsing Guide to the Greek New Testament* (Scottdale: Herald Press, 1971) goes verse by verse through the 25th edition of Nestle parsing verbs and words that bear the characteristics of verbs. To avoid the language limitations of all parsing works, Pierre Guillemette brought out a book based on Nestle[26] with a unique management of data and title to match. Anyone who knows English, French, Spanish, German, or Italian can use the work because of its unique system for identification of the components. Only the directions for use are given in the five languages signalled by the title: *The Greek New Testament Analyzed; Le Nouveau Testament Grec Analysé, Análisis del Nuevo Testamento Griego; Analyse des Griechischen Neuen Testaments; Il Nuovo Testamento Greco Analizzato* (Scottdale: Herald Press, 1986).

There is nothing like John Dewar Denniston's *The Greek Particles,* 2d ed. (Oxford: Clarendon Press, 1950) for the Koine, but see J. Blomqvist, *Greek Particles in Hellenistic Prose* (Lund: Gleerup, 1969), with some attention to papyri. Margaret E. Thrall, *Greek Particles in the New Testament: Linguistic and Exegetical Studies,* New Testament Tools and Studies 3 (Leiden: Brill, 1962) provides, among other instructive insights, acute observations about linguistic distribution.

For continuation beyond the beginning stage one can profit from Robert W. Funk's *A Beginning–Intermediate Grammar of Hellenistic Greek,* 3 vols. (Missoula, Mont.: Society of Biblical Literature, 1973; 2d printing, 1977).

The production of Greek grammars and other tools for beginners as well as advanced students will go on, but no one ought to undertake the task of preparing one without thorough immersion in Stanley E. Porter, *Verbal Aspect in the Greek of the New Testament, with Reference to Tense and Mood* (New York: Peter Lang, 1989). This is the first volume in a series that will merit ongoing attention: Studies in Biblical Greek, D. A. Carson, gen. ed.[25] Only those who think that laws governing perceptions of Greek grammar were codified on stone in the nineteenth century for eternal observance should ignore this book. The future is definitely on the side of this work, which takes a look

---

[25] For a rethinking of such phenomena as verbal aspect, bilingualism, linguistic register, literacy, etc., see Horsley, *New Documents,* vol. 5, passim; see also the work of K. L. McKay, cited in Porter (*Verbal Aspect,* 524), and the pioneering work by J. Mateos, *El Aspecto Verbal en el NT,* Estudios NT 1 (Madrid: Ediciones Cristiandad, 1977).

at Greek verbs from within the Greek language as used by those who spoke and wrote it, and not from the Procrustean ordinances of much traditional grammar. This study is definitely designed for those who teach the Greek language and for biblical scholars who claim to be able to teach others. May their ranks not be thinned by the first sentence in the author's preface: "The major assertion of this work in biblical Greek linguistics is that the category of synthetic verbal aspect—a morphologically-based semantic category which grammaticalizes the author/speaker's reasoned subjective choice of conception of a process—provides a suggestive and workable linguistic model for explaining the range of uses of the tense forms in Greek." Be assured, those who endure will find many a New Testament passage blossom in what may appear at first to be a desert.

To be properly prepared for the tidal waves of change that must inevitably make obsolete so much of what we take for granted in grammatical and lexical study, one must also take time out to read and inwardly digest *Linguistics for Students of New Testament Greek: A Survey of Basic Concepts and Applications* (Grand Rapids: Baker, 1988), by David Alan Black. No intimidation here. Anyone who can read an editorial page can understand this book, and the synchronic emphasis will cure almost any case of overexposure to diachronic presentation. On the other hand, those who are worried about being over-dosed with transformational semantic theory, a subset of the new linguistics, can find comfort in Jacob van Bruggen, *The Future of the Bible* (1978). The latter says of the KJV: "as a translation it is the most reliable one in use." He favors concordant translation and considers the "dynamic translation" procedures encouraged by Nida to be inimical to biblical truth.

Students of New Testament Greek frequently ask for guidance concerning grammars of ancient Greek in general. The standard is Eduard Schwyzer, *Griechische Grammatik: Auf der Grundlage von Karl Brugmanns Griechischen Grammatik,* vol. 1 (Munich: C. H. Beck, 1938; unrevised ed. with appendix of corrections and notes, 1953); vol. 2, ed. Albert Debrunner (1950); index vol. by Demetrius J. Georgacas (1953). For the broad scene there is no better one-volume reference grammar in English than Herbert Weir Smyth's *Greek Grammar,* rev. by Gordon M. Messing (Cambridge: Harvard University Press, 1956).

From this brief survey it is apparent that the user of the Greek New Testament is in an especially strategic position to mine its richly studded labyrinths. But tools to be effective must become extensions of the personality employing them. To aid in the achievement of maximum efficiency in the use of Greek grammars and lexicons is the burden of our next chapter.

And as a reward to all who faithfully take some of the trips suggested in this chapter and are therefore deserving of mirth-filled leisure with a cultural additive we recommend a puckish book written by Michael Macrone, *It's Greek to Me!* (New York: Harper Collins, 1991). But don't believe all of it!

CHAPTER EIGHT

The Use of Grammars and Lexicons

I N HIS *An Introduction to the Study of New Testament Greek,* James Hope Moulton relates how his little grammar got into the hands of a poor and almost crippled peasant in a country cottage. He had taught himself enough Greek to work through several chapters of the Gospel of John and used the added knowledge of the Bible to instruct and inspire the young people who gathered round him in the little room, which in Moulton's words "proved a very gate of heaven for many."

Grammars and lexicons are indeed keys that help unlock linguistic doors. It is the purpose of this chapter to suggest some of the possibilities of these versatile volumes and ways and means for using them to greater advantage.

THE LEXICON

OLD FRIENDS

It is a mistake to shun the lexicon as a graveyard haunted by columns of semantic ghosts or simply to fall back on it as on a codebook identifying words that did not appear in first-year-Greek vocabulary lists. The UBS dictionary (chap. 7) or Souter (chap. 7) will serve the latter purpose, but an interview with someone like Bauer calls for more earnest purpose. Every beginning Greek student knows the "meaning" of the word ὄνομα. Who would ever think of looking it up? But there is a fascinating discussion of this well-worn word in BAGD. Under I.4 (s.v. ὄνομα) this lexicon sketches the vivid associations made by the ancients between the name and the qualities possessed by a person or thing. The implications of all phrases involving the name of God or of Jesus are weighty. The mighty acts of the Creator and Jesus Christ combine into a single personal projection. To be baptized into the name of Jesus, as in Acts 2:38, involves something more than an initiation ceremony into an elite club. It embraces the realization that God offers in Jesus Christ a most unexpected rescue from the futility of rebellion and the breathtaking possibility of a new direction in life, guaranteed by Christ's irresistible assault on sin and death. The word ὄνομα, it goes without saying, does not itself "mean" all these things, but the lexicon invites consideration of contexts in which the word takes on specific meaning beyond the mere gloss. Those who wish to probe even more deeply might well follow up the repeated reference to W. Heitmüller, *Im Namen Jesu* (Göttingen, 1903). They will be surprised to learn that some of the formulaic phrases in which the term ὄνομα occurs are not necessarily of Semitic origin.

A word like "believe" may easily acquire a jaded ecclesiastical appearance, but Hebrew lexicons can do wonders for it. In its root form, אמן suggests activity that has to do with strengthening or being supportive in some way or other. In the *qal* only the participle is used, of one who gives support. The one who gives support may be a foster-mother or nurse. Thus, Naomi "takes care of" Obed, the son of Ruth and Boaz, and the kind of care that she gives is qualified in the context by a suggestion of tenderness. She held him close to her bosom (Ruth 4:16). The word may also be applied to pillars or door supports (2 Kings 18:16). The *qal* passive participle describes such as have found support and as a result have proved themselves steady. They can be said to be "faithful." Thus the psalmist complains that "the faithful have disappeared from humankind" (Ps. 12:2; 12:1 NRSV). In the *hiphil* the word means to "feel safe" because one is standing firm, hence, "trust, believe." The believers in God are the stable element in Israel. They have a firm support. Their stability comes not from their own resolute and unyielding obstinacy, but from the immovable undergirding of their covenant Redeemer. Out of this relationship develop faithfulness in disposition and reliable social conduct (*niphal*). Since context makes a large contribution to meaning, the Hebrew has no difficulty conveying it with a term that we are able to nuance with a variety of resources in English.

Almost everyone associates the expression "wait on tables" (Acts 6:2 NRSV) with food, but a look at BAGD under τράπεζα suggests the very strong probability that the apostles were entangling themselves in time-consuming bookkeeping. The apostles are then rejecting the role of bankers and not simply that of butlers.

LOCAL COLOR

One ought not only remain open to new and augmented appreciation of old friends; it is equally rewarding to understand their environment. The primary function of MM is to recreate the world in which the New Testament vocabulary was employed. This work is not a comprehensive lexicon but a discriminating selection of words that shed fresh light on the New Testament. In Acts

20:30 the apostle Paul views with agitation the inevitable arrival of false teachers. He says that people will rise within the group, speaking perverse things in an attempt to draw the disciples into their own following. The word ἀποσπαώ used in this passage, rendered "entice" by NRSV, is found, according to MM, in a papyrus of the third centuryB.C. The papyrus reads: "You wrote me not to withdraw the gang (of workmen engaged in the copper mines) from Philoteris before they had finished the work." The editors go on to note that "withdraw" in the sense of "breach of contract" is found in numerous formal documents. Between the lines of Acts 20:30, then, we note the suggestion that the disciples are under contract to serve the Lord Jesus Christ and that false teachers will urge them to break that contract. No new definition is attached to the word, but Paul's word undergoes rejuvenation and suggests to the expositor an appropriate contemporary legal illustration.

In Rom. 15:28 Paul informs the Roman congregation that he intends to complete the collection he has undertaken and will stop by on his way to Spain after he has made delivery to God's people in Jerusalem. The word used here for "making delivery" is σφραγίζω. The papyri suggest customs similar to the sealing of railroad boxcars. In one papyrus a shipmaster is instructed to write a receipt for grain shipped on a government transport, and he is to "seal a sample" to prevent the grain from being tampered with during transit. In another a merchant writes: "If you come, take out six *artabae* of vegetable seed, sealing it in the sacks in order that they may be ready." Paul will take all steps to ensure proper delivery of the collection and eliminate any cause for scandal.

The problem of the disorderly people or loafers in the Thessalonian congregations is sharpened by the material under ἀτακτέω in MM. In a papyrus dated A.D. 66 a contract of apprenticeship stipulates that the father must make good any days during which his son "plays truant" or "fails to attend." Similarly a weaver's apprentice must make up any days he is absent owing to idleness or ill health beyond the three-week vacation and sick leave allowed during the year. These papyri parallels to 2 Thess. 3:11 suggest that some Thessalonian employers were fuming at a message which in their judgment was capsizing the economic order.

Moffatt renders Gal. 3:1 as follows: "O senseless Galatians, who has bewitched you—you who had Jesus Christ the crucified placarded before your very eyes?" The NRSV reads: "It was before your eyes that Jesus Christ was publicly exhibited as crucified?" How does Moffatt arrive at the meaning "placarded" for προγράφω? Moulton-Milligan cites a papyrus in which a father, after the manner of our personal columns, requests that a public proclamation be posted to the effect that he will no longer be responsible for his son's debts. St. Paul's expression becomes transparent: "How in the world," he asks, "can you Galatians possibly pay any attention to these Judaizers? I practically set up before your eyes a billboard spelling out the love of the crucified Jesus. How much clearer could I put it?"

The world of the New Testament comes alive in the pages of this lexicon. The world of shopkeepers, of lonely widows, of traveling salespeople, of the lovelorn, of bankers, of merchants, and of politicians—in short, the dramatis personae of the New Testament—appears here. And because it is the same workaday world as that of our own century, with mainly names and places changed, *The Vocabulary of the Greek Testament* is a volume that more effectively than many others can bridge the chasm between pulpit and pew.

Find out where your friends are living!

PEDIGREE

Words are like people. To know them well one must meet them on their own level, in their own environment. In different circumstances they react differently. Like a face they take on varying expressions. Some of them move from place to place; some never return to their earlier familiar surroundings. But to know their past is to know a little better what makes them act as they do in the present. And the present that is our concern in this chapter is the hellenized world of the New Testament.

The Bauer lexicon is not intended to be a historical survey of New Testament Greek. It confines itself principally to citations from the New Testament. Moulton-Milligan deals only with the papyri, and to some extent with inscriptions. To see the family portrait one must go to LSJM (see chap. 7).

Some conception of LSJM's usefulness in Bible exposition may be gained from the study of a word such as κακοήθεια. St. Paul uses this word in a catalog of vices (Rom 1:29). BAGD offers the glosses "malice, malignity, craftiness." It is true that it submits Aristotle's definition, "κακοήθεια means always to assume the worst," but the reader must supply the translation. In LSJM similar information is presented, but under the cognate κακοήθης it is stated that the adjective is especially used in the sense of "thinking evil, prone to put the worst construction on everything." Might this be more illuminating than "malignity" in both Moffatt and the RSV, or "craftiness" in NRSV?

The very common word ἁμαρτάνω and its cognates provide another instructive study. In the *Iliad* 5.287 it is used of a spear missing its mark. In general it is used of failure to achieve one's purpose. Thus Odysseus in the underworld assures Achilles that Neoptolemus did not err in his words, and only Nestor and Odysseus were a match for him (*Odyssey* 11.511). Religious significance is attached to the word already as early as Homer. In the *Iliad* 24.68 Zeus alerts Hera to the fact that Hector never *failed* to offer pleasing gifts to the gods. The concept of actual wrongdoing and indiscretions committed against the gods appears in the *Iliad* 9.501. In biblical documents the implications of "sin" are more clearly defined in direct ratio to the increased understanding of God's moral nature and humanity's created responsibility, but the original idea of failure to achieve one's purpose sharpens the contrast between moral expectations and actual achievements. Ancient Hellenes had other ways of dealing with matters of behavior. In the Sacred Scriptures prophets unanimously proclaim that apart from an understanding of God's redemptive activity life is bound to end in disappointment and failure. Human endeavor without atonement is one long ramble. It lacks direction and orientation. Unless all of life is steered toward God and conditioned by God's designs, it goes off course, no matter how swift the speed or determined the direction. Again, ἁμαρτάνω by itself does not "mean" all these things, and there is nothing specifically "theological" about the term, but when a given context indicates awareness of divine interests, the student searches for resources in the receptor language that will express the meaning in a specific passage. Moved into the contemporary scene, strong are some of the warnings to humans who hurtle off along their own trajectory, swearing companionship to the wind.

The implications of Peter's choice of the word ἀποδοκιμάζω in 1 Peter 2:4, 7 can only be detected with the aid of LSJM, unless the student is fortunate enough to find a commentator who incorporates the material found in LSJM. Selwyn, who rarely leaves anything worth saying unsaid, omits discussion of the word in his commentary.[1] The first citation given in LSJM is Herodotus 6.130. In this account Cleisthenes addresses the suitors who seek the hand of his daughter. He has sent a proclamation throughout Greece announcing a contest for his daughter's hand. He has made trial of the suitors' manly bearing, their disposition and accomplishments. Now the time has come to declare his choice of a son-in-law. Of all the suitors Hippocleides impresses him most favorably, but on the night of the feast Hippocleides overbids his hand and in a shameless demonstration literally dances his wife away. Cleisthenes then silences the company and declares his reluctance to choose one and disqualify the others. But he must make a choice, and after announcing handsome consolation prizes he declares Megacles winner. The word used for disqualification in this account is ἀποδοκιμάζω. The rest of the suitors did not meet the specifications set by Cleisthenes.

Lysias 13.10, listed immediately after the Herodotus references, speaks of a certain Theramenes who had been disqualified for the office of general. From these parallels, as well as those listed under "2," one can with reasonable certainty assess the implications in Peter's choice of diction. Jesus is the candidate

---

[1] G. H. R. Horsley, *New Documents Illustrating Early Christianity,* vol. 5: *Linguistic Essays* (Macquarie University, N. S. W., Australia: Ancient History Documentary Research Centre, 1989), 93, thinks that the secondary literature in Bauer should be dropped in favor of other material but fails to consider the fact choice older studies might be overlooked were students dependent on current abstracts. Besides, the bibliographies in BAGD are extra. They do not preempt space. The book merely became a bit larger. It should also be noted that the second index volume of *TWNT* does not cite much literature before 1950, and insufficient account is taken of contributions this side of the Atlantic.

for Israel's highest office; nevertheless, humans declare him unworthy, unfit for the messianic task. Like a stone that does not pass the supervisor's scrutiny, he is rejected.

Of the making of many etymologies there was no end at the turn of the century, and often the resemblance of the word under discussion to its alleged ancestor was purely coincidental. But etymologies carry their own inherent fascination and often limn the meaning of a word in bold relief. That the word παρρησία is composed of the two words πᾶς and ῥῆσις and therefore literally means "saying everything" might not be recognized without the help of LSJM, in which we discover the components entered in parentheses. The references to the Athenian love of free speech help accent the type of fearlessness displayed by the apostles in Acts 4. They spoke the word as people who laid claim to the right of freedom of expression.

Learn to know the family tree!

A Notable Asterisk

The more comprehensive a lexicon becomes, the more complete is its listing of words. Koehler-Baumgartner signals the occurrences of certain words and forms with numbers in parentheses. BAGD simply places a single asterisk at the end of articles in which all occurrences in the New Testament and apostolic fathers have been noted, and a double asterisk when only New Testament passages are listed in full. Thus the student is spared the need for checking in an additional volume, in this case a concordance. At a glance one can see, for example, that μαθήτρια occurs only once in the New Testament (Acts 9:36). No other woman is described by this term in the New Testament. Even as her description so is Tabitha's character. She stood out as one rich in kind deeds and in almsgiving. She was an outstanding advertisement of Christian discipleship at its unselfish best.

Resource Material

One of the most valuable incidental features of BAGD is the bibliographical data found at the end of many of the articles. Enterprising use of the entries cited will open the door to a vast treasure trove of critical monographs, dissertations, and journal articles, as well as pages and chapters in significant books. If the subject is soteriology, a look at ἀπολύτρωσις, σῴζω, and σταυρός will yield more than twenty-five titles. The entries under 'Ιησοῦς, υἱός, χριστός, σωτήρ reveal references that illuminate with an almost enviable degree of comprehensiveness nearly every aspect of Christology. If a term paper calls for a study on miracles, consult the long list of titles under σημεῖον. For pros and cons of the North versus the South Galatian controversy, see the literature under Γαλατία. A check of φοβέω reveals that Mark 16:9-20 is rarely considered a part of the Mark autograph; Walter Bauer, Frederic G. Kenyon, and Colin H. Roberts debate the possibility of a lost ending. Julius Wellhausen, Alfred Firman Loisy, and Ernst Lohmeyer are among those who conclude that the Gospel of Mark terminated originally with ἐφοβοῦντο γάρ. Theodor Zahn and others were convinced that the evangelist was prevented from finishing his work. With the help of these and other discussions cited under φοβέω and γάρ students can more circumspectly weigh their own conclusions concerning the ending of Mark. Yet pragmatic considerations should not be the prime stimulus to more intensive and extensive investigation. One cannot describe the sheer edification provided by a trip through the realms of ἀλήθεια at the hand of Rudolf Bultmann's article in *ZNW* (see BAGD, s.v. and the list of abbreviations at the front of the lexicon). Some may object that space could have been saved for more lexical discussion by eliminating references to secondary literature, on the ground that current bibliographic aids can amply supply such information.[2] But the fact remains that many of the conclusions reached in the lexicon are based on some very informative exegesis done decades ago. Further, it is amazing how many cries of "eureka" are uttered by exegetes for "discoveries" that were made decades earlier by scholars listed under entries in BAGD. In a craft like ours the motto of the state of California ought to be used with practiced parsimony.

The reference to *ZNW* prompts a word of counsel. Lexicons like BAGD and BDB reflect the complicated structures of our times. Special signs and abbreviations are indispensable to a lexicon's system of communication. A little time spent pondering the introductory pages will spare users much unnecessary frustration, increase their enjoyment of the tightly wedged contents, and create a feeling of good will engendered by the knowledge that dollars were saved through decreased publishing costs.

THE GRAMMAR

Almost everyone who writes on the subject of grammar, especially Greek grammar, cites a few lines from Browning's "A Grammarian's Funeral":

> So, with the throttling hands of death at strife,
> Ground he at grammar.
> Still, through the rattle, parts of speech were rife;
> While he could stammer
> He settled *Hoti*'s business—let it be!

[2] Edward G. Selwyn, *The First Epistle of St. Peter,* 2d ed., reprint (London, 1955), ad loc.

Properly based Oun—
Gave us the doctrine of the enclitic De,
Dead from the waist down.

After quoting part of this dirge, Archibald T. Robertson goes on to assure his readers that grammarians are not such dull creatures after all and that they lead happy, normal lives. He then relates how the professor of Greek at Bonn reacted when he received a copy of the first volume of Basil Lanneau Gildersleeve's *Syntax of Classical Greek*. He brought it to the seminar and "clasped and hugged it as though it were a most precious darling (*Liebling*)." His reaction is understandable, for a grammar is like a woman who does not make the cover of *La Femme*—to appreciate her real charm and beauty requires sensitivity and repeated association.

TENSES

Develop a sensitivity to the nuances in Greek tenses and large areas of the New Testament will leap to life. The vivacity of the Greek language lies in its subtle distinction of tenses. They are a constant source of frustration to New Testament translators. Even John Bertram Phillips, who makes it a point to capture nuances often missed by other translators, erases the fine distinction between the present and the aorist of the verb μετανοέω in Luke 13:3, 5. The present tense in v. 3 suggests the interpretation: "Unless you begin to show some signs of repentance, you shall all perish in similar fashion." The aorist in v. 5 climaxes Jesus' warning and pinpoints the decisiveness of the hour: "Unless you make an immediate about-face, you shall all perish in exactly the same fashion."

In Luke 1:59 the imperfect ἐκάλουν lights up a roomful of people who were already speaking of "little Zechariah." They insisted on calling him after his father. Any other name was out of the question. Elizabeth's protest is vehement, οὐχί: "No! he is John!" One thinks of Strepsiades, who complained that his wife was insisting on adding (ἐτίθει) the word ἵππος to their son's name (Aristophanes, *The Clouds* 63–65).

A SIGNIFICANT CONDITION

One might easily overlook the clever point of attack described in the story of Jesus' temptation (Matt. 4:3; Luke 4:3). The conjunction εἰ at first sight seems to suggest that the devil is casting doubt on Jesus' divine sonship. But BAGD points out that (except in "unreal" conditions) εἰ with the indicative expresses "a condition thought of as real or to denote assumptions relating to what has already happened," and Matt. 4:3 is cited as a case in point. As Robertson (p. 1009), expresses it: "The temptation, to have force, must be assumed as true. The devil knew it to be true. He accepts the fact as a working hypothesis in the temptation." The diabolical strategy is evident. The devil hopes to steer Jesus along a path contrary to the divine objective. Jesus is to assert the powers that he admittedly has as the Son of God to his own advantage.

IMPERATIVES

Robertson had a flair for making grammar interesting, and one of his many fascinating discussions is in the area of negative prohibition (pp. 851–55). The phrase μή μοι κόπους πάρεχε (Luke 11:7) emerges as "quit troubling me." At Rev. 10:4 as John is about to take up his pen and write, he is warned by the angel: μὴ αὐτὰ γράψῃς. Robertson renders, "Do not begin to write." I would prefer, "No, don't write it." The hazard of time-consuming Oriental greetings can be captured by rendering the imperative in καὶ μηδένα κατὰ τὴν ὁδὸν ἀσπάσησθε (Luke 10:4) as "don't spend your time in chitchat with anyone along the way." The speaker's perception of the situation in the light of the context, not the tense per se, is what matters.[3]

A QUESTION OF CURIOSITY

The question addressed by the Samaritan woman to her townsfolk (John 4:29) is interestingly handled by Robertson. "There is certainly a feminine touch," he writes, "in the use of μή by the woman at Jacob's well when she came to the village. She refused to arouse opposition by using οὐ and excited their curiosity with μή" (p. 917; see also p. 1167). Her question might be rendered: "This couldn't be the Christ (the Messiah), could it?" In this and some of the preceding examples a grammarian's decision is available, but the student should not learn to expect a neat translation or explanation of every problem passage. Often the grammarian is content to provide the basic principles and essential data on the basis of which independent judgments can be formed. Using the information gained relative to the problem in John 4:29, for example, the student can proceed to a passage like Matt. 12:23. Here the crowds are represented as displaying astonishment in the face of Jesus' triumph over demonic controls. Messianic associations race through their minds, and they ask: "This

---

[3] On imperatives and aspect, see Stanley E. Porter, *Verbal Aspect in the Greek of the New Testament, with Reference to Tense and Mood* (New York: Peter Lang, 1989), 335–61.

can't be the son of David, can it?" Thereupon the opposition is quick to meet the rising tidal wave of messianic enthusiasm.

In all this it is necessary to remember that it is the interpreter's immediate responsibility to capture the use of language in the source document and not assume that the subtleties expressed in the Greek were necessarily prior to the present form of the document. In the interest of disciplined exegesis it is important to observe that in a given account it is Luke's, or Mark's, or John's Jesus, or whoever the character in the story may be, who acts and speaks. We do not know how the devil managed to communicate with Jesus, but we do know that in Matthew and Luke he used Greek. What their source or sources contained belongs to another phase of exegetical inquiry.

GOD OR HERO

The entire structure of Mark's Gospel is at stake in the view that is taken of the anarthrous υἱός in Mark 15:39. Does the centurion suggest that Jesus is one of many heroes, or does he rise to the occasion with a more significant appraisal? Ernest Cadman Colwell's fruitful discussion of the phenomenon involved here may be found by checking Moule, *An Idiom Book of New Testament Greek* (1959), via the index, s.v. "Article."

POINT OF KNOWLEDGE

To sense a difference between γινώσκω and ἐπιγνώσομαι in 1 Cor. 13:12 (*pace* Bultmann, *TDNT,* 1:703) is to feel the throb of this text. As Moulton paraphrases the verse: "Now I am acquiring knowledge which is only partial at best: then I shall have learnt my lesson, shall know, as God in my mortal life knew me."[4]

One must, of course, be on guard against overinterpretation. The verb συναντιλαμβάνομαι in Luke 10:40 prompted one enthusiastic expositor to capture the scene along these lines: "Here was Martha upbraiding the Lord: 'Why don't you tell Mary to get on the other side and take hold of this table so that we can move it.'" The fact is that compound verbs in the Koine many times do not communicate the kind of precision one might be led to infer from the heaping up of prepositions. Contexts must be carefully considered. Related types of inflated verbiage are apparent in contemporary English. Why is one tempted to say that a book is "entitled" rather than "titled"? Does one really imagine that "utilizing" a thing is somehow more important and distinctive

---

[4] James Hope Moulton, *Prolegomena,* 3d ed., *A Grammar of New Testament Greek* (Edinburgh: T. & T. Clark, 1908), 1:113

than "using" it? Perhaps some people when using the inflated forms do indeed sense a difference that prompts their choice.

Some will question the conclusion (see the debate registered in BAGD, s.v. ἀγαπάω and φιλέω), but it is this writer's judgment that the point of the repartee in John 21:15-17 is lost if the verbs ἀγαπάω and φιλέω sacrifice identity in a semantic merger. Jesus begins with the word ἀγαπάω, which is not necessarily the so-called higher word for "loving," which some think takes precedence over φιλέω. Rather, ἀγαπάω in numerous contexts refers to expression of interest in, or concern for, another, the kind of attitude that manifests an appreciation for community, without establishing an especially intimate relationship. On the other hand, the term φιλέω suggests in numerous contexts intimate companionship or expression of friendship. Hellenes placed a high value on friendship. Peter affirms intimacy. The third time, Jesus puts the question differently: "Do you count me your friend?" The affirmation made by Jesus at John 16:17 appears to be suspended. In short, the fact that the evangelist at times uses some pairs of words synonymously does not mean that at all times he uses them synonymously. Each context must be examined on its own terms.

A TROUBLESOME PARTICLE

The NRSV interprets 1 Cor. 12:2: "You know that when you were pagans, you were enticed and led astray to idols that could not speak." Despite the improvement over its predecessor's rendering, this is one of the less felicitous renderings of the version, and not only because of the insensitive use of the term "pagan," which is not offset by the alteration of RSV's "dumb" (idols). Moulton's discussion on the iterative ἄν (*Prolegomena,* 167) makes more lucid what the revisers have obscured and opens the way to serious consideration of history-of-religion data.

COMBINED ATTACK

A PERPLEXING ὅτι

The use of ὅτι in Luke 7:47 suggests a profitable use of grammars in conjunction with the lexicon. The context appears to demand the interpretation: "Since (ὅτι) she loved much, one can conclude that she first had her many sins forgiven." But does the New Testament support such a usage of ὅτι? At the end of the article on ὅτι BAGD lists passages in which the rendering "for" recommends itself. In one of these passages St. Paul states: "For I think that God has exhibited us apostles as last of all, as though sentenced to death"

(1 Cor. 4:9). Then he goes on to give the reason for his judgment. "Because we have become a spectacle to the world, to angels and to mortals" (NRSV). In view of our present situation as a spectacle to the world, it may be fairly inferred, says the apostle, that God intends us to appear at the end of the procession of doomed people. So also from the woman's great love for Jesus one may deduce the comprehensive forgiveness which elicited her love.

What additional light can be derived from the grammars? Either the index of quotations or the Greek-word index, or both, are convenient ports of entry to grammatical discussions. BDF does not cite Luke 7:47, but under ὅτι lists the causal force, with a reference to paragraphs 456, 1. 2; 480, 6. A feature of BDF, it should be noted, is the presentation in smaller type of detailed treatment, together with extensive references. Under the smaller numeral "1" some of the references noted in BAGD at the end of the article on ὅτι are cited. As noted above, Luke 7:47 is not included, but through the parallels BDF strengthens probability for the view presented.

In addition to consulting BDF, students may wish to discover what Robertson has to say on the matter. Under Luke 7:47 they will find seven page references. Until they grow accustomed to Robertson's arrangement of his material they are advised to look up each reference. They will find that the first relevant discussion appears on p. 962. A check under ὅτι in the index of Greek words and comparison with the text cited would also have revealed that pp. 962–66 present a detailed treatment of causal sentences. Perhaps to their surprise students will find that the οὗ χάριν and not the ὅτι of Luke 7:47 is referred to specifically in the paragraph titled "Paratactic Causal Sentences." But they will also note the caution that "the subordination of the ὅτι and διότι clauses is often rather loose" and that in at least one instance there is very little difference between ὅτι (1 Cor. 1:25) and γάρ (1 Cor. 1:26). Then follow some of the passages cited also in BAGD and BDF. With the parallel data before them, students are better prepared to make a critical inference.

Indeed, never will first-class grammars and lexicons be more welcome than when students find themselves caught in commentators' cross fire or bewildered by differences of viewpoint registered in Bible versions. When few reinforcing data are offered, adoption of a commentator's conclusion can be precarious, especially if, as in the case of Luke 7:47, an interpreter such as John M. Creed opts for a contrary view.[5] Creed thinks that the concluding absolution confirms the view that the woman's great love is responsible for the receipt of much forgiveness. But what evidence does he offer? Does Joseph A. Fitzmyer take one along a surer path of probability?[6] Check his line of proof, and if you have Moule at hand see the latter's "Notes on ὅτι" in *An Idiom Book of New*

---

[5] John M. Creed, *The Gospel According to St. Luke* (London: Macmillan, 1955), ad loc.

[6] Joseph A. Fitzmyer, *The Gospel According to Luke,* The Anchor Bible, 2 vols. (Garden City, N.Y.: Doubleday, 1981–85), ad loc.

Testament Greek (1959), 147. In any event the procedures outlined suggest how a little ingenuity and patience can rouse the dormant resources of mighty and lesser tomes to profitable service. Besides, there is the promise that students will do greater things than their teachers.

The lexicon and grammar can make a passage like Ps. 11:1-6 gleam with fresh brilliance. The fainthearted plead as excuse for their flight that the wicked are bending their bows (v. 2). Here יִדְרְכוּן, the imperfect tense, expresses the fear that envisions and anticipates the worst. "The wicked are in the process of bending their bows." In the next clause a perfect tense is used, כּוֹנְנוּ. Fear is intensified. The bow is already bent, and the arrow rests ready on the taut string. Faith meets this mounting fear with a vision of God's supremacy, beginning with v. 4. God sees it all. The word for seeing here is חָזָה. In Isa. 47:1 the verb is applied to observation of the stars. In Isa. 1:1 the seer peers as a prophet in an ecstatic state. Song of Solomon 7:1 MT (6:13 NRSV) speaks of the gaze fixed intently on a fair maiden. God, then, is viewed as one who watches attentively and vigilantly everything that occurs on the earth, and is not so oblivious as the fearful may think. On the contrary, God's eyelids "test" mere humans. The Hebrew word for "test" in Ps. 11:4, though not indubitably in Ps. 11:5, is בָּחַן. The verb is used metaphorically in Job 23:10 and Zech. 13:9. In Ps. 7:10 (7:9 NRSV) it expresses God's search of a human being's innermost self. Assurance is heightened by the reference to the divine eyelids, which are squinting to make out the scene more clearly. Such is God's concentration!

A CRITICAL EYE

We noted earlier that the task of the interpreter is never quite finished. Interpretation is an ongoing challenge, and the truth must out that even the most eminent and unbespectacled grammarians and lexicographers look betimes with vision blurred. This testimony to mortality imposes an earnest responsibility on students who may be tempted to succumb to uncritical dependence on what overwhelms them as the authoritative word. The humility evidenced is salutary; the intellectual surrender may be fatal.

A lexicon is really a sort of systematized concordance. Words in themselves are merely symbols. They are a medium of thought exchange. The task of lexicographers is to document the intellectual monetary system of a particular period in history. They endeavor to search out as many contexts as possible in which a given word is employed. They are forbidden under oath to impose another language symbol on a word until they discover from a close inspection of various contexts what that word represents. When the word appears only once they "cannot be holpen by conference of places," as the revisers of 1611 noted, but must make a learned guess. They may secure help from a translator who lived closer to the writing of the autograph, but must always allow for the possibility that almost any translator might also have been either forced or prone to make a guess. Thus Jerome renders ἐθελοθρησκία (Col. 2:23) with *superstitionis*. The lexicographer gathers from the context and from the components of ἐθελοθρησκία that the writer of Colossians is discussing some kind of free-wheeling cultic approach.

It would appear that the more contexts lexicographers have to explore and compare, the lighter their task and the higher their percentage of accuracy. In many cases this is true. Thus the word παραλογίζομαι occurs in a sufficient number of contexts to assure the lexicographer that "deception" is the basic idea conveyed by the word. Something is reckoned in alongside something else. The delusive element may be either a row of figures that is substituted for a bona fide list of expenditures or it may be a fallacious premise or argument. In either case "deception" is an intruding factor. In passages situated in mercantile contexts the lexicographer will say that the word means "reckon fraudulently, defraud"; in others involving questionable persuasive approaches, "deceive, delude." No one will dispute the correctness of these classifications or the distribution of the respective passages in BAGD. The word adapts itself easily to clear and convincing analysis. At the same time it is necessary to note that the one Greek word does not itself have all the "meanings" that we assign to it in the various translations we use for it. Totality-transfer is a sure route to distortion of an author's meaning.

With a word like μάρτυς the problem is more complex. BAGD suggests three major classifications: (1) a legal sense; (2) figuratively, of anyone who testifies to anything the individual has heard or seen; and (3) a martyr, as in Acts 22:20 and Rev. 2:13 with their references to Stephen and Antipas. But a study of the passages under "c" of the second classification casts suspicion on the equation of what appears a more fluid usage with a later technical meaning. Stephen and Antipas are called "martyrs" (μάρτυρες) not primarily because they testified by their violent deaths, which is what the word in its later technical sense implies, but because their lives rendered such sterling witness. In other words, one must keep a firm rein on easy assumptions.

Again, in 1 Peter 1:6 the writer uses the expression λυπηθέντες ἐν ποικίλοις πειρασμοῖς. BAG 2b rendered the word πειρασμός here with "temptation." But the context of the letter indicates that the writer is exhorting addressees who are profoundly distressed by the troubles to which they have been exposed because of their Christian allegiance. These troubles may indeed prove to be sources of temptation to sin, but at this point the writer is chiefly concerned about the perplexity such hardships have created in the minds of his readers. The participle λυπηθέντες, describing an attendant circumstance of pain, would appear to cast the decisive vote in favor of a "test" or "trial" of Christian endurance. The passage would then fall in the category of 1 Peter 4:12, as

BAGD partially grants by placing it in § 1 with the observation "perhaps," and alerting the reader to that possibility in § 2b.

Christmas radio skits often include a gruff, uncooperative innkeeper. Whether he is a legitimate member of the Christmas cast is questionable, *pace* BAG, which interprets the word κατάλυμα in Luke 2:7 as "inn." The more general meaning of "lodging" or "guestroom" is assigned to the other occurrence of this word in Luke's Gospel (22:11). It is true that both associations of the Greek word might have been intended by the evangelist, but in view of the fact that Luke 10:34 uses the technical term for an inn, πανδοχεῖον, the less precise term in Luke 2:7 appears designed. Instead of taking lodgings in the crowded large upper room they preferred the privacy of the lower quarters. Clearly lexicons are marvels of interpretive insight, but they are not infallible. Yet their creators try to be alert, and students will note BAGD's reappraisal of the use of the term in Luke 2:7.[7]

A similar critical approach must be applied to grammars. On page 595 of his "Big Grammar" Robertson cites passages in which the preposition εἰς is used to express aim or purpose. After stating that this is undoubtedly the use of εἰς in Matt. 26:28 (τὸ περὶ πολλῶν ἐκχυννόμενον εἰς ἄφεσιν ἁμαρτιῶν) he goes on to say: "But it by no means follows that the same idea is expressed by εἰς ἄφεσιν in Mk. 1:4 and Acts 2:38 (see Mt. 10:41), though that may in the abstract be true. It remains a matter for the interpreter to decide." Why these latter passages, but not Matt. 26:28, should be left to the mercy of the interpreter is not discussed. On page 523 Robertson gives the dative in Rom. 6:20 (ἐλεύθεροι τῇ δικαιοσύνῃ) the force of a locative, whereas the associative idea predominates. On the subject of ὅτι Robertson asserts that instances of consecutive ὅτι in the New Testament "are not numerous, but they are very clear" (p. 1001). He goes on to cite Mark 4:41; Matt. 8:27; Heb.2:6; and Luke 4:36, all of which are handled with considerably more reserve in BAGD and BDF.

At times, as students struggle for hours with a few phrases of Scripture, they will wonder whether it is worth all the trouble and whether it might not be better after all to take some "authority's"—perhaps a commentator's—word for it. Others will conclude that in this latter day of instant truth, word study is not for them, and they will just let the text express itself. In their naiveté they tend to forget that in the end they may be listening to themselves. It would be well for them to read Morton Smith's remarks delivered at a meeting of the American Academy of Religion in Dallas, in 1968.[8] And in the moment of lassitude let them remember that the advance troops in the battle for truth

---

[7] This observation about reappraisal serves also as a reminder to be precise about acronyms. It is remarkable how many errors occur in the exegetical literature due to confusion of editions of Bauer's lexicon. Frequently BAG is cited, without apparent awareness of a modification or correction in BAGD, which contains more than 20 percent new material.

[8] Morton Smith, "The Present State of Old Testament Studies," *JBL* 88 (1969): 19–35.

are always those who take nothing for granted. As Einstein said of himself, in accounting for some of his brilliant discoveries, "I accepted no axioms." Scientific lexical and grammatical study, as Philipp K. Buttmann once noted, is among the best antidotes against theological vagaries and somewhat sectarian and ideological interpretations to which, alas, even the most well-meaning commentators fall victim.

CHAPTER NINE

Bible Dictionaries

Certain scholars have rendered great service by providing the student of the Sacred Scriptures with interpretations of all Hebrew, Syrian, Egyptian, and other foreign expressions and names that are introduced without further explanation by the sacred writers. Eusebius through his historical investigations developing out of a concern for the divine books has also left us an indispensable tool. These men have done their work so that Christians need not search through many authors for information on some small point. But there is further need of someone with the proper qualifications to produce, in the interests of his fellow Christians, what would properly be called a labor of love. What I have in mind is a work that would carefully classify and accord individual treatment to the geographical locations, the flora and fauna, and the stones and unknown metals of Scripture.

S O WROTE ST. AUGUSTINE in his *De doctrina Christiana* (Migne, *PL* 34:62). Eusebius, bishop of Caesarea, had indeed written a book on geographical names in both the Old and New Testaments, Περὶ τῶν τοπικῶν ὀνομάτων τῶν ἐν τῆς θείᾳ γραφῇ, amplified by Jerome under the title *Liber de situ et nominibus locorum Hebraicorum* (Migne, *PL* 33:903–76), but the world waited more than a thousand years for fulfillment of Augustine's dream. Johann Heinrich Alsted (1588–1638) merits the title of pioneer in this area of biblical interpreters' aids.[1] After writing on almost every conceivable subject, including *Tabacologia: doctrina de natura, usu et abusu tabaci,* he must have been in fine fettle for his *Triumphus bibliorum sacrorum seu Encyclopaedia biblica* (Frankfort, 1625).

In the succeeding century the French Benedictine monk Antoine Augustin Calmet (1672–1757) published the first dictionary of consequence, *Dictionnaire*

---

[1] On the history of Bible dictionaries, see *The Jewish Encyclopedia* (New York: Funk & Wagnalls, 1907), 4:577–79; *Fuller Library Bulletin* nos. 20–23 (October 1953–September 1954); and Gert A. Zischka, *Index lexicorum: Bibliographie der lexikalischen Nachschlagewerke* (Vienna: Verlag Brüder Hollinek, 1959): 17–39. See also Bruce M. Metzger, "A Survey of Recent Research on the Ancient Versions of the New Testament," *NTS* 11 (1955): 1–16. On Eusebius's hand in the *Onomasticon* and on its value for topographical study, see Carl Umhau Wolf, "Eusebius of Caesarea and the Onomasticon," *The Biblical Archaeologist* 27 (1964): 66–96.

historique et critique, chronologique, géographique et littéral de la Bible, 2 vols. and 2 vols. supplement (Paris, 1722–28), reissued in 4 vols. (Geneva and Paris, 1730). The work was subsequently translated into English by Samuel d'Oyly and John Colson and published in a three-volume edition in London in 1732 under the title *An Historical, Critical, Geographical, Chronological, and Etymological Dictionary of the Holy Bible.* Numerous additions and some significant subtractions of rabbinic and Roman Catholic material were made by Charles Taylor in his edition published in London in 1795; in 1832–35 Edward Robinson prepared and published a condensed and revised seventh edition. Many later editions and translations have spread Calmet's work, and its influence is evident in most of the Bible dictionaries of the last century. Even today the work is not completely antiquated, for at its end is a long classified bibliography of interpretive aids, the like of which is difficult to find.

Johann Georg Benedikt Winer, *Biblisches Realwörterbuch zum Hand-gebrauch für Studirende, Kandidaten, Gymnasiallehrer und Prediger* (Leipzig, 1820; 3d ed. rev., 2 vols., Leipzig, 1847–48), broke new ground and remained the standard work for two generations in Germany. In England John Kitto, *A Cyclopaedia of Biblical Literature* (Edinburgh, 1843–45; 2d ed. Henry Burgess, 2 vols., Edinburgh, 1856; 3d ed. rewritten by William Lindsay Alexander, 3 vols., Edinburgh, 1862–66; Philadelphia, 1866), set novel patterns with emphases on the religion, literature, and archaeology of the New Testament. Biographical sketches of prominent Bible students and discussions of rabbinical lore such as the Talmud were for the first time considered substantial ingredients of a Bible dictionary. The works of both Winer and Kitto served as the basis for a number of articles in *Cyclopaedia of Biblical, Theological, and Ecclesiastical Literature,* ed. John M'Clintock and James Strong (see below).

William Smith, *A Dictionary of the Bible: Comprising Its Antiquities, Biography, Geography, and Natural History,* 3 vols. (London, 1860–63), soon overtook Kitto in popularity. Based on the language of the KJV, this dictionary was the first to contain a complete list of proper names in the Old and the New Testament and the Apocrypha. Its material on topography is superior to that on natural science. The dictionary was designed to be noncontroversial, and some of its subjects are represented by several articles, each treating the matter from a different point of view. A revised American edition by Horatio Balch Hackett, assisted by Ezra Abbot, was published in 4 volumes (New York, 1870) under the title *Dr. William Smith's Dictionary of the Bible; Comprising Its Antiquities, Biography, Geography, and Natural History.* Since then the multivolume work has spawned a number of one-volume editions. Being in the public domain, the multivolume work is still to be found as a reprint.

Deserving of more than passing mention is Thomas Kelly Cheyne and John Sutherland Black's *Encyclopaedia biblica: A Critical Dictionary of the Literary, Political, and Religious History, the Archaeology, Geography, and*

Natural History of the Bible, 4 vols. (London: Adam and Charles Black, 1899–1903). The great number of leading biblical scholars contributing to this work and the generally high degree of accuracy and completeness pervading it placed it high on scholars' lists, despite what some considered unnecessary skepticism and undue emphasis on conjectural criticism, complaints that seem inapposite after the space of a century of hermeneutical inquiry. The fact that a reprint was made about seventy-five years later (New York: Gordon Press, 1977) suggests the secure foundation of *EB*'s structure.

A less technical production designed also for the nonspecialist was undertaken by James Hastings, with the assistance of John Alexander Selbie, Andrew Bruce Davidson, Samuel Rolles Driver, and Henry Barclay Swete. The title, *A Dictionary of the Bible, Dealing with Its Language, Literature, and Contents, Including the Biblical Theology,* 4 vols. (New York: Charles Scribner's, 1898–1902; extra vol., 1904), abbreviated *HDB,* indicates the broad scope of this work. Beware of the hazard of "lust for the latest." Older works of this quality are not to be ignored. Jewish scholars like Wilhelm Bacher made signal contributions to this set, and Sir William Ramsay, who helped ancient Asia Minor come alive for New Testament students, contributed numerous articles of considerable durability to all of the volumes in this set.

A moderate type of French Roman Catholic biblical scholarship is represented in Fulcran Grégoire Vigouroux, *Dictionnaire de la Bible,* 5 vols. (Paris: Letouzey et Ané, 1895–1912; supplements by various editors, including Louis Pirot, beginning in 1928, André Robert, H. Cazellez, A. Feuillet, et al., 1928–). This carefully compiled dictionary will, despite the mold on some of its articles, meet the taste of students for gourmet fare. Bo Reicke and Leonhard Rost answer in German with historical flavor in *Biblisch-historisches Handwörterbuch: Landeskunde, Geschichte, Religion, Kultur, Literatur,* 4 vols. (Göttingen: Vandenhoeck & Ruprecht, 1962–79). Pseudepigraphic writings may be neglected in some small dictionaries, but not in *Gad Danske Bibel Lexikon,* ed. Eduard Nielsen and Bent Noack, 2 vols. (Copenhagen: G. E. C. Gad, 1965–66).

For those who read only English, and for all who wish a quick trip to knowledge in the fast-moving world of developments in biblical research, two works dominate the field. The first is *The Anchor Bible Dictionary* (*ABD*), ed. David Noel Freedman, and associates Gary A. Herion, David F. Graf, and John David Pleins, 6 vols. (New York: Doubleday, 1992). The discussion, for example, of the census recorded in Luke 2, one of two under the general entry "Census," is a model of fidelity to the state of knowledge and is quite representative of the responsible scholarship that floods this dictionary without sinking in bewildering verbiage the broader public that is purportedly envisaged by contributors to the Anchor Bible Series (AB).

Second, but not always in breadth of treatment, is *The International Standard Bible Encyclopaedia* (*ISBE*), rev. ed. Geoffrey W. Bromiley, with associates

Everett F. Harrison, Roland K. Harrison, and William Sanford LaSor, 4 vols. (Grand Rapids: Eerdmans, 1979–88). This is a "fully revised" edition of what had long been a fixture in ministers' studies.[2] A random comparison of entries suggests the importance of making use of more than one dictionary. For example, *ISBE* not only contains specific entries on Bible commentaries and Bible dictionaries but also lists outstanding commentaries at the end of each article on a biblical book, whereas *ABD* offers no such detailed information in these two categories. Although the number of volumes in *ABD* exceeds those in *ISBE,* the latter has eleven columns in the entry "Apostolic Council," and *ABD* only three under "Jerusalem, Council of." Moreover, it would be imprudent, as also the editors of *ABD* acknowledge, to ignore an earlier publication, *The Interpreter's Dictionary of the Bible* (IDB), 4 vols., edited by George Arthur Buttrick and respected associates (New York, Nashville: Abingdon, 1962). A supplement, ed. Keith Renn Crim (New York, 1976), preludes some of the topical interests that give a special stamp to *ABD.*

IDB is marked by such excellent scholarship that its entries remain sources of basic information, and its organization of data is in some respects preferable to that of *ABD.* For example, *IDB* contains an entire column (*ISBE* about a half column) on the use of the word "apple" in the English Bible (mainly RSV), whereas *ABD* directs its user—à la "find-the-treasure-in-the-dungeon computer game" —to "Flora, Biblical," where one hunts under a sylvan subheading "Fruit Trees, Nut Trees, and Shrubs" and finds the word "Apple," with a further direction to "see Apricot and Quince," both of which mercifully follow without requiring much further search, but offer only a few pits of information; and for "Apple of the Eye" (absent in *ABD*) one must go to *IDB,* which offers more information than *ISBE.* In short, no ministerial library (whether private or church) should be lacking any of the three. In the last analysis, *ABD,* when compared with *IDB* and *ISBE,* marks the boundary between an older fact-gathering emphasis with stress on synthesis and a developing attention to epistemological concerns; or, as the editors express it, "How do we know what we know about this topic?"

In the *Zondervan Pictorial Encyclopedia of the Bible,* 5 vols. (Grand Rapids, 1975), editors Merrill C. Tenney and Steven Barabas endeavored to reach a more sophisticated public and "supply more detail for scholarly study" than was envisaged for the earlier *The Zondervan Pictorial Bible Dictionary* of 1963. As stated in its preface, "the critical and theological position . . . is conservative." In addition to a profusion of black-and-white photographs, there are some spectacular expanses of color, including stunning exhibitions of numismatic items, following the entry "coat" (vol. 1, after p. 896).

---

[2] *The International Standard Bible Encyclopedia,* ed. James Orr, et al., 5 vols. (Chicago: Howard Severance Co., 1915; rev. ed. Melvin Grove Kyle, 1929).

ONE-VOLUME DICTIONARIES

For quick access to basic information one ought to have at hand a one-volume Bible dictionary, and the offerings are attractive. Breadth of treatment and objectivity win a nod in this category for *Mercer Dictionary of the Bible,* undertaken by the National Association of Baptist Professors of Religion, ed. Watson E. Mills (Macon, Ga.: Mercer University Press, 1990), whose topical outreach (note, for example, the entry "Bible and Liberation Movements"), when compared to the coverage in the valiant revision (New York: Charles Scribner's Sons, 1963) under Frederick Clifton Grant and Harold Henry Rowley of the one-volume edition of *HDB,* first published in 1909, indicates how far biblical studies moved in only two decades. Both works include articles or references to apocryphal and pseudepigraphical works. With *ABD,* the Mercer University Press publication manifests a strong interest in topical matters relating to hermeneutical developments in the last decades of the twentieth century.

A bit older, but displaying similar awareness of trends in scholarship, is *Harper's Bible Dictionary,* gen. ed. Paul J. Achtemeier (San Francisco: Harper & Row, 1985), copyrighted by the Society of Biblical Literature, with the RSV (1952) and the 2d ed. of RSV NT (1971) as reference base. Although more massive than an earlier *Harper's* by Madeleine Sweeny Miller and her husband John Lane Miller, it sometimes has less information than the latter. For example, the article "Gospel of Thomas" constitutes about two-thirds the content of the Miller's entry. On the other hand, the 1985 publication, reflecting new topical interests as in *ABD,* and with less emphasis on biblical minutiae, has two lengthy articles titled in sequence, "Sociology of the New Testament" and "Sociology of the Old Testament." Both of the former works reflect increasing ecumenical sympathies and awareness of the fluidity of canonical boundaries, features not found to a similar extent in *New Bible Dictionary,* ed. James Dixon Douglas and Norman Hillyer (Wheaton, Ill.: Tyndale, 1982). This is a completely revised and reset edition of *The New Bible Dictionary* (1962) and claims to be "written in a spirit of unqualified loyalty to Holy Scripture." Like most of the newer one-volume dictionaries it contains bibliographies.

Several European dictionaries have also invited interest. Louis Francis Hartman translated and adapted the 2d edition revised (Roermond, 1954–57) of Adrianus van den Born's *Bijbelsch Woordenboek* (Roermond, 1941) under the title *Encyclopedic Dictionary of the Bible* (New York, Toronto, London: McGraw-Hill, 1963), but special dogmatic pleading infects some of the fine scholarship. More reliable is K. Galling, *Biblisches Reallexikon=BRL* (Tübingen: J. C. B. Mohr [Siebeck], 1937; rev. ed., 1977), in the commentary series HAT. A German work, *Neues Bibel-Lexikon,* ed. M. Görg and B. Lang (Zurich: Benziger, 1988–), is based via its 1st edition (1951) on Born's work.

This work is designed to retire H. Haag's very respected *Bibel-Lexikon* (Zurich: Benziger, 1951–56; 2d ed., 1968).

Aware that we live in the "age of information," InterVarsity Press, the heirs of *A Dictionary of Christ and the Gospels,* brought out an entirely new work, *Dictionary of Jesus and the Gospels,* ed. Joel B. Green, Scot McKnight, and I. A. Marshall (Downers Grove, Ill.: InterVarsity, 1992).[3] Apart from articles on specific terms and subjects relating to Jesus, this work offers a wealth of encapsulated information on such topics as "Anti-Semitism," "Liberation Hermeneutics," "Rich and Poor," "Rhetorical Criticism," "Sociological Approaches to the Gospels," all with ample bibliography. Designed for a broad reading public, this work will certainly be quarried by all who labor in the fields of biblical learning.[4]

ENCYCLOPEDIC WORKS

In addition to the works already mentioned, reference should be made to publications that reflect special historical or ecclesiastical interests. The first of these in point of time is *Realencyklopädie für protestantische Theologie und Kirche,* ed. Johann Jakob Herzog, 21 vols. and index vol. (Hamburg, Stuttgart, and Gotha, 1854–68; 2d ed. Herzog, assisted by Gustav Leopold Plitt and after Plitt's death by Albert Hauck, 17 vols. and index vol., Leipzig, 1877–88; 3d ed. Albert Hauck, 21 vols. and index vol., Leipzig: Hinrichs, 1896–1909; 2 vols. supplement, Leipzig, 1913). The initial attempt to translate this monumental work into English under the editorial leadership of John Henry Augustus Bomberger miscarried for lack of funds (2 vols. through "Josiah"; Philadelphia, 1856–60). But a condensation and modification of Hauck's third edition was later published under the title *The New Schaff-Herzog Encyclopedia of Religious Knowledge, Embracing Biblical, Historical, Doctrinal, and Practical Theology and Biblical, Theological, and Ecclesiastical Biography from the Earliest Times to the Present Day,* ed. Samuel Macauley Jackson, with the assistance of Charles Colebrook Sherman and George William Gilmore, 12 vols. and index vol., New York and London: Funk &

---

[3] *A Dictionary of Christ and the Gospels, HDCG,* ed. James Hastings, with the assistance of John Alexander Selbie and John C. Lambert, 2 vols. (New York: Charles Scribner's Sons, 1906–8). A parallel volume, *Dictionary of the Apostolic Church,* 2 vols. (New York: Charles Scribner's Sons, 1916–18), HDAC, edited by the same scholars, endeavored to do for the rest of the New Testament what the former did for the Gospels, but it did not achieve the same degree of excellence.

[4] Although the newer works attract more attention, a salute is in order for J. L. McKenzie for a remarkable solo effort of permanent quality, *Dictionary of the Bible* (Milwaukee: Bruce Publishing Co., 1965), in which little ground is given up to hallowed but sometimes uninformed tradition.

Wagnalls, 1908–14; reprinted, Grand Rapids, 1949–50; with an extension of 2 vols., *Twentieth Century Encyclopedia of Religious Knowledge,* ed. Lefferts A. Loetscher, Grand Rapids: Baker, 1955). The name Schaff in the title continues to reflect the fact that the English edition is a reworking of a translation by Philip Schaff. *Evangelisches Kirchenlexikon: Kirchlich-theologisches Handwörterbuch,* ed. Heinz Brunotte and Otto Weber, 4 vols. (Göttingen: Vandenhoeck & Ruprecht, 1956–61), follows a similar pattern of presentation but with greater selectivity and on a less comprehensive scale; the biographical material in particular has been substantially curtailed.

More than compensating for the sparseness of the Brunotte-Weber production is the successor to Schaff-Herzog, namely, *Theologische Realencyklopädie.* Editors Gerhard Krause and Gerhard Müller, who began their work in 1967, with the first volume completed in 1977 (Berlin: de Gruyter), express the awareness of changes in approach to the very nature of scientific inquiry and also of shifts in theological positions that led to the publication of this work. Such awareness was coupled with the realization of seminal theological developments, especially in Scandinavia and North America. Some indication of the scope, as well as of undiminished Teutonic flair for interminable prose, is the fact that vol. 22 (1992) begins with the entry "Malaysia." A *Studienausgabe* of the first seventeen volumes and index volume became available in 1993 at the price of $795.00.

Only the highest praise and proper plaudits can be accorded the Roman Catholic productions distilling massively but masterfully the essence of encyclopedic knowledge continually collecting in archives throughout the world. *New Catholic Encyclopedia,* ed. William J. McDonald, et al., 14 vols. and index vol. (New York: McGraw-Hill, 1967), abbreviated *CE,* is appropriately titled. Not only does it antiquate *The Catholic Encyclopedia,* ed. Charles George Herbermann, et al., 15 vols. and index vol. (New York: Robert Appleton, Co., 1907–14; supplements, 1922ff.), but its ecumenical breadth embraces many fronts of contemporary encounter. An older work, *Dictionnaire de Théologie Catholique contenant l'Exposé des Doctrines de la Théologie Catholique, leurs Preuves et leur Histoire (DTC),* successively edited by Alfred Vacant, Joseph-Eugène Mangenot, and Émile Amann, began to appear in Paris in 1903. Reprinting began in Paris in 1909, and volumes of the text of fifteen volumes continued to appear until 1950. Its briefer Italian counterpart of Florentine origin, *Enciclopedia Cattolica,* abbreviated *EC,* includes a dozen volumes published over the relatively short span of 1948 to 1954. The bibliographies accompanying even the briefest articles help make the work an almost indispensable tool. The indexes in volume 12, cols. 2043–58, suggest the surfeit of biblical material available in this encyclopedia. Freer in expression is *Lexikon für Theologie und Kirche,* 2d ed. rev. Josef Höfer and Karl Rahner, 10 vols. and index vol. (Freiburg in Breslau: Herder, 1957–67). Michael Buchberger edited the previous ten-volume edition (Freiburg, 1930–38) of this work. A feature of the new edition is a continuation in three volumes (1966–68) containing texts and commentary of decisions made at Vatican II. Those who can read Spanish will profit from *Enciclopedia de la Biblia,* ed. Alejandro Díez Macho, Sebastian Bartina, and Juan Antonio Gutierrez-Larraya, 6 vols. (Barcelona: Garriga, 1963–65). This set includes articles on New Testament Apocrypha, contains one and one-half columns on targums, and is replete with bibliographies. There are some photographs in color, but most are black-and-white. It was a pleasure to see a picture of the famous inscription documenting the office of politarch in Thessalonica (6:966).

Not to be overlooked are three superior Jewish encyclopedias. The first of these is the elaborate and scholarly *The Jewish Encyclopedia,* prepared under the direction of Cyrus Adler, et al., and edited by Isidore Singer, 12 vols. (New York and London: Funk and Wagnalls, 1901–6), reprinted in 1907 and abbreviated *JE. The Universal Jewish Encyclopedia,* ed. Isaac Landman, 10 vols. and index vol. (New York: The Universal Jewish Encyclopedia, Inc., 1939–44), abbreviated *UJE,* has been drawn up in a more popular vein in the interest of Jewish public relations, and a major part of the work is devoted to modern Jewish life and biography. Both are in the main superseded by *Encyclopedia Judaica,* ed. Cecil Roth, 16 vols. (Jerusalem: Keter; New York: Macmillan, 1971–1972), followed by supplementary volumes.

Perhaps the most significant cooperative scholarly project of the Holy Land today is the publication of *Encyclopaedia Biblica: Thesaurus rerum Biblicarum alphabetico ordine digestus* 8 vols. and index vol. (Jerusalem: Bialik Institute, 1950–1988), begun with Umberto Moshe David Cassuto (d. 1951) as editor-in-chief and Eliezer Lipa Sukenik as head of an imposing editorial board. Published under the auspices of the Jewish Agency and the Museum of Jewish Antiquities at the Hebrew University in Jerusalem, the set is edited in the direction of a comprehensive survey of the field geographically, archaeologically, historically, sociologically, and politically. The format is pleasing to the eye, but Hebrew language purists may take exception to some of the semantic patterns. Students with only a smattering of Hebrew will be pleased to learn that most of the titles cited in the bibliographies appended to articles are in roman type. That most of the articles are written by Israeli scholars is further vivid testimony to a determined spirit of independence not limited to political aspiration.

As a rule of thumb one may say that much of what one can expect to find in the general Bible dictionary is not covered in these encyclopedias. For example, *HDB* has six pages on the "tabernacle of Israel," but *CE* under "Tabernacle" discusses the receptacle for vessels used in the reservation of the Sacrament. This circumstance is indicative of characteristic differences among Bible dictionaries and religious encyclopedias. The former concentrate on biblical terms and expressions, the latter on those phenomena characteristic of each of the sponsoring groups. Thus Schaff-Herzog spotlights scholars and other historically significant personages who have made distinct contributions inside the Reformation tradition. The Roman Catholic and Jewish encyclopedias do the same for distinguished men and women within the groups they especially target. On the other hand, a certain ecumenicity prevails, and instructive varying points of view may sometimes be obtained by checking in the encyclopedias of all three theological groups.

A work that combines the principal features of these encyclopedias with the detail one can expect to find in a Bible dictionary is the *Cyclopaedia of Biblical, Theological, and Ecclesiastical Literature,* ed. John M'Clintock and James Strong, 10 vols. (New York, 1867-81; and two-volume supplement, 1885–87). After the the the death of M'Clintock, the work from the third volume on was completed by Strong. A reprint by Arno Press (New York, 1969) has two photocopied pages of text per page in five volumes, exclusive of the supplement. A reprint by Baker reproduces the text complete in twelve volumes (Grand Rapids, 1968–70). This marvelous work not only lacks the parochialism of the previous encyclopedias, but it also discusses, for example, in addition to classical mythology, the subject of Japanese mythology.[5] Classical antiquities are generously treated. Even in matters where *CE* would possibly be assumed to have a monopoly M'Clintock-Strong should not be overlooked. "Stabat Mater," to take but one example, is treated by the latter in much greater detail. The M'Clintock-Strong production is indeed solid proof that many a scholar of yore did enviable work, and some of what was done so well will perhaps never be done better.

Because of expanding interests in contemporary biblical study, other works of an encyclopedic nature are gaining in popularity. A strong emphasis on Christian cult is present in *Dictionnaire d'archéologie chrétienne et de liturgie,* ed. Fernand Cabrol, Henri Leclercq, and Henri Marrou, 15 vols. (Paris: Letouzey et Ané, 1907–53). In this work the article on Abraham concerns itself with the appearance of Abraham in the intertestamental literature and in liturgy. An article on concordances appears, but the discussion centers on an early fragment consisting of passages taken from the Psalms and seemingly reflecting a rudimentary concordance effort. A bibliography directs the reader to later concordance developments.

A strong comparative theological interest is evident in *Die Religion in Geschichte und Gegenwart: Handwörterbuch für Theologie und Religionswissenschaft,* abbreviated *RGG.* The first edition, prepared under the lenient editorship of Friedrich Michael Schiele, appeared in 5 vols. (Tübingen: J. C. B. Mohr [Siebeck], 1909–13). Hermann Gunkel and Leopold Zscharnack saw the second edition through to publication in 5 vols. (Tübingen, 1927–31), made more serviceable with an index volume edited by Oskar Rühle (Tübingen,

---

[5] It is curious that *ABD* contains an entry "Biblical Scholarship, Japanese," but no other ethnic groups are considered. Why not Spanish or South American?

1932). Under the editorial guidance of Kurt Galling with Hans Freiherr von Campenhausen, Erich Dinkler, Gerhard Gloege, and Knud E. Løgstrup, a fully revised third edition began to appear in Tübingen on October 30, 1956, and was completed late in 1965. The seven volumes, the last a *Registerband* compiled by Wilfrid Werbeck, are relatively indispensable for the study of biblical theology and history of dogma. True, the scholars who produced the first edition adhered to the "history of religions" (*religionsgeschichtlich*) approach then popular, but the second and third editions reveal a return to more biblically oriented articles. All serious students of theology are forewarned that familiarity with the third edition of *RGG* breeds temptation to invest in a private set, for the seven volumes are a reference library worth many times the weight in poorer paper inked with ephemeral theological expression.[6]

Encyclopaedia of Religion and Ethics, edited by that master cataloguer James Hastings, assisted by John A. Selbie, et al., 13 vols. (New York: Charles Scribner's Sons, 1908–12) has given way to a revision under a new title, *The Encyclopedia of Religion,* ed. Mircea Eliade, 15 vols. and index vol. (New York: Macmillan, 1987). Abbreviated *EncRel,* this work concerns itself with almost every conceivable topic germane to the religions of the world and should be consulted on theologically significant biblical terminology. "Baptism," for example, is treated in its Hindu, Jewish, Moslem, and Polynesian contexts, to mention but a few.

WORDBOOKS

Related to the encyclopedic biblical works are the more specialized treatments of select words and their cognates, designed for the reader who is not familiar with the original biblical languages. Alan Richardson's *A Theological Word Book of the Bible* (New York: Macmillan, 1950; Macmillan Paperback 111, 1962) is in this category, along with Jean-Jacques von Allmen, *Vocabulaire biblique,* first published in Neuchatel in 1954. A translation of the second French edition (Neuchatel: Delachaux & Niestlé, 1956) was made by Philip J. Allcock, et al., under the title *A Companion to the Bible* (New York: Oxford University Press, 1958). A kind of miniature Kittel, edited by Edo Osterloh and Hans Engelland and featuring theologically significant terms found in Luther's translation and modern German versions, was first published in Göttingen in 1954 as *Biblisch-theologisches Handwörterbuch zur Lutherbibel und zu neueren Übersetzungen,* 3d ed. (Vandenhoeck & Ruprecht, 1964). Judicious use of the index prefacing this valuable work will aid greatly in

---

[6] One ought not despise an earlier edition of a work. For example, Hermann Gunkel has an excellent article on the Book of Lamentations in *RGG²*, which should be consulted in conjunction with the one by Hans-Joachim Kraus in *RGG³*.

locating significant references. *Bibeltheologisches Wörterbuch,* ed. Johannes B. Bauer (Graz, 1959; 3d ed., 2 vols., 1967), boasts such notable contributors as Jean Daniélou and Ceslaus Spicq but is deficient in methodology. This product of a period when interest in synthesis was high is available in English under the title *Sacramentum Verbi: An Encyclopedia of Biblical Theology,* 3 vols. (New York: Herder, 1970) and takes precedence over Xavier Léon-Dufour, *Vocabulaire de théologie biblique* (Paris: Cerf, 1962), which appears in English as *Dictionary of Biblical Theology* (New York: Desclée, 1967; rev. ed., New York: Seabury Press, 1973).

Developed especially in the interest of helpful proclamation of biblical thought is *Theologisches Begriffslexikon zum Neuen Testament,* published by R. Brockhaus in Wuppertal (vol. 1, 1967; vol. 2/1, 1969; vol. 2/2, 1971). Although a page of this wordbook bears some resemblance to one out of *TWNT* (see chap. 7), the method of presentation is different. *TBNT* uses German headwords, followed by one or more Greek words that fit under a given German term. For example, "Feindschaft (Hass)" presents in succession ἐχθρός and μισέω, each discussed by a different author. Through the rubric "Zur Verkündigung" at the end of selected entries the editors Lothar Coenen, Erich Beyreuther, and Hans Bietenhard show their concern to translate the meaning of the data from then to now. But many a user may wonder about the rationale. "Freude," for example, receives such a discussion, but not "Tier" (considering the environmental and other implications) and, oddly, not "Versuchung."

In the category of prosopography belongs O. Odelain and R. Séguineau, *Dictionnaire des noms propres de la Bible* (Paris: Cerf, 1978)=*Dictionary of Proper Names and Places in the Bible,* trans. and adapted by Matthew J. O'Connell (Garden City, N.J.: Doubleday, 1981)=*Lexikon der biblischen Eigennamen* (Düsseldorf, 1978). This work contains all the proper names to be found in the Old and New Testament of the Jerusalem Bible (original ed. of 1966), in almost 4,000 entries. Each item is defined in its historical and geographical context. Raymond J. Tournay's preface in this dictionary boasts of filling a "real need," for "until now we have had at our disposal only the indexes or lists of geographies or atlases of the Bible or histories of Israel." But Tournay fails to take note of a work by Thomas David Williams, *A Concordance of the Proper Names in the Holy Scriptures* (St. Louis: Herder, 1923), which cites the context for each entry and sometimes provides more detail than is found in Odelain-Séguineau. For example, s.v. "Tertullos," Williams first offers the information "Gr. Tertullos, diminutive of the Latin, Tertius—Third" and then gives New Testament details. The French work says nothing about the etymology.

CLASSICAL AND OTHER ANTIQUITIES

A richly-laden resource often overlooked is *Paulys Realencyclopädie der classischen Altertumswissenschaft,* ed. Georg Wissowa, reprinted (Stuttgart: J. B. Metzler, 1893–), frequently abbreviated RE in classical circles, but ordinarily PW by biblical scholars. Volume 20/2 carries the curious information that the Ethiopian church enrolled Pontius Pilate among the saints (June 25) and that Coptic tradition asserts that he died for the Savior. In vol. 23/1, cols. 1161–1220, Artur Weiser has a long and detailed discussion on the Psalms. For a less leisurely journey and for more current information, consult *Der Kleine Pauly: Lexikon der Antike von Paulys Realencyclopädie der classischen Altertumswissenschaft,* ed. K. Ziegler and W. Sontheimer, 5 vols. (Stuttgart: A. Druckenmüller, 1964–75). But for an even speedier trip one has available *The Oxford Classical Dictionary,* 2d ed. N. G. L. Hammond and H. H. Scullard (Oxford: Clarendon Press, 1970). Very respected as a permanent storehouse of information is Charles Victor Daremberg and Edmond Saglio, *Dictionnaire des antiquités grecques et romaines d'après les textes et les monuments,* 5 vols. and index (Paris: Hachette, 1877–1919).

More explicitly bridging the Greco-Roman world and Christian interests and quite ambitiously conceived is the indispensable *Reallexikon für Antike und Christentum: Sachwörterbuch zur Auseinandersetzung des Christentums mit der antiken Welt,* ed. Theodor Klauser, et al. (Stuttgart: Hiersemann, 1950–), abbreviated *RAC.* This work is designed to demonstrate the continuity and relation between the pre-Christian and early Christian periods. Thus the article "Diakon" discusses the history of the term deacon and pursues a proper interpretation of Acts 6:1-7 for three columns. The person of Abraham is first treated from the standpoint of the Old Testament, then of later Judaism, polytheism, the New Testament, patristic literature, Christian liturgy, Christian exorcism, and finally from the standpoint of Christian art, followed by the relevant literature. Fourteen columns are devoted to "Adoption," by Leopold Wenger and Albrecht Oepke, including a discussion of υἱοθεσία. Oriental, Greek-Roman, and Christian practices are first discussed, and then the metaphorical usage is traced. Perhaps a concern that it might not be completed before the parousia prompted Klauser to state in volume 9 (1976) that new policies had to be initiated. Some articles on less consequential matters had become so lengthy that the reader, he opined, might forget the topic under discussion. Apparently he underestimated what Horace once said about writers' potential for garrulity.[7] May one hope that the last entry, "Hoffnung," in vol. 15 (1991), presages greater obedience to editorial pleading.

---

[7] In his "Art of Poetry," after lambasting irrelevant narrative, Horace uses the analogy of pictorial art in his counsel to writers: "So, you know how to paint a cypress tree. But what's the point

THE USE OF BIBLE DICTIONARIES

The extraordinary range of material in all these tomes, both large and small, is utterly astonishing. The quality likewise is often exceptional, since the writers of such articles are usually chosen because of their competence in the particular area assigned to them. Limits of space, furthermore, discourage prolixity—the fortunes of *RAC* notwithstanding—which is sometimes a bane to intellectual digestion, proper correlation, and coherent assimilation.

The use one may make of these volumes will vary from time to time. Perhaps one of their chief values, in addition to the capsuling of information, is the select bibliographies the larger works offer on most subjects. These must, of course, be brought up to date, but not all the standard works of yesteryear are antiquated in all their parts, and the supplementary volumes will help keep one abreast. To save time in research, it is wise to go directly to any index or index volume appended to the work. If the dictionary includes an index of Greek terms, additional resources are opened. Thus one can readily find Benjamin Warfield's article on "Little Ones," *HDCG*, vol. 2, which illumines such passages as Matt. 18:6; Mark 9:42; and Luke 17:2. Most commentaries carry only a few lines of explanation. Warfield expends almost six columns in an effort to demonstrate that the phrase has reference to the humble disciples of Jesus.

It is wise to keep in mind the varying accents of the different dictionaries and encyclopedias. If, for example, the subject is "Baptism," it might be well to get the general picture out of one of the standard Bible dictionaries, but for specific Jewish considerations *JE* should be consulted. For an exalting religious experience as well as an unanticipated exegetical reward James Cooper's article on "Nunc Dimittis," *HDCG*, vol. 2, should be read, but for liturgical fortunes *CE* is the work to check.

A certain amount of ingenuity must be held in reserve to tap these catalogued treasures. A case in point, when looking for older material on concordances I had no difficulty in finding an excellent treatment under "Concordances" in M'Clintock and Strong, but I had to go to "Greek Language" to check on older editions of New Testament grammars and lexicons. Sometimes the encyclopedia is itself inconsistent. Schaff-Herzog, for example, carries an article on New Testament lexicons but none on New Testament grammars. Such differences in the selection and arrangement of material can be most frustrating.

Caution must be observed at all times in adopting views and conclusions that may have been antiquated by more recent findings—and most works are

---

if your client wants you to show him desperately swimming away from a wrecked ship? . . . In brief, design whatever you wish, but let simplicity and unity prevail" (lines 19–23). In the recording of it one is reminded of another exhortation: Physician, heal yourself.

obsolete even before they are published—but a Bible dictionary and related works judiciously used can greatly enrich one's knowledge and extend one's intellectual and spiritual horizons.

But is it really necessary to know about so many works? Needs vary, but for serious work one cannot be satisfied with partial evidence. Among the reasons a library has for maintaining an inventory of a vast range of books in a specific category is the fact that no one book contains all the information one needs or desires. This is especially true of Bible dictionaries. Be not entranced by dates, nor let the old be subject to disdain. To cite but one further example as invitation to vigilance: The Grant-Rowley revision of *HDB* (see above) distinguishes thirteen Eleazars, whereas one will search in vain in one or another dictionary for even a mention of the name. On the other hand, Grant-Rowley contains only a few bibliographies (see, e.g, entry "Jesus Christ"). The manner in which data are perceived and managed in the mind spells much of the difference between the old and the new productions. But the quantity of basic information differs from book to book. And learning to judge the quality of evidence as marshaled in a given book is part of one's maturation as a scholar.

CHAPTER TEN

Bible Versions

O F ALL THE AIDS at the disposal of the biblical interpreter, none outranks Bible versions. Intensified study of comparative philology and of the growing body of literature reflecting ancient versions has enlightened biblical scholars immeasurably by providing supporting evidence and parallel linguistic phenomena. Great caution will always be necessary in the reclamation of understanding through comparative philology, a highly technical study, which requires keen judgment and wide knowledge of the literature, but recovery of the lost meanings of many words has convinced scholars that they must become increasingly wary of simply proposing textual emendations to solve syntactical and lexicographical problems. To appreciate this shift in attitude among textual critics and to use these tools with skill, the student cannot avoid investigation of the history of ancient versions and careful analysis of their relative merits. Study of modern versions will develop that precision of expression and facility with language which is so essential for clear communication of the meaning of the sacred text.[1]

---

[1] For a general survey of Bible versions, see Ira M. Price, *The Ancestry of Our English Bible,* 3d ed. rev. William A. Irwin and Allen P. Wikgren (New York, 1956); Hugh Pope, *English Versions of the Bible,* rev. and amplified by Sebastian Bullough (St. Louis and London: B. Herder Book Co., 1952); *The Bible in Its Ancient and English Versions,* ed. Henry W. Robinson (Oxford, 1940); and William J. Chamberlin, *Catalogue of English Bible Translations: A Classified Bibliography of Versions and Editions Including Books, Parts, and Old and New Testament Apocrypha and Apocryphal Books,* Bibliographies and Indexes in Religious Studies 21 (New York: Greenwood, 1991). See also Harry M. Orlinsky and Robert G. Bratcher, *A History of Bible Translation and the North American Contribution* (Atlanta, Ga.: Scholars Press, 1991), one of the Society of Biblical Literature centennial volumes; the authors mention Luther's translation of the New Testament and state that it was made in three months, but do not take notice of an extraordinary achievement by Helen Spurrell. For a generally reliable guide on advantages or defects in fourteen of the most commonly used Bible versions, consult Jack P. Lewis, *The English Bible from KJV to NIV: A History and Evaluation,* 1st ed., 1981; 2d ed., "With new chapters on the NKJV, REB, and NRSV," Grand Rapids: Baker, 1991). For the ancient versions, George W. E. Nickelsburg, *Jewish Literature between the Bible and the Mishnah: A Historical and Literary Introduction* (Philadelphia, 1981), takes the literature down to ca. A.D. 200. For editions of the

For an introduction to versions, ancient and modern, one will do well to read John H. P. Reumann, *The Romance of Bible Scripts and Scholars: Chapters in the History of Bible Transmission and Translation* (Englewood Cliffs, N.J.: Prentice-Hall, 1965). This is one of a few scholarly books that one cannot lay down after reading a few pages. Information not ordinarily found in books on Bible translations is available in this selective survey of versions since the Septuagint, including those of Rabbi Akiba, Aquila, Tatian, Marcion, Luther, and many others. On Reumann's captivating story of "Philadelphia's Patriot Scholar," see above, chap. 4.

ANCIENT BIBLE VERSIONS

Next to the Septuagint, the outstanding Bible versions that mark early Jewish and Christian attempts to have the Sacred Scriptures speak to distinctive cultural situations are the targums, the Vulgate, and the Syriac Peshitta.

THE TARGUMS

During the dispersion of the Jews, Aramaic gradually came to be employed as the language of religion, and Jewish scholars proceeded to translate the Hebrew text into a somewhat artificial Aramaic halfway between biblical Aramaic and the spoken language of Palestine. These translations, or paraphrases, designed to explain the text, were called תַּרְגּוּמִים, from תַּרְגֵּם, "to translate." Later targums reflect less and less of the etymological derivation, for the reproduction of the original text gradually came to be of secondary importance, and the sacred text was made the vehicle for homiletic discourses, legends, allegories, and traditional sayings.

Since the targums were originally oral because of a deep-seated distrust among the Jews for competing Bible versions, the history of the various targum texts is difficult to document with conclusive evidence. Thus the authorship and date of origin of the *Targum Onkelos,* also called the *Judaic Pentateuch Targum* or the *Babylonian Targum,* are shrouded in obscurity. Yet this well-known paraphrase of the Pentateuch emerged and rose to a dominant position in the talmudic period about the fifth century A.D. because of its stricter

---

numerous old versions of the New Testament, see Bruce M. Metzger, *The Early Versions of the New Testament: Their Origin, Transmission, and Limitations* (Oxford, 1977). Part 1, Early Eastern versions, covers Tatian's Diatessaron, Old Syriac, Syriac Peshitta, Philoxenian and/or Harclean versions, Palestinian Syriac; the Coptic versions, Armenian, Georgian, Ethiopic, and minor Eastern versions. Part 2, Early Western versions, covers Old Latin, Vulgate, Gothic, Old Church Slavic, and minor Western (Anglo-Saxon, Old High German, Old Saxon) versions.

adherence to the Hebrew text, in the main the Masoretic. For the text of *Targum Onkelos,* see Alexander Sperber, *The Bible in Aramaic: Based on Old Manuscripts and Printed Texts,* vol. 1, *The Pentateuch According to Targum Onkelos* (Leiden: Brill, 1959). One of the mysteries of targumic tradition is a group of manuscripts that treat selected pentateuchal passages, hence the name *Fragmentary Targum.* Sperber's two volumes of *The Fragment Targums of the Pentateuch,* Analecta Biblica 76 (Rome: Pontifical Biblical Institute, 1980) present the texts and English translation, along with informative discussions.

The official Babylonian targum on the Old Testament prophetic writings is the targum linked in some rabbinic tradition with Jonathan ben Uzziel, one of the greatest disciples of Hillel in the first century A.D., and supposedly not extant in final written form till the fifth century. Some scholars claim that *Targum Jonathan* is actually a continuation of *Targum Onkelos,* but the translation is less literal than that of *Onkelos.*[2] Of special interest are the messianic associations the targumist establishes for Isaiah 53. Sperber, *The Bible in Aramaic,* vol. 2, contains *The Former Prophets According to Targum Jonathan* (1959); vol. 3, *The Latter Prophets According to Targum Jonathan* (1962).

In 1956 A. Díez Macho came across a copy of the Palestinian Targum, *Codex Neofiti 1,* in the Vatican library. It had been miscatalogued in 1892 as *Targum Onkelos.* Published in six volumes (Madrid and Barcelona, 1968-79), Díez Macho's edition of this Aramaic text of the Pentateuch, which, according to the colophon, was copied in 1504, contains translations in English, French, and Spanish. The "most paraphrastic of all the Pentateuchal targumim" is *Targum Pseudo-Jonathan,* a misnomer that arose out of a false resolution of an abbreviation. Instead of being ascribed to the author of the Babylonian *Targum to the Prophets,* it should be recognized as a recension of a Palestinian *Targum of the Pentateuch.* Various editions of this text have appeared, but the best is *Targum Pseudo-Jonathan of the Pentateuch Text and Concordance,* ed. E. G. Clarke, et al. (Hoboken, N.J.: KTAV, 1984).

Among the many document that have made the Cairo Genizah famous are seven fragmentary copies of pentateuchal targums, which are especially

---

[2] On ancient New Testament versions, also consult Bruce M. Metzger, *The Text of the New Testament: Its Transmission, Corruption and Restoration,* 3d ed. (Oxford: Oxford University Press, 1992); the main text reprints the edition of 1968, but updates it through an appendix. See also Kurt Aland and Barbara Aland, *The Text of the New Testament,* trans. Erroll F. Rhodes (Grand Rapids: Eerdmans, 1987), 181–217; Arthur Vööbus, *Early Versions of the New Testament: Manuscript Studies,* Papers of the Estonian Theological Society in Exile 6 (Stockholm: Estonian Theological Society in Exile, 1954). On the targums, see Bleddyn J. Roberts, *The Old Testament Text and Versions: The Hebrew Text in Transmission and the History of the Ancient Versions* (Cardiff: University of Wales Press, 1951), 197–213, with detailed bibliography, 307–9; John Bowker, *The Targums and Rabbinic Literature: An Introduction to Jewish Interpretations of Scripture* (Cambridge: Cambridge University Press, 1969). See also Paul Ernst Kahle, *The Cairo Geniza,* 2d ed. (Oxford: Basil Blackwell, 1959), 191–208.

valuable linguistically for the relative purity of their Palestinian Jewish Aramaic dialect. Some of the manuscripts alternate a portion of Hebrew text with a targum. Texts of five of the targums are included by Paul Kahle in his *Die Masoreten des Westens,* 2 vols. (Stuttgart: Kohlhammer, 1927–30), and all seven are included by M. L. Klein, *Geniza Manuscripts of Palestinian Targum to the Pentateuch,* 2 vols. (Cincinnati: Hebrew Union College Press, 1986).

The targumic Writings consist of (1) The Five Scrolls: Lamentations, Canticles, Ruth, Ecclesiastes, Esther; (2) Job, Psalms, Proverbs, Chronicles. In their treatment of the original text they display considerable variation. Paul de Lagarde edited them in *Hagiographa Chaldaice* (Leipzig, 1873), and Sperber includes the Five Scrolls and Chronicles in *The Bible in Aramaic,* vol. 4, pt. 1 (1968).[3]

General access for nonspecialists who merely want translations, some of which may vary in quality, will welcome J. W. Etheridge, *The Targums of Onkelos and Jonathan ben Uzziel on the Pentateuch: With the Fragments of the Jerusalem Targum* (Hoboken, N.J.: KTAV, 1968), as well as *The Aramaic Bible: The Targums,* directed by M. McNamara, to be completed in 19 vols. (Wilmington, Del.: Glazier 1987–).[4]

Aids to Study of the Targumic Literature

One of the best English grammars for study of targumic language is William Barron Stevenson, *Grammar of Palestinian Jewish Aramaic* (Oxford: Clarendon Press, 1924; 2d ed. with appendix by J. A. Emerton, 1962). Emil Kautzsch, *Grammatik des Biblisch-Aramäischen mit einer kritischen Erörterung der aramäischen Wörter im Neuen Testament* (Leipzig, 1884), and Karl Marti, *Kurzgefasste Grammatik der biblisch-aramäischen Sprache, Literatur, Para-*

---

[3] Sperber's 4th vol., pt. 1, *The Hagiographa: Transition from Translation to Midrash* (1963), contains the targums of Chronicles, Ruth, Canticles, Lamentations, and Ecclesiastes. In vol. IVB, *The Targum and the Hebrew Bible* (1973), Sperber discusses the relation of version to original text. On *Targum Onkelos,* see Philip S. Alexander, "Jewish Aramaic Translations of Hebrew Scriptures," *Mikra,* ed. Martin Jan Mulder (Assen: Van Gorcum; Philadelphia: Fortress Press, 1988), 217–18. ("Mikra" refers to the correct reading of the sacred words as handed down through the activities of numerous writers and copyists involved in the transmission of the sacred text.) The substance of Alexander's discussion is reproduced in his article "Targum, Targumim," *ABD* 6:320–31, but the latter does not include references to the text editions of the targums. Some correctives of Sperber's work are offered by the "Madrid School," which came into prominence under the leadership of Alejandro Díez Macho. See, e.g., Emiliano Martinez Borobio, *Targum Jonatán de los Profetas Primeros en traducion babilónica,* vol. 2: *I–II Samuel,* Textos y estudios "Cardenal Cisneros" 38 (Madrid: Instituto de Filología, 1987).

[4] For other targumic literature, see the secondary sources cited above, n. 2; also, Bernhard Grossfeld, *A Bibliography of Targum Literature,* 3 vols. (New York: KTAV, 1972–90); and the *Book List* of the Society for Old Testament Study. See also Orlinsky-Bratcher, *History of Bible Translation,* 1–6.

digmen, Texte und Glossar, Porta linguarum orientalium 18 (Berlin, 1896; 2d ed. rev., 1911; 3d ed. rev., 1925), may also lend expert assistance. Also helpful is M. H. Segal, *A Grammar of Mishnaic Hebrew* (Oxford: Clarendon Press, 1927).

Much appreciated is the work of a German lexicographer and rabbi at Breslau, Jacob Levy's *Chaldäisches Wörterbuch über die Targumim und einen grossen Theil des rabbinischen Schriftthums,* 2 vols. (Leipzig, 1867–68; 3d ed., 1881). Levy could not, of course, anticipate that the resources of this lexicon would assist students in understanding the literature of Qumran. Acquaintance with this work is presupposed in *Neuhebräisches und chaldäisches Wörterbuch über die Talmudim und Midraschim,* with additions by Heinrich Leberecht Fleischer, 4 vols. (Leipzig, 1876–89), an opus that laid the foundations for the scientific study of talmudic Aramaic. Marcus Jastrow, *A Dictionary of the Targumim, the Talmud Babli and Yerushalmi, and the Midrashic Literature* (London: Luzac; New York: Putnam, 1886–1903; 2d ed., New York, 1926; reprinted, 2 vols., 1943, 1950), is substantially an abridgment of Levy's lexicon. Works like Levy's are truly multipurpose, for they lend aid to students of Hebrew literature beyond the limited areas signaled by their titles. For the quick trip, take Gustaf H. Dalman, *Aramäisch-neuhebräisches Handwörterbuch zu Targum, Talmud und Midrasch,* 3d ed. (Göttingen: E. Pfeiffer, 1938; reprints).[5] The lexicon of abbreviations used by the sages is an especially useful feature.

For Qumran Aramaic, see J. A. Fitzmyer, *The Genesis Apocryphon of Qumran Cave I,* Biblica et Orientalia 18 (Rome: Pontifical Biblical Institute, 1966); Appendix II: "A Sketch of Qumran Aramaic," 173–206.

P. Nickels had good intentions when he aimed to help students of the New Testament explore new territory in *Targum and New Testament: A Bibliography together with a New Testament Index* (Rome: Pontifical Biblical Institute, 1967), but, as in the case of Billerbeck's commentary (see chap. 12), the student must cope with the problem of the dating of the material to which references are made.

THE LATIN VULGATE

The demand in the West for translation of the Greek Scriptures increased in direct ratio to the rising popularity of Latin as the foremost literary medium in the third and fourth centuries of our era. Some gauge of the proliferation

---

[5] The first edition of this work was edited by G. Dalman, assisted by P. Theodor Schärf, under the title ערוד החרש *Aramäisch-neuhebräisches Wörterbuch zu Targum, Talmud und Midrasch mit Vokalisation der targumischen Wörter nach südarabischen Handschriften und besonderer Bezeichnung des Wortschatzes des Onkelostargum* (Frankfurt a. Main, 1897).

may be gained from a work that was scheduled by the publisher Herder to cover twenty-seven volumes, *Vetus Itala: Die Reste der altlateinischen Bibel nach Petrus Sabatier neu gesammelt und herausgegeben von der Erzabtei Beuron* (Freiburg im B., 1949–). The corresponding work initiated by Adolf Jülicher for the New Testament, *Itala, das Neue Testament in altlateinischer Überlieferung* (Berlin: de Gruyter, 1938–), continues to devour time and has seen a number of shifts at the tiller.

The number of Latin translations assumed such massive, bewildering proportions that Damasus, Bishop of Rome (366–384), commissioned his secretary Eusebius Sophronius Hieronymus (St. Jerome) to undertake a revision based on a careful comparison with the Greek text. In his preface to the revision, Jerome documents the type of intellectual climate that may be observed whenever fresh words compete with hallowed associations. The danger is especially acute in the case of Bible versions that are employed in the liturgy of the church. Constant usage in sanctified contexts promotes a comfortable type of religious security, which is immediately jeopardized by anything novel. Jerome indeed expresses the trepidation of many an interpreter of Scripture who has known the complaint of the disturbed. How "dare he add, alter, or correct something in the ancient books"![6]

Like its counterparts in other languages, Jerome's version had to bide its time before it won general acceptance. It was not until the ninth century that ultimate emergence over its rivals was assured, and not until the Council of Trent in 1546 was it granted official recognition as the standard for the Roman Catholic Church. In the interval the text suffered considerable contamination.

The recovery of a purer Vulgate text is the object of two major critical editions. The first of these, *Novum Testamentum Domini nostri Iesu Christi Latine secundum editionem Sancti Hieronymi ad codicum manuscriptorum fidem,* was begun in 1878 under the editorial leadership of John Wordsworth with the assistance of Henry White. *Pars prior—Quattuor Evangelia* was published in Oxford: Clarendon Press, 1889–98; *Pars secunda—Epistulae Paulinae* followed in 1913–41. Both of the original editors died during the preparation of this second part, and the installments were completed by Alexander Ramsbotham, Hedley F. D. Sparks, and Claude Jenkins. *Pars tertia—Actus apostolorum, epistulae canonicae, apocalypsis Iohannis* appeared in 1954, with Sparks and Arthur Adams completing a truly magnificent project.

The second major undertaking is titled *Biblia Sacra iuxta Latinam Vulgatam versionem ad codicum fidem . . . edita.* Prior to this publication, texts of the Vulgate were based on the edition sponsored by Pope Clement VIII in 1592,

---

[6] From the "Epistula ad Damasum," in John Wordsworth and Henry White, *Novum Testamentum Latine: Editio minor* (Oxford: Clarendon Press, 1911), xiv. For an understanding of the Old Latin tradition with which Jerome's work had to compete, see Roberts, *Old Testament Text,* 237–46.

a revision of the 1590 edition under Pope Sixtus V. The responsibility for the newer edition was entrusted to a commission of Benedictines, who brought out the first volume (Genesis) in Rome in 1926. Each volume contains a triple critical apparatus. When complete, it promises to be another jewel in the order's crown and a permanent monument to Roman Catholic scholarship.

Best for desk-top use is *Biblia sacra iuxta vulgatam versionem,* 2 vols. (Stuttgart: Württembergische Bibelanstalt, 1969; 2d ed., 1975), edited by R. Weber. This fine edition includes Jerome's prefaces and an appendix, which embraces Prayer of Mannaseh, 3 and 4 Esdras, Psalm 151, and Letter to the Laodiceans. Users of the LXX will welcome the juxtaposed presentation of the Psalms according to both the LXX and the Hebrew text.

The "official" version for public use is *Nova Vulgata bibliorum sacrorum editio, Sacros. oecum. Concilii Vaticani II ratione habita iussu Pauli PP. VI recognita auctoritate Ioannis Pauli PP. II Promulgata* (Vatican City: Libreria Editrice Vaticana, 1979). The text of the New Testament of this edition is used in the diglot edition of Nestle[26].

A handy tool for moving back and forth from the Greek and Latin texts is Theodore A. Bergren's, *A Latin–Greek Index of the Vulgate New Testament.*[7]

Aids to the Study of Latin

Certain to meet most scholars' needs for guidance in the understanding of Latin words is the *Oxford Latin Dictionary,* ed. Peter Geoffrey William Glare. The printing began in 1965, but the first of the eight fascicles appeared in 1968, after a gestation period of thirty-seven years, with publication in one volume in 1982. The original assignment was treatment of "classical Latin from the beginnings to the end of the second century A.D.," but there was some fudging, and most of the jurists quoted in Justinian were patched in.

This dictionary in some respects supersedes *Harper's Latin Dictionary,* a work with a long and singularly checkered history and whose popularity was not necessarily a sign of exceptional scientific merit. It began as a translation by Ethan Allen Andrews of a work produced by Wilhelm Freund of Germany and appeared in New York (1850) under the title *A Copious and Critical Latin-English Lexicon, founded on the larger Latin-German lexicon of Dr. William Freund: with additions from the lexicons of Gesner, Facciolati, Scheller, Georges, etc.* A British revision and reprint was produced by the eminent collector of antique lore, William Smith. After John T. White and Joseph Esmond Riddle published a revised and enlarged version, *A Latin-English*

---

[7] The full title: *A Latin-Greek Index of the Vulgate New Testament based on Alfred Schmoller's 'Handkonkordanz zum griechischen Neuen Testament' with an Index of Latin Equivalents characteristic of 'African' and 'European' Old Latin Versions of the New Testament* (Atlanta: Scholars Press, 1991).

Dictionary (London, 1862), the firm of Harper and Brothers invited Charles Short, a classicist, and Charlton T. Lewis, a student of the classics and also editor of the *New York Evening Post* from 1868 to 1871, to do something more than a face-lifting of the "Andrews" lexicon.[8] Short worked on the letter *A,* and Lewis did the rest, and *Harper's Latin Dictionary,* popularly known as "Lewis and Short" or "Harper's" appeared in 1879. To meet the needs of the average student, Lewis prepared a smaller independent work, *A Latin Dictionary for Schools* (1888). No matter how recent the date on reprints of "Lewis and Short," the product is still an antique from the nineteenth century. But for one who needs less than the Oxford dictionary can offer and sometimes more it remains a valued tool for study of the Latin Vulgate and literature up to the time of the historian Magnus Aurelius Cassiodorus (d. ca. 580).

For a look at the ultimate in Latin lexicography, most students will search in a library for a most extraordinary work published by the distinguished firm of B. H. Teubner (Leipzig and Stuttgart). Dissatisfied with the state of Latin lexicography, the distinguished philologist Friedrich August Wolf called on colleagues at five universities to share the vision of a dictionary that would ultimately embrace all words found in Latin from its earliest stages to the beginning of the seventh century. A glimmer of what was to be appeared in the first fascicle, which contained the letter *A* through *abutor* (Leipzig, 1900). Known as *TLL,* for *Thesaurus linguae latinae,* fascicle 9 of vol. 5/1 interviewed *donec* in 1930. By 1950 editors were well in the middle of the letter *I.* Four years elapsed between the publication of vol. 10/2 fascicle 5 (1987) and the next fascicle (1991). An index of the ancient sources used for citations appeared in 1904. The entire work is certain to cost somewhat less than a Volkswagen, even though it is the Rolls Royce of lexicons. Those who do not expect to be alive when the work is completed can resort for the missing sections to *Lexicon totius latinitatis,* conceived by Aegidius Forcellini (1858–75).

Syriac Versions

Syriac is related to the Aramaic spoken in Palestine at the time of Jesus. The history of New Testament Syriac versions begins with Tatian's harmony of the Gospels, called the Diatessaron (ca. 170), the Gospel narrated διὰ τεσσάρων. The work is known to us chiefly through St. Ephraem's commentary on it and through two forms of an Arabic Diatessaron made from it. Preference for the separated Gospels was responsible for the circulation of a competing version known as the Old Syriac. This rendering of the four Gospels has come down to us in a palimpsest discovered in 1892 by Agnes Smith Lewis of Cambridge in the convent of St. Catherine at Mount Sinai and in a fragmentary

---

[8] Charles Short was also a member of the RV committee.

manuscript of the early fifth century discovered in 1842 in the monastery of St. Mary Deipara in the Nitrian desert west of Cairo. The latter was edited in 1858 by William Cureton, Semitics scholar and assistant keeper of manuscripts at the British Museum, from whom the manuscript derives the name Curetonian Gospels or Curetonian Syriac version.[9]

Both the Diatessaron and the Old Syriac were superseded by a version of the New Testament that, together with its Old Testament counterpart, is known as the Peshitta ("simple" or "vulgate"), the standard version of the ancient Syrian church. The origins of the Old Testament portion are shrouded in obscurity. In the case of the New Testament, many argue that orders issued by Rabbula, bishop of Edessa from 411 to 435, for a thorough revision of the Old Syriac in accordance with the then current Greek manuscript tradition played a significant role. Other Syriac versions were produced, but none enjoyed the popularity of the Peshitta. To fill the need of a critical edition, the Peshitta Institute of the University of Leiden began publication in 1972 of a long-term project, *The Old Testament in Syriac, according to the Peshitta Version,* under the editorship of P. A. H. de Boer and W. Baars. For a multitext adventure follow the fortunes of *Biblia polyglotta matritensia,* under the general editorship of Teófilo Ayuso Marazuela, begun with the publication of a description of the project (Madrid, 1957). In addition to the Hebrew Old Testament, LXX, and Greek New Testament, the project is to include targums, Syriac Old and New Testament, Vetus Latina, Spanish Vulgate, Coptic New Testament, and a translation in Castilian. A publication by the British and Foreign Bible Society, *The New Testament in Syriac* (1905–20), was designed for general use.[10]

The principal lexicon for Syriac studies is *Thesaurus Syriacus,* ed. Robert Payne Smith with the cooperation of Étienne Marc Quatremère, Georg Heinrich Bernstein, Georg Wilhelm Lorsbach, Albert Jakob Arnoldi, Carolus Magnus Agrell, Frederick Field, and Emil Roediger, 2 vols. (Oxford: Clarendon Press, 1879–1901). A supplement, collected and arranged by Smith's daughter, Jessie Payne Margoliouth, appeared in Oxford in 1927. Somewhat less formidable, but based on the thesaurus, is *A Compendious Syriac Dictionary,* also edited by Margoliouth (Oxford, 1903). More recent works include William

---

[9] On Syriac versions in general, see Roberts, *Old Testament Text,* 214–28 (Old Testament); Bruce M. Metzger, *The Text of the New Testament: Its Transmission, Corruption and Restoration,* 3d ed. (Oxford: Oxford University Press, 1992), 68–71, 269–70. For specialized study and bibliography, see, e.g., Arthur Vööbus, *Studies in the History of the Gospel Texts in Syriac,* CSCO 128, Subsidia 111 (Louvain: L. Durbecq, 1951).

[10] On the Peshitta, see P. B. Dirksen, "The Old Testament Peshitta," *Mikra,* 255–97. There is a a growing consensus that the Peshitta was translated from a Hebrew source text, not from an Aramaic targum. See also P. B. Dirksen's *An Annotated Bibliography of the Peshitta of the Old Testament,* Monographs of the Peshitta Institute 5 (Leiden, New York, Copenhagen, Cologne: Brill, 1989).

Jennings, *Lexicon to the Syriac New Testament,* rev. ed. Ulric Gantillon (Oxford, 1926), and Carl Brockelmann, *Lexicon Syriacum,* 2d ed. (Halle an der Salle: Niemeyer, 1928). Raimund Köbert, *Vocabularium Syriacum* (Rome: Pontifical Biblical Institute, 1956), deals with words from the New Testament Peshitta and chrestomathies and does for the Syriac version what Souter or the UBS dictionary does for New Testament Greek. Students look forward to the completion of *A Key to the Peshitta Gospels,* by Terry C. Falla. The first volume, "*'Alaph–Dalath*," appeared in 1991 (New Testament Tools and Studies 14, Leiden: Brill). Carl Brockelmann, *Syrische Grammatik: Mit Paradigmen, Literatur, Chrestomathie und Glossar,* 8th ed., *Lehrbücher für das Studium der orientalischen Sprachen,* IV (Leipzig: Harrassowitz, 1960), provides simple introduction but does not supplant A. Ungnad, *Syrische Grammatik mit Übungsbuch,* 2d ed. (Munich: Beck, 1932). Old but still inviting gratitude from students who need a reference grammar of Syriac but are weak in German is *Compendious Syriac Grammar* (London: Williams & Norgate, 1904), a translation by J. A. Crichton of Theodor Nöldeke's *Kurzgefasste syrische Grammatik,* 2d ed. (Leipzig, 1898). Also practical is Thomas Arayathinal, *Aramaic Grammar,* 2 vols. (Mannanam, India: St. Joseph's Press, 1957–1959). For textual-critical study one must use the immense resources of the microfilm collection of Syrian manuscripts at the Lutheran School of Theology at Chicago.

COPTIC TEXTS

For a millennium and a half a jar lay hidden in Egypt under a boulder about 10 km. from the modern city of Nag Hammadi, nearly 100 km. north of Luxor. In December 1945 its rest came to an end when two brothers from the hamlet of al-Qadot, the ancient site of Chenoboskion, came upon the jar as they were digging for nitrates. One of them, apparently in hope of seeing gold gleam before him, smashed it with his mattock, only to behold a library, the kind of which they had never seen before. From the large jar that they unearthed came twelve books or codices. These codices consisted of a series of papyrus leaves stitched together to form books, which were preserved in leather covers somewhat like our modern briefcases. Inside the cover of one of the codices were eight leaves from another codex, making a total of thirteen. Leaves that were not torn up or burned in ignorance of their value were later peddled for a pittance in Cairo. Not until November, 1953, was it made public that the last of the wandering remains of this primarily Gnostic library had come to rest, twelve through purchase, litigation, and confiscation in the Coptic Museum at Old Cairo, and one (Codex I) through private philanthropy in the C. G. Jung-Institut at Zurich.[11] As each installment of this codex was

---

[11] The part of the codex named in honor of Swiss psychologist Carl Gustav Jung appeared

published, the original portion was sent to the Coptic Museum. Finally, in 1975, all the codices, containing fifty-two separate tractates, were under the care of the Egyptian government.

Much patience has had to bridle curiosity before the ancient documents began to appear in print for close examination by philologists, church historians, historians of religion, and exegetes.[12] But thanks to the efforts of James M. Robinson and his associates, the kind of stranglehold that also choked the flow of knowledge from Qumran, strengthened by scholars' rivalry, was broken. In 1970 the Ministry of Culture of the Arab Republic of Egypt, in concert with UNESCO, named an international committee for the Nag Hammadi codices, whose principal task was to oversee the publication of photographic facsimiles, which subsequently appeared under the title *The Facsimile Edition of the Nag Hammadi Codices* (Leiden: Brill, 1972–79), thus opening the entire library for truly international study. The publication in 1984 of the *Introduction* volume, with addenda and corrections, completed the twelve-volume project. Members of the Coptic Gnostic Library Project under the auspices of the Institute for Antiquity and Christianity, Claremont, California, facilitated the production through reconstruction and conservation of the manuscripts in the Coptic Museum.

---

in a luxury edition, *Evangelium veritatis: Codex Jung f. VIII^v to XVI^v (p. 16–32), f. XIX^r–XXII^r (p. 37–43),* ed. Michel Malinine, Henri-Charles Puech, and Gilles Quispel, Studien aus dem C. G. Jung-Institut 6 (Zurich, 1956), providing plates; French, German, and English translations; comments; and indexes to the Greek and Coptic words. See reviews by Johannes Leipoldt, "Das 'Evangelium der Wahrheit,'" *TLZ* 82 (1957): esp. cols. 830–34; and Walter C. Till, "Bemerkungen zur Erstausgabe des 'Evangelium veritatis,'" *Orientalia* n.s. 27 (1958): 269–86. Pages 33–36, missing from the Jung Codex but later discovered among the papyri in Cairo, are photographically reproduced in Pahor Labib, *Coptic Gnostic Papyri in the Coptic Museum at Old Cairo,* vol. 1 (Cairo: Government Press, 1956), and were accorded appropriate treatment in a supplement to *Evangelium Veritatis,* published with the additional assistance of Till (Zurich, 1961). Perhaps the first complete translation is that of Till, "Das Evangelium der Wahrheit: Neue Übersetzung des vollständigen Textes," *ZNW* 50 (1959): 165–85. Robert McLachlan Wilson and Jan Zandee were called in to assist Malinine, Puech, Quispel, and Till in editing *De resurrectione (Epistula ad Rheginum),* the critical text and translations of further Codex Jung folios xxii^r–xxv^v, pp. 43–50 (Zurich, 1963). For further literature, see Ernst Haenchen, "Literatur zum Codex Jung," *TRu* 30 (1964): 39–82.

[12] An early but detailed survey of the documents found at Nag Hammadi, not all of which are indisputably Gnostic, is that of Henri-Charles Puech, "Les nouveaux Écrits gnostiques découverts en Haute-Égypte (Premier inventaire et essai d'identification)," *Coptic Studies in Honor of Walter Ewing Crum,* The Bulletin of The Byzantine Institute 2 (Boston: Byzantine Institute, 1950), 91–154. For the history of the discovery and peregrinations of the papyri, see studies by Puech, Gilles Quispel, and Willem Cornelis van Unnik in *The Jung Codex: A Newly Recovered Gnostic Papyrus,* trans. and ed. Frank Leslie Cross (London: Mowbray; New York: Morehouse Gorham Co., 1955), including bibliography. See also Walter C. Till, "New Sayings of Jesus in the Recently Discovered Coptic 'Gospel of Thomas,'" *Bulletin of the John Rylands Library* 41 (1959): 446–58.

In a dramatic signal of determination to let the world know what was in the documents, there appeared in 1977 an English translation of practically the entire Nag Hammadi library.[13] This publication was supervised by Marvin W. Meyer and coincided with the availability in 1977 of the entire library in facsimile, except for the *Cartonnage* volume, which appeared in 1979. (The flesh side of the leather used to bind the books was lined with used papyrus pasted to form thick cardboards called cartonnage, producing, as Robinson points out, "a hardback effect."[14]) At the same time the Claremont project was at work on its major scholarly effort, a seventeen-volume complete critical edition of the texts, *The Coptic Gnostic Library*, whose first volume appeared in Leiden (Brill, 1975): *Nag Hammadi Codices III, 2 and IV, 2: The Gospel of the Egyptians (The Holy Book of the Great Invisible Spirit)*, ed. Alexander Böhlig and Frederik Wisse in cooperation with Pahor Labib. This series, enhanced by three related manuscripts housed in Berlin, London, and Oxford, contains the edited Coptic text, with English translations, introductions, notes, and indexes.

In the light of advancing studies, with facts curbing conjectures, one early publication of a text from Nag Hammadi stands out, namely, a collection of sayings ascribed to Jesus and purportedly written by the apostle Thomas: *The Gospel According to Thomas: Coptic Text Established and Translated*, by Antoine Guillaumont, Henri-Charles Puech, Gilles Quispel, Walter C. Till, and Yassah ʿAbd al-Masīh (Leiden: Brill; New York: Harper, 1959). This edition contains the Coptic text (Sahidic dialect with lapses into Achmimic and Subachmimic) faced by a fairly literal but somewhat stiff translation. A publication by Robert M. Grant with David Noel Freedman, *The Secret Sayings of Jesus* (Garden City, N.Y.: Doubleday, 1960), subtitled *The Gnostic Gospel of Thomas* in Dolphin Book C163 (1961), places the *Gospel of Thomas* in the apocryphal gospel tradition and by careful comparative analysis of the literary style, exegetical methods, and theological content relates it to Gnostic, particularly Naassene, thought of the late second century. The book includes William R. Schoedel's more fluent English translation, with brief commentary by Grant on each of the sayings.[15]

---

[13] *The Nag Hammadi Library in English: Translated and Introduced by Members of the Coptic Gnostic Library Project of the Institute for Antiquity and Christianity, Claremont, California*, James M. Robinson, gen. ed.; 3d completely rev. ed. with an afterword by Richard Smith, managing ed. (Leiden: Brill, 1988; paperback, San Francisco: Harper, 1990). For the story of efforts to make the Nag Hammadi codexes available to the general public, see Hershel Shanks, "How to Break a Scholarly Monopoly: The Case of the Gospel of Thomas," *BAR* 16 (1990): 55.

[14] *The Nag Hammadi Library in English*, 14.

[15] The Coptic text, reproduced in Labib, *Coptic Gnostic Papyri* 1, plates 80–99, contains no word divisions—except for points or short slant lines above the last letter of many words—no sentence, section, or paragraph divisions. Although one might hope for scholarly agreement in dividing the text and numbering the sayings, the fact that various editors and authors have numbered

Students may find it interesting to compare one or the other of these early translations of the *Gospel of Thomas* with the one by Thomas O. Lambdin in *The Nag Hammadi Library* (pp. 126–38). One might also examine earlier conclusions in the light of those reached in later studies mentioned in bibliographies that have been industriously compiled, without a sign of tiring, by David M. Scholer, *Nag Hammadi Bibliography 1945–69* (Leiden: Brill, 1971), with on-going supplements. Scholer's compilation appears in the series Nag Hammadi Studies, ed. M. Krause, et al. (Leiden, 1971–). This series takes one into the corridors of a vast palace of learning relating to the Nag Hammadi literature and the implications of its contents.

There is a long future for well-pondered study of gnosticism, and Edwin M. Yamauchi endeavors to assist in the separation of fact from fancy in *Pre-Christian Gnosticism: A Critique of the Proposed Evidences* (Grand Rapids: Eerdmans, 1973; 2nd ed., Grand Rapids: Baker, 1983). For more general orientation in Gnostic studies, consult Kurt Rudolph, *Gnosis: The Nature and History of Gnosticisim,* trans. R. McL. Wilson and K. H. Kohn, ed. R. McL. Wilson (Edinburgh, 1984; paperback, San Francisco: Harper & Row, 1987).[16]

Of the six distinguishable groups of Coptic dialect in which Scripture is extant in varying degrees of completeness the Sahidic, spoken in southern or Upper Egypt, and the Bohairic, a literary rather than spoken language of northern or Lower Egypt, are of greatest interest to biblical scholars. Both

---

from 112 to 119(!) makes it necessary to note with special care what edition an author uses. For an annotated German translation with summary evaluation by veteran Coptist Johannes Leipoldt, see "Ein neues Evangelium? Das koptische Thomasevangelium übersetzt und besprochen," *Theologische Literaturzeitung* 83 (1958): cols. 481–95. For helpful bibliography, see Grant, *The Secret Sayings,* 199–201. The gospel was originally written in Greek. For a restudy of the Oxyrhynchus Papyri 1, 654, and 655 in the light of the Coptic translation, see Joseph A. Fitzmyer, "The Oxyrhynchus *Logoi* of Jesus and the Coptic Gospel According to Thomas," *Theological Studies* 20 (1959): 505–60, with extensive bibliography. On the literature in general, see Søren Giversen, "Nag Hammadi Bibliography, 1948–1963," *Studia Theologica* 17 (1963): 139–87; Ron Cameron, "Thomas, Gospel of," *ABD* 6:540.

[16] For a quick overview, see Rudolph's article in *ABD* 2:1033–40; and if time is limited, select a few items from Rudolph's bibliography, for example, the works listed under the names of U. Bianchi, W. Foerster, H. Jonas, E. Pagels, P. Perkins, G. Quispel, and R. McL. Wilson. For further exploration, *A Coptic Bibliography,* compiled by Winifred Kammerer, Elinor M. Husselman, and Louise A. Shier, General Library Publications 7 (Ann Arbor: University of Michigan Press, 1950). On Coptic versions, see, on the Old Testament, Roberts, *Old Testament Texts,* 229–33, and Kahle, *Cairo Genizah,* 258–61; on the New Testament, Metzger, *Text,* 79–81, 272–74. On the significance of the Nag Hammadi finds for biblical and Gnostic studies and on developments in Gnostic research, see Robert McL. Wilson, "The Gnostic Library of Nag Hammadi," *Scottish Journal of Theology* 12 (1959): 161–70; "Some Recent Studies in Gnosticism," *NTS* 6 (1959): 32–44; and his published dissertation, *The Gnostic Problem: A Study of the Relations between Hellenistic Judaism and the Gnostic Heresy* (London, 1958), with specialized bibliography cited there. For further literature, see Giversen, "Nag Hammadi Bibliography."

the fragmentary Sahidic version of the New Testament, the oldest and perhaps most important, and the Bohairic version, the latest and completely preserved, have been edited by George W. Horner and published in magnificent sets by Clarendon Press.[17]

A linguistic key to some of the vocabulary in the Nag Hammadi literature is offered by F. Siegert, *Nag-Hammadi Register: Wörterbuch zur Erfassung der Begriffe in den koptisch-gnostischen Schriften von Nag-Hammadi* (Tübingen: J. C. B. Mohr [Siebeck], 1982). This work provides a German index to Coptic and Greek words in the ancient texts. The editors of Corpus scriptorum christianorum orientalium (CSCO) have contributed greatly to biblical scholarship by including *Concordance du nouveau testament sahidique* in the Subsidia section of their impressive and reliable collection of basic Ethiopic, Arabic, Armenian, Coptic, Iberian, and Syriac texts, translations, and studies.[18]

Several studies may be recommended for learning the popular forms into which the Egyptian language evolved in the second century, and especially during the christianization of Egypt in the third and fourth centuries A.D. *An Introductory Coptic Grammar (Sahidic Dialect),* by Jack Martin Plumley (London: Home & Van Thal, 1948), offers a short but satisfactory treatment of the Upper Egyptian dialect. For those who handle German, Walter C. Till, *Koptische Grammatik (Saïdischer Dialekt), mit Bibliographie, Lesestücken und Wörterverzeichnissen* (Leipzig: Harrassowitz, 1955), also qualifies as a fine introductory guide. For more thorough study, Georg Steindorff, *Lehrbuch der koptischen Grammatik* (Chicago: University of Chicago Press, 1951), should

---

[17] *The Coptic Version of the New Testament in the Southern Dialect Otherwise Called Sahidic and Thebaic: With Critical Apparatus, Literal English Translation, Register of Fragments and Estimate of the Version,* 7 vols. (Oxford: Clarendon Press, 1911–24), and *The Coptic Version of the New Testament in the Northern Dialect Otherwise Called Memphitic and Bohairic: With Introduction, Critical Apparatus and Literal English Translation,* 4 vols. (1898–1905). Walter C. Till catalogued Coptic biblical fragments scattered in collections all over the world in "Coptic Biblical Texts Published After [Arthur Adolphe] Vaschalde's Lists," *Bulletin of the John Rylands Library* 42 (1959): 220–40. Vaschalde's lists of fragments of the Sahidic, Bohairic, Fayumic, and Achmimic versions are cited by Till (p. 220). For classified bibliographies of Coptic studies in general, see the annual lists published in *Orientalia.*

[18] The parts of the concordance are Louis-Théophile Lefort (1879–1959) *I. Les mots d'origine grecque,* CSCO 124, Subsidia 1 (Louvain, 1950); Michel Wilmet, *II. Les mots autochtones,* 1, CSCO 173, Subsidia 11 (1957); ibid., 2, CSCO 183, Subsidia 13 (1958); and ibid., 3, CSCO 185, Subsidia 15 (1959). Indexes to the concordance are provided by René Draguet in *Index copte et grec-copte de la concordance du nouveau testament sahidique,* CSCO 196, Subsidia 16 (1960). Rodolphe Kasser, ed. of *Papyrus Bodmer III: Évangile de Jean et Genèse I–IV,2 en bohaïrique,* CSCO 177, Scriptores coptici 25 (1958), French translation, CSCO 178, Scriptores coptici 26 (1958), published, in a new font suggesting its unusual script, the Coptic text and a French translation of Papyrus Bodmer 6 — as a Bohairic parchment of Proverbs, perhaps also fourth century, was named at Bibliotheca Bodmeriana, Cologny/Genève, Switzerland — under the title *Papyrus Bodmer VI: Livre des Proverbes,* CSCO 194, Scriptores coptici 27 (1960), and ibid., CSCO 195, Scriptores coptici 28 (1960).

be consulted. Those who would rather begin their appreciation of Coptic via English will welcome T. O. Lambdin's *Introduction to Sahidic Coptic* (Macon, Ga.: Mercer University Press, 1983). The standard lexicon is *A Coptic Dictionary,* ed. Walter Ewing Crum (Oxford: Clarendon Press, 1939),[19] but Crum does not provide etymological data.[20] Instead, he referred his readers to the first edition of W. Spiegelberg's, *Koptisches Handwörterbuch* (Heidelberg: C. Winter, 1921)[21] for such information, which is now even more accessible in J. Cerný, *Coptic Etymological Dictionary* (Cambridge: Cambridge University Press, 1976). Werner Vycichl, following the encouraging lead, traces the history of words in *Dictionnaire étymologique de la langue Copte* (Leuven: Peeters, 1983).

In English the student has available Bruce M. Metzger, *List of Words Occurring Frequently in the Coptic New Testament* (Grand Rapids: Eerdmans, 1962), and Richard Smith, *A Concise Coptic–English Lexicon* (Grand Rapids: Eerdmans, 1983).

For a brief period of time some attention was deflected from the Dead Sea Scrolls as certain scholars moved to speedy exploitation of Coptic sources. The initial impulse for such a shift had been given by specialists and non-specialists alike; scholarly debates and the eavesdroppings of journalists kept the option live. But certain lines for further research already sketched between the two communities and their literature helped to maintain the claim of the Scrolls. The Coptic papyri may appear to have less bearing than the Scrolls on the study of the New Testament, but further study of their contents may change some of the bias. Most certainly their importance for the study of early Gnosticism is not subject to challenge, and we are in a better position to recognize what "gnosticism" meant to "gnostics" rather than to their antagonists, thus far the more available informers. Would that more people developed both facility in the Coptic dialects and ability to dart about quickly in the complex thought world of Gnosticism.

---

[19] For the writings of this highly respected Coptic scholar (1865–1944), a laconic linguist tireless in research, see "A Bibliography of Walter Ewing Crum [1892–1943]," in *Coptic Studies in Honor of Walter Ewing Crum,* vii–xi.

[20] See Rodolphe Kasser, *Compléments au dictionnaire copte de Crum* (Cairo: Institut Français d'Archéologie Orientale, 1964), for supplementary material to Crum's work.

[21] W. Westendorf, *Koptisches Handwörterbuch, bearbeitet auf Grund des Koptischen Handwörterbuchs von Wilhelm Spiegelberg* (Heidelberg: C. Winter, 1965–77) is a revision of this work, with much additional material, which takes account not only of demotic or hieroglyphic Egyptian, but also related languages. To take account of discoveries since the publication of these works is the task of Janet H. Johnson, whose 2d ed. rev. of *Thus Wrote Onchsheshonqy: An Introductory Grammar of Demotic,* Studies in Ancient Civilization 45 (Chicago: University of Chicago Press, 1986) appeared in 1991. The basic reference works are William Spiegelberg, *Demotische Grammatik* (Heidelberg, 1925), and Wolja Erichsen, *Demotisches Glossar* (Copenhagen: Munksgaard, 1954); a supplement is to be published by the Oriental Institute of the University of Chicago.

ENGLISH VERSIONS

Forerunners of the King James Version

It is tempting to linger over the targums, the Vulgate, the Peshitta, Coptic texts, and other early versions, but we must proceed to the more immediate ancestry of the versions that dominate the biblical scene in the English-speaking world. The Vulgate is a vital genealogical link for the version nominally ascribed to John Wycliffe and completed about 1382. Just how much is Wycliffe's and how much the work of his followers is difficult to determine, but the greater part of the Old Testament appears to have been translated by one of Wycliffe's pupils, Nicholas of Hereford. The translation stimulated a reaction that was soon to become a trademark of the craft, for on May 4, 1415, thirty-one years after his death, the Council of Constance excommunicated Wycliffe and ordered his bones to be exhumed from consecrated ground. The digging done, the swirling waters of the River Swift rushed the ashes seaward.

The birth year of the English printed Bible is 1525. The same year William Tyndale, an exile from his beloved England, sent his translation of the New Testament to the presses. Shortly thereafter he set for himself the task of translating the Old Testament. His version of the Pentateuch appeared in 1530. The mold for the stately versions to follow, including that of the Authorized Version, was cast. The stature of the man warrants the inclusion here of a touching document written in 1535 from his prison cell:

> I believe, most excellent Sir, that you are not unacquainted with the decision reached concerning me. On which account, I beseech your lordship, even by the Lord Jesus, that if I am to pass the winter here, to urge upon the lord commissary, if he will deign, to send me from my goods in his keeping a warmer cap, for I suffer greatly from cold in the head, being troubled with a continual catarrh, which is aggravated in this prison vault. A warmer coat also, for that which I have is very thin. Also cloth for repairing my leggings. My overcoat is worn out; the shirts also are worn out. He has a woolen shirt of mine, if he will please send it. I have also with him leggings of heavier cloth for overwear. He likewise has warmer nightcaps: I also ask for leave to use a lamp in the evening, for it is tiresome to sit alone in the dark. But above all, I beg and entreat your clemency earnestly to intercede with the lord commissary, that he would deign to allow me the use of my Hebrew Bible, Hebrew Grammar, and Hebrew Lexicon, and that I may employ my time with that study. Thus likewise may you obtain what you most desire, saving that it further the salvation of your soul. But if, before the end of winter, a different decision be reached concerning me, I shall be patient, and submit to the will of God to the glory of the grace of Jesus Christ my Lord, whose spirit may ever direct your heart. w. TINDALUS[22]

---

[22] Jacob Isidor Mombert, *William Tyndale's Five Books of Moses Called the Pentateuch: Being a Verbatim Reprint of the Edition of M.CCCCC.XXX* (New York and London, 1884), li–lii.

On October 6, 1536, William Tyndale joined his predecessor. His last words were, "Lord, open the eyes of the King of England." Shortly thereafter his strangled body, too, was ashes.

The first printed English translation of the entire Bible appeared in 1535. The work of Miles Coverdale, it represents not so much a translation as an editorial achievement and is a significant link in the genealogy of the Revised Standard Version. The version is notable for its rhythmical prose and was preferred to the Authorized Version in the revision of the Book of Common Prayer. Some renderings, to be sure, will strike the modern ear as quaint. Thus in Judges 9:53 the woman "brake his [Abimelech's] braine panne." Psalm 14:1 (53:1) is rendered: "The fool hath said in his heart: Tush, there is no God." An ephod is an "overbody coat," and Ps. 91:5 reads: "Thou shalt not nede to be afrayed for eny bugges by night."[23]

There appeared in Antwerp in 1537 a large folio English Bible, mainly a compilation of Tyndale's unpublished manuscript of the Old Testament, his corrected edition of the New Testament, sections lifted out of Coverdale's Old Testament, and notes drawn largely from the distinguished Hebraist Konrad (Kürschner) Pellicanus (1478–1556). John Rogers, alias Thomas Matthew, a priest born ca. 1509 in Deritend, Birmingham, and later persuaded to Protestantism, was responsible for this quite unoriginal translation, which may generously be called the first authorized version. Matthew's Bible, dedicated "To the moost noble and gracyous Prynce King Henry the eyght," was temporarily licensed by the king for general reading, but the fact that more than half of the text was the often-anathematized work of William Tyndale later caused it to be denied the royal favor. The redress of Tyndale did not enhance the compiler's chance for longevity; on February 4, 1555, John Rogers was reduced to a heap of ashes. His combination of earlier texts, liberally issued by publishers who felt free to take great liberties with the text of the first edition, lived on to provide a common basis for later revisions.

A revision of Matthew's Bible, commissioned by worldly Thomas Cromwell, was made under the direction of Coverdale and appeared in 1539. Its great size (with cover 16½" x 11") was matched by its price, a princely sum of $15.00; booksellers found themselves overstocked. In the preface Archbishop Thomas Cranmer wrote:

> Here may all manner of persons, men, women, young, old, learned, unlearned, rich, poor, priests, laymen, lords, ladies, officers, tenants, and mean men, virgins,

---

[23] The word "bugge" is defined in *The Oxford English Dictionary* (Oxford, 1989), 2:626, s.v. "bug" 1a, as an "object of terror, usually an imaginary one; a bugbear, hobgoblin, bogy." On Coverdale's work, see James Frederic Mozley, *Coverdale and His Bibles* (London, 1953). The first facsimile edition of this version was published in 1975 (Folkestone, UK: Dawson) under the title *The Coverdale Bible 1535,* with an introduction by S. L. Greenslade. It reproduces the Holkham copy in the British Museum.

wives, widows, lawyers, merchants, artificers, husbandmen, and all manner of persons, of what estate or condition soever they be, may in this book learn all things what they ought to believe, what they ought to do, and what they should not do, as well concerning Almighty God as also concerning themselves and all other[s].[24]

Cranmer's associations with literary reminders of Tyndale involved the usual occupational hazard. He joined the elite company of those who had traded their ashes for beauty. But the "Great Bible" represented progress. It was the first English Bible "apoynted to the use of the churches," despite restrictions imposed a few years later.

A cross between Tyndale's version and the Great Bible, also influenced by John Calvin and Theodore Beza, as well as by the French Bibles of Jacques Lefévre d'Étaples and Pierre Robert Olivétan, was published in Geneva in 1560 by English reformers who sought refuge in Switzerland from Mary Tudor's regime. The version is notable for its introduction of Robert Stephanus's verse divisions of 1551 into the English New Testament, its use of italics for words not found in the original, and for its marginal notes written from an extreme Protestant point of view.[25] The rendering: "They sewed figge tree leaves together and made themselves breeches" (Gen. 3:7) is responsible for its well-known sobriquet, "Breeches Bible." The version was the Bible of Shakespeare and the Pilgrims.

Confusion created by the use of the Great Bible in the churches and of the Geneva Bible in the homes prompted English bishops to undertake revision of the Great Bible. The resulting version known as the "Bishops' Bible" first appeared in 1568, but it did not supplant the popular Geneva Bible. Nonetheless, as the second authorized Bible in England it made an indelible impression and served as the principal basis for the King James Version.

Meanwhile Roman Catholic pressure for a competing Bible version was strongly felt, and in 1582 the New Testament appeared at Rheims. The Old Testament was published in 1609–10, after the English College at Rheims had moved back to its former home in Douay. Hence this version is known in its entirety as the Douay-Rheims Bible or simply the Douay Bible.

Allusion to this version is seldom complete without reference to its heavy, Latinized style, which did not fail to leave its mark on the King James Version. Hebrews 13:16 is translated: "And beneficince and communication do not forget, for with such hostes God is promerited." But the version has its

---

[24] For Cranmer's preface, see Harold R. Willoughby, *The First Authorized English Bible and the Cranmer Preface* (Chicago: University of Chicago press, 1942), 38–50. For the quotation, see p. 44.

[25] On Robert Stephanus's versification, see above, chap. 1, p. 6; Metzger, *Text,* 104. *The Geneva Bible* (Madison, Wis.: University of Wisconsin Press, 1969), a facsimile of the 1560 edition, includes an informative introduction by Lloyd E. Berry.

lighter moments. Revelation 4:3 reads: "He that sate was like in sight . . . to the sardine." And Matt. 4:10 has a charm and dignity all its own: "Avaunt Satan." Later revisions eliminated many of these curiosities and introduced many improvements.[26]

THE KING JAMES VERSION

In 1611 appeared the version that was to parallel and rival the Vulgate in its theological influence and leave its mark on the literature and speech of all English-speaking men and women. King James I had called a conference of churchmen at his Hampton Court, and a Puritan named John Rainolds suggested that a revision of the English Bible be considered. King James I favored the proposal, and it was resolved to make the Bishops' Bible the basis for a new version. The version never claimed to be "authorized," but its use in the churches encouraged its survival in stiff competition with the Bishops' Bible and the Geneva Version, and in popular parlance it came to be "The Authorized Version."

One of the noteworthy characteristics of the KJV was the use of italics to indicate words not found in the original. The Geneva Bible was the first English version to follow this practice, which had been introduced by Münster in his Latin version of 1534.[27] An added feature was the introduction of marginal notes. First designed to provide additional comment, as the preface to the version of 1611 states, for "wordes and sentences" of certain "difficultie and doubtfulnesse," which "it hath pleased God in his divine providence, here and there to scatter,"[28] the reference column soon became a catchall for the findings of later revisers, including Bishop Lloyd's insertion in 1701 of Ussher's chronology. The appearance of the biblical page, as found in most editions, prompted Professor Moulton to say that the English Bible was the worst-printed book in the world. "Originally a stately and beautiful book, these embellishments of successive revisers have so crowded its pages with extraneous matter that as printed today it often looks more like a surveyor's manual than a work of literature."[29]

Not only did the version suffer accretions in external matters, but the text itself enjoyed revision from time to time. The last of these was made under

[26] See Hugh Pope, *English Versions,* 337–96.

[27] Ibid., 324–25.

[28] *Records of the English Bible,* ed. Alfred W. Pollard (London: Oxford University Press, 1911), 372. The preface is there printed in full (pp. 340–77).

[29] Edgar J. Goodspeed, *The Making of the English New Testament* (Chicago: University of Chicago Press, 1925), 49. Dewey M. Beegle, *God's Word into English,* rev. ed. (Grand Rapids: Eerdmans, 1965), 128–51, prints the neglected KJV preface in modern spelling.

the direction of Dr. Benjamin Blayney in Oxford in 1769, and it is primarily this edition that is known throughout the English-speaking world.

The King James Version or Authorized Version is justly praised for its stately diction, but simplicity and clarity are not always its chief merits. Criticism is not aimed at such an obvious mistake as "straining at a gnat" (Matt. 23:24), which, as Goodspeed said, remains perhaps the most famous misprint in literature. (But there have been British defenders of its legitimacy.) Nor is it so much the "thou" and "thee," and forms such as "cometh" and "willeth," as the heavy thump of ponderous Latin expressions and involved periods that discourage modern reading of the KJV. This is especially true of the New Testament epistles. The Gospels read with relative ease.

Other obscurities result from the inevitable passage of time, which erodes the edges of language and shapes it differently, so that the images and concepts evoked by the same semantic symbol are vastly different from those it once called forth. The phraseology of Mark 10:14 has its own hallowed contexts, but how many modern readers are really edified by the word "suffer" used in the sense of permit?

But it is not chiefly style and syntax that prompted the demand for further revision. The KJV was translated out of late medieval manuscripts. Shortly after its publication Codex Alexandrinus was presented to the king of England. Vaticanus (MS B) had remained unused in the Vatican library. The Ephraem palimpsest was first deciphered and published 1843–45 by Konstantin von Tischendorf (1815–74), who also rescued the greater part of Sinaiticus from oblivion. The need for a revision based on the new manuscript evidence was keenly felt.

REVISED VERSION

On June 22, 1870, the New Testament Company of the Commission for Revision of the English Bible began its work. Their version of the New Testament was published on May 17, 1881. Journalists considered it an occasion for contemplating the spectacular and after reconsidering achieved the unique. Officials of the *Chicago Tribune* first made special arrangements with Western Union to take the whole revision by telegraph, but concern for accuracy prompted a change of plans and postponement of the reprinting for twenty-four hours. On May 22, 1881, after ninety-seven compositors had labored steadily for twelve hours to set the type, the *Tribune* printed a sixteen-page supplement presenting the complete New Testament as just revised by the English and the American committee. Overcome by their achievement and filled with the spirit of the apocalypse, editors boasted that the public had the news that was, that is, and would be. The revision of the Old Testament consumed considerably more time, and it was not until May 19, 1885, that both testaments were published together.

American scholars had been invited to share in the task of revision, but not all their suggestions were incorporated in the text of the Revised Version (RV), many of them being relegated instead to an appendix. Moreover, the American revisers had agreed not to publish a revision of their own until fourteen years, counting from the time of the 1885 publication, had elapsed. In 1901 the American committees published a revised edition with their proposals incorporated in the text itself. This edition of the Revised Version came to be known as the American Standard Version.

Despite attempts at modernity, both the British and American editions of the Revised Version failed to achieve the objective of a truly contemporary version of Sacred Scripture. Moreover, the sands and rubbish heaps of Egypt were just beginning to give up a vast treasure store of linguistic material that was to make a completely new translation of the Scriptures, especially of the New Testament, imperative.

REVISED STANDARD VERSION/
NEW REVISED STANDARD VERSION

In 1928 the International Council of Religious Education acquired the copyright of the American Standard Version. A committee of scholars appointed by the council recommended a thorough revision of the 1901 version, embodying the best results of modern scholarship and in line with the King James-Tyndale tradition. The revision was authorized in 1937, and in 1946 the Revised Standard Version (RSV) of the New Testament was published. Both testaments were published in 1952;[30] a revision of the Apocrypha was added in 1957. Like its predecessors the Revised Standard Version (RSV), representing some of the best critical biblical scholarship when it was produced, aroused not only generous acclaim but also querulous suspicion and unmodified hostility. It is not surprising therefore that the traditional fate associated with Tyndale's offspring plagued also the revisers of this work, except that pages instead of bodies were burned, in more ways than one.

The use of the word "authorized" led some uninformed readers to conclude that the version had the sanction of a large and representative element in

[30] *An Introduction to the Revised Standard Version of the Old Testament (IRSVOT)* (New York: The International Council of Religious Education, 1952) and *An Introduction to the Revised Standard Version of the New Testament (IRSVNT)* (New York: The International Council of Religious Education, 1946), by the revision committee under chairman Luther A. Weigle, give the history of the RSV and include valuable hermeneutical and exegetical material. See also Ronald Bridges and Weigle, *The Bible Word Book: Concerning Obsolete or Archaic Words in the King James Version of the Bible* (Edinburgh, New York, Toronto: Nelson, 1960).

Christendom. This was not at all the case. The authorization indicated that the version was not a private enterprise, as was the case with contraband revisions of the American Standard Version, but had the approval and sanction of an organized ecclesiastical element, in this case the International Council of Religious Education and its associated members. Allegations regarding the theological bias of the revisers flew hither and yon after its publication, and data from the version were adduced in an attempt to prove that the version denied basic Christian truths. But careful examination suggests that the translators attempted to maintain a scientific objectivity in the handling of their data. On the other hand, warm claims of determined conformity with traditional belief are likewise critically inappropriate and unfair to the scholars responsible for the RSV. The fact that the revisers did not, for example, underrate, depreciate, or minimize expressions that emphasize the deity of Jesus Christ in the epistles does not mean that they unqualifiedly endorsed traditional theological positions. Rather, they permitted the original text to say what they were convinced it actually says and left to the critic and exegete the task of determining whether certain expressions experienced modifying or transforming theological development in the early church.[31]

Produced during a period of transition that would nudge the entire world in the direction of enormous social, intellectual, economic, and technological changes, the RSV was in effect hopelessly obsolete even upon publication. If the King James tradition was to stand up against the competition that developed, even in strongholds of fidelity to what was done in 1611, a thoroughgoing revision was mandatory, and all the more so since caves and sands were surrendering treasures that left no room for complacency in academia. Impelled also by theoretical explorations that were taunting scholars to move beyond the comfortable confines of standardized lines of inquiry, the Policies Committee of the RSV, a standing committee of the National Council of the Churches of Christ, in 1974 authorized the revision of the entire RSV Bible. This revision appeared in 1989 as *The Holy Bible containing the Old and New Testaments with the Apocryphal/Deuterocanonical Books: New Revised Standard Version* (NRSV).[32]

---

[31] On the RSV's approach to developments in scientific study of the Bible, see *IRSVOT,* 8, 11, 14, 27–28, 70–75; and *IRSVNT,* 11, 35, 41. See also Millar Burrows, *Diligently Compared: The Revised Standard Version and the King James Version of the Old Testament* (London, New York, Toronto: Nelson, 1964), which reflects the textual discipline behind departures from KJV.

[32] Bruce M. Metzger, Robert C. Dentan, and Walter Harrelson, participants in the NRSV revision include in *The Making of the New Revised Standard Version of the Bible* (Grand Rapids: Eerdmans, 1991) a brief history of the version and engage in frank discussion, including areas of disagreement, respecting approaches taken by the revisers. The scholars responsible for NRSV crossed denominational and confessional lines. Other notable ecumenical efforts include *Traducion Oecuménique de la Bible* (Paris, 1975) and *Die Bibel: Einheitsübersetzung der Heiligen Schrift, Altes und Neues Testament,* rev. ed. (Stuttgart, 1984). As in the case of the KJV, the translation

Since the RSV was the work of a committee, that version suffered somewhat from inconsistency, but the remarkable thing is that stylistic incongruities are not more noticeable. It often appears in most glaring form in the translation of proper names. When the name carries a special symbolical significance, it is translated, as in Hos. 1:6, "Not pitied" (RSV)="Loruhamah" (KJV). But unlike Moffatt, the RSV missed the wordplay on Achor (=dale of Trouble) in Hos. 2:15. And in Isa. 8:1, 3 the name Mahershalalhashbaz is borrowed from the KJV without benefit of translation, except in a footnote. Again, Moffatt caught the prophet's point: "Spoilsoonpreyquick." The revisers appeared to be uncertain as to the target public. Is it the holder of a pew or the specialist? It appears that the committee responsible for the NRSV endeavored to remove some of the inconsistencies but saw fit to retain others as being characteristic of the mixed set of documents known as the Bible. But it seems that an editorial subcommittee overrode some of the judgments of the scholars on the committee, and it would be a great service to the history of Bible scholarship to have these deviations documented. One suspects that in the matter of inclusive language there was much more debate than the final version suggests. Considerations of inclusiveness demanded some use of dynamic equivalence, the bane of traditionalists accustomed to concordant translation. Compare Ps. 41:5 in NRSV: "My enemies wonder in malice when I will die, and my name perish," with RSV: "My enemies say of me in malice, 'When will he die and his name perish?'"

In any case, students who look for help from the RSV/NRSV in the interpretation of a given text will do well to exercise their critical faculties with more than usual care at certain points. Occasionally a close inspection of the text will reveal a puzzling insensitivity of the translators of the RSV/NRSV to distinctions in verbal aspect. We shall have occasion to discuss some of these in the next chapter.

A casual comparison of RSV and NRSV readily brings to light a number of improvements in the latter. For example, NRSV removes the hybrid "ears of grain" (Mark 2:23) by rendering "heads of grain." The vagueness in RSV's rendering of Phil. 2:5 gives way to clarity. The task of finding others will improve a student's skill in penetrating the inner structure of a text.

With respect to verse divisions the NRSV removes some of the inconsistencies of which RSV was guilty, but in neither edition do the translators give any hint in the preface as to what authority is to be followed in the version. In Matt. 2:1, RSV included the word "saying" in v. 1, whereas in the KJV it appears as part of 2:2. In NRSV, the word is returned to v. 2 but in the form "asking." In the rendering of Luke 19:41, 42 both editions followed the KJV.

---

by Martin Luther required some modernization. The first results appeared in the "Lutherbibel" of 1956, which in the revised edition (Stuttgart, 1970) bears the title *Die Bibel nach der Übersetzung Martin Luthers revidiert 1956/1964 für Arbeit und Studium mit Schreibrand.*

On the other hand, in Matt. 15:5 (RSV and NRSV) the words about honoring one's father are represented in 15:6 of the KJV. At 1 John 5:7, RSV offered no hint in the apparatus that the translation given corresponds to part of 5:6 in the KJV, nor was any reason offered for the silent jettison of the "three that bear record in heaven, the Father, the Word, and the Holy Ghost" (v. 7 KJV). Although NRSV recovers the trinitarian formulation and accounts for the versification, it does so in a manner that adds little light to the textual problem. The margin states: "A few other authorities read (with variations) *7 There are three. . . .*" At the very least, the revisers ought to have indicated that Greek manuscript evidence for the expanded reading is of miserable quality.[33] Readers who compare the two revisions at Rom. 9:5 will wonder what made the NRSV committee adopt a reading contrary to the one in the RSV.

The text followed by the revisers in both testaments is admittedly eclectic. Endeavors to alert readers to the existence of textual problems exposed the RSV contingent to a charge of pomposity. What were users of the first edition of the New Testament (1946) to make of such pedantic and meaningless expressions as "many ancient authorities," "some ancient authorities," "many authorities, some ancient," and "a few ancient authorities" in support of a reading that departed from the one given in the text? Was one to infer from the observation "some" that many ancient authorities stood behind the RSV's choice of text? Conversely, could one legitimately infer from a marginal "many ancient authorities" that the support for the reading in the text is minimal? What was the revisers' methodology? Upon consideration of the matter, editors of the second edition of the New Testament of the RSV (1952), which incorporated a number of changes urged by various church bodies, opted for what looked like a neutral solution for the New Testament and replaced "some" and "many" with "other" to note variations. The result is that we then had notations reading variously "other ancient authorities," "other manuscripts," "other early authorities," or "other authorities." But why does the notation at, for example, 2 Peter 1:21 simply read "other authorities," when, for example, Codex Sinaiticus (א), to cite but one ancient authority, reads the marginal rendering? In annotations to Hebrews, "other manuscripts" appears alongside "other ancient manuscripts." At Acts 15:29 one encounters "other early authorities." What is the average Bible reader to make of all this? NRSV endeavored to improve matters, but further confusion results from an occasional marginal notation: "other authorities, some ancient" (see, e.g., Rom. 14:23 in both RSV and NRSV). Such notation is perplexing, especially since some manuscripts included in the endorsement of readings qualified with "other ancient authorities" are relatively not ancient. In brief, what do the revisers mean by ancient? Frequently RSV submitted an alternate reading in the margin,

---

[33] See Metzger, *Textual Commentary,* 716–18, with bibliography on the history of what has come to be known as the *Comma Johanneum.*

introduced by "Or.". In Rom. 1:1 the main text reads "servant." The margin reads: "Or *slave*." Since amateur readers are inclined to view the main text as having the philological advantage over the marginal readings, the RSV in effect wipes out one of the principal sources of strength in Paul's proclamation of a gospel that takes in all of humanity, including especially the marginalized. Paul says "slave," inviting the recognition of the entire Mediterranean world that he knows only one master. The NRSV at least admits that the Greek is to be rendered "slave," but the practice of using the abbreviation "Gk" followed by a gloss in italics without further explanation suggests to readers that the Greek means one thing and the text another. The RSV's clarifying note on 1 Cor. 11:10 is an exception to the practice, but NRSV forgot the century in which the translation was being made and reads: "Gr lacks *a symbol of.*" The further notation in NRSV: "Or *have freedom of choice regarding her head*" only adds to the reader's perplexity about the warrant for the text, not to speak of bewilderment over the linguistic principles involved. At 1 Cor. 6:9, RSV offered an explanation, albeit inadequate, for the use of the term "homosexuals"; NRSV not only obscures the contrasting types of behavior and distorts social history but does it without a marginal note. What much of this means is that committees responsible for versions serving various publics must deal more intensively with the question of popular versus technical exposition of a text, which is tantamount to asking: To what extent is consideration of political correctness legitimate in scholarly enterprise?

For the serious student, all this means that the NRSV and its predecessors provide a virtually endless stock of data for serious study. For ministers this means that they are professionally obligated to be able to give an answer to any amateur in their congregation who uses one of these versions and asks for professional assistance in deciphering the marginal conundrums or variations in rendering from one version to another. But if, in fact, it should be alleged that the average parishioner has little interest in such matters, perhaps future editions designed for the general public should drop the pedantic posturing and indicate in their prefaces that differences between versions can be traced to variations in manuscript evidence, but that the subject is too technical to treat in a book designed for the general public. At the same time, they must come clean respecting the necessity of engaging in—perish the thought—paraphrase and dynamic equivalence, and not cover up the fact with a high-sounding "or."

To develop some competence in textual criticism one should have at hand one or two of the most up-to-date critical texts. Among the many questions that might be asked by a parishioner may be one involving the text of Mark 2:17. Lovers of the KJV are still with us and will wonder about the loss of wording in RSV/NRSV in the rendering of that passage. These latter versions give no indication that εἰς μετάνοιαν has been omitted, despite the fact that many of the manuscripts used as evidence for other disputed readings support the words. (See also Luke 11:2, where NRSV corrects RSV's lack of marginal notation.)

On the credit side of NRSV one must note the effort made to choose language that is inclusive, albeit with mixed success. Also, we no longer read about "dumb" people (see RSV Mark 7:37) but "mute." On the other hand, less consideration is accorded people like lepers who are victims of prejudice. Despite the fact that the marginal note at Luke 17:12 informs us that "the terms *leper* and *leprosy* can refer to several diseases" the impact of the text, "lepers," will be felt especially in public assembly where no marginal notes are heard. On the other hand, at 1 Cor. 6:9 consideration is shown for same-sex orientation, with the text reading "male prostitutes," but without any marginal note indicating the tenuousness of the rendering (see above).

Departures from traditional readings and renderings are proportionately more numerous in the Old Testament translation in RSV/NRSV. The revisers make it their avowed aim to note all departures from the consonantal text either with references to the ancient versions or with a notation "Cn.," meaning correction or conjectural restoration. The absence of any marginal notations in such passages as Gen. 10:10 and 1 Kings 13:12 is perhaps an oversight. Departures from the pointing of the Masoretic Text are not noted. This imposes on the student the responsibility of distinguishing between those deviations from the KJV that are due to alteration of the MT's pointing and those that are the result of purely linguistic or syntactical inference and reasoning. On occasion the textual notation is not only inadequate but misleading. In the case of 2 Sam. 24:6 the RSV, followed by NRSV, is undoubtedly correct in reading "and to Kadesh in the land of the Hittites," inasmuch as Tahtimhodshi (KJV) is located in Erehwon and not in Palestine, but the reference to "Gk." presents a distorted picture. The reading is found in Lucian's recension of the Greek version but not in the traditional text of the LXX, for which the abbreviation "Gk." also does duty. A useful feature found in the RSV but not in the NRSV is the cross-referencing of Scripture passages used by New Testament writers. In this case RSV is a better multipurpose tool.

The significance of the NRSV cannot be overestimated, and we shall have more to say about its advantages as an interpretive aid. But other versions that this publication has cast into the shade require some consideration. Owing to the rapid proliferation of English versions in recent decades, our review must be sketchy. See handbooks on the history of the English Bible for further details and for information on versions not included in this survey.[34]

OTHER ENGLISH-LANGUAGE VERSIONS

The nineteenth century saw a number of noncommittee type versions of the Bible, but the most noteworthy is a version of the Old Testament, published

---

[34] See, e.g., Pope, *English Versions*, 585–600.

in 1885, whose claim to fame was obscured by the prestige of the RV, which appeared in the same year. At the age of fifty, the translator, Helen Spurrell, already accomplished in music, painting, and sculpture, decided to learn Hebrew with a view to translating the Bible of Israel. Using the unpointed Hebrew text as her base, "she made free use," observes Pope, "of the Samaritan Pentateuch and the Septuagint version, substituting their readings for that of the Hebrew text in a number of passages. . . . She printed her text in paragraphs, not in verses, with the poetical passages laid out as poetry—devices that had just been adopted in the Revised Version."

One of the more notable publications at the turn of the century exhibiting a move in the direction of more modern speech was *The Twentieth Century New Testament,* produced and published in London between the years 1898 and 1901 by an anonymous group of about twenty scholars.[35] The translation was based on the Westcott and Hort Greek text. A revised edition of this work appeared in 1904. Concern for tense distinctions and stylistic nuances marks this lively and still remarkably contemporary translation. The Gospels and epistles follow in the chronological order adopted by the translators, with a brief introduction preceding each book. *The Modern Speech New Testament: An Idiomatic Translation into Everyday English from the Text of "The Resultant Greek Testament"* (New York: Baker & Taylor, 1903), by Richard Francis Weymouth, edited with the assistance of Ernest Hampden-Cook, is also noted for awareness of tenses and, like its predecessor, displays exquisite literary taste. A fifth "newly revised" edition appeared in 1930.

About the same time, James Moffatt, who was to play a leading role in the production of the RSV until his death on June 27, 1944, brought out his *The Historical New Testament* (Edinburgh, 1901), in which not only the Gospels and epistles but all the New Testament documents were presented in the chronological order adopted by the prevailing criticism. Deference to liturgical traditions is apparent in the translation. A complete change showed up in his *The New Testament: A New Translation* (New York: George H. Doran, 1913). Based on Von Soden's text (see chap. 2), it was a modern-speech translation in every sense of the word, except for "thee" or "thou" in address to God. After the publication in 1924 of Moffatt's translation of the Old Testament, it was incorporated into the complete Moffatt Bible published in 1926. A final revision of both testaments appeared in 1935. The many reprintings this translation has enjoyed testify more eloquently than words to the impact that this translation has had on succeeding generations. As an independent piece of English literature Moffatt's pondered Bible translation ranks high; as a translation it is not only a monument to his learning and industry but provides an enchanting experience of the subtle nuances of Hebrew and Greek

---

[35] Kenneth W. Clark identifies some of the collaborators in "The Making of the Twentieth Century New Testament," *Bulletin of the John Rylands Library* 38 (1955): 58–81.

and far outweighs some commentaries whose many more pages deliver far less spiritual cargo. The critical fashions of the era during which Moffatt labored have somewhat dated his masterpiece, but a reading of his rendition of the prophets is like a flash back into history; few have caught their pulsating rhythm quite as well, despite the fact that he was more at home in Greek than in Hebrew. Sometimes he is carried away by the immediacy of the documents. John 19:5 reads: "So out came Jesus, wearing the crown of thorns and the purple robe; and Pilate said, 'Here the man is!'" Rarely does Moffatt obscure, as in his rendering of Matt. 26:26. It is understandable that the RSV/NRSV should repeatedly echo his outstanding version.

Helen Barrett Montgomery's *Centenary Translation of the New Testament* (Philadelphia: American Baptist Publication Society, 1924) is notable not only for being the first modern-speech translation by a woman but also for its arresting expression of the original, supported by vibrant captions for chapters. Check them, they're good. A year earlier William Gay Ballantine abandoned traditional verse divisions in *The Riverside New Testament: A Translation from the Original Greek into the English of Today* (Boston, New York: Houghton Mifflin, 1923; rev. ed., 1934). The year 1923 saw publication also of a New Testament translation by Edgar Johnson Goodspeed,[36] who served with Moffatt in the New Testament section of the American Standard Bible Committee. *The Old Testament: An American Translation,* edited by London-born Baptist John Merlin Powis Smith (1886–1932) and translated by him, together with Theophile J. Meek, Leroy Waterman, and Alexander R. Gordon, appeared in 1927. In 1931 the two translations were printed together as *The Bible: An American Translation.* A revised edition, directed by T. J. Meek, appeared in 1935. Further amplification came in 1939 by adding Goodspeed's *The Apocrypha: An American Translation,* first published separately (Chicago: University of Chicago Press, 1938). The title of the whole work was then changed to *The Complete Bible: An American Translation* (1939). The translations of both testaments are genuinely American, yet not colloquial. A high literary quality pervades the rendering of the Old Testament, and Goodspeed does not fail to revive for readers the vibrancy of the papyri. Occasionally he lets himself be whisked away in pursuit of a contemporary rendering. At Acts 8:28-29 the eunuch "is sitting in his car, reading the prophet Isaiah." Whereupon the Spirit orders Philip, "Go up and stay by that car."

The New Testament in Basic English appeared in New York in 1941. This unique translation was prepared by a committee under the direction of the British Old Testament scholar Samuel Henry Hooke, working in conjunction

---

[36] The intensity of Goodspeed's scholarly outreach is captured in James Cook's *Edgar J. Goodspeed—Articulate Scholar* (Chico, Cal.: Scholars Press, 1981). This biography should be read in connection with Goodspeed's own intriguing map of his life, *As I Remember* (New York: Harper, 1953).

with the British psychologist and educator Charles Kay Ogden of the Ortho-logical Institute, who selected the 850 words used in the regular vocabulary of Basic English. Despite being limited to a select 1,000 words to express the 5,500-word Greek vocabulary, the version recreates the richness of the New Testament message with remarkable deftness. The complete Bible in Basic English was published in 1949 (Cambridge, UK: Cambridge University Press).

In the same decade Roman Catholic translators made significant contribu-tions. A revision of the Challoner-Rheims version of the New Testament was published in Paterson, N.J., in 1941. The format of this version based on the Latin Vulgate and known as the Confraternity Edition of the New Testament is a worthy model for biblical publication, but the text retains an antique flavor. The Old Testament followed in four volumes (1952–69). The entire publica-tion project bears the title: *The Holy Bible: Confraternity of Christian Doctrine* (Paterson: St. Anthony Guild Press, 1941–69). In a notable break from dependence on the Latin Vulgate and in a series of editorial moves that parallels the history of the KJV and developments in scientific approach to the biblical texts, the U.S.A. Bishops' Committee of the Confraternity of Christian Doctrine in effect retired *CCD* and cleared the way for *The New American Bible*, 2 vols. in one (Paterson: St. Anthony Guild Press, 1970). Its subtitle, *Translated from the Original Languages with Critical Use of All the Ancient Sources,* indicates the radical break with tradition.[37] The framed notation on the title page, "With Textual Notes on Old Testament Readings," deserves special attention, for it refers to a section (pp. 325–451) following the New Testa-ment portion. These textual notes, lamentably absent in later editions, offer a marvelous opportunity for comparative analysis of all Old Testament transla-tions. Since the New Testament portion of NAB had not received the careful attention accorded the Old Testament, the sponsoring committee urged a revision of the former, which appeared in 1986 as *The New American Bible: Revised New Testament* (Northport, N.Y.: Costello Publishing Co.; Grand Rapids: Eerdmans). This revised translation of the New Testament, together with the Old Testament portion of NAB, is now included in an Oxford Univer-sity publication, *The Catholic Study Bible: The New American Bible,* ed. Donald Senior, Mary Ann Getty, Carroll Stuhlmueller, John J. Collins (New York/Oxford: Oxford University Press, 1990). This edition has instructive essays, notes, and maps, which readers of any ecclesiastical tradition can use with profit to mind and spirit.

---

[37] On advances in Roman Catholic scholarship, see *The Biblical Heritage in Modern Catholic Scholarship,* ed. John J. Collins and John Dominic Crossan (Wilmington, Del.: Glazier, 1986), ten essays in a volume honoring Bruce Vawter on his sixty-fifth birthday. See esp. John L. McKenzie, "American Catholic Biblical Scholarship 1955–1980," 211-33; Walter Harrelson, "A Protestant Looks at Catholic Biblical Scholarship," 234–55.

Ronald A. Knox followed the Confraternity Edition of the New Testament with *The New Testament of our Lord and Saviour Jesus Christ: Newly Translated from the Vulgate Latin at the Request of Their Lordships, the Archbishops and Bishops of England and Wales* (New York: Sheed & Ward, 1944), a title that smoothly conceals some hierarchical infighting vis-à-vis the Confraternity Edition. The translation combines bold, independent judgment with occasional singular disregard for critical discussions. Thus the sufferings mentioned in 1 Peter 1:11 are associated with the Christian rather than with Christ, but the text of John 7:53 — 8:11 is printed without allusion to the textual problem. Weymouth used square brackets, and *The Twentieth Century New Testament* printed the passage at the end of the Gospel. Knox climaxed his indefatigable labor with the publication of his version of the Old Testament in two volumes in 1949. James A. Kleist and Joseph L. Lilly have endeavored to meet the need for a truly modern Roman Catholic English translation of the New Testament (Milwaukee: Bruce Publishing Co., 1954). Their translation is based on Jesuit Jose Maria Bover's *Novi Testamenti biblia Graeca et Latina* (Madrid, 1943). On the whole the translation by Kleist of the four Gospels is more felicitous than the translation by Lilly of the remainder of the New Testament.[38]

The New Jerusalem Bible, ed. Henry Wansbrough (Garden City, N.Y.: Doubleday, 1985), supersedes *The Jerusalem Bible,* ed. Alexander Jones, et al. (Garden City, N.Y.: Doubleday, 1966), which in the main reproduced the one-volume edition of *La Sainte Bible* (Paris, 1961) and took account of initiatives exhibited at the Second Vatican Council. A revision of this last publication displayed even more scholarly responsibility, appearing under the title *La Bible de Jerusalem: La Sainte Bible traduite en français sous la direction de l'Ecole Biblique de Jérusalem* (Paris, 1973) and begetting a multinational progeny including, in addition to the English of 1985, versions in German (1969), Portuguese (1976), Spanish (1977), and Italian (1985).

The New Testament in Modern English of John Bertram Phillips (New York: Macmillan, 1958; rev. ed., 1973) has enjoyed extraordinary popularity. In a review of this translation we once referred to its interpretation of the linguistic data as "transegesis."[39] By this hybrid we meant to convey the thought that Phillips's work is not only translation, but in many respects an exegesis that makes more precise what other translators may prefer to leave somewhat ambiguous. Phillips in his introduction does indeed express annoyance over the prospect of being charged with interpreting rather than translating the Greek text, but he is in good company and need make no apologies, for, as Moffatt once said, "A real translation is in the main an interpretation," and even the RSV/NRSV translators occasionally indulge themselves (e.g., 1 Cor.

---

[38] See F. Danker's review of this volume in *CTM* 29 (1958): 473–74.
[39] Ibid., 30 (1959): 541–42.

16:12). Yet it must be granted that because of frequent extended interpretations or paraphrases it is more difficult to infer the original from Phillips's rendering than from any other translation or version mentioned in this chapter. On the other hand, Phillips did not aim at writing a "pony" for students of Greek.

In general Phillips achieves his objective to communicate the New Testament in contemporary idiom. His transegesis is lucid and arresting, often brilliant. Only on occasion is the meaning of the original distorted, as in the rendering of "strict governess" for παιδαγωγός (Gal. 3:24; "custodian" RSV). Since the equation suggests an unflattering portrait of British governesses, we interpose a word in their defense. Phillips seeks to avoid theological clichés, but thoroughness and consistency in the avoidance of stereotyped phrases and words are not the chief merits of his work. The stained-glass or ecclesiastically sanctioned terms "bless" and "grace" appear frequently; a "holy kiss" is cooled to nothing more than an anachronistic "handshake" (1 Thess. 5:26). With sensible paragraphing the book invites sustained reading. A student's paperback edition (New York, 1965) remedied for reference work the absence of verse divisions and enumeration in earlier editions. Phillips's translation, though not designed for liturgical use, has much to contribute as another tool for Bible study.

Hugh J. Schonfield claimed that his *The Authentic New Testament,* Mentor Book MD 215 (New York: New American Library, 1958), was the first published English translation of the New Testament by a Jew. With it the student may see old, familiar sights through eyes more accustomed to poring over the Old Testament. Generous use of rabbinic lore challenges inquiry into words and customs that once seemed self-evident. Critical discussions spanning almost a century are reflected consistently; in this respect the translation is even more useful than Moffatt's New Testament, though Schonfield, who follows no particular manuscript or critical edition, is not always up-to-date. His effort to convey the atmosphere of New Testament times is carried even to elimination of traditional chapter and verse divisions.

British scholars, long recognized for competence and sympathy in rendering the Greco-Roman classics, directed their talents to a truly new translation of the Bible into twentieth-century English. Efforts such as the KJV, RV, RSV, NRSV are revisions, not translations. The first portion of the British work, *The New English Bible: New Testament* (Oxford and Cambridge, 1961), abbreviated NEB, was "officially commissioned by the majority of the British Churches," and was greeted with international acclaim.[40] Any burning seems

---

[40] For detailed study of the first edition of NEB New Testament in relation to RSV, see F. Danker, "The New English Bible," *CTM* 32 (1961): 334–47. On Jewish translating, see Harry M. Orlinsky, "The New Jewish Version of the Torah: Toward a New Philosophy of Bible Translation," *JBL* 82 (1963): 249–64; Theophile J. Meek, "A New Bible Translation," ibid., 265–71. *New English*

to have been confined to words. The translation of the entire Bible, complete with the Apocrypha, and with limited revision of the New Testament, appeared in 1970. Like the RSV, the NEB required substantial revision, especially in the Old Testament, and in 1989 *The Revised English Bible with the Apocrypha* (REB) was published in Oxford. For a sampling of reassessments made in this edition, see the treatment of Ps. 81:16 and compare the notes on Psalm 87. Enjoying much broader ecclesiastical participation than the first edition, REB commands the attention of all who welcome scholarly integrity wedded to sensitivity for the sound of language well-tuned.

Translators who aim at translation, not an interlinear crutch for readers lame in Greek, so often hear charges of "interpretive paraphrase." But the very essence of translation is interpreting a document with reasonably equivalent expressions of the language into which it is translated. Retreat into evasive albeit ecclesiastically sanctioned ambiguity or churchly correctness is conscientiously avoided in NEB/REB. The NEB is significant historically for at least two reasons. It climaxes individual production of modern-speech versions with a committee project representative of much of Christendom, and it moves as a vanguard for ecclesiastical concern to catapult the Christian message clear of medieval encasements. A translation that makes the Apocalypse as good a "read" as H. G. Wells's fantasies, and the Book of Acts as racy as some modern novels, can hardly be charged with low aim.

A source of frustration in evaluating the RSV has been the lack of an authoritative printing of the Greek text used. In contrast, R. V. G. Tasker's edition of the Greek text underlying the New Testament portion of NEB, *The Greek New Testament: Being the Text Translated in the New English Bible 1961* (Oxford and Cambridge, 1964) is a thoughtful contribution to scholarly examination of the new translation. The appendix, which includes discussion of the variants recorded in the footnotes, should be of interest to beginners in textual-critical studies as well as to merely curious readers. A corresponding volume for the Old Testament appeared in 1973, *The Hebrew Text of the Old Testament: The Readings adopted by the Translators of the New English Bible.*

Scholarly unobtrusiveness and gracious simplicity are among the virtues of Charles Kingsley Williams, *The New Testament: A New Translation in Plain English* (Grand Rapids: Eerdmans, 1963), based on Alexander Souter's *Novum Testamentum Graece* (Oxford, 1910). Except for 167 additional words defined in a glossary, Williams limits himself to the words listed in the *Interim Report*

Bible, New Testament, Concordance, comp. Edith Grace Elder (London, 1964), retitled *Concordance to the New English Bible: New Testament* in the 2d printing (Grand Rapids: Zondervan, 1965), supplements existing concordances of other versions for locating passages in NEB. Syntactical and grammatical niceties were rendered with a finesse not found in its nearest rival, the RSV, but NRSV closed much of the philological and aesthetic gap.

on Vocabulary Selection (London, 1936). Consciously colloquial but less felicitous than Williams in style is William F. Beck, *The New Testament in the Language of Today* (St. Louis: Concordia Publishing House, 1963), whose chief strength lies in keen awareness of tenses. Beck's version of the Old Testament, valued also by members of the NRSV committee for its nuancing of the Hebrew text, joined his translation of the New Testament, with some revision of the latter, in *The Holy Bible: An American Translation* (New Haven, Mo.: Leader Publishing Company, 1976; rev. ed., Cleveland: Biblion, 1988).

Not to be snubbed is the *New World Translation of the Hebrew Scriptures, Rendered from the Original by the New World Bible Translation Committee* (Brooklyn: Watchtower Bible and Tract Society of New York, Inc., 1950–63). The translation of the New Testament appeared first (1950) and was then combined in 1963 with the various volumes of the Old Testament (1953, 1955, 1957, 1958, 1960). The "orthodox" do not possess all the truth, yet one does well to "test the spirits."

Succumbing to the relentless movement of change in the post–1950s, various groups of scholars whose constituencies favored progress without radical departure from tradition brought their energies to bear on Bible translation in a more modern mode. After the encouraging reception accorded Gerrit Verkuyl's rendering of the New Testament (Berkeley: J. J. Gillick & Co., 1945), a staff of translators — among them Gleason L. Archer, William Sanford LaSor, J. Barton Payne, Merrill F. Unger, et al. — produced a version whose quality of rendering was matched by the sagacity expressed in many of its notes: *The Holy Bible: 'The Berkeley Version' in Modern English* (Grand Rapids: Zondervan, 1959; revised in 1969 as *The Modern Language Bible*).

In 1965 a "transdenominational" group of scholars met at Palos Heights, Illinois, and set in motion procedures that led to the publication of *The Holy Bible, New International Version* (Grand Rapids: Zondervan, 1978), with generous funding from what is now the New York International Bible Society. To this version goes a large measure of credit for breaking some of the hold that the KJV had on much of the English-speaking public, especially in more traditionally oriented circles.

Awareness of developments in linguistics since the end of the nineteenth century is exhibited especially in *Good News Bible with Deuterocanonicals/ Apocrypha: The Bible in Today's English Version,* published by the American Bible Society (New York, 1979). The first installment of this publication was translated by Robert G. Bratcher, special secretary to the translations department of the society, in association with a committee of biblical scholars. It appeared in 1966 as *Today's English Version of the New Testament: A Translation Made by the American Bible Society,* also published as *Good News for Modern Man,* a title not destined for longevity. Those for whom "the word is the thing" and correspondence-rendering the ideal option will resist this version at many a turn of phrase. But those who welcome a challenge to entrenched semantic conclusions will find in this translation a host of opportunities for renewed understanding through the medium of dynamic equivalence.

In *The Discovery Bible: New American Standard New Testament* (Chicago: Moody Press, 1977), Gary Hill invites amateurs to share in the linguistic process. He offers a coding system that highlights words in red, and in some instances with numerals that guide one to an appended "Synonym Glossary," thereby assisting readers to catch some of the *"emphasis, mode of action,* and *synonym distinction"* in the underlying Greek. For example, Luke 6:43 reads (we use italics for Hill's red lettering): "For there is no *good* tree which produces *bad* fruit; nor, on the other hand, a *bad* tree which produces *good* fruit." The specific Greek words for "good" and "bad" are readily found in the glossary.

For new insights into the Old Testament, use *Tanakh: A New Translation of the Holy Scriptures According to the Traditional Hebrew Text* (Philadelphia: Jewish Publication Society, 1985).

Finally, for the grand tour, see *The Cambridge History of the Bible,* a three-volume work published in inverse order: vol. 3, *The West from the Reformation to the Present Day,* ed. Stanley Lawrence Greenslade (Cambridge: Cambridge University Press, 1963); vol. 2, *The West from the Fathers to the Reformation,* ed. Geoffrey William Hugo Lampe (Cambridge, 1969); vol. 1, *From the Beginnings to Jerome,* ed. Peter R. Ackroyd and Christopher Francis Evans (Cambridge, UK, 1969; New York, 1970). On a vast scale the authors depict the origins and place of the Bible in literary, artistic, liturgical, and theological history.

The long history of Bible versions documents the human estimate of the sacred words. Here is light shed from many angles. Here ancient words and antique phrases crackle with fresh meanings. Here is the distilled essence of entire lifetimes devoted to learning. In Bible versions is some of the most precise scholarship one will ever find, for here men and women on whom the world's most critical eyes were fixed have labored. One has only to develop the skill of using these basic products of the interpreter's art to enter into their very studies. To the furtherance of that end we dedicate our next chapter.

---

[41] On modern editions of the Bible, see Margaret T. Hills, *The English Bible in America* (New York: American Bible Society and The New York Public Library, 1961).

CHAPTER ELEVEN

The Use
of English Bible Versions

MODERN BIBLE VERSIONS are especially useful as aids to interpretation because of the precision demanded by the discipline. In the case of versions undertaken by a group of scholars the result represents an even greater wealth of philological and exegetical learning than is possible in a strictly private or individual translation, unless the translator be a Moffatt or a Goodspeed.

A convenient way to make systematic use of modern Bible versions is first to write out your own translation of a given passage, leaving a space of perhaps three or more lines between each line of translation. After you have completed your translation consult one or more modern-speech translations in addition to the REB and the NRSV. Throw in the KJV, if you wish. Note any variations in these versions above the word or phrase in your own translation, with the source of the variant clearly indicated through abbreviations of your choice, Gd (Goodspeed), etc. Be on the alert for variations in punctuation, alterations of tense, departures in syntax, and linguistic changes. The resulting comparison will not only alert you to your own specific lexicographical and grammatical problems, but you will also have within focus the troublesome phrases or passages of your text. In many instances you will note the aptness of an interpretation that never struck you as peculiarly fitting before. In other cases you will be forced to investigate a word or phrase that you took for granted for many years.

GRAMMAR

Versions are helpful, first of all, in alerting one to nuances tinging the never drab clauses of the original, especially the significant overtones of tenses. Compare, for example, the KJV, RSV, NRSV on the rendering of the last verb in Matt. 21:38b. Which of the three has the least robust rendering? Which of these renderings would find support in Moulton's grammar or in BDF?

Compare RSV and NRSV at Mark 9:38, and then check *The Twentieth Century New Testament* on the passage.[1] The comparative and analytic study of versions will repay the user in grammatical dividends.

LINGUISTIC AID

The rash of New Testament translations sets the craft on fire with a zeal to communicate. The competition has yielded some philological gain. Take, for example, the word τετελειωμένων in Heb. 12:23. Is the thought here that the people have now reached moral maturity, or did the author have something else in mind? The NRSV ambiguously reads, "the spirits of the righteous made perfect"; but Goodspeed's rendering, which specifies exactly what the writer had in mind, was available decades earlier: "the spirits of upright men now at last enjoying the fulfillment of their hopes." This rendering, but one of many in the NRSV that shortchange perceptions of the biblical writers, highlights the limitations of committee-directed versions and the need to use other versions for comparison, not to speak of other tools that are available for tuning in on the finer aspects of the text.

The word πρηνής in Acts 1:18 might elicit no special inquiry. On the other hand, a look at Goodspeed and Moffatt, after checking RSV/NRSV, might suggest that the latter's marginal reading, "swelling up," has real merit, but that "falling headlong" is preferable. The context seems to favor a reference to "swelling." An umpire is needed. BAGD cites LSJM for offering "swollen" as a possibility, but a look at that lexicon indicates that the British scholars are guessing, and BAGD prudently points out that "other examples" in the sense of "swollen" are lacking. The German Bauer, BAAR, saves space by ignoring all sponsors of "swollen," except Zigabenus, and states that the rendering "swollen" is linguistically untenable. Conclusion: until other data are forthcoming, RSV/NRSV win on this one, but so do many of their predecessors. One of my favorite versions, *The New Life Testament,* translated by Gleason H. Ledyard for Native Americans (Custer, SD: American Indian Mission, Inc., 1969), reads: "And falling down head first, his body broke open and his insides ran out."

A careful study of versions will aid in the development of precision in the understanding and expression of the meanings of words and may prompt students to undertake lexical and concordance studies of words that they might otherwise have supposed they comprehended thoroughly.

---

[1] For criticism of the judgments of the revisers of the RSV in matters of grammar, see Allen P. Wikgren, "A Critique of the Revised Standard Version of the New Testament," *The Study of the Bible Today and Tomorrow,* ed. Harold R. Willoughby (Chicago: University of Chicago Press, 1947), 388–91.

PUNCTUATION

It has been our experience that students are likely to overlook the placement of such prosaic marks as commas and other punctuation used to clarify syntax. The case of Rom. 9:5 is too well known for reiterative comment. A comparison of translations of Matt. 8:7 suggests an interesting point of interpretation. Most versions attribute a declarative statement to Jesus: "I will come and heal him." But Kleist suggests the possibility of reading the Greek text as a question: "Am I to come and cure him?" In this he shares an awareness that is registered in numerous editions of the Nestle text. The punctuation is really significant. If Jesus employs a question, then the centurion's faith is similar to that of the Syrophoenician woman. Instead of immediately receiving a reassuring word from Jesus he hears a rebuff, "What, you want me to come down?" "Oh, no," says the centurion, "I know I'm not worthy of that, but say only the word." The question of the validity of Kleist's interpretation can be explored in connection with application of literary-critical approaches, such as narrative analysis, that are standard fare in any literary inquiry.

In Matt. 3:3; Mark 1:3; and Luke 3:4 we have what appear to be word-for-word echoes of Isa. 40:3. A closer study of the position of the colon in each of these passages in the NRSV alerts one to the skillful use by the evangelists of the LXX version of the Isaiah passage.

The revisers of the RSV/NRSV do not appear to share the thinking of those responsible for the comma after the words "faithful men" in the KJV (2 Tim. 2:2). Faithfulness does not necessarily assume or guarantee pedagogical ability, but the teaching ability that one already possesses should be faithfully employed. The RSV/NRSV accentuates the latter insight by dropping the comma. Failure to note the difference in the versions might lead one to superficial understanding of the verse.

More serious expository implications inhere in the omission of a comma in the KJV after the phrase "who hath abolished death" (2 Tim. 1:10). The RSV/NRSV appears to make the gospel responsible for all the benefits outlined in the verse. But which version is more faithful to the μὲν—δέ construction? Compare also the theological significance of the punctuation in 2 Cor. 5:19 in KJV, RSV/NRSV, REB, and then compare the marginal notes on this passage.

In Ps. 49:11 a change of a semicolon (KJV) to a comma (RSV), combined with a slight change in syntax, alters the sense of the passage completely. According to the KJV and the American Translation the wicked parade their pride by calling their lands after their own names. Here one can observe the influence of Moffatt on the RSV/NRSV, which makes the point that graves are the dwelling places of the wicked, despite their previous spacious real estate holdings.

Of special significance is the use of quotation marks in the interpretation of John 3. Students may well explore what christological viewpoints or critical views of the fourth evangelist's treatment of ecclesiastical tradition concerning Jesus of Nazareth are reflected in the divergent typographies of the RSV and NRSV.

TEXTUAL CRITICISM

The approach of translators to textual data is an additional fruitful area of study for the inquiring student. Were it not for Phillips's rendering "And thou Bethlehem, land of Judah" (Matt. 2:6), few readers even of the original would be aware of the fact that the RSV/NRSV with its rendering "in the land of Judah" (KJV) is practically approving the conjecture γῆς supplied by Johannes Drusius in the seventeenth century.

Long acquaintance with the KJV in 1 John 4:19 made the adjustment to "We love, because he first loved us" (RSV/NRSV) difficult for some auditors and readers. But the variation compels reassessing the textual evidence, and a study of other translations, including Goodspeed and Moffatt, indicates that the revisers of the KJV were on the right track in their preference for the reading of Vaticanus. God's love is the source of and motivation for the love shown by God's people.

In John 19:29 Goodspeed, Moffatt, and NEB adopt Camerarius's conjecture "javelin, spear." The RSV does not even hint at this intriguing possibility. Compare REB's treatment, and check the discussion in BAGD.

Where were the letters of recommendation mentioned in 2 Cor. 3:2 written? On the hearts of the Corinthians or on the heart of Paul? We never took a second look at Sinaiticus when we first read this verse, until the RSV jolted us to the realization that the logical place for the spiritual writing of letters recommending Paul's ministry is in the lives of the Corinthians, as the latter part of the verse seems to affirm. Yet why did NRSV return to the KJV reading? Count on commentators to debate this one.

In Ps. 137:5 the KJV renders "let my right hand forget her cunning." The RSV/NRSV, following Moffatt's guidance, transposes the letters of the consonantal text and in place of תִּשְׁכַּח ("forget") reads תִּכְחַשׁ ("wither"), one of the readings considered probable in *BHS*.

Versions can indeed render timely assistance in alerting one to significant problems of the text and consequently of interpretation.

EXEGESIS

For the general exegetical task, versions and translations will be found stimulating as well as helpful. The KJV merely transliterates the mysterious

"Sheshach" of the MT in Jer. 25:26. Moffatt rendered this word "Babylon." The RSV, which again follows Moffatt here, states in the margin that the Hebrew term is "Sheshach," a cipher or cryptogram for "Babylon." The NRSV, following a policy of reverting RSV's translation of bynames, returns to KJV's transliteration. A comparison of NRSV and other versions at Ps. 41:9 brings to the surface a problem that might be overlooked. What does it mean to "lift the heel against" someone? REB interprets: "exults over my misfortune." What is the social history of the paralinguistic gesture? Compare Psalm 109 in RSV and NRSV and note the change in the source of imprecations. Why does the NRSV read in 109:6, "They say"? Can the rendering "angelic powers" by REB in Ps. 29:1 be justified? What help do the lexicons give in these matters?

Mark 7:4 reads quite differently in the RSV (following KJV) from the rendering found in Goodspeed, Moffatt, or NRSV. One would hardly guess that the divergent interpretive translations hinge on a mere preposition in the original. The KJV/RSV states that the Pharisees purified themselves on their return from market. The others affirm that the Pharisees purified what they purchased at market. If one has overlooked the problem, a comparison of these versions may initiate a profitable philological investigation.

The renderings of Jesus' replies in Matt. 26:25, 64 (RSV) might suggest that Jesus appreciated the practicality of timely evasions. The student is compelled to investigate the force of the idiom σὺ εἶπας when comparing the unequivocal "You are right!" and "It is true," respectively, of Goodspeed's translation with "You have said so" (RSV/NRSV). Also compare Moffatt's rendering.

To whom does the term θέλημα in 1 Cor. 16:12 refer? Daringly injecting God into the verse, the RSV indicates in a footnote that the reader is being subjected to transegesis rather than strict translation. The NRSV takes a second look at the passage.

What church did Paul greet after he had arrived at Caesarea (Acts 18:22)? Here the KJV/RSV offered no help. On the contrary, its rendering suggests that he went up to the heart of the harbor town and met with the Christians. Goodspeed's geography is much clearer: "When he reached Caesarea, he went up to Jerusalem and paid his respects to the church, and then went on to Antioch." The NRSV likewise does well in not shying away from transegesis in this case.

"Abide in me, and I in you" (John 15:4). What does this word of Jesus as cited in the KJV and RSV mean? It is a literal rendering of the original, but can it be called a translation? *The Twentieth Century New Testament* reads: "Remain united to me, and I will remain united to you." Goodspeed renders "You must remain united to me and I will remain united to you." No commentator could do better, but the NRSV comes close.

What are the "seventy weeks" of Dan. 9:24? The RSV gives expression to a great weight of critical opinion by rendering "seventy weeks of years." Without comment, the NRSV returns to the KJV.

THEOLOGY

A comparison of versions often suggests theological concerns or problems. The fortunes of 1 Peter 2:8 at the hands of translators are a case in point. The Vulgate renders, "Lapis offensionis et petra scandali, his qui offendunt verbo, nec credunt, in quo et positi sunt" ("a stone of stumbling and a rock that will ensure a fall for those who stumble at the word and do not believe, as is their destiny"). The KJV's "which stumble at the word, being disobedient, whereunto also they were appointed" is substantially followed by the RSV/ NRSV. Moffatt expresses the divine predestination even more bluntly: "they stumble over it in their disobedience to God's word. Such is their appointed doom." Phillips, on the other hand, softens the tone with, "Yes, they stumble at the Word of God, for in their hearts they are unwilling to obey it—which makes stumbling a foregone conclusion." The interpretation one adopts bears solidly on the view one takes of the lines of thought in 1 Peter.

The omission by the RSV/NRSV, along with Moffatt and Goodspeed, of Acts 8:37 (KJV) is not without importance for one seeking to understand the convictions of the writer of Acts on Baptism. Standing as it does in a footnote in the RSV/NRSV, the verse documents an early problem in the mission program of God's people.

CRITICAL METHODOLOGY

Translations are bound to reflect the critical presuppositions of the scholars responsible for them. The RSV/NRSV, as we have stated, engages the critical resources of some of the most eminent Old and New Testament scholars. The student should learn to assess properly the results of their labors.

The use of modern English pronouns in the RSV to refer to Jesus in the Gospels and in a passage like Acts 9:5 aroused considerable response in a number of Christian communities. According to the chair of the RSV revisions committee, it was decided "after two years of debate and experiment" to abandon archaic forms "except in language addressed to God."[2] This statement led to unwarranted charges that the revisers intended to deny the deity of Jesus Christ. The fact of the matter is that the revisers were simply attempting to reflect a critical point of view regarding first-century reaction to Jesus of Nazareth. Inasmuch as the conviction that Jesus was the Son of God

---

[2] *An Introduction to the Revised Standard Version of the New Testament* (New York: The International Council of Religious Education, 1946), 56.

presumably developed, according to the revisers, after the death of Jesus, the archaic forms were used in most of the other New Testament writings where Jesus is addressed directly (see Acts 9:13).

The National Museum at Athens displays the evolution of the human form in Greek sculpture from severe constraint to the rhythmic freedom exhibited in the famous discus thrower. Similarly, committee-type Bible versions go through series of changes—with some dictated by political and cultural awareness. The RSV producers eliminated much archaic form but left a few contours for those who would have felt dismay over too much familiarity in address to the Deity. But no anxiety about allegations of contempt was felt by the NRSV committee. Faced with numerous inconsistencies in the RSV, as well as philological reality, the NRSV translators left not a single "thee," "thou," "thine," "art," "hast," or "hadst" for future deletion.[3]

Support for an early second century dating of 2 Peter may be found in 2 Peter 1:1 (RSV/NRSV). The student will note the significant attribution of deity to Jesus Christ, "of our God and Savior Jesus Christ," in contrast to "of God and our Saviour Jesus Christ" (KJV). The revisers evidently were convinced that the late date of 2 Peter warranted a phrasing that would accurately reflect growing Christian concern for unqualified documentation of the deity of Jesus.

The predominating view that Ephesians is probably a circular or catholic letter finds expression in the omission of the words "in Ephesus" in the RSV. The NRSV reverts to the reading in the KJV (Eph. 1:1). Which tool would be especially helpful for determining the rationale behind the decision?

To be fair in the process of criticism one must keep in mind the purpose of a translation. If it is to be used in public worship certain constraints and considerations not imposed on translations for private reading apply. At the same time, the very recognition of such constraints and political considerations implies that one cannot appeal to committee-type versions as a first line of defense for a philological position on the ground that they are produced by groups of eminent scholars.

To derive greater benefit and to feel forcefully the critical impact written into a Bible version it is important to consider not only isolated passages and translations of individual words but also to grasp the total intellectual framework into which the version fits. When this is sympathetically but critically done, the version will display more than a transfer of ancient meanings to contemporary tongues. It will truly prove an efficient tool for Bible study.

Although, for pedagogical reasons, discussion in this chapter is limited to English Bible versions, it should be obvious that all Bible versions, ancient or modern, can be used to ferret out problems and suggested solutions, which can then undergo further investigation at the hand of other tools. Indeed, the more one uses, the richer will be the dividends.

---

[3] For problems connected with the use of archaic English pronouns, see the RSV renderings in Ps. 110:4; Matt. 16:16; 22:44 (cf. Ps. 110:1); Heb. 5:6.

CHAPTER TWELVE

Judaica

THE DIVORCE OF CHURCH and synagogue has left its mark on the history of interpretation. Not until the twentieth century was any concerted effort made to reestablish communications. The losses to both sides have been many and great, but fortunately some of them are not irrecoverable. The publication of *Ancient Judaism and the New Testament* (New York: Macmillan, 1959), in which the distinguished Anglican theologian Frederick C. Grant rebukes the Christian church sharply for failure to assess adequately its immense debt to Judaism, was an attempt to mend the breach. In the same spirit we propose to encourage the Christian student and minister to develop a more sympathetic awareness of the vast resources buried in Jewish literature and to explore afresh the interpretive values enshrined in the synagogue.

The loss of Jewish political independence in 586 B.C. imposed on Judaism a struggle for national survival. When apocalyptic hopes were dashed and revolutionary uprisings failed to usher in a new golden age, the only rallying points left were the laws and ordinances that made Judaism a stronghold of distinctive cultural phenomena. The history of Israel in the lands of its dispersion is the history of a nation painfully growing up as "the people of the Book," bound to the Torah. That history has left its indelible impression on the New Testament writings. One cannot read a page without moving, or reeling, in the realm of Jewish ideas and thought patterns. To understand the New Testament, one must be familiar with the growth of Judaism and with the development of the postcanonical literature in which Israel's longings found expression.

Our earliest formal history comes from the pen of Flavius Josephus (A.D. 37/38–ca. 100), the author of four major volumes: an autobiography, a history of the Jews from earliest times to the war with Rome (*Antiquities*), a history of the Jewish War, and a book of apologetics (*Against Apion*). Benedict Niese's *Flavii Josephi opera, Editio Maior,* 6 vols. and index vol. (Berlin, 1885–95), with a full critical apparatus, is a highly valued edition of the Greek text, but his *Editio Minor,* 6 vols. (Berlin, 1888–95), is given high marks by Karl H. Rengstorf (see below). In the absence of Niese's editions students will find very serviceable a newer German edition, with translation, an introduction, and notes, ed. O. Michel and O Bauernfeind, *Flavius Josephus: De bello judaico/Der jüdische Krieg*, 3 vols. (Darmstadt: Wissenschaftliche Buchgesellschaft, 1959–69). With the Greek the Loeb Classical Library offers an English translation begun by Henry St. John Thackeray (d. 1930), continued by Ralph Marcus (d. 1956) from the fifth volume and by Allen Wikgren in the eighth, and completed by Louis H. Feldman, 9 vols., with general index in the last (Cambridge, Mass.: Harvard University Press, 1926–65).[1] The history of philological work on Josephus is in part a tale of unfulfilled dreams, with mountains of paper left for a few specialists to sift. Karl Heinrich Rengstorf tells the arresting story in a work that a young visitor to a certain lexicographer's study termed "humongous," with price to match: *A Complete Concordance to Flavius Josephus*, 4 vols. (Leiden: Brill, 1973–83). A separate volume by A. Schalit, *Namenwörterbuch zu Flavius Josephus* (Leiden, 1968), registers the proper names. Dedicated to exploration of philological terrain, Thackeray and Marcus began *A Lexicon to Josephus* (Paris, 1930–), but the project outlived them, as well as H. R. Moehring of Brown University, to whom the baton had been passed.

Heavily dependent on Josephus is Emil Schürer's classic introduction to the history of the Jewish people, *Geschichte des jüdischen Volkes im Zeitalter Jesu Christi,* 3d and 4th ed., 3 vols. and index vol. (Leipzig: J. C. Hinrichs'sche Buchhandlung, 1901–11). The second German edition was translated into English (1885–91), but new discoveries, among them the Qumran manuscripts and the Bar Kokhba documents, solicited refinement of older perspectives and stimulated the publication of what H. H. Rowley conceived of as a "new Schürer." Encouraged by Matthew Black, the revision was carried out by Géza Vermès and Fergus Millar under the title *The History of the Jewish People in the Age of Jesus Christ (175 B.C.–A.D. 135),* 3 vols. (Edinburgh, T. & T. Clark, 1973–87). The third volume was issued in two parts, the second of which also contains an index of names and subjects. When reading this work, as well as many others that compare basic theological perceptions in Christianity and Judaism, it is necessary to be aware of tendencies to make disparagement of the latter a platform for aggrandizement of the former. Given such caution, and taking account of the fact that one is not privileged to adopt opinions wholesale without taking account of the primary sources (especially tannaitic documents of the type cited below), one may profitably use the vast

---

[1] Ralph Marcus carefully outlines recent progress in our knowledge of Josephus and suggests reasons for the importance of Josephus for current and future biblical scholarship in a fine summary sketch, to which a helpful bibliography has been appended, "Josephus, Flavius," *Twentieth Century Encyclopedia of Religious Knowledge: An Extension of The New Schaff-Herzog Encyclopedia of Religious Knowledge,* ed. Lefferts A. Loetscher (Grand Rapids: Baker, 1955), 1:614. See also the bibliographies by Heinz Schreckenberg, *Bibliographie zu Flavius Josephus* (Leiden: Brill, 1968), supplementary volume (1979); and Louis H. Feldman, *Josephus: A Supplementary Bibliography* (New York: Garland, 1986).

amount of information contained in these volumes. This same stricture applies, in general, to all scholarly productions, even to those that endeavor to right the wrongs of their predecessors, for objectivity is like the Holy Grail, and who is totally worthy?[2]

Max Leopold Margolis and Alexander Marx, *A History of the Jewish People* (Philadelphia: Jewish Publication Society of America, 1927), is a more extensive, albeit far less detailed, survey, covering the period from Abraham ca. 2,000 B.C. to the opening of the Hebrew University of Jerusalem on April 6, 1925. The book has an extensive bibliography and helpful chronological tables.

In his *Early Israel in Recent History Writing: A Study in Method,* Studies in Biblical Theology 19 (London: SCM Press; Chicago: Alec R. Allenson, 1956), 17 n. 1, John Bright expressed the hope that his teacher William Foxwell Albright would go on to write a comprehensive and up-to-date replacement for earlier, now antiquated works. Bright spoke for himself and without embarrassment to his master in *A History of Israel* (Philadelphia: Westminster Press, 1959), in which he emphasized both the religious and the political factors shaping Israel. In his 3d rev. ed. (London, 1981) he took some account of developments in Pentateuchal criticism and considered new data relative to Israel's origins and "conquest accounts." For a different viewpoint, echoing Wellhausen, see Giovanni Garbini, *History and Ideology in Ancient Israel,* trans. John Bowden (New York: Crossroad, 1988). The histories of Israel currently being written are many, and the two books just mentioned to some extent represent polarities in the discussion. Given the problems of chronology exhibited in the biblical records, it is not likely that an acceptable history of Israel designed for the general reader will soon be written, but the first major work in English since Bright's effort, *A History of Ancient Israel and Judah,* by J. H. Hayes and J. M. Miller (Philadelphia: Westminster, 1986), moves in that direction. As archaeological contributions become more generally recognized by scholars of the text there will be more dialogue between diggers and readers, and new data will most certainly emerge to give more light to all who seek answers when so much is murky.

Many primary source materials for the history of the Jews in Egypt are now published in attractive format in the systematic collection *Corpus papyrorum Judaicarum (CPJ* or *CPJud),* ed. Victor A. Tcherikover with Alexander Fuks

---

[2] William O. E. Oesterley and Theodore H. Robinson, *A History of Israel,* 2 vols. (Oxford: Clarendon Press, 1932); Robert Henry Pfeiffer, *History of New Testament Times: With an Introduction to the Apocrypha* (New York: Harper, 1949), pt. 1; and Wilhelm Bousset, *Die Religion des Judentums im späthellenistischen Zeitalter,* 3d ed. rev. Hugo Gressmann, HNT 21 (Tübingen: J. C. B. Mohr [Siebeck], 1926), remain helpful adjuncts to Schürer's work. On distortions foisted on their successors by scholars such as F. Weber, E. Schürer, P. Volz, and others, see E. Parish Sanders, *Paul and Palestinian Judaism,* passim. On G. F. Moore's "scathing criticism" of Schürer, see Richard Bavier, "Judaism in New Testament Times," in *The Study of Judaism: Bibliographical Essays* (New York, 1972), 12. This bibliographical work by various contributors takes account of secondary literature relating to Judaism from New Testament times to the modern period.

(Cambridge, Mass.: Harvard University Press, 1957–64). The first volume adds a very detailed sketch of "the historical development of the Jewish people in Egypt during the Hellenistic-Roman-Byzantine age" ("Prolegomena," 1–111; quoted from p. 1) to papyri related to Jews and Jewish affairs during the Ptolemaic period. The second volume includes relevant papyri of the early Roman period; the third presents documents of the late Roman and Byzantine period, but without the anticipated *papyri magici*. Helpful references to learned discussions supplement the commentary accompanying each document. A corresponding type of publication for epigraphs was compiled by Jean-Baptiste Frey, *Corpus inscriptionum iudaicarum* (*CII*), 2 vols. (Rome: Institute of Christian Archaeology, 1936, 1952).

George Foot Moore[3] relies heavily on Schürer in his documentation of Pharisaic Judaism, *Judaism in the First Centuries of the Christian Era*, 3 vols. (Cambridge, Mass.: Harvard University Press, 1927–30), acknowledged as one of the finest works on Jewish religion. Moore lays stress on tannaitic materials as sources for the study of "normative Judaism" (a disputed term), an approach followed also by Robert Travers Herford, a Christian scholar noted for his knowledge of rabbinics, who insisted in his *Judaism in the New Testament Period* (London: Lindsey Press, 1928) that 90 percent of Jesus' teachings were of Pharisaic origin. See also his *Christianity in Talmud and Midrash* (London: Williams & Norgate, 1903; reprint, Clifton, N.J.: Reference Book Publishers, 1965).

Joseph Bonsirven in *Le Judaïsme Palestinien au temps de Jésus Christ* (Paris: G. Beauchesne, 1934–1935) contends that Diaspora Judaism, with the exception perhaps of Philo, made little impression on either Christianity or Judaism.

William Farmer's *Maccabees, Zealots and Josephus: An Inquiry into Jewish Nationalism in the Greco-Roman Period* (New York: Columbia University Press, 1956) is an instructive study suggesting a probable connection between the nationalists of Josephus's day and the Maccabees.

The Pharisees are the object of Louis Finkelstein's specialized treatment in *The Pharisees: The Sociological Background of Their Faith*, 2 vols., 2d ed. rev. (Philadelphia: Jewish Publication Society of America, 1940), but his confidence in being able to deduce the structure of pre–A.D. 70 Pharisaism from tannaitic materials requires assessment under careful scrutiny of those sources.

THE INTERTESTAMENTAL PERIOD: APOCRYPHA AND PSEUDEPIGRAPHA

The first important period of Jewish literary production apart from the canonical Hebrew writings is known as the intertestamental period, which

---

[3] Moore's middle name, Foot, is frequently misspelled "Foote."

covers roughly the two centuries preceding and the century following Jesus Christ.[4] The chief religious literary products of this period are known as the Apocrypha and pseudepigrapha. "Apocrypha" comes from the word ἀπόκρυφον, meaning "hidden away." The books in this classification were identified as such either because they were considered too profound for the uninitiated or because they were viewed as spurious or sectarian. The term has come to be applied technically to the noncanonical writings attached to the Old Testament Greek and Latin versions.

Technically, a pseudepigraphical writing is a literary work that claims the authorship of someone other than the real writer, who prefers to remain anonymous for his work's sake, and which nevertheless need not be labeled "forgery." The term "pseudepigrapha" is used loosely and is generally applied to all Jewish productions of the intertestamental period that never enjoyed the status granted the Apocrypha but nevertheless stood in some relationship to these writings. The twofold division is not at all fortunate, for all the writings here under consideration are in effect pseudepigrapha, but no one has been able to introduce a satisfactory substitute. Nor is there a hard and fast line of demarcation even with respect to the Apocrypha, for the Vulgate and editions of the LXX vary in their inclusion of materials.[5]

For many years the standard translation incorporating most of these writings was Robert Henry Charles, ed., *The Apocrypha and Pseudepigrapha of the Old Testament,* 2 vols. (Oxford: Clarendon Press, 1913), but Paul Riessler's translation of the intertestamental literature, *Altjüdiches Schrifttum ausserhalb der Bibel übersetzt und erläutert* (Augsburg: B. Filser, 1928), was in some respects even more complete. Superseding all previous translation work and much of earlier historical treatment is *The Old Testament Pseudepigrapha,* ed. James H. Charlesworth, 2 vols. (Garden City, N.Y.: Doubleday, 1983–85). This work provides translations of the texts, many of which will swim into some student's ken like a new planet, and directs readers to the sources underlying them. The contents of this work are reflected in the list below.

The Dropsie College edition of Jewish apocryphal literature, which began with the publication of the text and translation of 1 Maccabees, ed. Sidney S. Tedesche and Solomon Zeitlin (New York: Harper, 1950), has continued to expand with publications from various firms, but many of the original texts that are hard to come by are not available in this series, and for others more

---

[4] On the subject of intertestamental studies, see John Coert Rylaarsdam, "Intertestamental Studies since Charles's Apocrypha and Pseudepigrapha," chap. 2 in *The Study of the Bible Today and Tomorrow,* ed. Harold R. Willoughby (Chicago: University of Chicago Press, 1947), 32–51; see also R. A. Kraft and G. W. E. Nickelsburg, eds., *Early Judaism and Its Modern Interpreters,* The Bible and Its Modern Interpreters 2 (Philadelphia: Fortress Press; Atlanta: Scholars Press, 1986).

[5] On the pseudepigrapha and their genres, see Albert-Marie Denis, "Les genres littèraires des pseudépigraphes d'Ancien Testament. Essai de classification," in *The First International Colloquium on the Dead Sea Scrolls,* ed. Z. J. Kapera, Folia Orientalia 25 (Warsaw, 1988).

modern treatments are desirable. Scholars are therefore grateful for the Greek texts of numerous documents that are available in the series Pseudepigrapha Veteris Testamenti Graece (PVTG, published in Leiden: vol. 1, *Testamenta XII Patriarchum: Edited According to Cambridge University Library Ms Ff 1.24 fol. 203a–261b, With Short Notes,* ed. Marinus de Jonge (1964; 2d ed. with some corrections, 1970); vol. 1/2, *The Testaments of the Twelve Patriarchs: A Critical Edition of the Greek Text,* ed. de Jonge (1978); vol. 2, *Testamentum Iobi,* ed. S. P. Brock, and *Apocalypsis Baruchi, Graece,* ed. J.-C. Picard (1967); vol. 3, *Apocalypsis Henochi, Graece,* ed. M. Black, and *Fragmenta pseudepigraphorum quae supersunt graeca: Una cum historicorum et auctorum Judaeorum hellenistarum fragmentis,* ed. Albert-Marie Denis (Leiden: Brill, 1970). Gratitude should also be expressed to Scholars Press for constantly pursuing scholars to produce texts and translations of such works, which are so important for understanding the contextual thought world of the New Testament. To keep abreast, students should consult the periodic advertisements from Scholars Press for publications entered under "Society of Biblical Literature Texts and Translations: Pseudepigrapha Series" (Atlanta, Ga., 1972–).

Among introductions to the Apocrypha and pseudepigrapha, Robert Henry Pfeiffer, *History of New Testament Times with an Introduction to the Apocrypha* (New York: Harper, 1949), is the most thorough. William O. E. Oesterley, *An Introduction to the Books of the Apocrypha* (New York: Macmillan 1935), and Charles C. Torrey, *The Apocryphal Literature: A Brief Introduction* (New Haven: Yale University Press, 1945), are also helpful. Aage Bentzen, *Introduction to the Old Testament,* translated from the Danish (Copenhagen: G. E. C. Gad, 1941) and revised by the author, 2 vols. (Copenhagen, 1948–49; 2d ed. with corrections and supplement, 2 vols. in 1, Copenhagen and London, 1952; 3d ed. [1957]), carries briefer but nevertheless meaty information (see 2:218–52). This volume is especially valuable for its studious elucidation of the sometimes neglected literary forms of the Old Testament and for its inclusion of relatively inaccessible Scandinavian material. Paul Volz, *Die Eschatologie der jüdischen Gemeinde im neutestamentlichen Zeitalter,* 2d ed. (Tübingen: J. C. B. Mohr, 1934), is the standard discussion of the eschatological accents in the intertestamental writings. For the study of New Testament biblical theology many consider it almost indispensable. For the boundlessly energetic, A.-M. Denis, *Introduction aux pseudépigraphes grecs d'ancien Testament,* Studia in Veteris Testamenti Pseudepigrapha 1 (Leiden, 1970), opens the way to pursuit of knowledge in many directions. For the quick tour, see David Syme Russell, *The Old Testament Pseudepigrapha: Patriarchs and Prophets in Early Judaism* (Philadelphia: Fortress Press, 1987).[6]

---

[6] See also Nikolaus Walter, "Jewish-Greek literature of the Greek period," in *The Cambridge History of Judaism,* vol. 2: *The Hellenistic Age,* ed. W. D. Davies and Louis Finkelstein (Cambridge, UK: Cambridge University Press, 1989), 385–408.

In the following list of Apocrypha and pseudepigrapha Rahlfs's edition of the LXX is occasionally mentioned to alert the student to the specific pseudepigraphic items included by that editor and to note certain peculiarities of citation or arrangement of materials. The abbreviations "Charlesworth" and "Denis" encode specific collections cited above.

The Apocrypha

Historical

1 Esdras (or Greek Ezra), an expanded version of Ezra-Nehemiah (MT). In the Vulgate, 1 Esdras=Ezra; 2 Esdras=Nehemiah; 3 Esdras=Greek 1 Esdras; and 4 Esdras=the pseudepigraphic apocalypse.
1 and 2 Maccabees (for 3 and 4 *Maccabees* see below under pseudepigrapha).

Historical Romances

Tobit
Judith

Wisdom Literature

Ecclesiasticus, or The Wisdom of Sirach (*Siracides*)
The Wisdom of Solomon (*Sapientia*)

Additions to Canonical Books

a. Miscellaneous
Baruch
The Epistle of Jeremiah
(For the Prayer of Manasseh=Rahlfs, *Odae* 12, see below under pseudepigrapha)
b. Additions to the Book of Daniel
The Prayer of Azariah (Rahlfs, Dan. 3:26-45)
The Song of the Three Children (Rahlfs, Dan. 3:52-90)
Susanna
Bel and the Dragon

c. Additions to the Book of Esther (indicated in Rahlfs by letters of the alphabet accompanying the number of the canonical verse either following or preceding the interpolations).

The Pseudepigrapha

In the following list those marked with an asterisk are extant in Greek. "Denis" refers to Albert-Marie Denis, ed., *Fragmenta pseudepigraphorum quae supersunt graeca* (Leiden: Brill, 1970).

Legends

> *Letter of Aristeas**
> *Jubilees* (fragments in Denis*)[7]
> *Martyrdom and Ascension of Isaiah* (Greek fragment 2:4 — 4:4 in Denis*)
> *Joseph and Aseneth**
> *Life of Adam and Eve**
> Pseudo-Philo
> *Lives of the Prophets*
> *Ladder of Jacob*
> *4 Baruch* (*Paraleipomena Jeremiou**)
> *Jannes and Jambres* (fragments in Denis*)
> *History of the Rechabites**
> *Eldad and Modad* (in *Shepherd of Hermas* 2.3.4; Denis*)
> *History of Joseph**

Testaments (Some with Apocalyptic Material)

> *Testament of the Twelve Patriarchs**
> *Testament of Job**
> Testaments of the Three Patriarchs
> > *Testament of Abraham**
> > *Testament of Isaac*
> > *Testament of Jacob.*
> *Testament of Moses* (=*Assumption of Moses;* Latin text, but some Greek fragments*, Denis)
> *Testament of Solomon**
> *Testament of Adam*

Apocalypses and Related Literature

> *1 Enoch* (*Ethiopic Enoch;* some Greek fragments*, Denis)[8]

---

[7] The first edition of the Ethiopic text of *Jubilees* since the publication by R. H. Charles in 1895 was done by James C. VanderKam, *The Book of Jubilees,* Scriptores Aethiopici 88, 2 vols. (Leuven: Peeters, 1989).

[8] The limited text base of E. Isaac's translation in *The Old Testament Pseudepigrapha* (ed. Charlesworth) invites preference for the rendering of Matthew Black in *The Book of Enoch or*

2 Enoch (Slavonic Enoch)
3 Enoch (Hebrew Enoch)
*Sibylline Oracles**
Treatise of Shem
Apocryphon of Ezekiel (fragmentary, Denis*)
Apocalypse of Zephaniah (fragmentary, including a citation ascribed to
   Clement of Alexandria; Denis*)
4 Esdras (in the Vulgate; for Greek fragments, see Denis, *Fragmenta,*
   130–32*)
*Greek Apocalypse of Ezra**
Vision of Ezra
Questions of Ezra
Revelation of Ezra
*Apocalypse of Sedrach**
2 Baruch (or *Syriac Baruch;* a Greek papyrus fragment in Denis*)
*3 Baruch**
Apocalypse of Abraham
Apocalypse of Adam
Apocalypse of Elijah (for Greek fragments, see Denis*)
*Apocalypse of Daniel**

Poetry

More *Psalms of David* (Psalm 151* Rahlfs; 152–155)
Prayer of Mannaseh (*Odes* 12* Rahlfs)
*Psalms of Solomon** (Rahlfs)
Hellenistic Synagogal Prayers*
*Prayer of Joseph** (Denis)
*Prayer of Jacob**
*Psalms of Solomon** (Rahlfs)
Odes of Solomon (of forty-two odes, only no. 11 is extant in Greek; for
   the text, see "Papyrus Bodmer XI," in *Papyrus Bodmer X–XII,* ed. Michel
   Testuz [Cologny-Genève: Bibliotheca Bodmeriana, 1959])

Wisdom Literature

Ahiqar
Life of Aesop (fragments in Denis*)

I Enoch: A New English Edition with Commentary and Textual Notes (Leiden: Brill, 1985),
which takes account of Aramaic fragments (see J. T. Milik, *The Books of Enoch: Aramaic
Fragments of Qumrân Cave 4* [Oxford: Clarendon Press, 1976]) and the Greek fragments (see
Black, *Apocalypsis Henochi Graece* [Leiden: Brill, 1970], 1–44; for addenda and corrigenda of
the latter, see Appendix B in Black's later work). For some of the shortcomings in Black's book,
see the review by George Nickelsburg in *JBL* 107 (1988): 342–44.

*3 Maccabees** (Rahlfs)
*4 Maccabees** (Rahlfs)
Pseudo-Phocylides* (Denis)
The *Sentences* of the Syriac Menander

Fragments of Lost Judeo-Hellenistic Works (for the texts, see Denis, *Fragmenta*)

Philo the Epic poet* (not strictly pseudepigraphic; Eusebius, *Praeparatio Evangelica* [*PrEv*] 9; Denis, 203–4).
Theodotus* (Eusebius, *PrEv* 9; Denis, 204–7)
*Orphica** (see Denis, 163–67)
Ezekiel the Tragedian* (not strictly pseudepigraphic; Eusebius, *PrEv* 9.28-29; Denis, 207–16)

Pseudo-Greek Poets* (see Denis, 161–74)[9]
Aristobulus* (in Eusebius; Denis, 217–28)
Demetrius Judaeus* (Eusebius, *PrEv* 9, and Clement of Alexandria, *Stromata* 1.141.1–2; Denis, 175–79)
Aristeas the Exegete* (Eusebius, *PrEv* 9.25.1-4, and addition in Job 42:17a–e, Rahlfs; Denis, 195–96).
Eupolemus* (Eusebius, *PrEv* 9, and Clement of Alexandria, *Stromata* 1.141.4.; Denis, 179–86)
Pseudo-Eupolemus* (Eusebius, *PrEv* 9; Denis, "Anonymus quidam," 197–98)
Cleodemus-Malchus* (Josephus, *Antiquities,* 1.239-41=Eusebius, *PrEv* 9.20.2–4; Denis, 196–97)
Artapanus* (Eusebius, *PrEv* 9; Denis, 186–95)
(Pseudo-)Hecataeus* (Josephus, in *Contra Apionem;* Denis, 199–200)[10]

The textual indexes in Jean Daniélou, *The Theology of Jewish Christianity,* trans. and ed. John A. Baker, The Development of Christian Doctrine Before the Council of Nicaea, I (London: Longman & Todd; Chicago: Regnery Co., 1964), offer a practical point of entry into the hermeneutical techniques of

[9] Included are fragments from Jewish writers ascribed to classical authors. The sequence in Denis, *Fragmenta,* 161–74: Aeschylus; Sophocles; Euripides (=Euripides/Philemon, in Charlesworth, *Old Testament Pseudepigrapha,* 2:827–28); Orpheus (cited as *Orphica* in Charlesworth); Pythagoras; Diphilus, pp. 168–69 (=Diphilus/Philemon/Euripides in Charlesworth, 2:828–29); Menander (=Philemon/Menander in Charlesworth, 2:829–30); Diphilus, p. 171 (=Diphilus/Menander in Charlesworth, 2:829); Euripides; (Hesiod) Homer; Callimachus, pp. 171–72 (=Various Epic Poets, Charlesworth, 2:823–24).

[10] Denis, *Fragmenta,* 157–60, also includes *Letters* of Heraclitus, nos. 4 and 7, thus giving them a Jewish provenance, but see Schürer, *Geschichte,* 3/1:695, citing V. Martin's new papyrus evidence, *Museum Helveticum* 16 (1959): 77–117.

many pseudepigraphic writers and early ecclesiastical writers, with frequent glances at the canonical texts.

Indispensable for searching the mass of philological data in the pseudepigrapha is Albert-Marie Denis, *Concordance grecque des pseudépigraphes d'ancien testament: Concordance, corpus des textes, indices* (Louvaine-in-Neuve: Université Catholique de Louvain, 1987). Alongside it one can make use of the lexical help provided by Christopher Abraham Wahl, *Clavis librorum Veteris Testamenti apocryphorum philologica* (Leipzig, 1853); for the reprint of this work (Graz: Akademische Druck- und Verlagsanstalt, 1972) Johannes Baptista Bauer contributes an index of words used in fragments of *Greek Enoch, Psalm of Solomon, Apocalypse of Moses, Paralipomena of Jeremiah, Apocalypse of Baruch, Testament of Abraham* A, B; *Testament of Job, Testament of Solomon, Greek Apocalypse of Ezra, Apocalypse of Sedrach.*

Not strictly intertestamental but in a related category are apocryphal writings bearing specifically on the New Testament. Wilhelm Schneemelcher's thorough revision of Edgar Hennecke, *Neutestamentliche Apokryphen in deutscher Übersetzung,* 3d ed., 2 vols. (Tübingen: J. C. B Mohr [Siebeck], 1959–64), incorporated much new Coptic material. An English translation appeared in two volumes under the title *New Testament Apocrypha,* trans. and ed. R. McL. Wilson, 2 vols. (Philadelphia: Westminster, 1963–65). Wilson's edition improved the German factually, expanded the bibliography, and overshadowed Montague Rhodes James's less complete collection in *The Apocryphal New Testament: Being the Apocryphal Gospels, Acts, Epistles, and Apocalypses with Other Narratives and Fragments* (Oxford: Clarendon Press, 1924). But the rapid pace of discoveries and further pondering of a vast assemblage of data required such extensive revision of Hennecke-Schneemelcher that a 5th rev. German ed., 2 vols (1987–89), bore only the name of Schneemelcher. To keep pace, Wilson brought out a revised edition of his translation of the first volume, "rigorously checked and revised against the new German edition" (Cambridge, UK: James Clarke & Co.; Louisville: Westminster Press, 1991). Students who prefer their apocrypha in French can resort to François Amiot, *La Bible apocryphe: Évangiles apocryphes* (Paris: A. Fayard, 1952), which ranges beyond the gospel material.

Since (Hennecke-) Schneemelcher does not contain original texts, the student must consult the sources as listed, for example, in the front matter of BAAR and the English editions of Walter Bauer's lexicon. New Testament students owe an immense debt of gratitude to Aurelio de Santos Otero for bringing together so much that wanders without much notice in the byways of learning. His collection of apocryphal gospel material, *Los evangelios apocrifos: Colección de textos griegos y latinos, versión crítica, estudios introductorios, commentarios e ilustraciones,* 6th ed. (Madrid: Biblioteca de Autores Christianos, 1988), includes a general introduction, followed by the texts, for which de Santos Otero first offers a translation and then the Greek or Latin form of the text. Included are such works as the *Infancy Gospel of James* (*Protevangelium of James*), *Gospel of Pseudo-Thomas* (*Infancy Gospel of Thomas*), and the *Acts of Pilate* (*Gospel of Nicodemus*), for which students have long been dependent on the edition of Constantine Tischendorf, *Evangelia Apocrypha: adhibitis plurimis codicibus graecis et latinis maximam partem nunc primum consultis atque ineditorum copia insignibus,* 2d ed. (Leipzig, 1876). But all later editions of apocryphal gospel texts attest the permanence of Tischendorf's work. The discovery of a papyrus text of the *Infancy Gospel of James,* published by Michel Testuz, *Papyrus Bodmer V: Nativité de Marie* (Cologny-Geneva: Bibliotheca Bodmeriana, 1958), led to one of the few extensive revisions of Tischendorf's work. Relentless in pursuit of resolutions for problems raised by variations in textual tradition forms, Émile de Strycker corrected some errors in Testuz's edition in an endeavor to offer a "provisional" early form of the text, *La forme la plus ancienne du protévangile de Jacques: Recherches sur le Papyrus Bodmer 5 avec une édition critique du texte grec et une traduction annotée,* Subsidia Hagiographica 33 (Brussels: Société de Bollandistes, 1961).

An extraordinary treasure-trove for understanding the New Testament in the light of Jewish thought and experience in the Hellenistic world is the output of the great Jewish thinker Philo Judaeus, available in the standard edition by Leopold Cohn, Paul Wendland, and Siegfried Reiter, *Philonis Alexandrini opera quae supersunt,* 6 vols. and index vol. by Hans Leisegang (Berlin, 1896–1930). Leisegang's index to Philo's vocabulary is less complete than G. Mayer's *Index Philoneus* (Berlin: de Gruyter, 1974). Those who use German have a translation available in *Die Werke Philos von Alexandria in deutscher Übersetzung,* ed. L. Cohn, 5 vols. (Berlin, 1909–29). The French offer Roger Arnaldez, et al., eds., *Les oeuvres de Philon d'Alexandrie,* 35 vols. (Paris: Cerf, 1961–73). An English translation of the works of Philo, begun by Francis Henry Colson (d. 1943) and George Herbert Whitaker, reached completion in 1962 in ten volumes and two supplementary volumes, ed. Ralph Marcus (Loeb Classical Library; Cambridge, Mass.: Harvard University Press). A few treatises in Armenian still await translation. Secondary entry to Philo's mind can be made through Samuel Sandmel, *Philo of Alexandria: An Introduction* (New York: Oxford University Press, 1979), or via J. Daniélou, *Philon d'Alexandrie* (Paris: A. Fayard, 1958). The more ambitious will find Philo quite compelling in E. R. Goodenough, *An Introduction to Philo Judaeus* (New Haven, Conn.: Yale University Press, 1940; 2d ed. rev.; Oxford: Blackwell, 1962).[11]

---

[11] On a Latin text of Pseudo-Philo, *Liber Antiquitatum,* an anonymous work that was erroneously attributed in the course of time to Philo of Alexandria, see Daniel J. Harrington, "Philo, Pseudo-," *ABD,* 5:344–45. Harrington, et al., also edited the text, accompanied by J. Cazeaux's French translation, *Pseudo-Philon: Les Antiquités bibliques,* 2 vols. (Paris: Cerf, 1976). For studies on Philo, see Roberto Radice and David T. Runia, *Philo of Alexandria: An Annotated Bibliography 1937–1986,* 2d ed. (Atlanta: Scholars Press, 1992).

THE RABBINIC PERIOD

From the intertestamental period we move on to the modern era of "normative" Judaism. In the second century A.D. a compilation of selected Jewish traditions, consisting of extensive reinterpretations of the written law to meet the needs of changing times, was begun by Akiba and completed by Jehudah ha-Nasi with the help of his academy. The result was the Mishnah (מִשְׁנָה) from שָׁנָה, meaning the repetition of something that has been heard. The Mishnah is a systematic code divided into six orders, or *sedarim* (סְדָרִים). Each *seder* (סֵדֶר) is divided into treatises or tractates (מַסֶּכְתּוֹת), which in turn are subdivided. The sponsors of the Mishnah are called Tannaites, from תְּנָה, to teach the oral law. Their successors in the third to the fifth centuries are the Amoraim (אָמוֹרָא, teacher), who concentrate on the explanation of all the legal ramifications of the Mishnah. Since their work may be said to "complete" the Mishnah and to stand in the relation of commentary to text it is called the Gemara (גְּמָרָה, from גְּמַר, "to complete"). Together the Mishnah and the Gemara form the Talmud (תַּלְמוּד, from לָמַד, "to study"), a word first applied alternately to the Gemara. Both Palestinian and Babylonian rabbis worked on supplementing the Mishnah; quite naturally two Talmuds came into existence. The Talmud growing in Palestine never reached completion. The Babylonian Talmud fared better and represents a much more full and thorough treatment of the Jewish discussions covering roughly the period A.D. 100–500; it was completed about A.D. 600. The commentary in the Talmud is of two kinds: halakah and haggadah. Halakah (from הָלַךְ, "to go") embraces all exposition of law. Haggadah (הַגָּדָה, from הִגַּד, "to explain") includes all nonhalakic materials, such as parables, prayers, fables, legends, meditations, allegories, and the like. Halakah strives for the achievement of moral excellence; haggadah aims at edification. Halakah seeks to influence the will; haggadah addresses its appeals to the intellect, the imagination, the understanding.

Details on the Talmud and other Jewish works of this period may be found in Hermann Leberecht Strack, *Einleitung in Talmud und Midrasch,* 7th ed. rev. by Günter Stemberger (Munich: Beck, 1982), long a standard introduction to the subject of Jewish exposition, a work replete with bibliographies. After the publication of the 5th ed. rev. (Munich, 1920), Strack worked on further revision up to the time of his death, and the total harvest was garnered in a translation based on Strack's revisions of his fifth edition and issued in Philadelphia in 1931 by the Jewish Publication Society of America as *Introduction to the Talmud and Midrash,* to all intents and purposes a sixth edition of the original. A translation of the Strack-Stemberger edition was made by Markus Bockmuehl (Edinburgh: T. & T. Clark, 1991; Minneapolis: Fortress Press, 1992).

The Hebrew text of the Mishnah, with Philip Blackman's parallel English translation (London: Mishnah Press, 1951–57), was reissued in a revised, enlarged edition (New York: Judaica Press, 1964). The work, titled *Mishnayoth,* embraces seven very readable volumes, but does not antiquate Canon Herbert Danby's excellent translation, *The Mishnah* (London: Oxford University Press, 1933), complete with introduction and brief explanatory notes. Students skilled in Hebrew will welcome Chanoch Albeck and Henoch Yalon, "The Six Orders of the Mishnah Explained and Pointed," as the Hebrew title (Jerusalem and Tel Aviv: Bialik Institute, 1952–59) is rendered. Especially attractive for novices because of its more literal rendering of the Hebrew and a glossary of mishnaic terms is Jacob Neusner's *The Mishnah: A New Translation* (New Haven: Yale University Press, 1988). Nevertheless, for sustained study of the Mishnah it is necessary to consult Karl Heinrich Rengstorf and Leonhard Rost, eds., *Die Mischna: Text, Übersetzung und ausführliche Erklärung* (Berlin: Töpelmann, 1910–), which offers the Hebrew text, a German translation, and informed comment. For further adventurous exploration of mishnaic labyrinths it is necessary to use a basic tool such as *Thesaurus Mishnae: Concordantiae verborum quae in sex Mishnae ordinibus reperiuntur,* compiled by Chayim Yehoshua Kasovsky, 3 vols. (Jerusalem, 1956–58; 2d ed., 4 vols., Jerusalem: Massada, 1967). For a grammar of mishnaic Hebrew see Segal's work (p. 166, above).

In 1939 Gerhard Kittel and K. H. Rengstorf began a double-level collection, *Rabbinische Texte,* which includes German translation and comment on the tannaitic Midrashim and the Tosefta. The latter is an anthology of tannaitic texts parallel to the Mishnah but without canonical status and larger in scope. The first complete and unabridged English translation of the *Midrash Rabbah,* a large collection of fact, legend, and sermonic material, appeared in ten volumes, edited by Harry Freedman and Maurice Simon (London: Soncino, 1939). For samples of contents and for light on the Midrashim, see Jacob Neusner, *A Midrash Reader* (Minneapolis: Fortress Press, 1990).

The first translation of the "entire" Talmud in English was published by the Soncino Press of Great Britain under the title *The Babylonian Talmud* (London, 1935–52). The thirty-five attractive volumes were capably edited by Isidore Epstein. Far more ambitious in scale is this editor's parallel-text version, *Hebrew-English Edition of the Babylonian Talmud* (London: Soncino Press, 1960–). Meanwhile, on this side of the Atlantic, J. Neusner accepted editorial responsibility for a production through Scholars Press that is to number 36 volumes in the Brown Judaic Studies series under the title *The Talmud of Babylonia: An American Translation,* whose first volume appeared in 1984 (Atlanta: Scholars Press). Navigation on the "Sea of Talmud," as that reservoir of rabbinic learning and lore is often called, can gain steerage through use of אזנים לתורה, *Subject Concordance to the Babylonian Talmud,* compiled by Lazarus Goldschmidt (1871–1950) and edited by Rafael Edelmann (Copenhagen: Munksgaard, 1959). Goldschmidt's purportedly exhaustive subject index, which may be considered a fitting climax to the career of this

Orientalist and bibliophile to whom we owe a scholarly edition of the text and a German translation of the Babylonian Talmud, 9 vols. (Berlin, Leipzig, The Hague: by various publishers, 1897–1935), orders key words in context according to subject.

Somewhat closer to the New Testament in time (ca. A.D. 450) is the formation of the Palestinian Talmud. Parts of this Talmud became available for the first time in German in August Wünsche's translation, *Der jerusalemische Talmud in seinen haggadischen Bestandtheilen zum ersten Male in's Deutsche übertragen* (Zurich, 1880). More ambitious in scope is the cooperative translation enterprise headed by Martin Hengel, *Übersetzung des Talmud Jerushalmi,* with the first volume appearing in 1980 (Tübingen: J. C. B. Mohr [Siebeck]). The first volume of an English translation of the Palestinian Talmud, *The Talmud of the Land of Israel,* appeared in 1982 (Chicago: University of Chicago Press), with some translations done by the editor, J. Neusner.

Since the Babylonian Talmud contains much material that postdates the period of formation of New Testament documents, especially careful use of its contents, as noted below on the use of Billerbeck's commentary, is mandatory for the student who makes judgments about Jewish matters in the New Testament.

In *Talmud and Apocrypha* (London: Soncino Press, 1933) Robert Travers Herford compares and contrasts talmudic and apocryphal writings as he attempts documentation of their emanation from a common source in post-captivity Judaism. Haggadic amplifications of biblical accounts wait to fascinate and inform in Louis Ginzberg, *Legends of the Bible* (New York: Simon and Schuster, 1956), a shorter version of his seven-volume *The Legends of the Jews* (Philadelphia: Jewish Publication Society, 1909–38). *A Rabbinic Anthology* (New York: Macmillan, 1938; reprint, New York: Meridian Books, 1960), translated and edited by Claude Joseph Goldsmid Montefiore and Herbert Martin James Loewe, offers a topical sampling of rabbinic wisdom.

The interpretive possibilities of the rabbinic writings for the understanding of the New Testament are exploited and correlated in many excellent publications.[12] Claude J. G. Montefiore's *The Synoptic Gospels,* 2d ed. rev., 2 vols. (London: Macmillan, 1927), contains much helpful comment. His *Rabbinic Literature and Gospel Teachings* (New York: Macmillan, 1930) supplements his study of the Synoptics. In *Studies in Pharisaism and the Gospels* (Cambridge, UK: Cambridge University Press, 1924), Israel Abrahams compares the doctrine of the rabbis to the teachings of Jesus. An apologetic tone stiffens his determined defense of Pharisaism.

In *The Teachings of Jesus: Studies of Its Form and Content* (Cambridge,

---

[12] On the history of rabbinic studies and their application to problems of New Testament interpretation, see Jan Willem Doeve, *Jewish Hermeneutics in the Synoptic Gospels and Acts* (Assen: Van Gorcum, 1954), 5–51.

UK: Cambridge University Press, 1931; 2d ed., 1935; reprints, 1951, 1955), and *The Sayings of Jesus* (London: SCM Press, 1949), Thomas Walter Manson makes brilliant use of rabbinic materials throughout, but especially to expose the deep and adventitious root system, which finds its apex in the concept of the fatherhood of God.[13]

The German Moravian and later Lutheran Gustaf Hermann Dalman has drawn many a student into his debt with a pair of incisive works elucidating New Testament concepts and incidents against the elaborate background of rabbinic materials, *Die Worte Jesu* (Leipzig, 1898) and *Jesus-Jeschua* (Leipzig, 1922). The first was translated into English by David Miller Kay as *The Words of Jesus* (Edinburgh: T. & T. Clark, 1902); the second by Paul Philip Levertoff as *Jesus-Jeshua* (New York: Macmillan, 1929). Bo Reicke, in his *Neutestaentliche Zeitgeschichte* (Berlin: de Gruyter, 1965; 3d ed., 1982), sketches the broader Hellenistic landscape; Werner Foerster, in *From the Exile to Christ: A Historical Introduction to Palestinian Judaism,* trans. Gordon E. Harris (Philadelphia: Fortress Press, 1964), the Jewish milieu, in which the ministry of Jesus takes on fresh perspective. In *Die apostolische und nachapostolische Zeit* (Göttingen, 1962), the first part of a promising four-volume manual edited by Kurt Dietrich Schmidt and Ernst Wolf and titled *Die Kirche in ihrer Geschichte,* author Leonhard Goppelt discusses factors that helped shape the postapostolic church.

Of historical interest is Joseph Gedaliah Klausner, ardent Zionist, prolific writer, and even candidate for the presidency of Israel in 1949, who rendered opinions on the birth of Christianity as seen from the ward of Judaism. *Jesus of Nazareth: His Life, Times, and Teaching,* trans. Herbert Danby (New York: Macmillan, 1925), was composed originally in modern Hebrew and published in Jerusalem in 1922. In it Klausner defended the classic contention of Julius Wellhausen that Jesus was a Jew, not a Christian. In his second notable work, *From Jesus to Paul,* trans. William F. Stinespring (New York: Macmillan, 1943), Klausner brands Paul the culprit responsible for the establishment of Christianity separate from Judaism. In *The Messianic Idea in Israel: From Its Beginning to the Completion of the Mishnah,* trans. W. F. Stinespring (New York: Macmillan, 1955), Klausner endeavors to turn the weight of prophetic realism against authoritarian materialism in Zionist social policy. Needless to say, his tracing of the evolution of Christianity is based mainly on Jewish sources, many of which definitely merit the attention of Christian scholars. For balance, read William David Davies, *Paul and Rabbinic Judaism: Some Rabbinic Elements in Pauline Theology* (London: SPCK, 1948; 2d ed., 1955).

---

[13] *The Sayings of Jesus* was originally published as the middle portion of *The Mission and Message of Jesus: An Exposition of the Gospels in the Light of Modern Research* (New York: E. P. Dutton, 1938), of which the other contributors were Henry Dewsbury Alves Major and Charles James Wright. The 1949 edition of *The Sayings of Jesus* contains additional notes.

For detailed critical analyses of the use of rabbinic materials relative to New Testament interpretation, the student should consult Morton Smith, *Tannaitic Parallels to the Gospels,* Journal of Biblical Literature Monograph Series 6 (Philadelphia: Society of Biblical Literature, 1951); Jan Willem Doeve, *Jewish Hermeneutics in the Synoptic Gospels and Acts* (Assen: Van Gorcum, 1954); and Edward Earle Ellis, *Paul's Use of the Old Testament* (Edinburgh: Oliver and Boyd, 1957). These books are important for understanding the basic exegetical principles used by Paul and other New Testament writers in their approach to the Old Testament and its interpretation.

Other standard discussions include Paul Fiebig's study of parables, *Die Gleichnisreden Jesu im Lichte der rabbinischen Gleichnisse des neutestamentlichen Zeitalters* (Tübingen, 1912), and his investigation of miracles, *Jüdische Wundergeschichten des neutestamentlichen Zeitalters* (Tübingen: J. C. B. Mohr [Siebeck], 1911). His *Jesu Bergpredigt* (Göttingen: Vandenhoeck & Ruprecht, 1924) sheds light on numerous expressions in the Sermon on the Mount. Ismar Elbogen, *Der jüdische Gottesdienst in seiner geschichtlichen Entwicklung* (Frankfurt am Main, 1913; 3d ed., 1931; reprint, Hildesheim, 1962), contributes notably to the history of liturgy.

Final mention is reserved for Hermann L. Strack and Paul Billerbeck, *Kommentar zum Neuen Testament aus Talmud und Midrasch,* 5 vols. (Munich: C. H. Beck, 1922–28; 2d ed., 4 vols. in 5, rabbinic index, and index of scribes with geographical index, 1954–61), abbreviated Billerbeck, since Billerbeck was chiefly responsible. This work is not for amateurs, but when used with awareness of its distortions of Jewish perspectives, lamentably weak documentation of tannaitic sources, and assumption that relatively late rabbinic materials are reliable indicators of first-century Judaism, Billerbeck can offer some interesting parallels to New Testament data.[14]

Among the ancient sources for Jewish history are the fragments of Jewish writers found especially in Josephus and Eusebius and collected by Felix Jacoby in *Die Fragmente der griechischen Historiker* (*FGrHist*) (Berlin and Leiden, 1923–). Important also are the thoughts collected from antiquity in Menaham Stern, *Greek and Latin Authors on Jews and Judaism,* with introductions, translations, and commentary, 3 vols. (Jerusalem: Israel Academy of Sciences and Humanities, 1974–)

---

[14] G. F. Moore's evaluation remains beyond challenge: "For vast collections made for a wholly different purpose the reader may resort to Strack-Billerbeck, Kommentar zum Neuen Testament aus Talmud und Midrasch . . . ; but he should be warned that the critical sifting of this miscellany devolves upon him who uses it for any particular purpose" (*Judaism,* 3:viii). In a number of works, E. P. Sanders echoes Moore.

INTERPRETIVE VALUES

Not only do the Apocrypha and pseudepigrapha make absorbing reading; very often they can throw a great deal of light on some obscure New Testament expression. Take, for example, the evangelist's use of the word δικαιόω in Luke 7:29. The rare use of the word with reference to human justification of God is repeatedly documented in the *Psalms of Solomon* (2:15; 3:5; 4:8; 8:7, 26). In the light of these passages, in which God's people are said to recognize the justice of all of God's actions, it is clear that Jesus intends to say that the common people recognize God's sovereignty and humbly surrender to divine claims by submitting to a baptism of repentance, whereas some more sophisticated hearers refuse to acknowledge their need for a change of heart.

At Jude 6 the Nestle editors cite the *Book of Enoch* 10:6. The purpose of this reference is clear when the apocalyptic writing is consulted. In Robert H. Charles's edition, *The Book of Enoch* (Oxford: Clarendon Press, 1912), 22–25, the apocryphal version of the attempt of evil angels to inflict a race of giants on the earth by consorting with the daughters of men is related as follows:

> (4) And again the Lord said to Raphael: "Bind Azâzêl hand and foot, and cast him into the darkness: and make an opening in the desert, which is in Dudael, and cast him therein. (5) And place upon him rough and jagged rocks, and cover him with darkness, and let him abide there for ever, and cover his face that he may not see light. (6) And on the day of the great judgement he shall be cast into the fire. (7) And heal the earth which the angels have corrupted, and proclaim the healing of the earth, that they may heal the plague, and that all the children of men may not perish through all the secret things that the Watchers have disclosed and have taught their sons. . . ." (11) And the Lord said unto Michael: "Go, bind Semjaza and his associates who have united themselves with women so as to have defiled themselves with them in all their uncleanness. . . . (15) And destroy all the spirits of the reprobate and the children of the Watchers, because they have wronged mankind." (Enoch 10:4-15)

The reading of *Enoch* 1:9 alongside Jude 14 and 15 will prove similarly instructive.

The Sermon on the Mount is a good starting point for investigations in the rabbinic literature. David Daube draws attention to the probable significance of Jesus' introductory formula for the citation of traditional legal positions. At first sight the words of Jesus "You have heard . . . but I say unto you" (see Matt. 5:21ff.) suggest that Jesus is substituting his own novel legislation for the older, accepted legislation. But a study of rabbinic approaches to Scriptural injunctions (as in Mekilta on Exod. 20:12) indicates that Jesus is rejecting a mere literal application of the original precept, which in its bald form is narrow compared with the one accepted in its stead. "To hear" means "to take literally." At one level, the Matthew expression is to be translated, "You have literally understood" or "You might understand literally." Some difficulties arising in the Matthean account from the fact that not all words in Jesus' quotations can be traced to specific Old Testament passages may be solved through careful application of this interpretation. For example, in Matt. 5:21 Jesus makes the pronouncement: "You shall not kill, and anyone who kills shall be in danger of the judgment." The latter part of the statement is not found in the Old Testament. The problem is solved substantially if the words in 5:21b are interpreted as the scribes' own expansion of the Torah. Jesus' formula, then, introduces not only Old Testament quotations but also certain scribal amplifications. Rabbi Judah the Prince illustrates the procedure. Commenting on the expression "And the Lord came down from Mount Sinai," he explains: "I might hear this as it is heard, I might understand this according to its literal meaning. . . . But thou must say: If the sun, one of the many servants of God, may remain in its place and nevertheless be effective beyond it, how much more He by whose word the world came into being."

The importance of Judah the Prince's interpretation of such words is evident from the context. Jesus claims to uphold the Law and to fulfill it. Instead of repealing and discarding the old legislation, he sharpens the appropriate understanding of it. In place of a limiting literal approach he substitutes a broad, liberal approach and an attitude that is a willingness to embrace anything encompassed by the Mosaic legislation. Not the effectiveness or the time-honored character of the Law but Jesus' own person lends authority to its precepts.[15]

Sensitivity to insights suggested by or derived from the rabbinical literature will prove rewarding in the study of New Testament thought. Morton Smith (*Tannatic Parallels*, 152–60) discusses what he terms "parallels with a fixed difference." These are series of parallel passages in which the common denominator of the New Testament passages remains consistently different from topical parallels in the rabbinic literature. One of these series of topically parallel passages proposes the extraordinary claims of Jesus. Thus in Matt. 10:25 Jesus says to His disciples: "It is sufficient for the disciple that he become as his teacher." In *Sifra* 25:23 it is stated that God says to Israel: "You are my servants." *Sifra* comments: "It is enough for the servant that he be as his master." In Matt. 25:35 and 40 Jesus says to the righteous at the last judgment: "For I was hungry, and you gave me something to eat. . . . I tell you, since you have done this to one of the least of these my brothers, you have done it to me." *Midrash Tannaim* 15:9 parallels this with "so the Holy One, blessed be He, said to

---

[15] David Daube, *The New Testament and Rabbinic Judaism* (London: University of London, Athlone Press, 1956), 55ff. Although it is weak in Gospel criticism, this work provides detailed examples illustrating the potential of rabbinic materials as resources for understanding obscurities and pregnant allusions in the New Testament.

Israel, 'My children, whenever you feed the poor I count it up for you as if you fed me.'" Other passages of a similar nature are discussed by Smith and seem to admit the conclusion that the church's picture of Jesus Christ as Lord may be documented indirectly also from parallels in rabbinic literature.

A knowledge of Jewish hermeneutics can be helpful in appreciating some of Paul's elaborate argumentation. In Romans 4 Paul is anxious to prove that faith alone, apart from the deeds of the Law, can justify a person before God. To convince a Jew he must show first of all that Abraham believed; second, that he secured forgiveness of sins; and third, that he experienced this as a non-Jew.

He chooses Abraham as exhibit A. Genesis 15:6 proves the first proposition: ἐπίστευσεν δὲ᾽Αβραὰμ τῷ θεῷ, καὶ ἐλογίσθη αὐτῷ εἰς δικαιοσύνην (Rom. 4:3). But what benefit accrued to Abraham? The word ἐλογίσθη reminds the apostle of Ps. 32:1, 2 (Rom. 4:7, 8), where the same word occurs, and it is exactly this transfer from one passage to another via a common word or phrase, which is known as גְּזֵרָה שָׁוָה (gezerah shawa), the second of Hillel's seven hermeneutical principles. (See Strack, *Introduction to the Talmud*, 94, or Doeve, *Jewish Hermeneutics*, 61–75.) Humans are not charged (ἐλογίσθη) with sin. That is the benefit. But does this apply to an uncircumcised Gentile? This is the third proposition yet to be answered. Again the apostle makes use of Hillel's second *middah*, or hermeneutical rule, but this time in reverse, "Yes, of course, for (γάρ) we say faith was counted to Abraham for righteousness." What the psalmist has said applies to Abraham according to the principle of inference based on the analogy of words, and the benefit was conferred on him before his circumcision. Hence, the righteousness of faith is secured not only for the Jew but also for the Gentile—apart from the Law.

The devastating argumentation employed by Jesus in John 7:23 can be fully appreciated only if a passage like the following is consulted:

> Circumcision and all its preliminaries supersede the Sabbath: this is R. Eliezer's view. Whence does R. Eliezer learn this? . . . Because Scripture saith, *and in the eighth day the flesh of his foreskin shall be circumcised,* (implying) even on the Sabbath. . . .
>
> Now, the Rabbis disagree with R. Eliezer only in respect of the preliminaries of circumcision; but as for circumcision itself, all hold that it supersedes the Sabbath: whence do we know it?—Said 'Ulla, It is a traditional law; and thus did R. Isaac say, It is a traditional law.
>
> An objection is raised: How do we know that the saving of life supersedes the Sabbath? R. Eleazar b. 'Azariah said: If circumcision, which is (performed on but) one of the limbs of man, supersedes the Sabbath, the saving of life, *a minori* must supersede the Sabbath![16]

---

[16] Seder Mo'ed, Shabbath, xix, 131b, 132a, *Shabbath,* II, trans. Harry Freedman, *The Babylonian Talmud,* ed. Isidore Epstein, vol. 8 (London: Soncino Press, 1938), 660.

Finally, Strack-Billerbeck, *Kommentar,* 1:783f., cites rabbinical material that files sharp the point of Matt. 18:10: "Take care that you despise not one of these little ones which believe in me, for I tell you their angels do always behold the face of my Father who is in heaven." According to some rabbis even the angels, only the highest of whom have the honor of standing in the presence of God, are not privileged to look on God's glory. In the saying of Jesus the curtain veiling God from the view of human beings and angels is drawn aside; even the lowliest has the assurance of a personal audience before heaven's king.

CHAPTER THIRTEEN

CONTEXTUALITY
I. *Archaeology*

ONTEXUALITY AND NETWORK hit the high notes in the last decades of the twentieth century. Parts I and II of this chapter strike a common theme. In Part I we examine tools for study of archaeology relating to the lands of the Bible. In Part II we concentrate on two specific types of documents, most of them in Greek, namely, papyri and epigraphs. Many of these are the products of amateur or professional exploration of ancient sites. Since all ancient documents are artifacts, the second portion of Part II deals with advances in the sociological study of such productions, with some attention paid to applications of literary-critical theory to the understanding of more formal literary pieces.

ROLL CALL

Little did a French officer of engineers named Bouchard realize, when he accepted assignment in Napoleon Bonaparte's expedition to the Nile delta (1798–99), that a stone would assure him a place in history. In August, 1799, spades under Bouchard's control turned up a black basalt stele near the town of Rosetta (Rashid) in Egypt's western delta. The Rosetta Stone, as it came to be named, bore inscriptions in Greek and two forms of Egyptian writing, the complicated hieroglyphic and the more popular demotic. After this discovery the Near East seemed reconciled to the unveiling of its ancient past, and archaeological campaigns continued to gain access to the remote niches in which history often hides.

The who's who of archaeology and related studies glitters with the names of prestigious professional excavators as well as of amateurs who called attention to things long hidden in a past reluctant to disclose itself. There are the names of Claudius James Rich, who wrote his first "Memoir on the Ruins of Babylon" in 1812 and later sniffed the elusive greatness of Nineveh; of J. D. Åkerblad and Silvestre de Sacy, who determined the value of certain demotic characters on the Rosetta Stone and thus broke ground for the decipherment of Egyptian hieroglyphics on the Rosetta Stone by Jean François Champollion in 1822; of Heinrich Schliemann, that "brilliant amateur" who went in search of Homer's Troy;[1] of Sir Henry Creswicke Rawlinson, who at the risk of his life on a forbidding rock face at Behistun made entrée possible into Assyrian and Babylonian literatures; of Austen Henry Layard,[2] generous colleague of Paul Émile Botta, exposed to many dangers, who headed for northern Mesopotamia in 1845 in search of Nineveh with 60 pounds sterling in his pocket, but had to settle at first for Calah; of Samuel Birch, who reported to Great Britain's Society of Biblical Archaeology in 1870 that he was able to reinforce the identity of the Hebrew kings Omri, Ahab, Jehu, Menahem, Pekah, Hoshea, Hezekiah, and Manasseh; of Archibald Henry Sayce, through whose lecture in 1880 before the Society of Biblical Archaeology a nation that had been dead for three thousand years sprang to life in headlines throughout England; of Jacques Jean Marie de Morgan, discoverer of Hammurabi's Code at Susa (Persepolis), and Jean Vincent Scheil, who transcribed and translated it in 1902; of B. Hrozný, who on November 24, 1915, broke the news that he had deciphered the Hittite language; of John Garstang, historian of the Hittites, examiner of Egyptian embalming practices, and spur to the excavators of Jericho and archaeological excavators generally; of James Henry Breasted, the founder and a director of the Oriental Institute of the University of Chicago; and of many others who do not merit ungracious ignorance of their achievements simply because we know some things better today.[3]

---

[1] Schliemann's digging at Hissarlik was the first scientific excavation of an ancient site. He was in error about having found Troy. And he did not gaze on the face of Agamemnon at Mycenae.

[2] Layard was extraordinarily free of the envy and jealousy that permeates some scholarly crafts. Unfortunately his own country was free of generosity and foresight, which would have given Layard the opportunity to engage in the more scientific and methodical type of excavation that he desired. As a result Layard's work was more in the nature of bureaucratic pillaging. For a stirring account of Layard's excavations and what he had done to help fill the British Museum with some of its most amazing treasures, see H. V. Hilprecht, *Explorations in Bible Lands During the 19th Century* (Philadelphia: A. J. Holman, 1903), 88–128; 157–63. For Egyptologists, some of whom like J. D. Åkerblad, S. Birch, P. Botta, J. de Morgan, and J. Scheil also researched other areas, see Warren R. Dawson and Eric P. Uphill, *Who Was Who in Egyptology,* 2d rev. ed. (London: Egypt Exploration Society, 1972); among those mentioned is Joseph Ernest Renan, author of *Vie de Jésus,* who was very supportive of procedures for the preservation of monuments, some of which had suffered shocking destruction under the Viceroys.

[3] Contrast Albright's appeciation of Wilhelm Gesenius, *Scriptura linguaeque Phoeniciae monumenta quotquot supersunt* (Leipzig, 1837). He called it an "epochal book," in which, he asserted, Gesenius had collected all accessible documents in accurate copies and interpreted them on the basis of sound epigraphical method, profound grammatical knowledge, and balanced judgment. See also his praise of F. K. Mover's four-volume work, *Die Phönizier* [?] (1841–56), in which Mover collected everything known at the time about the Phoenicians and their colonies, much of it drawn from classical sources (W. F. Albright, "The Role of the Canaanites in the History of Civilization," appendix 1 in *The Bible and the Ancient Near East: Essays in Honor of William*

MODERN DEVELOPMENTS

Archaeology has come a long way since Giovanni Battista Belzoni (1778–1823), an explorer of incredible strength, used a battering ram to burst into a pyramid at Giza. To Sir William Matthew Flinders Petrie (1853–1942), the lay "dean of the diggers," goes the credit for initiating a really new phase in archaeological research. He recognized the essential nature of ancient tells, the artificial mounds created by successive occupations of a site and developed the "potsherd yardstick" in its fuller implications during his digging at Tell el-Hesi in 1890. In spite of his lax labor policies toward those tilling the debris under his indulgent guidance, Petrie rescued sufficient evidence to establish that also unpainted pottery, unstable stylistically and subject to subtle but significant changes of design even at the hands of would-be imitators, provides a convenient index to the relative dating of widely separated strata, especially when synchronized with the ceramic phases of surrounding ancient but contemporary cultures. The method was viewed with suspicious caution at first, and since Petrie's time it has been greatly refined and modified, with the result that much of our Near East chronology of antiquity attains a high level of accuracy.

Yet even such progress as was made by Petrie is forced to fade somewhat in the face of a veritable revolution that has taken place in the last decades of the twentieth century. And if it is ever true that a little knowledge is a dangerous thing, especially the student of archaeology ought to heed the sober warning implicit in this maxim. A deficiency in critical judgment or a dearth of information carefully culled from reliable sources can be calamitous or at least extremely embarrassing. It is therefore imperative that students lose no time in seeking out authoritative guidance. With the help of reliable interpreters of the ancient data they will see the biblical narrative leap to life under their steady gaze, and what they see will enrich their total spiritual understanding, stimulate cultural sympathies, and awaken an alertness and sensitivity to the vibrant beat of history. For archaeology is more than discovery of artifacts and words inscribed on sherd or stone.

"New Archaeology" and "Biblical Archaeology"

For a starter to assist in appreciating the scope of the task, we recommend the article, "Archaeology, Syro-Palestinian and Biblical," by William G. Dever, *ABD*, 1:354–67, which distills the information in his *Recent Archaeological Discoveries and Biblical Research* (Seattle: University of Washington Press,

---

Foxwell Albright, ed. G. Ernest Wright [Garden City, N.Y.: Doubleday, 1961], 328–62). This article is a revision of one published in 1942.

1990), a revision of a series of lectures designed to acquaint the general public with progress in archaeological studies.[4] As one does with any advertisement of promising new directions, it is necessary to maintain a respectful willingness to test and sift and then hold fast to that which is good. "Archaeology," declares Dever, "is not merely an antiquarian pursuit, the discovery of fascinating relics; it is an intellectual inquiry, one that seeks to penetrate and illumine human experience in the past. Thus *theory*—by which we mean not 'speculation,' but the basic way in which the discipline of archaeology sees itself—is clearly fundamental" (*ABD*, 1:354).

The principal issue is here laid out clearly: archaeology, a social science discipline that shares the synchronic interests of prehistoric archaeology, must take account of the many contexts in which individual aspects of ancient life have their significance. On expedition staffs, says Dever, in an observation that reminds one of the vision of Alexander the Great for advancing knowledge, one typically might find "geographers, geomorphologists, climatologists, paleobotanists and paleozoologists, physical and cultural anthropologists, historians of technology, computer programmers, and still other specialists in fields formerly thought quite remote from archaeology" (*ABD*, 1:355). The application of such a multidisciplinary approach—with emphasis on anthropological and ecological orientation—to archaeological inquiry involving matters of interest to biblical students is of a piece with the general trend, beginning in the 1960s, to move biblical study in numerous areas away from the narrow base traditionally associated with seminary training. In other words, interest in archaeology as a support base for historical judgments about biblical data is no longer a major concern of "biblical" archaeology. Technology, social and economic history, and demography—these are focal points of the newer archaeology. Within its theoretical framework, even animal bones and the pollen count in a mud brick provide significant data for determination of cultural patterns. As for written documents and artifacts that may be seen in a museum, they are but a fraction of the total witness to human activity.[5]

To accommodate the demands for such rigorous inquiry, the term "Syro-Palestinian Archaeology" came into vogue in the 1970s. Such delimitation was in part a reaction to far-ranging attempts on the part of "biblical archaeologists" to cover all of Near Eastern studies, of which even an Albright could not achieve mastery. A further contributing factor was biblical archaeology's lack of a clear-

---

[4] See Dever, *Recent Archaeological Discoveries*, 33–36, on the history of the emergence of Syro-Palestinian archaeology as a discipline, distinct from the less defined form of biblical archaeology. An article by W. S. LaSor, "Archeology," *ISBE*, 1:235-44, well describes the techniques, but one ought to follow the reading of it with exposure to Dever's work. For a nontechnical statement of Dever's thinking, see "Archaeology and the Bible—Understanding their Special Relationship," *BAR* 16 (1990): 52–58, 62.

[5] For a popular presentation of the new archaeological approach, see Thomas E. Levy, "How Ancient Man First Utilized the Rivers in the Desert," *BAR* 16 (1990): 20–31.

cut identity, without which academic "discipline" has little meaning in an era of unparalleled burgeoning data. Moreover, it was thought to be too parochial, while also failing to solve basic historical problems connected with the patriarchal, Mosaic, and conquest eras.

What does all this mean for biblical scholarship? Need there be a great divide between the way archaeology is done by archaeologists throughout the world and the interests of biblical scholarship, which has long relied on documents and artifacts to shed light on biblical texts? Dever suggests that the latter is possible if it be acknowledged that certain textual remains are "curated artifacts," among which the Bible is the prime exemplar. As Dever indicates in connection with the problem of using the Bible as a database for historiography, this is not a demeaning term, but a statement of fact: the Bible is one of many relics from antiquity. By "curated" he means that it is like a carefully preserved artifact, which is "repaired and/or altered and usually put to a somewhat different use from that for which it was originally intended."[6] In other words, to do archaeology objectively when taking account of biblical data, one must not begin with presumption of historicity in a biblical account and then do archaeology to endorse it. Again, this does not mean that the Bible is given second-class status, but that recognition of archaeology's concentration on the larger context in which the Bible took shape can provide a broader base on which the biblical material takes on "immediate, vivid, flesh-and-blood reality." Understood in this sense, the term "new archaeology," when applied to archaeology done with an interest in biblical content, can be useful in assessing what has taken place in the history of "biblical archaeology," namely, the exploration and excavation of areas and sites that are of interest to students of the Bible.

Paul W. Lapp explains in a popular presentation, *Biblical Archaeology and History* (New York: World Publishing Co., 1969), the close association of "biblical archaeology" and "biblical theology" in terms of the "acts of God." The term "biblical archaeology," he points out, is pertinent if one means archaeology of the biblical period, but in the minds of some, he warns, it means a separate discipline because it deals with the Bible, "a book apart from all other books."[7] Awareness of his observation will protect an amateur from being felled in the crossfire of terminological debate and constantly changing theoretical perceptions respecting the task of archaeology, for the term "new archaeology" is itself in process of becoming a linguistic artifact.[8] In short,

---

[6] Dever, *Recent Archaeological Discoveries,* 10.

[7] Lapp, *Biblical Archaeology,* 62. Lapp cites Werner Keller, *The Bible as History: Archaeology Confirms the Book of Books,* as a case study for apologetic interest.

[8] For a critique of "new archaeology," see Paul de Courbin, *Qu'est-ce que l'archéologie? Essai sur la nature de la recherche archéologique* (Paris, 1982); now in English, *What Is Archaeology? An Essay on the Nature of Archaeological Research* (Chicago: University of Chicago Press, 1988).

the newer approaches suggest that a dialogue between those who espouse the older interests and those who favor the newer can enrich all participants. Also, much could perhaps be gained if the term "biblical archaeology" were applied to archaeological activity or discussion in connection with geographical areas generally associated with data contained in the Bible.

ALBRIGHT AND . . .

Biblical archaeology, in the sense of archaeology involving matters of interest to Bible students in the United States, begins with Edward Robinson, who in 1838 and 1851 rediscovered more than two hundred long lost biblical sites by using Arabic place-names. In 1870 the American Palestine Exploration Society came into being. In its statement of purpose appear the words: "for the illustration and *defense* of the Bible."[9] This statement was a departure from the text of the British Palestine Exploration Society. Through the efforts of William Foxwell Albright, whose achievements and breadth of understanding as an Orientalist are not likely to be surpassed, biblical archaeology reached its zenith. His thought-provoking presentation on the relation of archaeology to the historical task remains a staggering achievement: *From the Stone Age to Christianity: Monotheism and the Historical Process,* 2d rev. ed. (Baltimore: Johns Hopkins University Press, 1946; Anchor Book A100, Garden City, N.Y.: Doubleday, 1957), a book which was all the more notable because so little had been done in Israelite historiography. A sequel, *Archaeology and the Religion of Israel: The Ayer Lectures of the Colgate-Rochester Divinity School, 1941* (Baltimore, 1942; 3d ed., 1953), presents the religion of Israel in its historical context. Albright considered archaeology an adjunct of biblical studies, but not of the type exhibited in a work like that of W. W. Prescott, *The Spade and the Bible: Archaeological Discoveries Support the Old Book* (New York: Revell, 1933). Similarly, W. S. LaSor defines biblical archaeology as "the study of any of the material remains of man's activity that may properly be used to shed further light on the biblical story."[10]

In *The Archaeology of Palestine* (1st ed., 1949; Penguin Book A199, Harmondsworth, 1951; rev. ed., Gloucester, Mass.: P. Smith, 1971), Albright outlines the history of the "discovery" of Palestine and then fills in the detail of successive stages of Palestinian history as unearthed by the archaeologist's spade. For a *Festschrift* published in honor of Albright, *The Bible and the Ancient Near East* (New York: Doubleday, 1961), a book full of nourishing thought and data, George E. Mendenhall submitted an article, "Biblical History in Perspective." While praising the master, he had a sense of the future:

[9] Dever, *Recent Archaeological Discoveries,* 13.
[10] W. S. LaSor, "Archaeology," *ISBE,* 1:235.

"The impact of other disciplines, especially the social sciences, upon biblical history has not yet been fully felt; here again, Albright has been in many respects a pioneer. The future will no doubt see further application of other disciplines and their methods in the study of ancient Israel, but this process has tended to be rather slow, since most scholars are more interested in the immediate religious concerns of their subject matter" (pp. 35–36). In Albright's work one senses the prudence that knows how to use the winds of change for forward movement and guard against the gusts that blow away the best of the past.[11]

Some of Dever's conclusions will most certainly be liable to correction and modification, especially in respect to the alleged demise of biblical archaeology. One is under obligation therefore to add some observations respecting one of the most articulate communicators of the contributions made by archaeologists of Bible lands and sites, namely, George Ernest Wright (1909–74), Shechem's deliverer from obscurity, protégé of Albright, Dever's teacher, and advocate of the Neo-Orthodox Biblical Theology movement. Wright's semi-popular *Biblical Archaeology* (1st ed., 1957; 2d ed. rev., Philadelphia: Westminster Press, 1962), at first sight might discourage further attention from those who think that "new archaeology" has said the last word. Its opening paragraph proclaims: "The biblical archaeologist may or may not be an excavator himself, but he studies the discoveries of the excavations in order to glean from them every fact that throws a direct, indirect or even diffused light upon the Bible. He must be intelligently concerned with stratigraphy and typology, upon which the methodology of modern archaeology rests. . . . Yet his chief concern is not with methods or pots or weapons in themselves alone. *His central and absorbing interest is the understanding and exposition of the Scriptures*" (emphasis ours). Words like this coming from an archaeologist, especially American, were not too well accepted in Germany. On the other hand, this work is so filled with readable information relating to the biblical texts and presented in such an arresting manner that it can be ignored only with great loss to the student who passes it up for more ephemeral fare. For the fact remains that those whose main task includes exposition of the Bible will make use of those aspects of archaeological study which illuminate a biblical text, while at the same time taking into account the larger scene and the "total dynamics of cultural change."[12]

---

[11] Albright's bibliography fills an entire book: David Noel Freedman, assisted by Robert McDonald and Daniel L. Mattson, *The Published Works of William Foxwell Albright: A Comprehensive Bibliography* (Cambridge: American Schools of Oriental Research, 1975).

[12] In fairness to Wright it must be noted that he saw the future moving in. See his "What Archaeology Can and Cannot Do," *Biblical Archaeologist* 34 (1971): 70–76. For Dever's tribute to Wright, see "Biblical Theology and Biblical Archaeology: An Appreciation of G. Ernest Wright," *HTR* 73 (1980): 1–15. For an appreciative assessment of Wright's contributions to archaeology, but with sensitivity to new directions, see Philip J. King, "The Influence of G. Ernest Wright on the Archaeology of Palestine," in *Archaeology and Biblical Interpretation: Essays in Memory*

Well known beyond Great Britain for indefatigable zeal in probing the mysterious fortunes of Jericho and her corrections of Garstang's conclusions, Kathleen M. Kenyon has earned general respect for her ability to interpret technical archaeological matters for a public beyond her peers. In *Archaeology in the Holy Land* (New York: Frederick A. Praeger, 1960; 4th ed., New York: W. W. Norton, 1979), she shows her mastery of evidence as she traces the history of Palestine from prehistoric times to the postexilic period. For a focus on work done in Palestine since 1940, consult *The Bible and Recent Archaeology* (1978; rev. ed. P. R. S. Moorey, Atlanta: John Knox Press, 1987), which Kenyon developed out of a series of four lectures delivered at Oberlin College. Covering archaeological activity from ca. 3000 to the Herodian period, Kenyon proceeds on the premise that archaeological study provides a constant stream of new information for better reconstruction of the ancient society of the lands of the Bible. In this work one observes a salute to postmodern developments.[13] Finding support in Sir Mortimer Wheeler's adage "The archaeologist may find the tub but altogether miss Diogenes," propaganda for the Wheeler-Kenyon school, without excessive politeness to colleagues in the profession, was made by Hendricus J. Franken and C. A. Franken-Battershill in *A Primer of Old Testament Archaeology* (Leiden; New York: Brill, 1963). In *The Archaeology of the Land of Israel,* trans. Anson F. Rainey (Philadelphia: Westminster Press, 1982; orig. Hebrew, Jerusalem, 1978), Yohanan Aharoni adopts Kenyon's stratigraphic designations in a study that takes him from prehistoric times to the destruction of the First Temple.

POST-KENYON PERIOD

In *Archaeology of the Land of the Bible 10,000–586 B.C.E.* (New York: Doubleday, 1990) the purpose of Amihai Mazar is to "present a comprehensive, updated and as objective as possible picture of the archaeological research of Palestine relating to the Old Testament period" (p. xv). This book appears in the Anchor Bible Reference Library, which is a third component of the

---

of Dr. Glenn Rose, ed. Leo G. Perdue, Lawrence E. Toombs, and Gary Lance Johnson (Atlanta: John Knox Press, 1987), 15–29. One who reads this book will gain an impression of how the Bible comes alive as it is understood within the social and cultural matrices that gave it shape. To bridge academia and the public square Wright launched the *Biblical Archaeologist* in 1938 for lay people.

[13] For a synthesis of previous work done at Jericho, see Piotr Bienkowski, *Jericho in the Late Bronze Age* (Warminster, UK: Aris & Phillips, 1986). After careful study, including microscopic examination of shards, Bienkowski concludes that evidence of occupation in the Late Bronze Age (ca. 1550–1200) is problematical. For a different view, see B. G. Wood, "Did the Israelites Conquer Jericho? A New Look at the Archaeological Evidence," *BAR* 16 (1990): 44–58. On the date of the destruction suggested by Garstang, see K. M. Kenyon, in *Encyclopedia of Archaeological Excavations in the Holy Land,* 4 vols. (Jerusalem, 1975–1978), 2:564 (entry "Jericho").

Anchor Bible group and serves "as a supplement to the cutting edge of the most recent scholarship." Mazar puts the big question (p. xvi), ostensibly to students who can learn the basics of archaeological study through this book: Should archaeology of the Holy Land be regarded as an individual discipline or is it just another branch of Near Eastern archaeology?

To mark the one-hundreth anniversary of the first stratigraphic excavation in the Land of Israel, an excavation in 1890 that saw the beginning of scientific archaeological investigation in Israel, the Open University of Israel published a collection of essays under the editorship of Amnon Ben-Tor. A revised translation by R. Greenberg of the Hebrew-language edition appeared under the title *The Archaeology of Ancient Israel* (New Haven: Yale University Press, 1992). Ben-Tor notes previous attempts at a synthesis: Albright's *Archaeology of Palestine,* which he praises as one of the best introductions to sites and life in ancient Palestine; Kenyon's *Archaeology in the Holy Land;* and Aharoni's *The Archaeology of the Land of Israel.* Now, Ben-Tor notes, we have a team effort.[14] A variety of approaches, covering the Neolithic, Chalcolithic, and Early Bronze ages, finds enrichment through magnificent photographs and line drawings. Among the items included in the bibliography students may find especially helpful Ian Hodder, *Reading the Past* (Cambridge, UK: Cambridge University Press, 1986; 2d ed., 1991) and Roland de Vaux, "On Right and Wrong Uses of Archaeology," in *Near Eastern Archaeology in the Twentieth Century: Essays in Honor of Nelson Glueck,* ed. James A. Sanders (Garden City, N.Y.: Doubleday, 1970), 64–80.

In an endeavor to meet some of Albrecht Alt's concerns about a firmer footing for a history of Israel's origins, Israel Finkelstein produced *The Archaeology of the Israelite Settlement* (Jerusalem: Israel Exploration Society, 1988). He may not have arrived at the origins, but he has deeply probed Iron Age settlements and ensures that the recording of the history of Israel's beginnings be heavily dependent on archaeological data.

IN THE PUBLIC SQUARE

Numerous books await opportunity to give students and interested members of the general public access to what is otherwise the secret lore of specialists. Some of them are written by people who are not themselves professional archaeologists but have the knowledge and skill necessary for reliable communication in the public square. Among them are Jack Finegan and Millar Burrows. In *Light from the Ancient Past: The Archeological Background of the Hebrew-Christian Religion* (Princeton: Princeton University Press, 1946;

---

[14] Amnon Ben-Tor, ed., *The Archaeology of Palestine,* trans. R. Greenberg (New Haven: Yale University Press, 1992), xix.

2d ed. rev. with account taken of many new excavations, 1959), Finegan fills in and relates many details with much better than average archaeological ability and insight. In *The Archaeology of the New Testament: The Life of Jesus and the Beginning of the Early Church* (Princeton: Princeton University Press, 1969) he explores sites relating to stories about Jesus and John the Baptist. And in *The Archaeology of the New Testament: The Mediterranean World of the Early Christian Apostles* (Boulder, Colo.: Westview Press, 1981), he exhibits the findings of archaeologists relating to traditions about John, Paul, and Peter.

Millar Burrows answered one of his own questions in a book of considerable merit: *What Mean These Stones? The Significance of Archeology for Biblical Studies* (New Haven: American Schools of Oriental Research, 1941), which came with the American Schools of Oriental Research seal of acceptance and depicts with numerous illustrations the practical value of archaeology in biblical interpretation.

André Parrot, the well-known excavator of the city of Mari on the Upper Euphrates and curator-in-chief of the Musées nationaux de France, has also done much to acquaint lay readers with the various results of scholarly archaeological research. Excavations by Parrot and later by J. Margueron yielded over twenty thousand cuneiform texts. Parrot's series, Studies in Biblical Archaeology, begun with *The Flood and Noah's Ark,* trans. Edwin Hudson (New York: Philosophical Library, 1955), is written with enthusiasm and abounds in illustrations.

For those who cannot explore the British Museum, there is no better collection of photographs of its most spectacular artifacts derived especially from nineteenth-century excavations than T. C. Mitchell's *Biblical Archaeology: Documents from the British Museum* (Cambridge, UK/New York: Cambridge University Press, 1988). A brief commentary accompanies each photographed exhibit or document. Document 18 pictures a restored text of the "Moabite" stone, which records an inscription by King Mesha of Moab, based on the copy of the text published by Theodor Nöldeke, in 1870, who succeeded in purchasing it for the Berlin museum. Delivery was frustrated by international politics and the stone was subsequently smashed by local Bedouin. Fortunately a squeeze had been taken before this act of vandalism. Numerous fragments were joined and the original stele can be seen in the Louvre. Unfortunately it appears that there was no Solomon in the vicinity to resolve the dispute. The stele mentions Omri's "oppression" and that Mesha mounted a rebellion.[15] Mitchell's document 7 exhibits a letter found at Amarna in which Yapahu, the ruler of Gezer, asks for help against a marauding group of "Hapiru." Were

---

[15] Detailed information on Moab and the inscription is provided in essays edited by Andrew Dearman, *Studies in the Mesha Inscription and Moab* (Atlanta: Scholars Press, 1989). The inscription has generated an extensive bibliography. Wright, *Biblical Archaeology,* 156, credits the discovery to a young French archaeologist, Charles Clermont-Ganneau, in 1868.

these people connected with the "Hebrews"? Document 26 in Mitchell's collection features the "Annals of Sennacherib," found at Nebi Yunus (Nineveh) by a Colonel Taylor in 1830. The annals make no claim that Jerusalem was taken, but for a different perspective on the campaign see 2 Kgs 18:17–19:36 and Isaiah 36–37. Treaty formulas have long been a topic of discussion, and it is important to note when viewing the "Vassal Treaty of Esarhaddon," king of Assyria, 680–669 B.C., in document 28, that usage varies between treaty and covenant forms used in the second millennium and the first millennium B.C. How little there is in common between the early chapters of Genesis and Mesopotamian epics of creation and the flood can be seen from a reading of the accounts pictured in documents 3 (Atrahasis Epic) and 32 (Enuma Elish). The caption, "Fragments of an Unknown Gospel," in no. 55, refers to two pages of papyrus (Papyrus Egerton 2), which were written about A.D. 150.

The method of presentation followed by Gaalyah Cornfeld and David Noel Freedman in *Archaeology of the Bible: Book by Book* (San Francisco: Harper & Row, 1976) is clear from the title, but the results are somewhat muddied for the unsophisticated reader, who must keep in mind that the traditional sequence of books has little to do with the actual chronology of things and events recorded in them.

For the general reader who finds it difficult to adjust to the cultural conditionedness of the Bible, there is a helpful 101-page introductory piece by Raymond Edward Brown, *Recent Discoveries and the Biblical World* (Wilmington, Del.: Glazier, 1983), which tells the reader what archaeology is about and discusses some of the principal sites worked on since the Second World War. After reading this book, take a look at Leslie J. Hoppe's answer to the question *What Are They Saying About Biblical Archaeology?* (New York: Paulist Press, 1984). Programmed for beginners who desire to know how archaeologists reach conclusions about matters relating to biblical data is *The Old Testament and the Archaeologist* (Philadelphia: Fortress Press, 1981; London: SPCK, 1983), by Hubert Darrell Lance, who has a knack for bringing to the light matters shrouded in the mist of the past.

MISCELLANY

One of the more notable books zooming in on a specific feature of the ancient world is Hershel Shanks, *Judaism in Stone: The Archaeology of Ancient Synagogues* (San Francisco: Harper & Row, 1979). More technical is Lee Israel Levine, *Ancient Synagogues Revealed* (Jerusalem: Israel Exploration Society, 1981). Lionel Casson is recognized for his knowledge of maritime data, and his *Ships and Seamanship in the Ancient World* (Princeton, 1986) is an invitation to interesting sailings into the past. The lack of an introduction or sourcebook in the English language for study of early Christian archaeology prompted Graydon F. Snyder to produce *Ante Pacem: Archaeological Evidence of Church Life Before Constantine* (Macon, Ga.: Mercer University Press, 1985). Besides producing a very informative text, Snyder lists important secondary literature, some of which would escape notice without his guidance.

A basic resource for chronological work is Robert W. Ehrich, *Chronologies in Old World Archaeology* (Chicago: University of Chicago, 1965), which concentrates on 5000–1400 B.C. For those who find themselves frustrated when confronting the varying chronological systems used in the ancient world, Jack Finegan, a master of times and seasons, provides a key to the data in *Handbook of Biblical Chronology: Principles of Time Reckoning in the Ancient World and Problems of Chronology in the Bible* (Princeton: Princeton University Press, 1964). For further enlightenment on calendaric matters, consult E. J. Bickerman, *Chronology of the Ancient World,* 2d ed. (Ithaca, N.Y.: Cornell University Press, 1980).

Before contemplating a "dig," get acquainted with Martha Joukowsky's *A Complete Manual of Field Archaeologists: Tools and Techniques of Field Work for Archaeology* (Englewood Cliffs, N.J.: Prentice-Hall, 1980).[16] Students wishing to keep abreast of archaeological developments will find a reliable publication in *The Biblical Archaeologist* (*BA*), published by the American Schools of Oriental Research. Designed for the nonspecialist, the *Biblical Archaeology Review* (*BAR*) serves copy that is pleasing to the eye and composed to make one wise. With *BAR* one can keep up with current explorations and vigorous debates relating to archaeology and biblical topics. The Dead Sea scrolls are among the many interesting subjects receiving coverage in *BAR*. Its sister publication, *Bible Review* (*BR*), is pitched to a broader reading public.[17]

THE LAND

GEOGRAPHY

Geography is the science that studies the earth's surface and its physical features, climate, and distributions of plant and animal life, and takes account of their varying effect on populations, cultures, and industries. The vital role played

---

[16] Joukowsky's work is generous with bibliography on a host of topics, pp. 543–607. On methodology, see also W. G. Dever and H. D. Lance, eds. *A Manual of Field Excavation: Handbook for Field Archaeologists* (Cincinnati: Hebrew Union College–Jewish Institute of Religion, 1978), based on work at Gezer (1964–71).

[17] The Biblical Archaeology Society's *New Testament Archaeology Slide Set,* ed. Dan P. Cole (Washington, D.C., 1986), provides, in addition to the fine photographs, a manual with informative articles drawn from *BAR* and *BR*.

by topographical and other features in the history of lands and peoples is signally exhibited in the fortunes of Palestine and its inhabitants.

Since Edward Robinson's epoch-making trip through Palestine in 1838, the land has been subject to ever closer scrutiny; today only a few ancient sites remain unidentified. Much that was previously written on the geography of Palestine is therefore considerably antiquated but retains some advantages that derive from scrutiny prior to increasing industrialization and natural changes wrought by time's relentless course. George Adam Smith, *The Historical Geography of the Holy Land in Relation to the History of Israel and of the Early Church,* first published in 1894, 4th ed. (London, 1896), still remains, in its broader outlines, an accurate and in every respect a most captivating account. For encyclopedic information on the physical characteristics of Palestine, consult Denis Baly, *The Geography of the Bible* (New York: Harper, 1957; "complete revision," 1974). Baly's *Geographical Companion to the Bible* (New York: McGraw-Hill, 1963) shows how geography impacted the lives of the people portrayed in the biblical record.

Long a standard reference work is Félix Marie Abel, *Géographie de la Palestine,* 2 vols. (Paris: Libraire Lecoffre, J. Gabalda, 1933, 1938). This work is cited frequently in a fine textbook by Yohanan Aharoni, *The Land of the Bible: A Historical Geography,* trans. A. F. Rainey (Philadelphia: Westminster Press, 1967; 2d ed., 1979; rev. A. F. Rainey, 1980), which takes the reader down to the Persian period. For continuation past that period, consult Michael Avi-Yonah, *The Holy Land from the Persian to the Arab Conquests (536 B.C. to A.D. 640): A Historical Geography,* trans. and rev. A. F. Rainey (Grand Rapids: Baker, 1977; orig. Hebrew, 3d ed., Jerusalem, 1962). In Martin Noth, *The Old Testament World,* trans. Victor I. Gruhn (Philadelphia: Fortress Press, 1966), a review of Old Testament texts and versions plus a survey of methods of textual critical work round out a savory blend of geographical and historical knowledge, with some accent on cultural details. The broader reading public will take delight in H. Donner, *Einführung in die biblische Landes- und Altertumskunde* (Darmstadt: Wissenschaftliche Buchgesellschaft, 1976), and for those who wish to delve further, this book contains ample bibliographies.

For a look at the flora and fauna along the way see Michael Zohary, *Plants of the Bible: A Complete Handbook to all the Plants* (New York: Cambridge University Press, 1982) and Garland Bare, *Plants and Animals of the Bible* ([London]: United Bible Societies, 1969). As in the identification of ancient colors, determination especially of botanical items is not done without risk, but both of these works offer needed guidance. In addition to discussion of botanical entities under nine headings, with relevant biblical texts, the first book includes two hundred full-color plates "taken in the natural habitat." Bare's compilation, without pictures, was prepared for the Thailand Bible Revision Company, but all biblical students can use it with profit, not least of all for the value of its lengthy bibliography. All terms are transliterated and briefly defined in the lead column, with scientific equivalents noted, when ascertainable. Other columns include biblical references, translation in KJV and RSV, Thai/Southeast Asia equivalent, and two columns of workbook space. An ambitious book by George Cansdale, *All the Animals of the Bible Lands* (Grand Rapids: Zondervan, 1970), requires some philological correctives but provides much useful information.

SITES

Specific sites come up for treatment in numerous publications. Over four hundred Palestinian sites are discussed in *The New Encyclopedia of Archaeological Excavations in the Holy Land,* 4 vols. (Westwood, N.J.: Prentice-Hall, 1993), edited by Ephraim Stern, assisted by Ayelet Gilboa, both from the University of Jerusalem, with Joseph Aviram, of the Israel Exploration Society, as editorial director.[18] The list of contributors reads like a who's who in archaeology. For authoritative information on sites of interest to students of Greek literature, as well as of places mentioned in the New Testament, there is nothing that surpasses *The Princeton Encyclopedia of Classical Sites,* ed. Richard Stillwell with William L. MacDonald and Marian Holland McAllister (Princeton: Princeton University Press, 1976).

Several earlier classic treatments also deserve mention. Heading the list is Gustaf Hermann Dalman, *Orte und Wege Jesu,* 3d ed. rev. (Gütersloh: C. Bertelsmann, 1924). The translation of this edition into English by Paul P. Levertoff, *Sacred Sites and Ways: Studies in the Topography of the Gospels* (New York: Macmillan, 1935), includes additional matter and is one of the finest introductions to the land of Jesus. Conjectures still bridge many gaps in our knowledge of the history of Jericho, but Miss Kenyon's digging—see the joint expedition reports, prepared with the help of colleagues, in Excavations at Jericho, vols. 1–5 (London, 1960–83)—has done much to undermine John Garstang's claim to have found the victim walls of Joshua's campaigns. The expeditions and detailed explorations of Nelson Glueck, who dedicated much of 1932–47 to study of ancient Transjordan, are documented with text, photography, and drawings in several editions of *The Annual of the American Schools of Oriental Research.* Supplementary results of his intensive study of

---

[18] The first edition of this work was originally published in Hebrew, 2 vols. (Jerusalem, 1970). Michael Avi-Yonah (d. 1974) helped mark the fiftieth anniversary of the Israel Exploration Society for the English-speaking world with an English-language edition under the title *Encyclopedia of Archaeological Excavations in the Holy Land,* 4 vols. (Englewood Cliffs, N.J.: Prentice-Hall, 1975–1978); M. Avi-Yonah edited the first two volumes, and after his death Ephraim Stern saw volumes 3 and 4 through publication.

the Jordan River area are to be found in *The Other Side of the Jordan* (New Haven: American Schools of Oriental Research, 1940), *The River Jordan* (Philadelphia: Westminster Press, 1946; rev. ed., New York: McGraw-Hill, 1968), and *Rivers in the Desert: A History of the Negev* (New York: Farrar, Straus and Cudahy, 1959). Glueck visited more than 1,500 sites, whose identification is in the main accepted by other scholars.

Sites and biblical references are linked in a series of essays produced by various scholars for *Archaeology and Old Testament Study: Jubilee Volume of the Society for Old Testament Study, 1917–1967,* ed. David Winton Thomas (Oxford: Clarendon Press, 1967).

ATLASES

Numerous atlases provide the basic cartographical materials for a more reliable and appreciative survey from a distance of the Palestinian landscape both ancient and modern. Atlases of Bible lands range from collections of only maps to maps accompanied by archaeological researches relating, as the case may be, to land areas, population movements, military campaigns, cultic practices, and numerous other topics. Meriting prime consideration is *The Harper Atlas of the Bible,* gen. ed. James B. Pritchard (New York: Harper & Row, 1987), published in Great Britain as *The Times Atlas of the Bible* (1987). This is a marvelous combination of masterfully produced photographs combined with informative text—the next best thing to visiting a museum of antiquities. In keeping with developments in the space age, some of the maps take account of the curvature of the earth and replace flat projection with a more realistic one. Also, the position of north varies on such maps, depending on the subject that is depicted. But there are a sufficient number of maps with traditional orientation. A rewritten and more concise version of this atlas appeared under the title, *The Harper Concise Atlas of the Bible,* ed. James B. Pritchard (New York: Harper & Row, 1991), which makes use of dates in the third edition of *The Cambridge Ancient History* and also information on dates and terminology in the *Encyclopedia of Archaeological Excavations in the Holy Land,* vol. 4, ed. M. Avi-Yonah and E. Stern (Englewood Cliff, N.J.: Prentice-Hall, 1978). Of older works one may still consult with profit G. Ernest Wright and F. V. Filson, *The Westminster Historical Atlas to the Bible,* rev. ed. (Philadelphia: Westminster Press, 1956). A special feature of Lucas Hendricus Grollenberg, *Atlas of the Bible,* trans. and ed. Joyce M. H. Reid and Harold Henry Rowley (New York: Nelson, 1956), is annotated maps that blend history and topography in remarkable fashion. Magnificent photographs contribute to its excellence.[19]

---

[19] This atlas originally appeared in Holland as *Atlas van de Bijbel* (Amsterdam, 1954) and

Detailed discussion of geographic and topographic references from Genesis to Revelation may be had in Emil G. Kraeling, *Rand McNally Bible Atlas* (Chicago: Rand McNally, 1956), which is designed primarily for advanced students. A remarkable feature of *The Macmillan Bible Atlas,* by Yohanan Aharoni and Michael Avi-Yonah (New York: Macmillan, 1968; rev. ed., 1977), is a handsome collection of 262 territorial maps prepared by cartographers and other specialists associated with Carta, at Jerusalem. Each of these maps illustrates a portion of text, ordinarily a paragraph of 150 to 200 words. Many of the texts and maps relate to individual campaigns and conquests. "The Sortie of the Moabites . . ." (no. 133) traces the route of invasion, and below the text is a photograph of the Mesha stele, which one can decipher without difficulty. Map no. 177 charts the travels of Zenon, to whom historians owe so much of their knowledge about the era of Ptolemy II, and the text offers a brief biography of this ardent collector of business documents.

More general guidance is found in the compact *Oxford Bible Atlas,* ed. Herbert G. May with Robert W. Hamilton and G. N. S. Hunt (London, 1962; 3d ed. rev. John Day, New York: Oxford University Press, 1984) and in F. F. Bruce, *Bible History Atlas* (New York: Crossroad, 1982). In *Atlas of Israel,* published by the famed house of Elsevier (Amsterdam, London, New York, 1970), even the paper, ink, and color mixes originated in Israel. An official work of the State of Israel, the atlas includes not only detailed description in standard categories of geographical documentation but also a history of Israel from prehistoric times to the present. Also of exceptional merit is J. Monson, et al., *Student Map Manual: Historical Geography of the Bible Lands* (Jerusalem/Grand Rapids: Zondervan, 1979). For quick locating within 48 pages, use *Hammond's Atlas of the Bible Lands,* ed. Harry Thomas Frank (Maplewood, N.J.: Hammond, 1977; new ed., 1984).

For broader documentation of the ancient world, consult Antonius A. M. van der Heyden and Howard H. Scullard, *Atlas of the Classical World* (New York: Nelson, 1959). This atlas, which deals exclusively with polytheistic Greco-Roman antiquity, is important for understanding the context in which Christianity was born and to which it took many directions of return. Its section on Hellenism serves as a bridge to Frederik van der Meer and Christine Mohrmann, *Atlas of the Early Christian World,* trans. and ed. Mary F. Hedlund and Harold H. Rowley (New York: Nelson, 1958), which illuminates the early church. For key sites relating to Acts and Paul's letters, consult Moses I. Finley, *Atlas of Classical Archaeology* (New York: McGraw-Hill, 1977).

---

in French as *Atlas de la Bible* (Brussels, 1954), on which the translation is based. Grollenberg's redesigned, compact *Shorter Atlas of the Bible,* trans. Mary F. Hedlund (New York: Nelson, 1959) was also published as *The Penguin Shorter Atlas of the Bible* (Baltimore: Penguin, 1978). Old, but a marvelous repository of contours and descriptions, is *The Survey of Western Palestine,* by C. R. Conder and H. H. Kitchener, 3 vols. (London, 1881–1883; reprint, Tel Aviv, 1970).

The general reader will appreciate Clemens Kopp, *The Holy Places of the Gospels* (New York: Herder, 1963), a translation by Ronald Walls of *Die heiligen Stätten der Evangelien* (Regensburg: Pustet, 1959)—something like taking a bus tour through the Gospels. To follow St. Paul in a similar way, use Henri Metzger, *St. Paul's Journeys in the Greek Orient,* trans. S. H. Hooke (London: SCM Press, 1955. For Jerusalem and environs, take the tour with John Wilkinson, *The Jerusalem Jesus Knew: An Archaeological Guide to the Gospels* (Nashville: Nelson, 1983).[20]

THE LITERATURE OF THE NEAR EAST: TABLETS AND SHERDS

UGARIT

In 1822, J. F. Champollion published his successful deciphering of Egyptian hieroglyphics. H. C. Rawlinson followed this astounding feat with a publication in 1851 of 112 lines of the Babylonian text of the Behistun inscription. Since then other languages and dialects, including the stubborn Hittite, have surrendered their secrets. But the discovery of clay tablets at the site of ancient Ugarit has had perhaps the most far-reaching effects on our understanding of the larger religious context in which Israel's history must be written. In 1928 in the region of Ras Shamra, about 12 km. north of the port of Latakia, in Syria, an Arab peasant struck a slab of stone with his plough and uncovered traces of an ancient tomb containing a number of potsherds and some small undamaged vessels. An expedition was sent out under the direction of Charles Virolleaud, who soon focused his attention on a nearby mound. Subsequent excavations under the leadership of Claude F. A. Schaeffer brought to light a remarkable civilization, documented by literary, religious, lexical, legal, and commercial texts, written variously in Akkadian, Hurrian, Sumerian, and Ugaritic. Of these languages the Akkadian, that is, Babylonian and Assyrian, were well known; Sumerian was partially known; and some slight acquaintance with Hurrian had already been achieved by scholars; but Ugaritic was entirely new. Professor Hans Bauer of Halle soon inferred that the language was of Semitic origin and tracked down a few words, but Edouard Paul Dhorme and Charles Virolleaud merit the credit for raveling the skein of the Ras Shamra alphabet. In *The Cuneiform Texts of Ras Shamra Ugarit* (London, 1939) Claude F. A. Schaeffer discusses the history of Ugarit and the types of documents found at Ras Shamra and relates the discovery to the interpretation

---

[20] For a far-ranging summary of archaeological work, from Rome to the Indus River, see the various articles on archaeology in *ISBE,* 1:235-283. In *ABD* it is necessary to check under each site entry.

of the Old Testament. Godfrey Rolles Driver, *Canaanite Myths and Legends* (Edinburgh: T. & T. Clark, 1956), gives a transliterated text and translation of the poems, and supplements the literature with observations on philology and grammar and a Ugaritic glossary. An even more comprehensive sampling is to be found in Cyrus H. Gordon, *Ugaritic Literature: A Comprehensive Translation of the Poetic and Prose Texts* (Rome: Pontifical Biblical Institute, 1949), which includes epistles, diplomatic and administrative texts, and veterinary prescriptions and inventories in addition to the myths and legends. To keep up with developments, follow *Ugarit-Forschungen: Internationale Jahrbuch für die Altertumskunde Syrien-Palästinas* (Neukirchen-Vluyn, 1969–). In the use of Ugaritic materials for interpretation of the biblical text, the student will do well to heed Albright's caution against overenthusiastic attempts to find biblical names and places documented in Canaanite shards.[21] Prudence demands a check against standard Ugaritic grammars and glossaries.[22]

El-Amarna

In another part of the world, on the eastern bank of the Nile River, a Bedouin woman in 1887 came upon some clay tablets near the village of Hajji Qandil, about 300 km. south of Cairo. Scholars called the location of the tablets "el Amarna," after the name of the Bedouin tribe. These "dead files" of international state correspondence come from the reigns of Amenophis III, Akhenaten, and Tutankhamen. Numerous other tablets came to light in the course of illegal trading and serious excavation, and Jørgen Alexander Knudtzon, with Otto Weber (commentary) and Erich Ebeling (indexes) issued *Die El-Amarna Tafeln mit Einleitung und Erläuterungen,* Vorderasiatische Bibliothek 2 (Leipzig: J. C. Hinrichs'sche Buchhandlung, 1907–1915). This work held the field until William L. Moran edited *Les lettres d'El-Amarna,* Littératures anciennes du Proche-Orient 13 (Paris: Cerf, 1987). An English-

---

[21] See Albright's admonition in connection with Ugaritic texts in *The Archaeology of Palestine,* Penguin Book A199 (Harmondsworth, 1951), 235.

[22] See Albright, *Archaeology of Palestine,* 109. Edmond Jacob, *Ras Shamra-Ugarit et l'Ancien Testament,* Cahiers d'Archéologie biblique 12 (Neuchatel: Delachaux & Niestlé, 1960), and Arvid S. Kapelrud, *The Ras Shamra Discoveries and the Old Testament,* trans. George W. Anderson (Norman, Okla.: University of Oklahoma Press, 1963), long ago set an example for sober method. For ongoing work at Ugarit, see the journal *Syria* in the section "Chronicles archéologique"; and *Annales archéologique arabes syriennes* (Damascus). Also consult the series Ugaritica, of which no. 1 appeared in 1939 (Paris, edited by Schaeffer). See also *The Harper Atlas of the Bible,* 44–45. John Huehnergard, *The Akkadian of Ugarit,* Harvard Semitic Studies 34 (Atlanta: Scholars Press, 1989), offers a description of the orthography and grammar of documents written in Akkadian syllabic cuneiform. In an earlier work *Ugaritic Vocabulary in Syllabic Transcription,* Harvard Semitic Studies 32 (Atlanta: Scholars Press, 1987), the same author dealt with the lexicon of the Ugaritic-Akkadian dialect.

language edition of this French work was published by Moran with corrections, expansions, and updating, *The Amarna Letters* (Baltimore: Johns Hopkins University Press, 1992).

MARI

Mari, an ancient city of Mesopotamia situated on the west bank of the Euphrates about 315 km. southeast of Haran, was first accorded archaeological recognition after the discovery of a statue fragment by Bedouins. André Parrot began excavating in 1933, and since then more than twenty thousand cuneiform texts from the Old Babylonian period have come to light. Detailed reports on this city began to flow again after J. Margueron's researches, beginning in 1979.[23]

EBLA

To the northwest of Mari and about 60 km. southwest of Aleppo lies Ebla, a major city of the third millennium B.C., which was discovered in 1964 at Tell Mardikh. Thousands of cuneiform tablets with details about international trade and politics over the area extending from Lower Meopotamia to Palestine for the period from ca. 2400 to 2250 B.C. have come to light. A portion of the texts are lexical. Early conclusions about some place-names have had to be abandoned, and geographical names associated at first with Palestine are now shifted elsewhere. In *Ebla: An Empire Rediscovered,* trans. Christopher Holme (Garden City, N.Y.: Doubleday, 1980), Paolo Matthiae gives a first-class tour of this long-buried empire. The excitement generated by the discoveries is reflected in the nine-page bibliography compiled by Giovanni Pettinato, *A New Look at History,* trans. C. Faith Richardson (Baltimore: Johns Hopkins University Press, 1991). Pettinato's book discusses the history of Ebla and provides a translation of some of the texts. For further shortcuts to things Eblaite, consult *Eblaitica: Essays on the Ebla Archives and Eblaite Language,* vol. 2, ed. C. H. Gordon and Gary A. Rendsburg (Winona Lake, Ind.: Eisenbrauns, 1990), which begins with a memorial tribute by Gordon to Claude Frédéric Armand Schaeffer (1898–1982) and ends with a "Corrigenda et Addenda to *Eblaitica I*" (1987), plus indexes of Ebla texts and biblical

---

[23] For a summary of the significance of Mari, see the articles by J. Margueron and Jean-Marie Durand under the entry "Mari," *ABD,* 4:525–36; bibliography by Brian E. Keck under the same entry, 4:536–38.

references to this and the first *Eblaitica* volume, edited by Gordon, Rendsburg, and Nathan A. Winter (1987). A third volume appeared in 1992.[24]

HITHER AND YON

When scholars first took account of a text from the Bible (Numbers 22–24) in the light of a plaster inscription dating to the 8th century B.C., the stage was set for production of a large secondary literature. Dating to the end of the 8th century B.C., the inscription relates to a certain "Balaam" who served as a divine seer at an Iron Age temple in the East Jordan Valley. Its discovery at Tell Deir 'Alla "caused a curious sensation," according to Baruch A. Levine. Apart from some linguistic similarities, the inscription and the biblical recitals have little in common.[25]

A marvelous collection of translations of texts from a multitude of sites is offered in *Ancient Near Eastern Texts Relating to the Old Testament* (*ANET*), ed. James B. Pritchard (Princeton: Princeton University Press, 1950; 2d ed. rev., 1955; 3d ed., 1969). A companion set, *The Ancient Near East in Pictures Relating to the Old Testament* (*ANEP*) (Princeton: Princeton University Press, 1954; 2d ed., with supplement, 1969) contains about 750 pictures, with explanations, mirroring the world of the texts. The problem of making available additions and revisions to purchasers of other editions without issuing larger revised editions at considerable cost to both publisher and the earlier purchasers was partially solved through the publication of *The Ancient Near East: Supplementary Texts and Pictures Relating to the Old Testament* (Princeton: Princeton University Press, 1969), which includes the additions and corrections noted in the second and third editions of *ANET*, as well as one hundred additional pictures to supplement *ANEP*. On the other hand, the careful student will note that the supplementary volume does not include the corrections that could be made in the plates for the main work. An abridgement of *ANET* and *ANEP* became available in *The Ancient Near East: An Anthology of Texts and Pictures*, 2 vols. (Princeton: Princeton University Press, 1958, 1975). The cross-references make it easy to use in connection with the parent texts. Through books like these the amateur joins the experts at the site.

---

[24] See also C. H. Gordon, "Ebla as background for the Old Testament," in *Congress Volume Jerusalem 1986*, ed. J. A. Emerton, Supplements to Vetus Testamentum 40 (Leiden: Brill, 1988).

[25] See Baruch A. Levine, who discusses the implications of the inscription for Bible students: "The Balaam Inscription from Deir 'Alla : Historical Aspects," in *Biblical Archaeology Today: Proceedings of the International Congress on Biblical Archaeology, Jerusalem, April 1984* (Jerusalem: Israel Exploration Society in cooperation with ASOR, 1985), 326–39; André Lemaire provides a transcription and translation, "L'inscription du Balaam trouveé à Deir 'Alla: Epigraphie," ibid., 313–25 (bibliography, 322–23 n. 4).

Pritchard and company do what Hugo Gressmann, *Altorientalische Texte zum Alten Testament,* 2 vols.; 2d ed. (Berlin and Leipzig: de Gruyter, 1926–1927), long did for German students—provide a collection of Egyptian, Akkadian, Sumerian, and Hittite texts and a representative selection of Ugaritic documents. More recent discoveries, coupled with advances in the understanding of longer-known texts, constantly encourage new renderings, and Stephanie Dalley has provided them in *Myths from Mesopotamia: Creation, the Flood, Gilgamesh, and Others,* The World's Classics Series (Oxford and New York: Oxford University Press, 1991). This collection of the principal Mesopotamian myths, including the Atrahasis myth (from an old Babylonian version first published in 1969), the Epic of Creation (Enumah Elish), the Epic of Gilgamesh, the Descent of Ishtar, and others less well known.[26]

We are tempted to present a full-dress review of other Semitic languages deciphered during the last century, but Pritchard's assemblage of texts and pictures provides easy access to this exciting corpus of literature, of which some documents, it must be granted, receive more extended treatment in Alexander Heidel's discussion of creation narratives in *The Babylonian Genesis: The Story of the Creation* (Chicago: University of Chicago Press, 1942; 2d ed., 1951), and *The Gilgamesh Epic and Old Testament Parallels* (Chicago: University of Chicago Press, 1946; 2d ed., 1949).[27]

EVERYDAY LIFE

Recent decades have seen the publication of much helpful material on the total setting of the life and history of the Scriptures. To be acquainted with these is of great importance if one is to understand more fully a given period, event,

---

[26] For the Atrahasis epic, see the text in *ANET,* 104–6. For text and commentary on the "Enuma Elish," see Anton Deimel, *"Enuma Elis" und Hexaémeron,* Sacra Scriptura antiquitatibus orientalibus illustrata 5 (Rome, 1934; 2d ed., 1936); see also *ANET,* 60–72. For Semitic inscriptions, consult the *Corpus Inscriptionum Semitica,* whose beginnings can be traced to Renan's enthusiasm and organizing ability: see Albright, appendix 1, in *The Bible and the Ancient Near East: Essays in Honor of William Foxwell Albright,* ed. G. Ernest Wright (Garden City, N.Y.: Doubleday, 1961), 328–62; see esp. p. 330. *Ancient Hebrew Inscriptions: Corpus and Concordance,* Graham I. Davies (Cambridge, UK: Cambridge University Press, 1991) covers 1000 B.C.–200 B.C. and includes such texts as the Lachish and Arad letters, the Siloam tunnel inscription, and the texts discovered at Kuntillett Ajrud. Charles-F. Jean and Jacob Hoftijzer, *Dictionnaire des inscriptions sémitiques de l'ouest* (Leiden: Brill, 1965), covers a broad range of "Northwest" Semitic languages. See also Émile Puech, "Palestinian Funerary Inscriptions," *ABD,* 5:126–35.

[27] Besides *ANET,* take advantage of J. H. Breasted, *Ancient Records of Egypt,* 5 vols. (Chicago, 1906–1907; reprint, New York: Russell & Russell, 1962). The general reader will delight in D. Winton Thomas, *Documents from Old Testament Times* (Edinburgh, 1958), and the "reader centered" compilation by Victor H. Matthews and Don C. Benjamin, *Old Testament Parallels: Laws and Stories from the Ancient Near East* (New York: Paulist Press, 1991).

or passage of the Bible. The following are selected titles from the mass of materials available under several headings.

For one whose curiosity spurs inspection of the menus, wardrobes, and daily lives of these ancient people, there is no substitute for Gustaf H. Dalman, *Arbeit und Sitte in Palästina,* 7 vols. (Gütersloh: C. Bertelsmann, 1928–42), whose value is enhanced by the author's intimate understanding of rabbinic materials. For more rapid reading use Joachim Jeremias, *Jerusalem in the Time of Jesus,* trans. F. H. and C. H. Cave (Philadelphia: Fortress Press, 1969), and Willy Corswant, *A Dictionary of Life in Bible Times,* trans. Arthur W. Heathcote (New York: Oxford University Press, 1960) from the French edition (Neuchatel: Delachaux & Niestlé, 1956) and completed and illustrated by Édouard Urech. Not to be ignored is Kurt Galling's *Biblisches Reallexikon,* 2d rev. ed. (Tübingen: J. C. B. Mohr [Siebeck], 1977), in the series Handbuch zum Alten Testament (see chap. 15). Galling features cultural topics and matters relating to daily life in this work, which is designed for both nonspecialists and specialists. Musical instruments and beauty aids are only two of a host of items picturing life in Palestine, including Phoenician and Syrian areas. An index helps one explore the interesting topical presentations. Victor H. Matthews, *Manners and Customs in the Bible* (Peabody, Mass.: Hendrickson, 1988), recreates some of the social world of the Bible in an illustrated chronological presentation; each chapter sketches the historical and physical setting of the time period and the basic elements of its social world. In *Archaeology in Biblical Research* (New York: Abingdon, 1965), Walter G. Williams pierces for nonspecialists the mystique of archaeology with an excellent account of archaeological achievements and procedures up to the time of the writer. Besides featuring cultural realia, including musical instruments, Williams sheds light on the role of prophets in various societies.

More given to topographic description and matters of archaeological interest such as sites and structures is *Dictionnaire archéologique de la Bible* (Paris: Hazan, 1970), under the general editorship of Abraham Negev, who enjoys among others the collaboration of Yohanan Aharoni, William G. Dever, Nelson Glueck, and Ruth Yacobi; available also in English: *Archaeological Encyclopedia of the Holy Land* (New York: Putnam, 1972). In *Jewish Symbols in the Greco-Roman Period,* 13 vols. (New York and Princeton, 1953–68), Erwin Ramsdell Goodenough sought the religious attitudes of Jews in the Greco-Roman world through investigation of symbols on archaeological remains. An abridged edition by J. Neusner bears the title *Jewish Symbols in the Greco-Roman Period* (Princeton: Princeton University Press, 1988). Goodenough's collection of data will outlive his conclusions; see Morton Smith, "Goodenough's Jewish Symbols in Retrospect," *JBL* 86 (1967): 53–68.

INTERPRETIVE VALUE

In *The Archaeology of Palestine,* W. F. Albright relates the story told by a farmer whom he once met in a hotel in Nazareth. This farmer was the superintendent of a rural Baptist Sunday school; his neighbor was superintendent of a Methodist Sunday school. One day the two men entered into a heated discussion on the merits of Baptism by sprinkling versus Baptism by immersion. The Methodist eventually countered with a question that he supposed would clinch his argument. Where in Jerusalem was there a place large enough to immerse all the Pentecost converts? The disturbed Baptist farmer finally proposed that his neighbor cultivate his farm while he sailed for Palestine to investigate the possibility. "He travelled steerage," relates Albright, "and walked over Palestine in order to save money. He was stabbed and robbed by Arab villagers near Nablus; he nearly died of dysentery contracted in a cheap Jewish hostel at Tiberias. But no matter, his eyes shone as he described the success of his mission and told of measuring the Mamilla Pool at Jerusalem and of estimating that it could have held the entire multitude at Pentecost. Of course there was no point in telling him that the pool in question is mediaeval, since there undoubtedly were a number of large reservoirs in Jerusalem at that time. His last words as we parted were, 'So I'm going back to convert my Methodist brother!'"[28] The farmer might have conserved his time and energy by pointing out that ten thousand people can be immersed in a single cistern.

Occasionally archaeological discoveries can help us fill in details that are ignored by the biblical text. In 2 Kgs. 18:14 we read the laconic statement: Sennacherib "arrived at Lachish." What is the reality? The archaeological record is a story of terrible destruction. Men and women leave with their goods; Assyrian archers provide cover for a battering ram; captives are impaled within sight of the defenders.[29]

What is Solomon's "Millo" (1 Kgs. 9:15, 24)? A look into various resources mentioned in this chapter will reveal the diversity of opinion that an excavation can engender.

---

[28] *Archaeology of Palestine,* 8–9.

[29] See John Gray, *Archaeology and the Old Testament World* (Toronto and New York: Nelson, 1962), plate 15, on the siege of Lachish, taken from Sennacherib's palace at Nineveh. Gray includes the text of the inscription describing the campaign of 702–701 B.C. (the celebrated Taylor prism), 156–57. For a clearer outline of the scene, see Wright, *Biblical Archaeology,* figures 115–117, pp. 165–66. The illustrations in Wright are borrowed from Layard, *Monuments of Nineveh,* plates 21–23. Wright does not cite the date of Layard's work, which first appeared in London in 1849 (a second series of photographs was used in an edition of 1853, after a second expedition). Gray, who makes many connections with the biblical text, aims at introducing "students, clergy, and interested laymen to the mind of ancient Israel in her historical and cultural environment."

It is true, Albright points out time and again, that archaeology in the main confirms the substantial accuracy of the historical picture transmitted by the biblical documents. Unquestionably they approach the longevity of the patriarchs with far greater restraint than in some Sumerian accounts, in which, for example, a king named En-Men-Lu-Anna ruled 43,200 years. Also, from documents other than the Bible, we now know that Belshazzar was a historical figure. But much more important than the confirmation of isolated points is archaeology's contribution to a broader appreciation of the complex environment in which Israel grew up culturally and spiritually. There is no question that the Old Testament prophets borrowed Egyptian, Babylonian, and Canaanite literary forms to express themselves. Study of the cultural and spiritual matrix in which their thought took shape helps us better to understand their message and to appreciate their profound inspiration by comparison.

For those who have the sympathy and cultural sensitivity requisite for profitable investigation of remote societies, archaeology can serve as a kind of time machine to traject them into the past and help them try to relive Israel's experience. Even as archaeology has a sobering effect on scholars who attempt compression of the Fourth Gospel into Hellenistic molds, its study can do a great deal to prevent extraction of Moses, Jesus, or Paul from their historical situations in the interest of private intellectual or dogmatic considerations. As Millar Burrows has expressed it, "Archeology helps to tie exegesis down to historical fact."[30] Without the archaeological discipline the interpreter's task cannot be properly executed.

TEXTUAL CRITICISM

Among the specific contributions of archaeological investigation one might mention a few of the many linguistic problems eliminated with its assistance.

Even the word "tell," without which an archaeologist can hardly be expected to give his bearings, was once misunderstood. The KJV renders Joshua 11:13: "But as for the cities that stood still in their strength. . . ." The RSV/NRSV, relying on new discoveries, reads more accurately: "But none of the cities that stood on *mounds* [emphasis ours] did Israel burn. . . ." The discovery of a weight inscribed with the word "pim" and equivalent to two-thirds of a shekel has clarified 1 Sam. 13:21 (see RSV/NRSV).[31]

In 1 Kgs. 10:28 the RSV/NRSV reads: "And Solomon's import of horses was from Egypt and Kue." The KJV renders the word מִקְוֵה with "linen yarn." But the inscription of Zakar refers to the region of Cilicia as "Kue." Only a

---

[30] *What Mean These Stones? The Significance of Archeology for Biblical Studies* (New Haven: American Schools of Oriental Research, 1941), 291.

[31] See Mitchell, document 37, p. 74 ("Paym Weight"). The word *pîm* can be vocalized *paym*.

change in vowel pointing is required to read this place-name in the Hebrew text supported by the LXX and the Vulgate.

CULTURAL PARALLELS

The highlighting of parallel cultural factors, as we have already indicated, is one of the most valuable contributions made by the archaeologist. But it is important to remember that parallel lines never meet. In other words, two phenomena may relate to one another in terms of common cultural inheritance, or they may have originated independently. Deductions about origin or dependency should not be made without careful consideration of other data.

The story of Rachel's theft of Laban's teraphim (Gen. 31:34) can now be reinvestigated with a better understanding of her motives. From the so-called Nuzi tablets it appears that there was a close cultural association between the family gods and the right of inheritance. Perhaps Rachel was motivated not so much by piety or superstition, suggests M. Burrows, as by a shrewd concern that her husband secure the inheritance rights.[32] Laban's cries of distress over the loss of his household deities may also quaver with economic overtones.

In Gen. 37:35 Jacob breaks into the following lament at the news of Joseph's alleged death: "I shall go down to Sheol to my son, mourning" (RSV). A similar reaction is observable in Lutpan, Baal's overseer, who announces the death of Baal and then ends his dirge: "I will go down into the earth."[33]

A further document found at Ras Shamra discusses the treatment of ailing horses. One of the remedies proposed is a kind of pressed fig cake, called *debelah.* As Schaeffer pointed out, it would perhaps be lacking in respect to suggest that Hezekiah (Isaiah 38) was successfully cured by a horse remedy, but the fact remains that the prophet attended his cure with the use of an old-fashioned remedy prescribed long before by the veterinarians at Ugarit.[34] Do we perhaps have a parallel to Naaman's experience (2 Kings 5)? And one might also ask whether modern-day sun worshipers feel themselves demeaned by using sunscreen balm packaged for use on cows' udders, instead of pricier lotion advertised for general use and perhaps even less effective.

The list of prices suggested by the merchants of Ugarit documents the age-old bargaining spirit reflected in Abraham's concern for the Cities of the Plain. The Ugaritic document with prices suitable for almost every type of customer reads:

The price,	Good price,
High price,	Stiff price,
Low price,	Fair price,

[32] *What Mean These Stones?* 91, 259.

[33] G. R. Driver, *Canaanite Myths and Legends,* Old Testament Studies 3 (Edinburgh, 1956), 109.

[34] *The Cuneiform Texts of Ras Shamra Ugarit* (London, 1939), 41.

Poor price,   Price in the town, etc.[35]
Fixed price,

Or take these tender words, written by a son to his mother and document-ing a side of Ugaritic character that is not often appreciated: "I lay my devo-tion at the feet of my mistress, so far away. May the gods protect you and keep you safe and sound. Behold, Kelal is with me. He is well and so I am. I am resting now, and my journey is finished. My mistress, may you send me all news of your health in answer to your servant."[36]

"Remember the days of old, consider the years of many generations" (Deut. 32:7).

II. *Papyri, Epigraphy, Social-Scientific Criticism, Social World*

Ever since the Renaissance, the remains of Greek writing have suffered from increasingly unscientific classification. An artifical distinction developed between so-called classical writings and other Greek and Latin productions. The title of Herbert Jennings Rose's sketch of authors and their works, *A Hand-book of Greek Literature from Homer to the Age of Lucian,* indicates the chronological span, but the contents display the pervading elective factor.[37] As Rose states in the preface, "the vast Christian and the considerable Jewish literature written in Greek have been wholly omitted, not that they lack importance, but that they represent a different spirit from that of the Greeks themselves, and are best handled in separate works." Translation: there is a great divide between the literature of Hellenic polytheists and their imitators and the works of Jewish and Christian writers. In reply one can point out that the spirit of Lucian is quite different from that of Homer and Plato. In short, ideology rather than scientific classification accounts for the omission.

Unfortunately, the demarcation also led to an artificial distinction between "literary" and "documentary" production, without sufficient consideration

---

[35] *Cuneiform Texts,* 40.

[36] *Cuneiform Texts,* 42. For further comparison — and contrast — of Ugaritic and biblical faith and culture see, for example, the type of study done by Norman C. Habel, *Yahweh versus Baal: A Conflict of Religious Cultures: A Study in the Relevance of Ugaritic Materials for the Early Faith of Israel,* Concordia Seminary, St. Louis, Graduate Study 6 (New York: Bookman Associates, 1964).

[37] The first edition of Rose's book appeared in 1934 (London: Methuen); 4th ed. rev., 1951; reprint with minor corrections, 1956.

accorded the varieties of expression and content in inscriptions and papyri. From 1839 on there was some publication of texts of ancient authors, but classicists lost interest when texts did not come forth in great number. Among the discoveries were some from Herculaneum that added to our knowledge of Epicurus; then came Hyperides, followed in 1891 by Herodas (Herondas), and Aristotle's Constitution of Athens; and in 1897 Bacchylides, with profound implications for the history of Hellenistic poetry. These latter finds aroused immediate interest, as did the fragments of many ancient writings that either filled in missing lines or offered variants of a known text. But after the initial excitement died down, the documents drawn up on papyrus in political bureaus, on the counters of industry, or in busy thoroughfares by illiterates seeking the assistance of local scribes, were left in the hands of papyrologists, as were fragments of pottery called ostraca. Those that were inscribed on stone, metal, or decorated pottery were generally recognized as the province of epigraphists. To numismatists was left the study of legends on coins.

In itself such allocation of data was not reprehensible. The damaging feature was the lack of communication that developed between the various groups of specialists. Hence it came to pass that the same phenomenon observable in "biblical archaeology," with its narrow interest in illumination of the biblical text, befell "classical" study, which lost sight of the broader scene of Hellenic influence. One of the casualties, the New Testament, a Greek classic of the ages, had long before found its place at the bottom of the literary scale in the minds of those who were devoted to the nuanced cadences of Plato and Demosthenes, and any attempts at demonstrating the association of its text with the nonliterary papyri inadvertently succeeded in confirming opinions about its alleged banality. Basil Lanneau Gildersleeve, a classicist for whom the Bible was a second language, commented with tongue in cheek in an essay on translators' improvements of their source documents: "How much fewer fastidious souls would have been saved, if the Greek of the New Testament had not been transposed into the organ notes of the Authorized Version. Only the robuster sort can forgive ἐάν with the indicative and associate with the riffraff of worse than plebeian names that figure in the last chapter of the Epistle to the Romans." Indeed, could the New Testament be at all considered within any linguistic mainstream? According to G. H. R. Horsley, "one classicist of international reputation indicated" at a conference held in America in 1985 "that by '*koine*' he meant only the New Testament."[38]

Disdain for barbarisms in the writing of the unwashed masses had manifested itself as early as the second century in the broadsides of anti-Christian champions of Hellas. But not until the Renaissance did the debate on the quality of New Testament Greek reach the flowering stage. At the polar points

---

[38] G. H. R. Horsley, *New Documents Illustrating Early Christianity.* Vol. 5: *Linguistic Essays* (N.S.W., Australia: Macquarrie University, 1989), 41.

were the purists, who endeavored to defend New Testament usage in terms of Attic usage, and the Hebraists, who insisted on its Semitic character.[39]

By the end of the eighteenth century the Hebraists appeared to have won the exchange, and the laurels went to them for most of the nineteenth century. It is not suprising, therefore, that when Adolf Deissmann (see chap. 8) confronted *Aufklärungsland* with his exposition of biblical texts in the light of the papyri and epigraphs, many were the called, but few the chosen. Among the grammarians who saw the light were James Hope Moulton and Archibald T. Robertson (for their grammars see chap. 7).[40] But resistance in favor of a special kind of biblical Greek with heavy Semitic accent was not easily dismissed, and even the massive array of evidence so ponderously piled up by Robertson could not stay the tide. Not many years were to pass before the four-volume grammar begun by Moulton lost its Hellenic soul in the third and fourth volumes produced by Nigel Turner, who explicitly affirmed that "Bibl. Greek is a unique language with a unity and character of its own,"[41] and even raised the specter of a "Holy Ghost language."[42] Others could be forgiven for not seeing the light that dawned from the East, but Turner erred against Deissmann's better knowledge by reducing New Testament linguistic complexities to "Christian Greek."

Unfortunately, some biblical scholars lack a first-hand acquaintance with papyri, and to many of them inscriptions are a closed book; and so the hazard of overemphasis on Semitic features continues to imperil a balanced understanding of New Testament Greek. The major hope for diversion of the debate into more productive channels probably lies in the recognition of the phenomenon of bilingualism. That is, bilingualists are able to make use of two languages, but some of their expressions may deviate from the norm of either language as a result of their familiarity with more than one language.

Reference was made in chap. 7 to some of the principal grammatical and lexical resources for exploration of papyri and inscriptions. In what follows we concentrate on a background sketch of these two media and directions for locating collections of papyri.

---

[39] Horsley, *New Documents,* 5:38–39). Adolf Deissmann's article "Papyri" in *Encyclopaedia biblica* (above, chap. 9), 3:3556–63 states well the case for the future.

[40] A. T. Robertson, *A Grammar of the Greek New Testament in the Light of Historical Research,* 4th ed. rev. (New York: George H. Doran, 1923), 76–77; on "The Fiction of Jewish Greek," see Horsley, *New Documents,* 5:5–40.

[41] Nigel Turner, *A Grammar of New Testament Greek by James Hope Moulton,* vol. 3: *Syntax* (Edinburgh: T. & T. Clark, 1963), 4.

[42] Turner, *Grammar,* 9.

PAPYRI[43]

Papyrus (*Cyperus Papyrus*), derived from a marsh plant in the Nile valley, was the writing material most used in the ancient world. As Eldon J. Epp noted in a captivating contribution to a volume in honor of Joseph Fitzmyer, papyrus is remarkably durable. Thor Hyerdahl constructed his second ship, the *Ra II*, out of eight tons of papyrus and sailed from Morocco to Barbados in fifty-seven days, a journey of 3,270 miles.[44] Most of the documents written on this material come from ruined buildings and rubbish heaps. Others have been found in tombs, and some have been taken from mummy wrappings. Long ago, the poet Wordsworth expressed a poignant longing:

> O ye, who patiently explore
> The wreck of Herculanean lore,
> What rapture! could ye seize
> Some Theban fragment, or unroll
> One precious, tender-hearted, scroll
> Of pure Simonides.
>
> That were, indeed, a genuine birth
> Of poesy; a bursting forth
> Of genius from the dust:
> What Horace gloried to behold,
> What Maro loved, shall we enfold?
> Can haughty Time be just?

Wordsworth alludes to a discovery that took place in 1752 at Herculaenum, Italy, where a library of Epicurean writings, including especially Philodemus,

---

[43] Albert Thumb, *Die griechische Sprache im Zeitalter des Hellenismus* (Strassburg: Karl J. Trübner, 1901), 181–83, notes the significant role played by Gustav Adolf Deissmann (see above, chap. 7) in appreciation of papyri and inscriptions for interpretation of the Greek Bible. For entry into the world of papyrology, see O. Montevecchi, *La Papirologia* (Turin, 1973); E. G. Turner, *Greek Papyri: An Introduction*, rev. ed. (Oxford, 1980); F. Danker, *A Century of Graeco-Roman Philology* (Atlanta: Scholars Press, 1988), 115–28, hereafter cited as *Century*. For information on the "Duke Data Bank of Documentary Papyri," see John J. Hughes, *Bits, Bytes & Biblical Studies* (Grand Rapids: Zondervan, 1987), 579–80. C. K. Barrett, ed., *New Testament Background: Selected Documents* (London: SPCK, 1957), includes, among other items that have a bearing on New Testament topics, Pliny's description (*Natural History* 13.68–83) of the preparation and use of papyri.

[44] E. J. Epp, "The New Testament Papyrus Manuscripts in Historical Perspective," in *To Touch the Text: Biblical and Related Studies in Honor of Joseph A. Fitzmyer, S.J.*, ed. Maurya P. Horgan and Paul J. Kobelski (New York: Crossroad, 1989), 261–88, with frequent reference to the excellent study by E. G. Turner, *Greek Papyri: An Introduction* (Oxford, 1968). Epp points out that papyrus texts of the New Testament were for many decades snubbed in favor of the great parchment uncials.

was unearthed. The poet's prayer was answered in a different way, as prayers often are. In 1896 there were unearthed at Al-Kussiyah fourteen epinician odes and six dithyrambs authored by Bacchylides. Bishop Joseph Barber Lightfoot (1828–1889), "one of the first to vindicate the Greek of the New Testament as the genuine *lingua franca* of the Graeco-Roman world of that day,"[45] in 1863 echoed Wordsworth's thought: "if we could only recover letters that ordinary people wrote to each other without any thought of being literary, we should have the greatest possible help for the understanding of the language of the NT generally."[46] Had he lived a bit longer, he could have celebrated the recovery of such and other kinds of everyday communication at numerous sites in Egypt.

As the abbreviation lists in the major lexicons indicate, the number of published papyri is staggering, and only a few notable sites and corpora can here be mentioned. Some of the early Christian documents cited in BAGD were found in an ancient rubbish heap at Behnesa, located about 120 miles south of Cairo. This was the site of the ancient Oxyrhynchus, capital of the nome that bore its name. There, in 1897, Bernard Pyne Grenfell and Arthur Surridge Hunt found Roman office records that had been put to the torch, but the sands moved in, put out the fire, and preserved the fragments for all time, some in the very baskets in which they were carried out to be burned. Ever since 1898 texts from this treasure of retrieval have been transcribed, translated, and annotated in volumes that appear with gratifying regularity. Since the texts in the series, The Oxyrhynchus Papyri, are entered under a continuous numbering system, it is customary to cite only the number of a specific papyrus, not the volume of the series.

In 1933 John Garrett Winter called attention to the University of Michigan's outstanding collection, an inventory of more than five thousand items, in a time-defying account titled *Life and Letters in the Papyri* (Ann Arbor: University of Michigan Press, 1933). Among the papyri in the Michigan collection are statements of account from the Zenon archive (P. Mich. 1=P. Mich. Zen.), found in 1915 at Philadelphia in the Fayum, on the edge of the desert. This archive takes its name from the confidential business manager of Apollonius, a minister of finance under Ptolemy II. Zenon was meticulous in maintaining his files and fortunately did not believe in shredding. When he transferred his office to Philadelphia, he took with him his mass of correspondence, which remained intact, like the "dead files" of Tell el-Amarna, for more than two millennia. Other shares of the Zenon hoard went to Columbia University and

---

[45] George R. Eden and F. C. MacDonald, eds., *Lightfoot of Durham: Memories and Appreciations* (Cambridge, UK: Cambridge University Press, 1932), 8.

[46] James Hope Moulton, *A Grammar of New Testament Greek,* vol. 1: *Prolegomena,* 3d ed. (Edinburgh: T. & T. Clark, 1908), 242.

the British Museum. Columbia's share began to be published in 1934 in P. Col. Zen. I.[47]

Many of the papyri consist of occasional letters, and they are frequently made the basis of comparison for study of New Testament letters. It is true that papyrus letters reflect some of the basic epistolary conventions, but for detailed analysis of rhetorical structures in the Pauline and most other New Testament correspondence one must examine the structures of more formal literary texts. More attention therefore needs to be paid to the more formal type of letter preserved in texts other than papyri, including especially Rudolf Hercher's epistolary collection.[48] Another resource that is almost totally neglected in New Testament study is the multitude of letters inscribed on stone (see below).

A notable collection of papyri relating to Jewish economic and social life, customs, institutions, and political experience is available in *Corpus Papyrorum Judaicarum* (*CPJ*), ed. Victor A. Tcherikover (d. 1958) and Alexander Fuks, 3 vols. (Cambridge: Harvard University Press, 1960). Of special historical importance in this collection are nos. 153 ("The Letter of Claudius to the Alexandrians," a reprint of P. Lond. 1912, which is frequently cited in BAGD) and 154–59 ("Acts of Alexandrian Martyrs"), in volume 2.

A wealth of material from the Bar Kokhba (Cochba) period sheds light not only on political circumstances but on linguistic interchange in the second century. A detailed report on discoveries that included correspondence of the resistance leader is given by Joseph A. Fitzmyer, *Essays on the Semitic Back-ground of the New Testament* (London: Geoffrey Chapman, 1971), 305–54. Since the publication of Fitzmyer's report, Naphtali Lewis edited the bulk of the so-called Babatha archive, discovered at Naḥal Ḥever, about four and a half km. south of Engedi. These documents, dating from the time of the Bar Kokhba revolution (A.D. 132), belonged to Babatha the daughter of Simeon and her family and deal with matters of property and lawsuits involving Babatha.[49]

George Milligan's *Here & There Among the Papyri* (London: Hodder and Stoughton, 1922) has long served as a popular introduction to the papyri for

---

[47] On Zenon, see Willy Clarysse and Katelijn Vandorpe, *Zenon: Een Grieks Manager in de Schaduw van de Piramiden* (Leuven, 1990); available from the authors in Leuven. These letters in Greek may be profitably compared with the Egyptian letters in Edward Wente's collection from various periods in Egyptian history, *Letters from Ancient Egypt,* ed. Edmund S. Meltzer, SBL Writings from the Ancient World 1 (Atlanta: Scholars Press, 1990).

[48] R. Hercher, *Epistolographi Graeci* (1873). The literature on ancient epistolary forms and New Testament letters is extensive: see "Letters: Greek and Latin Letters," *ABD,* 4:290–93, bibl.); John L. White, *Light from Ancient Letters* (Philadelphia: Fortress Press, 1986), bibl. 221–24.

[49] *The Documents from the Bar Kokhba Period in the Cave of Letters, Greek Papyri,* ed. Naphtali Lewis. *Aramaic and Nabataen Signatures and Subscriptions,* ed. Yigael Yadin (d. 1984) and Jonas C. Greenfield (Jerusalem: Israel Exploration Society, 1989).

students of the New Testament and at the same time has stimulated appetites for more information of the type found in Winter's book (see above). Beginners on the road to further papyrological adventure will also find the first two volumes of Arthur Surridge Hunt and Campbell Cowan Edgar, *Select Papyri* (Loeb Classical Library), an encouragement to further inquiry.[50]

For setting up shop on one's own, *A Greek Papyrus Reader* (Chicago: University of Chicago Press, 1935), by Edgar J. Goodspeed and Ernest Cadman Colwell, has proved to be a helpful and interesting medium. The Greek vocabulary at the back of the book offers sufficient guidance to decipher the texts, which afford glimpses into numerous facets of ancient Egyptian life, bureaucratic and private.[51] Humorless reviewers, who equate a dash of levity as poison to the well of learning, are ever with us. In a review of this work, in *The Classical Journal* 32 (1936–37), 303–4, the reviewer observed that the introductions were "sometimes rather facetious," and he suggested that "playful references" to contemporary experience like the depression and the machine age "might well have been replaced [he does not say, 'accompanied by'] a little more information about the documents." The fact is that the "playful" items consist of only a few words. The reviewer probably was unacquainted with Goodspeed's lighter side, which adds sparkle to his autobiography, *As I Remember* (New York: Harper, 1953). As for Colwell, his reputation for wit requires no recital.

For those who can learn without the benefit of Attic salt we recommend the far more thorough guide by P. W. Pestman, *The New Papyrological Primer, being the Fifth Edition of David and Van Groningen's Papyrological Primer* (Leiden: Brill, 1990). In the late 1930s the legal historian Martin David and the Greek philologist Bernard Abraham van Groningen, no majors in parochialism, conceived the idea of a "Papyrological Primer." Their four editions provided many students with an authoritative base for entry into papyrology. This fifth edition is, in Pestman's words, a "new and modernized version. Papyrology being constantly on the move, an entirely new primer is the result. I have tried to write it in the spirit of my teachers, intending to show how fascinating Greek Papyrology really is, and why."[52] The eighty-one Greek texts, preceded by an introduction worthy of its name, are arranged in chronological order and illustrate various aspects of life in Hellenistic, Roman, and Byzantine Egypt. A brief commentary and explanatory notes accompany each text.

[50] Volume 1 contains "Non-Literary Papyri: Private Affairs"; vol. 2, "Non-Literary Papyri: Public Documents." The 3d vol., ed. D. L. Page, contains "Literary Papyri: Poetry."

[51] The second impression, 1936, includes corrections submitted by F. Wilbur Gingrich. Some of Goodspeed's knowledge of the papyri is distilled in his solution of difficulties faced by translators, *Problems of New Testament Translation* (1945), frequently cited in BAGD.

[52] The 1st ed. was titled *Papyrologisch Leerboek* (1940), which was translated into English for a 2d ed., *Papyrological Primer* (1946; 3d ed., 1952; 4th ed., 1965). If *Pestman's Primer* is not available, consult Eric Gardner Turner, *Greek Papyri: An Introduction,* rev. ed. (Oxford, 1980).

A glossary of Greek words assists the student in the interpretation of texts. After spending time with the Goodspeed–Colwell *Reader* or Pestman's *Primer,* students might well try their hand at decipherment of script in one of the biblical documents published in the series Bodmer Papyri.

Pestman's *Primer* is also of value for making acquaintance with the principal works, primary and secondary, relating to papyrology. The standard list for identification of papyrus publications is *Checklist of Editions of Greek Papyri and Ostraca,* ed. John F. Oates, et al., 3d ed. (Chico, Calif.: Scholars Press, 1985). Since decipherments of many papyrus texts appear in periodicals, some of them frequently unavailable to scholars, a warehouse for gathering such texts was developed, beginning in 1915: *Sammelbuch Griechischer Urkunden aus Ägypten,* successively published by Friedrich Preisigke, Friedrich Bilabel, Emil Kiessling, and H.-A. Rupprecht. Scholars frequently offer corrections of texts that have been published, and these are collected in *Berichtigungsliste der griechischen Papyrusurkunden aus Ägypten,* ed. F. Preisigke, et al. (1922–).[53] Detailed access to the latter is made possible by Willy Clarysse, et al., *Konkordanz und Supplement zu Berichtigungsliste,* vols. 1–7 (Leuven, 1989). An anthology of papyri frequently cited in BAGD is *Grundzüge und Chrestomathie der Papyruskunde.* Ulrich Wilcken was responsible for vol. 1: *Historischer Teil* (1912); Ludwig Mitteis for vol. 2: *Juristischer Teil* (1920). The collection by F. G. Kenyon, et al., *Greek Papyri in the British Museum,* 5 vols. (London, 1893–1917) also receives repeated mention in BAGD.

Although publications of newly discovered papyri, as well as better readings of some that were previously published, make updating of standard works a necessity, the names of Friedrich Preisigke and Edwin Mayser still spell glory for Germany. *Wörterbuch der griechischen Papyrusurkunden mit Einschluss der griechischen Inschriften, Aufschriften, Ostraka, Mumienschilder usw. aus Ägypten,* 3 vols. (Berlin, 1925–31), begun by Friedrich Preisigke (d. 1924) and continued by Emil Kiessling, deals exclusively with the papyri. Two supplements have been published, and a fourth volume, undertaken in 1944, was completed in 1992. To fill some gaps, Winfried Rübsam published *Supplement I* (Amsterdam, 1969–71; *Supplement II* was published in 1992.

Anxious to unpack the grammatical world of the papyri, Stanislaus Witkowski published his *Prodromus grammaticae papyrorum graecarum aetatis Lagidarum, Abh. der phil. klass. der Akademie zu Krakau* (1897), 196–260, but it was in Edwin Mayser's work that awareness of the evolution of the Greek language reached a high point. Scholars have long been dependent on his incomplete *Grammatik der griechischen Papyri aus der Ptolemäerzeit: Mit Einschluss der gleichzeitigen Ostraka und der in Ägypten verfassten Inschriften* for analysis of Koine material relating to the Septuagint and New Testament.

---

[53] Work on vol. 9 is to be completed with the help of a computer.

The title indicates the breadth of its data base: papyri, potsherds, and stone monuments.

Despite Mayser's achievement, the flood of Egyptian data and developments in linguistics invite new appraisal of old conclusions. A total of 32,284 ancient documents, including papyri, mummy labels, ostraca, and inscriptions, can lay some claim to responsibility for conclusions reached in Francis Thomas Gignac, *A Grammar of the Greek Papyri of the Roman and Byzantine Periods:* I, *Phonology* (Milan: Istituto Editoriale Cisalpino—La Goliardica, 1976); II, *Morphology* (1981). Analysis of syntax, the real test of a grammarian's feel for language, is scheduled for the third and fourth volumes. When completed, Gignac's work will certainly supersede much that is in Mayser.

Long holding the field for concentration on use of the papyri for exposition of the New Testament is *The Vocabulary of the Greek Testament: Illustrated from the Papyri and Other Non-Literary Sources,* by James Hope Moulton and George Milligan (London: Hodder & Stoughton, 1914–29; one-volume edition, 1930), cited as MM. At the twentieth International Congress of Papyrologists (Copenhagen, August 23–29, 1992), Prof. G. H. R. Horsley called attention to a proposal made to Moulton by Gustav Adolf Deissmann, in a letter dated January 12, 1907. Declining a request by Moulton to collaborate on a lexicon, Deissmann apparently thought of producing one with strong emphasis on epigraphic material and therefore encouraged Moulton to concentrate on papyri. Sidetracked by various academic tasks and other projects, Deissmann never produced his *opus vitae.* But Moulton, heeding Deissmann's counsel, teamed up with Milligan and produced a work that has long serviced New Testament scholars. Unfortunately, there was a liability in Deissmann's suggestion: because of the preponderance of papyrus references in MM, students concluded, as Horsley points out, that epigraphic material was relatively less important for New Testament study.

Among specialized studies, Theodor Nägeli's *Der Wortschatz des Apostels Paulus: Beitrag zur sprachgeschichtlichen Erforschung des Neuen Testaments* (Göttingen: Vandenhoeck & Ruprecht, 1905) is of abiding interest for students of the New Testament. Nägeli saw the significance of Adolf Deissmann's researches, and in this classic little work he made a penetrating search of Pauline writings to determine the linguistic range in his diction. Much of Paul's usage, Nägele found, corresponds to expressions in papyri and epigraphs. Six decades later Lars Rydbeck concentrated on grammatical phenomena in a study titled *Fachprosa, vermeintliche Volkssprache und Neues Testament zur Beurteilung der sprachlichen Niveauunterschiede im nachklassischen Griechisch* (Uppsala, 1967). In this book Rydbeck demonstrates that certain expressions in documentary papyri and the New Testament that have at times been deemed to be colloquial or Semitic are found in the early imperial period in writers of technical prose, including, for example, Pedanius Dioscurides (pharmacologist),

Didymus of Alexandria (literary expert), and Heron of Alexandria (inventor and mathematician).

For a detailed survey of work done in Greek papyrology, see Orsolina Montevecchi, *La Papirologia* (Turin, 1973), reprinted with *Addenda* (1988). The list of periodicals and serials serving researchers is long, but students should be able to find one or the other of the following in their libraries: *Aegyptus, The Bulletin of the American Society of Papyrologists, Chronique d'Égypte,* and *Zeitschrift für Papyrologie und Epigraphik.* For other periodicals, serials, and reference works, see Pestman, *Primer,* xviii–xxi.

Further appreciation of the extent to which papyri can be used in New Testament study can be gleaned from the series *New Documents Illustrating Early Christianity,* ed. G. H. R. Horsley, 5 vols. (Macquarie University, N.S.W., Australia, 1981–89), in which the student can see the propylaeum to a new Moulton–Milligan. The first four volumes add to the evidence in MM and BAGD (see chap. 7) for epigraphical and papyrological data that can be used in exposition of the New Testament. The fifth volume contains Horsley's scintillating essays on the Koine, with sharp critique of philological deterioration in the syntactical portion of Moulton's *Grammar* (see chap. 7). In keeping with developments in "new archaeology," a sixth volume (1992) of *New Documents,* ed. by S. R. Llewelyn with the collaboration of R. A. Kearsley (1992), initiated a new series, with a modest shift from philology to social history. The documents in this sixth volume illustrate family relations, slavery, the Roman bureaucracy and military, medicine and magic, and other topics.

As in the field of archaeology, there are signs of discontent among some scholars who have an interest in papyri but take a negative view of what appears to them a purely antiquarian approach. Defenders of the faith, on the other hand, fear that the discipline of strenuous philological research will lose out to anthropological and sociological approaches as students opt for a less rigorous academic program. The years ahead will determine how well theoretical understanding of papyrology as a discipline can cohabit with the demands of a fragment of papyrus for sharply honed paleographic skills and nuanced lexical, grammatical, and historical knowledge.

As for the important role that papyri have played in establishing the text of the New Testament, see above (chap. 2). In New Testament textual studies the prestigious parchments will not command the adoration once accorded them. Papyri tend to "rock the boat." We now know how volatile the text of Homer was in ancient times and that many texts transmitted during the Middle Ages are unreliable. Be prepared for a variety of changes. Our electronic data bases are only beginning to be earnestly probed.

In view of all the illumination of ancient nooks and crannies through knowledge gained from the papyri, one can only sigh for how much more we could have known had not some desert folk in 1778, to cite but one moment of inadvertent destruction of pathways to the past, burned about fifty scrolls "for the aromatic smell they gave forth in burning." Goodspeed wondered whether their finders thought they would make a good tobacco. So he proposed to George Milligan, his houseguest at the time, that they experiment by burning some tiny pieces of papyrus that had no writing on them. Upon sniffing the fumes, Goodspeed concluded that they "smelled just like brown paper." Fortunately for the history of philology, the Arabs probably made a similar discovery and stuck to higher-quality pipe tobacco, for they spared one roll, which was published as the *Charta Borgiana* (1788), an account of forced labor of peasants on the Nile embankment at Arsinoe in the years 191–92.[54]

EPIGRAPHY[55]

The term "epigraphy" derives from the Greek preposition ἐπί, meaning "on" or "upon," and the verb γράφειν, "to write." Epigraphy is the scientific study of ancient writings or inscriptions made on a durable surface, such as stone, wood, metal, or pottery. The word "inscription" is derived from the corresponding Latin term *inscriptio*. In chap. 13 reference was made to inscriptions relating to languages other than Greek; here the focus is on the latter, and especially those found on stone.

Besides their value to palaeographists, who find them of great interest in charting the history of the Greek alphabet and Greek script, inscriptions possess an enormous historical value. One of the most notable examples is the so-called Gallio Inscription.[56]

Heads of state used inscriptions to acquire immediate public attention for extraordinary correspondence, declarations, or decrees. One of the most famous is the *Res Gestae Divi Augusti,* a report made by Caesar Augustus near the end of his life on his administration of the Roman Empire and deposited with the Vestal Virgins. A translation in Greek was incised at a number of sites in the Mediterranean world. Especially important for the study of epistolary form is Charles Bradford Welles, *Royal Correspondence in the*

---

[54] F. Danker, *Century,* 126–28; see Milligan, *Here & There,* 10; E. J. Goodspeed, *As I Remember* (New York: Harper, 1953), 102–3. Forty-three texts from Karanis are known as P. Kar. Goodspeed (=P. Chic. Goodspeed).

[55] For general orientation, see entries "Epigraphy, Greek" and "Epigraphy, Latin" in *OCD; ISBE,* "Inscriptions," 2:831–39; Danker, *Century,* 91–114. For details on the various corpora, see Jacob J. E. Hondius, *Saxa Loquuntur: Inleiding tot de Grieksche Epigraphik* (Leiden: A. W. Sijthoff, 1938). For grammatical study, E. Schweizer, *Grammatik der pergamischen Inschriften: Beiträge zur Laut- und Flexionslehre der gemeingriechischen Sprache* (Berlin, 1898); Leslie Threatte, *The Grammar of Attic Inscriptions,* vol. 1: *Phonology* (Berlin: de Gruyter, 1980).

[56] On the importance of reading evidence aright, see Dixon Slingerland, "Acts 18:1–18, The Gallio Inscription and Absolute Pauline Chronology," *JBL* 110 (1991): 439–49; for the text, see *SIG*² 801D; Hans Conzelmann, *Acts,* Hermeneia (Philadelphia: Fortress Press, 1987), 152–53.

Hellenistic Period: A Study in Greek Epigraphy (New Haven: Yale University Press, 1934). Included in this corpus are letters from, among others, Antigonus I, Lysimachus, and Ptolemy II, Ptolemy III, and Ptolemy IV. One of the assets that students of the New Testament should readily welcome is the alphabetized appendix of selected vocabulary. In some respects, these letters are more helpful than the papyri for the interpretation of certain features in St. Paul's letters.

Excellence, or *aretē* (ἀρετή), practically synonymous with an exemplary sense of civic responsibility, and frequently equated with beneficence, was celebrated in a variety of documents. A commemoration thereof can be called an aretalogy, a term that ought not to be applied exclusively, as it sometimes is, to observance of a deity's achievements. Aretalogy is a genus of laudation with a variety of recipients of praise and honor. The *Res Gestae* is an autobiographical aretalogy. In contrast to the simple dignity of the Augustan prose is the "bacchantic dithyrambic prose," as Eduard Norden termed it, of Antiochus I of Commagene.[57] About the middle of the first century B.C. he defied the ravages of time by engraving directions for cultic observance at his burial shrine. One need not go to Qumran to find a lengthy sentence like the one in Ephesians 1:3-14. Antiochus I expected far more suspense from his readers. His verbal torrent is also worth looking at in connection with St. Paul's boasting in 2 Corinthians.[58]

Thousands of stones record the wishes of heads of state, the recognition of athletes and artists for exceptional performance, the honors accorded physicians and bureaucrats for services faithfully rendered, the praises heaped on philanthropists for an endless variety of public works and other types of contributions, including especially the staging of public shows and festivals. Many record the activities of clubs and associations.[59] In *Benefactor* we have tried to go beyond Nägeli, standard lexicons, and wordbooks in suggesting a number of points of contact between such documents and the New Testament. But only a beginning has been made, and the stones, unyielding as they may be in other ways, will be forced to give up their treasures to those who insist on probing their diction and syntax beyond the boundaries of lexical glosses. Four main resources await the mining. The first is William Dittenberger, ed., *Sylloge Inscriptionum Graecarum* (=*SIG*) 4 vols., 3d ed. (1915–

---

[57] Eduard Norden, *Die Antike Kunstprosa,* 2d ed. (Leipzig: Teubner, 1909), 1:145. For the text, see *OGIS,* 381; a portion of it is also printed in *Hellenistic Greek Texts,* ed. Allen Wikgren, with the collaboration of Ernest Cadman Colwell and Ralph Marcus (Chicago: University of Chicago Press, 1947), 137–40; translation in Danker, *Benefactor,* no. 41.

[58] Awareness of Hellenic background helps one understand the theme of boasting in 2 Corinthians; see F. Danker, *Augsburg Commentary on the New Testament: II Corinthians* (Minneapolis: Augsburg, 1989).

[59] For inscriptions relating to Greek clubs and associations, see Erich Ziebarth, *Das griechische Vereinswesen* (Leipzig: S. Hirzel, 1896) and Franz Poland, *Geschichte des griechischen Vereinswesens* (Leipzig: Teubner, 1909). For the Roman scene, Jean-Pierre Waltzing, *Étude historique sur les corporations professionnelles chez les Romains,* 4 vols. (Louvain: C. Peeters, 1895–1900).

24).[60] This work includes decrees issued by heads of state as well as by clubs and associations, various kinds of honorary documents, cultic rules and regulations, to cite but a few. The second is *Orientis Graeci Inscriptiones Selectae* (*OGIS*), by the same editor, 2 vols. 1903–1905. This corpus contains most of the types found in *SIG*[3], but with concentration on documents relating to conditions and circumstances in the divided empire of Alexander the Great. Included is the edict of Tiberius Julius Alexander (*OGIS* 669), which made possible a more reliable history of first-century Ptolemaic Egypt. The third is *Inscriptiones Graecae* (Berlin, 1873–) of which vols. 2 and 3 (*editio minor=IG*[2]) are the more frequently cited portions. The fourth is *Supplementum Epigraphicum Graecum,* begun in 1923 under the editorship of Jacobus J. Hondius, assisted by P. Roussel, Antonin Salač, Marcus N. Tod, and Erich Ziebarth. This series, like the *Sammelbuch* for papyri, brings together in one place the fruits of epigraphic labors published in books, bulletins, and journals, and in a variety of languages. Many of these publications would be inaccessible, outside of a few universities, for general perusal. Besides the inclusion of entire new texts, the series reports suggestions made by reviewers and other critics for improvement of texts previously published. Students will also see references to the great collection made by August Boeckh, *Corpus Inscriptionum Graecarum,* 4 vols. (Berlin, 1825–1877), which was superseded by *IG.* The Roman world is recollected in *Corpus Inscriptionum Latinorum* (Berlin, 1863–), begun by Theodor Mommsen. Under the editorship of H. Dessau, many of these became available in three volumes (5 parts) to a wider public in *Inscriptiones Latinae Selectae* (Berlin, 1892–1916).[61]

For an introduction to epigraphic study, consult Arthur Geoffrey Woodhead, *The Study of Greek Inscriptions* (Cambridge: Cambridge University Press, 1959; 2d ed., 1981). More basic is B. F. Cook, *Greek Inscriptions* (Berkeley and Los Angeles: University of California Press, 1987). A stand-by in German is Günther Klaffenbach, *Griechische Epigraphik* (Göttingen: Vandenhoeck & Ruprecht, 1957). For Latin inscriptions, see Giancarlo Susini, *The Roman Stonecutter: An Introduction to Latin Epigraphy* (Oxford: Basil Blackwell, 1973).

Biblical students frequently encounter the name of Sir William Ramsay in connection with the study of St. Luke's and St. Paul's writings. Many of his books have been reprinted but not his most useful one for philological study of the New Testament, *The Cities and Bishoprics of Phrygia.* Because of insufficient evidence, only one volume in two parts appeared (Oxford, 1895–97).[62]

---

[60] The 2d ed. (1898–1901), signified by *SIG*[2], is used for inscriptions that were not repeated in *SIG*[3].

[61] For other notable corpora, see the list of abbreviations in BAGD.

[62] As an introduction to *Bishoprics,* the student ought to consult Ramsay's *The Historical*

Since the ultimate in excellence was exhibited by helpful deities, who in turn became the models for human beneficence, inscriptions dedicated to such deities as Isis and Sarapis are in bountiful supply. Although some students of St. John's Gospel may not realize it, they owe much to Werner Peek for his publication of texts relating to Isis, *Der Isishymnus von Andros und verwandte Texte* (Berlin: Weidmann, 1930).[63]

Precisely because memorials on stone were thought to resist the ravages of time, Pericles voices a poigant note in his oration over the fallen heroes at Marathon when he observes that beyond the limited space of pillared praise all the earth is their sepulcher (Thucydides 2.43.3). Tombstones are one of the most generous sources for glimpses into mind and soul. Richmond Lattimore collected and categorized a great number of Greek and Latin sepulchral inscriptions in very readable form, with accompanying translations and ample bibliography, in *Themes on Greek and Latin Epitaphs* (Urbana: University of Illinois Press, 1962).[64]

One would like to say much more, but sufficient guidance has here been given for biblical students to find an endless variety of possibilities from which to choose for further inquiry. If the twentieth century was the age of the papyri for stimulation of biblical studies, the twenty-first century belongs to inscriptions, and probably also to patristic writers.

There are a number of specialized works for the study of epigraphs. Eduard Schweizer's inheritance was *Grammatik der pergamischen Inschriften: Beiträge zur Laut- und Flexionslehre der gemeingriechischen Sprache* (Berlin: Weidmannsche Buchhandlung, 1898). In a 43-page study, Gottfried Thieme, *Die Inschriften von Magnesia am Mäander und das Neue Testament: Eine sprachgeschichtliche Studie* (Göttingen: Vandenhoeck (Ruprecht, 1906), discusses words and phrases that writers of the New Testament have in common with inscriptions found at Magnesia, western Asia Minor. The inscriptions themselves were edited by Otto Kern, *Die Inschriften von Magnesia am Maeander* (Berlin: W. Spemann, 1900). This latter collection, together with the inscriptions from Priene, located in the same general area, ed. F. Frhr. Hiller von Gaertringen, with C. Fredrich, H. von Prott, H. Schrader, Th. Wiegand, and H. Winnefeld, *Inschriften von Priene* (Berlin: Georg Reimer, 1906), provide excellent starters for probing the types of documents and the kinds of diction and phraseology that illuminate so much of the New Testament.

Geography of Asia Minor, Royal Geographic Society, Supplementary Paper 4 (London, 1890). For a list of this eminent scholar's contributions to our knowledge of ancient Asia Minor, see the biography by W. Ward Gasque, *Sir William M. Ramsay: Archaeologist and New Testament Scholar* (Grand Rapids: Baker, 1966).

[63] For entry into the literature relating to Isis, see Jan Bergman, *Ich bin Isis: Studien zum memphitischen Hintergrund der griechischen Isisaretalogien,* Acta Universitatis Upsaliensis, Historia Religionum 3 (Uppsala: University of Uppsala, 1968).

[64] Originally published as vol. 28, nos. 1–2, Illinois Studies in Language and Literature.

Useful for determining the Roman understanding of Greek words for political entities and titles used in Roman bureaucratic parlance is Hugh John Mason, *Greek Terms for Roman Institutions: A Lexicon and Analysis,* American Studies in Papyrology 13 (Toronto: Hakkert, 1974). In the Greek-to-Latin glossary, Mason shows some of the distribution of usage in papyri and inscriptions along with references to recognized Greek authors. Selected terms, a number of which occur in the Book of Acts, are then discussed. A Latin-to-Greek reverse index completes this very helpful book.

SOCIAL-SCIENTIFIC CRITICISM[65]

Before the 1960s most biblical interpretation was diachronic; that is, it was pursued with historical questions in mind. When was a document written? Where was it written? Who wrote it? How many hands were involved in its production? What editorial processes are discernible? What do we know about the history of the text, especially the variants that we encounter in it? What is the probability for accuracy concerning events described in it? What are the truth claims in these historically conditioned documents, or what theologically significant material can we glean from them. Such were the questions asked, to various degrees of interest, by those who considered themselves practitioners of historical-critical exegesis.[66] As the influence of the newer linguistics, with its interest in synchronic study of a document, drew up alongside increasing awareness of anthropology and sociology as instruments for finding significance in ancient documents, some historical-critics began to look for ways in which their approach might take a new lease on life, somewhat along the theoretical lines taken by practitioners of the newer archaeology.

Not that the phenomenon of social inquiry came on the scene like Athena from Zeus's brow. Before the battle took shape, drum rolls were heard in many quarters. Johann Gottfried Herder, the brothers Grimm (Jacob and Wilhelm), and later especially Hermann Gunkel and other form-critics alerted interpreters to the importance of folk interest in the production of basic patterns of

---

[65] For a sketch of social-scientific study of the Bible, see "Sociology," *ABD,* 6:79–99; John H. Elliott, *What Is Social-Scientific Criticism?* Guides to Biblical Scholarship Series (Minneapolis: Fortress Press, 1993), with comprehensive bibliography (hereafter, *Social-Scientific Criticism*). See also Elliott's article, "Social-Scientific Criticism of the New Testament: More on Methods and Models," *Semeia* 35 (1986): 1–33; the entire issue, with additional contributions by Bruce J. Malina, Leland J. White, and Jerome H. Neyrey, is devoted to social-scientific criticism of the New Testament and its social world.

[66] See Edgar Krentz, *The Historical-Critical Method* (Philadelphia: Fortress Press, 1975). See also Hermann Bengston, *Introduction to Ancient History,* trans. R. I. Frank and Frank D. Gilliard (Berkeley: University of California Press, 1970).

literature. And the University of Chicago had initiated a line of inquiry about similar matters by Shirley Jackson Case and Shailer Matthews.

In *Die apostolische und nachapostolische Zeit* (Göttingen: Vandenhoeck & Ruprecht, 1962), the first part of a promising four-volume manual edited by Kurt Dietrich Schmidt and Ernst Wolf and titled *Die Kirche in ihrer Geschichte,* author Leonhard Goppelt discussed factors that helped shape the postapostolic church.

Martin Hengel, *Judaism and Hellenism: Studies in Their Encounter in Palestine during the Early Hellenistic Period,* 2d ed., trans. John Bowden, 2 vols. (Philadelphia: Fortress Press, 1974), traced the development of Judaism in the intertestamental period in an effort to "illuminate the social, religious and historical background from which primitive Christianity emerged." The first volume consists of text, the second of notes and bibliography. Elias Bickermann, *The Jews in the Greek Age* (Cambridge: Harvard University Press, 1988), reads the influence of Hellenism on Jews a bit differently from Martin Hengel.

Félix Marie Abel covered some of the same ground that is traveled by Hengel, but in the second volume of his *Histoire de la Palestine depuis la conquête d'Alexandre jusqu'-à l'invasion arabe,* 2 vols. (Paris: J. Gabalda, 1952), he continues the story to the time of the vanquishing Arabs.

Lacking in all these and related studies was a theoretical framework for understanding the diverse phenomena. Required was a firmer grasp of the social totality. Serving as bellwether in the 1960s was E. A. Judge's *The Social Pattern of the Christian Groups in the First Century* (London: Tyndale Press, 1960), a book whose brevity belies its import. In 1973, a working group, led by Wayne A. Meeks and Leander E. Keck, was formed to explore the social world of early Christianity, with initial focus on developments at Antioch-on-the Orontes from its beginning until the fourth century. In their view social-science disciplines appeared to provide an approach that transcended attempts either to establish truth claims in the biblical canon or to extract meaning merely on the basis of a socio-historical analysis. To illustrate: It is one thing to know the historical circumstances that are implied by the Book of Revelation; it is another to know what varieties of social circumstances might account for the kinds of concerns and issues expressed in the book, as well as for the kinds of communities to which a book of that nature would be of interest. Once one makes such determination, one is well on the way to explicating the text. In other words, as John Hall Elliott and others have pointed out, something more than historical-critical inquiry as traditionally understood is needed. The task requires a much more comprehensive approach that goes beyond social description to holistic inquiry, namely, social-scientific analysis.[67]

---

[67] For a description and critique of selected sociological approaches to the study of the Bible, see the literature cited in n. 29. On the social setting in general, see Carolyn Osiek, *What Are They Saying About the Social Setting of the New Testament?* (New York: Paulist, 1984).

Drawing on the contributions of cultural anthropology, the sociology of knowledge, and the relevant research of the social sciences, sociologically oriented exegetes view biblical texts as records of social interchange. The ways in which people think about things have effects on their lives, and their experiences and perceptions of reality in turn determine their thought processes and, ultimately, the meanings of the texts they produce. Therefore, to do exegesis properly one must examine a text as much as possible within its total contextuality. Social-scientific study is concerned with the ways in which the various dimensions of life—economic, political, and ideological—interact with one another so as to produce the social phenomena that constantly emerge and develop in the course of history. The production of texts in their endless variety is a part of this social interaction. Hence, by using a "model" drawn from field research, as is done by archaeologists who extrapolate from known systems, one can begin to diagnose a related phenomenon at another point in time or place.

Such an approach invites consideration, if not immediate conviction, because human beings in community display certain patterns of behavior that can be classified and used for understanding related modes of behavior. When such methodology is applied to the explication of texts, it can, as Elliott points out, be termed "social-scientific criticism." In this way social-scientific interpretation complements historical-critical inquiry. The latter asks in diachronic fashion the journalist's basic what-when-where questions; the former inquires with synchronic awareness: how, why, and wherefore. In his book *A Home for the Homeless: A Sociological Exegesis of 1 Peter, Its Situation and Strategy* (Philadelphia: Fortress Press, 1981), reissued in a paperback edition with a new introduction and subtitle: *A Social-Scientific Criticism of I Peter, Its Situation and Strategy* (Minneapolis: Fortress Press, 1990), Elliott shows how one might answer the latter questions. At the same time, as Elliott affirms, social-scientific criticism "is an *expansion,* not a replacement of conventional historical-critical method. It *complements* the other subdisciplines of the exegetical enterprise (text criticism, literary criticism, form and genre criticism, historical criticism, tradition and redaction criticism, theological criticism, reception criticism) through its attention to the social dimensions of the text, its contexts of composition and reception, and their interrelationships."[68]

Since Elliott's work on 1 Peter is the first to apply social-scientific criticism to an entire document of the Bible, it deserves recognition as a guiding tool for such an approach. Used in association with his extended definition, *What Is Social-Scientific Criticism?* (Minneapolis: Fortress Press, 1993), it will help the digger for truth find treasure in other ancient textual earth.[69]

[68] Elliott, *Home,* xix.
[69] Elliott's *What Is Social-Scientific Criticism?* is one of many in Guides to Biblical Scholarship, published by Fortress Press, Minneapolis. For introductions and bibliographies to the growing

In addition to Elliott's studies, one must make the acquaintance of Gerd Theissen's *Sociology of Early Palestinian Christianity,* trans. John Bowden (Philadelphia: Fortress Press, 1978), a popularization of pioneering essays published in a variety of periodicals. Theissen analyzes the interaction of the Jesus movement with Jewish Palestinian society in general. His first note (p. 120) takes account of some earlier studies down to 1974. As reflected in a later study, *The Gospels in Context: Social and Political History in the Synoptic Tradition,* trans. Linda M. Maloney (Minneapolis: Fortress Press, 1991), Theissen's approach lacks the social-scientific thrust exhibited in Elliott's work.[70]

To meet the needs of "contemporary college-educated persons" who require some bridgework from their own technical areas of inquiry to the strange world of biblical texts, Bruce J. Malina has designed *Christian Origins and Cultural Anthropology: Practical Models for Biblical Interpretation* (Atlanta: John Knox Press, 1986). This is the "big picture" approach versus atomistic exegesis, with the framework adopted from Mary Douglas.[71] Like Elliott, Malina goes beyond Theissen to higher levels of conceptualization for more adequate explanation of social data. Many items in the bibliography (pp. 208–20) are seedplots for later "discoveries." See also his important earlier study, *The New Testament World: Insights from Cultural Anthropology* (Atlanta: John Knox Press, 1981).

SOCIAL WORLD

Not to be confused with social-scientific study are the numerous productions that offer a view of social circumstances and institutions without reference to the theoretical framework described above.

---

number of varieties of approaches to exposition of the biblical text, this is the series to consult. In addition, the chapter on commentaries in the present work will introduce the student to numerous products of such approaches. For application of social-scientific analysis to a Gospel, see Halvor Moxnes, *The Economy of the Kingdom: Social Conflict and Economic Relations in Luke's Gospel* (Philadelphia: Fortress Press, 1988). See also the essays in *The Social World of Luke-Acts: Models for Interpretation,* ed. Jerome H. Neyrey (Peabody, Mass.: Hendrickson, 1991).

[70] In a review article in *CBQ* 41 (1979): 176–81, Bruce Malina lists some of Theissen's publications that underlie *Sociology of Early Christianity;* he also charges Theissen with falling short of in-depth sociological study. For further critique of Theissen, see J. H. Elliott, "Social-Scientific Criticism of the New Testament and Its Social World: More on Method and Models," *Semeia* 35 (1986): 1–33. Elliott's well-screened bibliography includes references to basic works that antedate application of social-scientific models to biblical studies. It is, of course, the nature of scientific inquiry that one generation sows and another harvests, and each in turn becomes obsolete. The same issue of *Semeia* also contains articles that make use of social-scientific models in the study of Matthew, Mark, 1 Corinthians, and 3 John.

[71] See Mary Douglas, *Natural Symbols: Explorations in Cosmology* (New York: Pantheon Books, 1970; reprint, 1973); *Cultural Bias,* Occasional Paper No. 35 of the Royal Anthropological Institute of Great Britain and Ireland (London: Royal Anthropological Institute, 1978).

Anthologies are a useful medium for gaining entry to ancient social worlds. In *New Testament Background: Selected Documents* (London: SPCK, 1956, and reprints), C. K. Barrett samples a broad variety of ancient texts that reveal somewhat the intellectual and religious milieu in which the New Testament took shape. A sourcebook by Mary R. Lefkowitz and Maureen B. Fant, *Women's Life in Greece and Rome* (Baltimore: John Hopkins University Press, 1982), offers translations of selections from Greek and Roman authors, papyri, and epigraphs relating to women. As in this work, so also in Ross S. Kraemer's *Maenads, Martyrs, Matrons, Monastics: A Sourcebook on Women's Religions in the Greco-Roman World* (Philadelphia: Fortress Press, 1988), woman's history begins to leap out of texts frequently ignored by male writers concerned with social institutions. For original texts on the social positions of women, consult H. W. Pleket, *Epigraphica*, vol. 2: *Texts on the Social History of the Greek World*, Textus Minores 41 (Leiden: Brill, 1969). Documentation from Roman and Greek sources for many aspects of slavery is available in Thomas Wiedemann's *Greek and Roman Slavery* (Baltimore, 1981). For "sacred texts of the mystery religions of the ancient Mediterranean world," consult Marvin W. Meyer, *The Ancient Mysteries: A Sourcebook* (San Francisco: Harper, 1987).

Inscribed decrees, diplomatic and private correspondence, and selections from Greek and Roman authors on political and economic matters dominate a sourcebook by M. M. Austin, *The Hellenistic World from Alexander to the Roman Conquest: A selection of ancient sources in translation* (Cambridge, UK: Cambridge University Press, 1981). Through these documents one can gain a clearer image of the kind of world that later on shaped the context within which Christianity learned to communicate. This author's *Benefactor: Epigraphic Study of a Graeco-Roman Semantic Field* (St. Louis: Clayton Publishing House, 1982) goes further and relates selected decrees and other inscribed documents to biblical documents, thereby demonstrating the important role played by the reciprocity–patronage system. Many other documents are included in Naphtali Lewis and Meyer Reinhold, *Roman Civilization*, 2 vols. (New York: Harper, 1966).

In *Goddesses, Whores, Wives, and Slaves: Women in Classical Antiquity* (New York: Schocken Books, 1975), Sarah B. Pomeroy embeds translations from Greek and Latin literature in her discussion of the fortunes of women in the ancient Mediterranean world. More theoretically oriented, with repeated emphasis on the theme of patriarchy, is Elisabeth Schüssler Fiorenza's *In Memory of Her: A Feminist Theological Reconstruction of Christian Origins* (New York: Crossroad, 1984). Status of children, wet-nursing, and theories of conception in the ancient Roman world are but a few of the topics discussed in a collection of essays edited by Beryl Rawson, *The Family in Ancient Rome: New Perspectives* (Ithaca, N.Y.: Cornell University Press, 1986).

Rawson's two sets of bibliographies will amaze the student who might be tempted to underestimate the importance of the topic.

A number of books include within their covers a miscellany of topics. Everett Ferguson, *Backgrounds of Early Christianity* (Grand Rapids: Eerdmans, 1987), offers a judicious sampling of primary and secondary sources on a broad range of topics relating to politics, religion, culture, and intellectual currents.

Robert M. Grant's *Gods and the One God* (Philadelphia: Westminster Press, 1986) is the first of nine volumes in Library of Early Christianity, edited by Wayne A. Meeks. This series includes chapters on the New Testament in its social environment (John E. Stambaugh and David L. Balch) and early biblical interpretation (James L. Kugel and Rowan A. Greer); a sourcebook on moral exhortation (Abraham J. Malherbe); studies on letter writing in antiquity (Stanley K. Stowers); the moral world of the first Christians; a look down the pathway from the Maccabees to the Mishnah (Shaye J. D. Cohen); studies on the literary environment of the New Testament (David E. Aune);[72] and Christology in context (M. de Jonge).

Greeks, Romans, and Christians: Essays in Honor of Abraham J. Malherbe, ed. David L. Balch, Everett Ferguson, and Wayne A. Meeks (Minneapolis: Fortress Press, 1990), collects the thoughts of numerous scholars on Hellenistic philosophy, rhetorical influences on portions of Pauline correspondence, and other points of contact between Christianity and Hellenism. The book concludes with a bibliography of Malherbe's many efforts to contextualize Christianity.

Some of Arnaldo Momigliano's choice essays on religion in the Greco-Roman world are collected in a book titled *On Pagans, Jews, and Christians* (Middletown, Conn.: Wesleyan University Press, 1987). See also John Ferguson, *The Religions of the Roman Empire* (Ithaca, N.Y.: Cornell University Press, 1970), and W. Burkert, *Greek Religion,* trans. J. Raffan (Cambridge: Harvard University Press, 1985).

For the grand scene one ought to make the acquaintance of William Woodthorpe Tarn, *Hellenistic Civilization,* 2 vols., 3d ed. rev. by Tarn and G. T. Griffith (London: E. Arnold, 1952), an old but vibrant work. In *The Harvest of Hellenism* (New York: Simon and Schuster, 1970), F. E. Peters records "A History of the Near East from Alexander the Great to the Triumph of Christianity."

Where did Christians live in Rome? Who were their neighbors? What nationalities did they represent? What social distinctions prevailed? What can be learned about the people listed in Romans 16? These are a few of the questions Peter Lampe endeavors to answer, with guidance to a vast literature, in

---

[72] See also Aune's *Prophecy in Early Christianity and the Ancient Mediterranean World* (Grand Rapids: Eerdmans, 1983), a study of early Christian prophetic activity and expression against the background of prophetic roles in Israel, early Judaism, and the Greco-Roman world.

Die stadtrömischen Christen in den ersten beiden Jahrhunderten, Wissenschaftliche Untersuchungen zum NT 2/18, 2d rev. ed. (Tübingen: J. C. B. Mohr [Siebeck], 1989), which will also appear in English. Wayne A. Meeks discusses the social world of the apostle Paul in *The First Urban Christians* (New Haven: Yale University Press, 1983). What are the implications of St. Paul's activity as an artisan? Ronald F. Hock, *The Social Context of Paul's Ministry: Tentmaking and Apostleship* (Philadelphia: Fortress Press, 1980), answers with full command of the ancient social and economic context. Derek Tidball stages a broader scene in *The Social Context of the New Testament: A Sociological Analysis* (Grand Rapids: Academic Books, 1984). For a bridging of Pauline usage and Greco-Roman legal interest, consult Francis Lyall, *Slaves, Citizens, Sons: Legal Metaphors in the Epistles* (Grand Rapids: Academic Books, 1984).

Sumptuously adorned is *A History of Private Life,* I: *From Pagan Rome to Byzantium,* ed. Paul Veyne, trans. Arthur Goldhammer (Cambridge: Harvard University Press, 1987). This is the first of five volumes in a series that has the private sector from polytheistic Rome to the present time as its core topic. The general editors, Philippe Ariès and Georges Duby, have designed the series for the general public, and students who desire to check the validity of many of the generalizations found in this work will be frustrated by the paucity of notes. On the other hand, the bibliography (pp. 647–55) lists some of the choicest scholarly discussions on Greco-Roman social-historical topics. In addition to cultivating knowledge of Paul Veyne's informative section, "The Roman Empire" (pp. 5–234), students will profit from Peter Brown's instructive chapter, "Person and Group in Judaism and Early Christianity" (pp. 253–67).

Two works that are constantly mined, overtly or covertly, cannot escape mention. David Magie provides a large supply of social data in *Roman Rule in Asia Minor to the End of the Third Century after Christ,* 2 vols. (Princeton: Princeton University Press, 1950). The other, Mikhail Ivanovich Rostovtzeff's *The Social and Economic History of the Roman Empire,* 2 vols. (1926;, 2d ed. rev. P. M. Fraser, Oxford: Clarendon Press, 1957), invites some discount for ideological perspective.

Before making pronouncements about social customs in Asia Minor it is well to note what William Ramsay said in *Asianic Elements in Greek Civilisation: The Gifford Lectures in the University of Edinburgh 1915–1916* (London: John Murray, 1927), a book replete with sagacious comment on kinship and custom, that one must be careful about looking "through European-Greek binoculars badly focused on an Asian object" (p. 141). For further appreciation of this scholar's knowledge of Mediterranean society, consult his insightful comments in *The Social Basis of Roman Power in Asia Minor,* prepared for the press by J. G. C. Anderson (Aberdeen: Aberdeen University Press, 1941).

Standing out from among many works is *The Future of Early Christianity: Essays in Honor of Helmut Koester* (Minneapolis: Fortress Press, 1991), a mosaic of contextualization by thirty-nine colleagues and students of Helmut Koester, with its generous and fruitful contributions to the study of Christian origins and history. This handsome volume refracts many of the hues that are part of the variegated pattern portrayed in the present chapter and those that have gone before. Edited by Birger A. Pearson, this collection touches, among other things, on textual criticism, archaeology, exegetical questions, early Christian literature, Gnosticism, Judaica, papyrology, and epigraphy.

At the beginning of chap. 13 we called the roll of a number of pioneers who laid the foundation for others who came later into the vineyard of inquiry. One of the hazards encountered at the end of the twentieth century is the ease with which those who have labored in the heat of day can be forgotten. Out of much that could be mentioned, we refer especially to work done by the *Religionsgeschichtler,* the proponents of the history-of-religions approach to biblical interpretation. Younger students who do not read German can scarcely know how much of the work of the *Religionsgeschichtler* has entered into the mainstream of biblical studies. Included in that goodly company of scholars who defied time's erasures by producing pyramids of ageless research are Richard Reitzenstein, Albrecht Dieterich, and others in *Archiv für die Religionsgeschichte,* an inexhaustible quarry of learning.[73] Students who know the meaning of gratitude will add to this list the names of other scholarly benefactors who deserve a place in abiding memory.

CONTEXTUALIZATION OF THE READER

Whereas the Enlightenment set the reader of the Bible outside the precincts of the text, hermeneutical theory in the closing decades of the twentieth century focused attention on the reader's immediate involvement in the text. Since detailed exploration of this subject would excessively expand the present work, it is sufficient to call attention to a few basic resources out of a rapidly expanding bibliography. Little known in biblical circles, but important for understanding the shift that has taken place, is the collection of essays in *Contemporary Literary Hermeneutics and Interpretation of Classical Texts/ Herméneutique littéraire contemporaine et interprétation des textes classiques,* ed. Stephanus Kresic (Ottawa: University of Ottawa Press, 1981). The two-part article, "Biblical Criticism," *ABD,* 1:725–36, by J. C. O'Neill and William Baird, sketches historical developments, describes a variety of historical-critical

---

[73] For other classics, see the list in Helmut Koester, "Epilogue: Current Issues in New Testament Scholarship," in *The Future of Early Christianity: Essays in Honor of Helmut Koester,* ed. B. Pearson (Minneapolis: Fortress Press, 1991), 467–68 n. 1; for an assessment especially of R. Reitzenstein's research on Iranian mythology, see Carsten Colpe, *Die religionsgeschichtliche Schule* (Göttingen: Vandenhoeck & Ruprecht, 1961).

and literary-critical approaches, and provides guidance to the basic literature. In "Reader Response Theory," *ABD*, 5:625–28, Bernard C. Lategan features the development in literary studies that "focuses on the relationship between text and receiver." For more detailed probing of this method of understanding a text, consult Edgar V. McKnight, *Post-Modern Use of the Bible: The Emergence of Reader-Oriented Criticism* (Nashville: Abingdon Press, 1988). In *Mark and Method: New Approaches in Biblical Studies* (Minneapolis: Fortress Press, 1992), Janice Capel Anderson and Stephen D. Moore serve as editors of a series of essays on modern developments in criticism. Robert Fowler's chapter on Mark in this book invites attention to the detailed discussion in his *Let the Reader Understand: Reader-Response Criticism and the Gospel of Mark* (Minneapolis: Fortress Press, 1991). Other chapters in *Mark and Method* round out some of the principal emphases in contemporary inquiry, including feminist criticism. Especially revealing is the title of the second essay, by Elizabeth Struthers Malbon, "Narrative Criticism: How Does the Story Mean?" Jack Dean Kingsbury well exhibits application of literary-structural awareness in two works published by Fortress Press: *Conflict in Mark* (Minneapolis, 1989) and *Conflict in Luke* (1991), both with the subtitle: *Jesus, Authorities, Disciples*. For an overview of a variety of approaches to the Old Testament, see *The New Literary Criticism and the Hebrew Bible,* ed. J. Cheryl Exum and David J. A. Clines (Valley Forge, Penn.: Trinity Press, 1993).

Between the "New Archaeology" and "New Criticism" there appears to be no epistemological division. But in practice the latter more than the other democratizes the effort to understand, and interpretation becomes less and less an elitist undertaking.

CHAPTER FOURTEEN

The Dead Sea Scrolls

I N THE SPRING of the year 1947 two young shepherds were grazing their sheep and goats in the vicinity of Qumran. As one of them was looking for a stray sheep, so the story goes, he casually cast a stone into a small opening in one of the cliffs. The shattering sound echoing from the cave, soon to be heard around the world, sent him scurrying off in fright, but the lure of possible buried treasure brought him and his companion back to find only rolls of decaying leather in jars that lined the floor of the cave, now famous as Qumran cave 1. Among these scrolls was a copy of the prophecy of Isaiah and a commentary on Habakkuk. In just a few years the mists of legend have shrouded much of the story; much that was written about these ancient scrolls right after their discovery will seem to some future generation crude attempts to appraise what can be evaluated only with fact-filtering time, disciplined judgment, and chastened caution.

Since the first discoveries in cave 1, ten other caves were relieved of their treasures. One of the more notable is cave 4, from which the fragments of close to five hundred manuscripts were removed in 1952. Cave 11 was discovered in 1956. As more and more of the finds were published and discussed, the Qumran picture came into clearer focus. Besides those discovered at Qumran, other fragments were found at Masada, Wadi Murabba'at, Naḥal Ḥever, Naḥal Ṣe'elim, and Naḥal Mishmar.

As must be expected when dealing with discoveries of this type, many a jerry-built construction was forced very early to topple at the impact of a fact. The report of Yigael Yadin on the excavation of King Herod's palace and environs, "The Excavations of Masada—1963/64: Preliminary Report," *Israel Exploration Journal* 15 (1965), relieved some writers of their anxiety about the antiquity of the Dead Sea Scrolls.[1]

---

[1] Solomon Zeitlin expressed his verdict of forgery in "The Fallacy of the Antiquity of the Hebrew Scrolls Once More Exposed," *JQR* 52 (1962): 346–66; idem, "History, Historians and the Dead Sea Scrolls," *JQR* 55 (1964): 97–116. Yigael Yadin expressed himself further in *Masada: Herod's*

Nor has the manner of the Scrolls' entry into the public square brought honor to academia. In his well-known study *Introduction to the Talmud and Midrash,* Hermann L. Strack describes the refusal of Solomon Leb Friedland (Friedländer) to permit others, including Strack, to inspect a Spanish talmudic manuscript of the year 1212 A.D.[2] History repeated itself in connection with the sporadic publication of many of the Dead Sea Scroll fragments. For chapters in the sorry tale, see Hershel Shanks, *Understanding the Dead Sea Scrolls: A Reader from the Biblical Archaeological Review,* ed. Hershel Shanks (New York: Random House, 1992).[3] Helping to break the "monopoly on the still-unpublished Dead Sea Scrolls" was the reconstruction of unpublished scrolls by Ben Zion Wacholder and Martin G. Abegg, eds., *A Preliminary Edition of the Unpublished Dead Sea Scrolls: The Hebrew and Aramaic Texts from Cave Four,* fascicle 1 (Washington, D.C., 1991). Fascicle 2 appeared in 1992. Published by the Dead Sea Scroll Research Council, Biblical Archaeological Society, Washington, D.C., these two fascicles coordinate with the 2-volume set of photographs published by the Biblical Archaeology Society under the direction of Robert H. Eisenman and James M. Robinson, *A Facsimile Edition of the Dead Sea Scrolls: Prepared with an Introduction and Index,* 2 vols. (Washington, D.C., 1991), containing 1,785 plates. The publication of 4QMMT in this set (vol. 1, fig. 8, p. xxxi) led to acerbic litigation.

Excellent English introductions to the Qumran scrolls, besides the work by Shanks, include Yigael Yadin, *The Message of the Scrolls* (1957), ed. James H. Charlesworth (New York: Crossroad, 1992); Frank Moore Cross, Jr., *The Ancient Library of Qumran and Modern Biblical Studies: The Haskell Lectures, 1956–1957* (Garden City, N.Y.: Doubleday, 1958; rev. ed., Anchor Book A272, 1961); and Jozef T. Milik, *Ten Years of Discovery in the Wilderness of Judaea,* trans. John Strugnell, Studies in Biblical Theology 26 (London: SCM Press; Naperville, Ill.: Alec R. Allenson, 1959). Cross includes much

---

Fortress and the Zealots' Last Stand, trans. Moshe Pearlman (New York, 1966). Others who labored to bring light in the early years include J. A. Sanders, *The Psalms Scroll of Qumran Cave 11 (11Qpsᵃ),* Discoveries in the Judaean Desert of Jordan 4 (Oxford: Clarendon, 1965), which includes a Hebrew text of Sirach 51:13-20*b*, 30*b*. A more popular edition of the Oxford work was published under the title *The Dead Sea Psalms Scroll* (Ithaca, N.Y.: Cornell University Press, 1967), and in a postscript Sanders presents a fifth fragment, not included in the Oxford text of the Psalms scroll but recovered in a kidnap-case atmosphere by Yigael Yadin, who first published the fragment in *Textus* 5 (1966). In appendix 2 Sanders catalogues and indexes the premasoretic Psalter texts, followed by a premasoretic Psalter bibliography in appendix 3. Joseph A. Fitzmyer, *The Genesis Apocryphon of Qumran Cave 1: A Commentary,* Biblica et Orientalia 18 (Rome: Pontifical Biblical Institute, 1966), early demonstrated the contribution made by Qumran to our knowledge of Aramaic.

[2] Pp. 68–69.

[3] In a chapter from the *Reader* titled "Is the Vatican Suppressing the Dead Sea Scrolls?" 275–90, Shanks challenges the conspiracy theory advanced by Michael Baigent and Richard Leigh, *The Dead Sea Scrolls Deception* (New York: Summit Books, 1991).

textual criticism; Milik concentrates on Essene history. Both survey master-fully the scroll study during a decade of international scholarly investigation and furnish numerous bibliographical references. In the same breath one must mention Millar Burrows, *More Light on the Dead Sea Scrolls* (New York: Viking, 1958), whose cautious approach and sober evaluations have in some respects been vindicated. Menahem Mansoor packed much into a stimulating syllabus, *The Dead Sea Scrolls: A College Textbook and a Study Guide* (Leiden; Grand Rapids: Eerdmans, 1964; 2d ed., 1983, a reprint with altered subtitle, "A Textbook and Study Guide," and three additional chapters: "The Temple Scroll," "Masada," and "The Case of Shapira's Missing Dead Sea (Deuteronomy) Scroll of 1883"). Also useful is Roland Kenneth Harrison's careful, concise *The Dead Sea Scrolls: An Introduction* (New York: Harper, 1961), with selected bibliography. Aramaic expert Matthew Black—unlike Burrows, who does not find his understanding of the New Testament greatly affected by study of the scrolls—traces genetic connections between Qumran and church in *The Scrolls and Christian Origins: Studies in the Jewish Background of the New Testament* (New York: Scribner, 1961), while Lucerta Mowry, *The Dead Sea Scrolls and the Early Church* (Chicago: University of Chicago Press, 1962), compares the two communities, with repeated emphasis on redemption and Pharisaism, but leaves open the "how and when of the connections" (p. 246). In a kind of scrollwork anthology, *The Meaning of the Qumrân Scrolls for the Bible: With Special Attention to the Book of Isaiah* (New York: Oxford University Press, 1964), William Hugh Brownlee inscribes the relevance of Qumran for understanding the text, canon, geography, and exegesis of both testaments. The association of John's Gospel with Qumran thought is explored in *John and the Dead Sea Scrolls,* ed. James H. Charlesworth (New York: Crossroad, 1991). In *The Dead Sea Scrolls After Forty Years* (Washington, D.C.: Biblical Archaeology Society, 1991) the public receives an invitation to overhear four scholars (Hershel Shanks, James C. VanderKam, P. Kyle McCarter, Jr., and James A. Sanders) discuss some very interesting matters, including the mysterious 4QMMT and technical problems connected with the "Copper Scroll," in a symposium at the Smithsonian Institution.

Theodor H. Gaster, *The Dead Sea Scriptures: In English Translation, with Introduction and Notes,* 3d ed. rev. and enlarged (Garden City, N.Y.: Double-day, 1976), and, with more detailed comment, André Dupont-Sommer, *The Essene Writings from Qumran,* trans. Géza Vermes (Oxford, 1961), supply in English many of the chief documents.[4] Vermes's own fluent translation of the principal texts is in *The Dead Sea Scrolls in English,* Pelican Original ASS1 (Baltimore, 1962; 3d ed., New York: Viking Penguin, 1987). To fill a void created by scholars who for decades held unpublished fragments, Robert

---

[4] The translation is from the 2d rev. and enlarged ed. of *Les Écrits esséniens découverts près de la mer Morte* (Paris, 1959).

Eisenman and Michael Wise published *The Dead Sea Scrolls Uncovered: The First Complete Translation and Interpretation of 50 Key Documents Withheld for Over 35 Years* (Rockport, Mass.: Element, 1992). In 1993 appeared the first volume of an 8-volume series (The Princeton Theological Seminary Dead Sea Scrolls Project, gen. ed. James H. Charlesworth): *The Dead Sea Scrolls: Hebrew, Aramaic, and Greek Texts with English Translations,* vol. 1: *The Rules,* ed. James H. Charlesworth, et al. (Tübingen: J. C. B. Mohr [Paul Siebeck]; Louisville: Westminster/John Knox). Eduard Lohse contributes a number of documents from caves 1 and 4 in pointed Hebrew text with facing German in *Die Texte aus Qumran: Hebräisch und deutsch, mit masoretischer Punktation, Übersetzung, Einführung und Anmerkungen* (Darmstadt: Wissenschaftliche Buchgesellschaft, 1964).[5]

In 1821, the Oxford University Press published the first complete translation of the Ethiopic Enoch into a European language. Seventeen years later, the translator, Richard Laurence, published the text of one of the three Ethiopic codices brought by the English traveler J. Bruce from Ethiopia, then known as Abyssinia. In the course of centuries, portions of this work became known in Greek, Latin, Coptic, and Syriac; but at the beginning of September, 1952, J. T. Milik, persistent prober of caves, found the first Aramaic fragments of Ethiopic Enoch. In a sumptuous edition, *The Books of Enoch: Aramaic Fragments of Qumrân Cave 4* (Oxford: Clarendon Press, 1976), Milik, in collaboration with Matthew Black, offers, besides the texts and annotations, a fascinating historical introduction, plates for checking his decipherment, an appendix consisting of diplomatic transcriptions, and indexes, one of which is an Aramaic-Greek-Ethiopic glossary. When using this work it is wise to keep in mind that Milik's text is to a large extent reconstructed, as indicated by the square brackets. Two years later M. A. Knibb, with the assistance of E. Ullendorf, published *The Ethiopic Book of Enoch: A New Edition in the Light of the Aramaic Dead Sea Fragments,* 2 vols. (Oxford: Oxford University Press, 1978) and in the process made obsolete the text and translation by R. H. Charles. About the same time, the Israel Exploration Society published a Hebrew edition of the highly prized Temple Scroll (11QT) from cave 11 (3 vols. with supplement; Jerusalem, 1977). The same society published an English-language edition, *The Temple Scroll,* in three volumes with a supplement (Jerusalem, 1983), but with corrections and additions in vols. 1 and 2.

In *The Dead Sea Scrolls of St. Mark's Monastery,* vol. 1 (New Haven: American Schools of Oriental Research, 1950; corrected reprint, but inferior photographs, 1953)—a work dedicated to Mar Athanasius Yeshur Samuel, Syrian archbishop-metropolitan of Jerusalem and Hashemite Jordan—M.

---

[5] The text includes 1QS, 1QSa, 1QSb, CD, 1QH, 1QM, 1QpHab, 4QPBless ["patriarchal blessing"], 4QTestim, 4QFlor, 4QpNah, 4QpPsa [=4QpPs37], and 16 pages of brief notes.

Burrows, assisted by John C. Trever and William H. Brownlee, set forth in photographs and transcriptions the texts of two major documents from Qumran: the almost-intact Isaiah scroll (1QIsaᵃ) and a commentary on Habakkuk (1QpHab). A second volume, of which only the second fascicle appeared (1951), contained the Manual of Discipline (=Rule of the Community, 1QS).[6]

Fragments were not forgotten amid the attention accorded the more glamorous texts. Systematic gathering, especially from Murabbaʿat and Qumran caves 1–11, took place in the series Discoveries in the Judaean Desert of Jordan, beginning in 1955 (Oxford: Clarendon) with the publication of *Qumran Cave I*, ed. D. Barthélemy and J. T. Milik. Others, including R. de Vaux, P. Benoit, and J. Strugnell, have provided editorial continuity.

Featured by E. L. Sukenik in *The Dead Sea Scrolls of the Hebrew University* (Jerusalem: Hebrew University and Magnes Press, 1955) are black-and-white photographs, accompanied by transcriptions, of 1QIsaᵇ (an Isaiah scroll), 1QM (War Scroll), and 1QH (Thanksgiving Hymns). This publication from Magnes Press appeared a year earlier in a modern Hebrew edition under the auspices of the Bialik Foundation (Jerusalem, 1954).

Some fragmentary columns of Job 17:14–42:11 in Aramaic found a masterful first printing in *Le targum de Job de la grotte XI de Qumrân*, ed. J. P. M. van der Ploeg and A. S. van der Woude, with the collaboration of B. Jongeling (Leiden: Brill, 1971).

Complicating the mysteries of Qumran is the question of the influence of a text known as the Damascus Document on the thought and cult of communities at Qumran. Near the beginning of the twentieth century, S. Schechter published the *editio princeps* of this document, otherwise known as the Zadokite Document, in *Documents of Jewish Sectaries*, 2 vols. (Cambridge, UK: Cambridge University Press, 1910). J. A. Fitzmyer added a prolegomenon in KTAV's reprint (New York, 1970).

Helpful in interpreting fragmentary sections is *Rückläufiges hebräisches Wörterbuch*, ed. Karl-Georg Kuhn with Hartmut Stegemann and Georg Klinzing (Göttingen: Vandenhoeck & Ruprecht, 1958), a companion to *Konkordanz zu den Qumrantexten*, ed. Karl-Georg Kuhn with Albert-Marie Denis, Reinhard Deichgräber, Werner Eiss, Gert Jeremias, and Heinz-Wolfgang Kuhn (Göttingen, 1960), supplemented in *Revue de Qumran* 4 (1963): 163–234.

In this chapter we have endeavored also to keep alive the memories of those who made early efforts to bring important discoveries to the world's attention.

---

[6] Color and black-and-white photographs of the three documents published by Burrows appear in F. M. Cross, et al., eds., *Scrolls from Qumran Cave 1: The Great Isaiah Scroll, The Order of the Community, The Pesher to Habakkuk: From Photographs by John C. Trever* (Jerusalem: Albright Institute of Archaeological Research and the Shrine of the Book, 1974).

Scholars have been inspired to let down such a flood of literature that in 1958, *Revue de Qumran,* a journal devoted specifically to the study of the scrolls, began to appear in Paris with articles in French, German, and English. In the journal *Biblica* Peter Nober annually offers valuable discussion of bibliographical additions. Via *The Dead Sea Scrolls: Major Publications and Tools for Study,* rev. ed., SBL Resources for Biblical Study 20 (Atlanta: Scholars Press, 1990), J. A. Fitzmyer urges students to peer into publications of many lands for guidance in finding the wealth of arcane lore that these scrolls have hoarded for them.

In these publications advanced students may find full details on texts and critical editions. But nonspecialists are not without resources. For the generalist there is a broad range of information in *Understanding the Dead Sea Scrolls: A Reader from the Biblical Archaeological Review,* ed. Hershel Shanks (New York: Random House, 1992). Apart from the editor, a dozen contributors to the *Biblical Archaeological Review* and its sister publication, *Bible Review,* among them Otto Betz, Frank Moore Cross, Lawrence H. Schiffman, and Yigael Yadin, ensure the absence of dullness in this miscellany, which includes details of the discovery, stories of intrigue, descriptions of selected scrolls, suggestions for solution of long-standing problems facing readers of biblical texts, recital of academic blundering, and an antidote to sensationalism.[7]

THE SCROLLS AND
OLD TESTAMENT TEXTUAL CRITICISM

As late as 1947 a scholar lamented: "In the realm of textual criticism it seems that our work is all but over. The reason for this is not, of course, that the textual critic has succeeded in solving all the many problems of the text of the Old Testament. At times it would appear that some of the most crucial

---

[7] For pre-1970 literature, see *Bibliographie zu den Handschriften vom Toten Meer,* BZAW 76 (Berlin, 1957; 2d ed., 1959) and BZAW 89 (1965), in which Christoph Burchard catalogs 4,459 articles and books plus hundreds of related review articles. William S. LaSor, "Bibliography of the Dead Sea Scrolls, 1948–1957," *Fuller Library Bulletin* 31 (Fall 1958), arranges entries by subject; B. Jongeling prepared a sequel: *A Classified Bibliography of the Finds in the Desert of Judah 1958–1969* (Leiden: Brill, 1971). See also Craig R. Koester, "A Qumran Bibliography: 1974–1984," *Biblical Theology Bulletin* 15 (1985): 110–20. Herbert Braun, "Qumran und das Neue Testament: Ein Bericht über 10 Jahre Forschung (1950–1959)," *Theologische Rundschau* n.s. 28 (1962): 97–234; 29 (1963): 142–76, 189–260; 30 (1964): 1–38, 89–137, offers practically a Qumran commentary on the New Testament at the hand of the scholarly literature. The catena-like comments are reprinted in vol. 1 of *Qumran und das Neue Testament,* 2 vols. (Tübingen, 1966); the 2d vol. contains theological reflection on themes involving the relation of Qumran texts and the New Testament. To learn which scrolls or fragments have been published and where the photos and transcriptions of them are to be found in learned publications, see the guidelist by J. A. Sanders, "Palestinian Manuscripts 1947–1967," *JBL* 86 (1967): 431–40.

and tantalizing of the corrupt passages are also those on which textual criticism can shed the least light. The truth is that we have simply exhausted the materials with which we can carry on our attempts to recover the original text of the Old Testament writings. There is, of course, always the remote hope that the discovery of new manuscripts will help to clarify a few more difficulties."[8] After a few months that hope was strikingly fulfilled in the finds at Qumran.

To understand the importance of the Dead Sea Scrolls for Old Testament studies, one must recall that in the latter part of the nineteenth century Paul Anton de Lagarde had maintained that about A.D. 100 the rabbis succeeded in extracting an authoritative Hebrew text from the fluid textual tradition, and that this text then was made the standard for subsequent copies. It therefore became practically impossible to gain access to the premasoretic textual tradition except through the LXX, the Targums, Aquila, and Jerome, the Samaritan Pentateuch, and some of the apocryphal and pseudepigraphical literature. The LXX itself posed almost insuperable problems for textual critics because of its pollution through the usual alterations of well-meaning or careless copyists and because of its contamination in some recensions by revision according to the prevailing Hebrew text. Even if we are justified in assuming that in given instances we have succeeded in rescuing the original Greek text, we cannot consistently conclude from readings that deviate from the received Hebrew text that the translators must necessarily have based their work on variant Hebrew manuscripts, for as we have already noted, their principles and techniques of translation and their linguistic competence may have been responsible for some of the variations that continue to vex us.

A Greek and a Hebrew encampment formed when scholars lined up quite readily behind David ben Naphtali Hirsch Fränkel (1707–1762), German rabbi and pioneer commentator on the Palestinian Talmud, and later behind Max Loehr (1864–1931), German exegete and archaeologist, on the side of the massive masoretic tradition. Other scholars collected behind Paul Anton de Lagarde (1827–1891) and Julius Wellhausen (1844–1918) with the common claim that the Greek versions ought to be used as correctives of the modifying masoretic confusion of the Hebrew text. For a time it seemed that the traditionalists were bound to win the battle, but an uncalled truce came about with the revelations of Qumran. The Isaiah scroll was found—nothing startling developed! Except for the often unavoidable scribal errors and a few variations, which are reflected in modern translations, there was no essential difference between the new scroll and the Masoretic Text. It was tempting to oversimplify the textual problem with the efficiency of overgeneralization and conclude that what applied to Isaiah's prophecy might be applied with equal

---

[8] Frederick C. Prussner, "Problems Ahead in Old Testament Research," *The Study of the Bible Today and Tomorrow,* ed. Harold R. Willoughby (Chicago: University of Chicago Press, 1947), 179–80.

validity to other books as well. It was forgotten at the time that Isaiah was not among the books whose texts in the LXX diverge greatly from the MT. Diggings at cave 4 undermined the prevailing overconfidence in the accuracy of the MT and turned over correctives that could not be shoveled surreptitiously to one side. We now have conclusive evidence gleaned from fragments of Joshua, Samuel, and Kings that the linguists translating into Greek were working with a text or texts distinguishable from the MT. Not idiosyncrasy but fidelity to the text they had before them accounts for many variations noted in a comparison of the LXX with the MT.[9]

An instructive example comes to the fore in 1 Sam. 21:5 (21:4 AV). Moffatt had expressed the problem of a conditional sentence lacking an apodosis by leaving the sentence incomplete: "If only the young soldiers have kept clear of women—." The LXX (Vaticanus) completed the sentence: εἰ πεφυλαγμένα τὰ παιδάριά ἐστιν ἀπὸ γυναικός, καὶ φάγεται. As Cross points out, the variants καὶ φάγονται and καὶ φάγετε also appear. Corresponding to these words completing the sentence in the Old Greek, the Qumran fragment reads ואכלתם ממנו "If the young men have kept themselves from women, *then ye may eat of it* [italics ours]." The Masoretic Text, concludes Cross, "arises from haplography and cannot be defended on the principle of *lectio difficilior*."[10]

In the apparatus to 1 Sam. 23:11 Kittel states that the words הֲיַסְגִּרֻנִי בַּעֲלֵי קְעִילָה בְיָדוֹ are probably due to dittography, a view held since Julius Wellhausen, and suggests that the omission of these words in the LXX may be a preservation of the original reading. The omission of the words in 4QSam[b] strikingly confirms not only the reading of the LXX (Vaticanus) but also the critical restoration of the passage by textual scholars.[11]

Of even greater significance is the discovery of portions of Jeremiah that display the shorter text heretofore found only in the Greek version. In Jeremiah 10, for example, the Qumran Jeremiah (4QJer[b]) omits four verses also omitted in the LXX and follows the LXX in shifting the order of a fifth verse. The longer recension is also found among the Qumran manuscripts.[12]

A remarkable example from the Isaiah scroll is Isa. 53:11. Here the LXX reads the word φῶς. Scholars had suggested that אוֹר be inserted after the word

[9] Material in this paragraph is primarily from Frank Moore Cross, Jr., *The Ancient Library of Qumran and Modern Biblical Studies: The Haskell Lectures, 1956–1957*, rev. ed., Anchor Book A272 (Garden City, N.Y.: Doubleday, 1961), 161–94. On *Qumran and the Hebrew text*, see F. M. Cross and S. Talmon, eds., *Qumran and the History of the Biblical Text* (Cambridge: Harvard University Press, 1975), a scintillating collection of essays on connections between Qumran and the Hebrew and Greek texts of the Old Testament.

[10] Frank M. Cross, "The Oldest Manuscripts from Qumran," *JBL* 74 (1955): 147–72. See esp. pp. 167, 168.

[11] Cross, "The Oldest Manuscripts," 170.

[12] Cross, *The Ancient Library of Qumran*, 186–87.

יִרְאֶה to read: "he will see light." An earlier proposed reading (see the *apparatus criticus* in *BH*) has now been confirmed by 1QIsaᵃ and 1QIsaᵇ.[13]

In Deut. 32:8 the RSV reads at the end of the verse "according to the number of the sons of God." The margin directs one to compare the Greek, whereas the Hebrew reads "Israel." The NRSV has "according to the number of the gods," with the following marginal data: "Q Ms [Qumran manuscript] Compare Gk [Greek] Tg [Targum] MT [Masoretic Text] *the Israelites*." The MT reads בְּנֵי יִשְׂרָאֵל, "sons of Israel." In one of the chapters of *Understanding the Dead Sea Scrolls,* Ronald S. Hendel calls attention to a Dead Sea scroll fragment that contains the reading בני אלוהים, "sons of God" (see also Job 38:7; cf. 1:6; 2:1; Ps. 29:1; and compare renderings in RSV/NRSV).[14]

THE SCROLLS AND THE NEW TESTAMENT

Ever since their discovery the scrolls have been ransacked for parallels to New Testament thought. One of the most fruitful discussions has centered in the Gospel of John, which, it has been charged, reflects almost every conceivable Hellenistic trend. Now it appears that the writer of the fourth Gospel and the related epistles has drawn from streams that run very close to those at Qumran and flow from the headwaters of Palestinian Judaism. (See, e.g., 1QS 3:13-26 and 1 John 3 and 4.)

Some of the New Testament's use of the Old Testament has long proved puzzling because of unabashed wrapping of New Testament history in Old Testament prophetic utterances. The Qumran community's recording of its own history according to Old Testament outlines now provides a helpful parallel. Thus the community applies Isa. 28:16 to itself (1QS 8:1-19). In the light of this practice John the Baptist's preaching in the wilderness is understandable (Matt. 3:1). The Qumran community of the new covenant sets its course into the desert in fulfillment of Isa. 40:3.

Luke 2:14 has long been a vexing problem. The problem appears now almost certainly solved in view of the scrolls' use of the phrases "sons of (God's) good pleasure" and "chosen of (God's) good pleasure" (cf. 1QH 4:30-38; 11:7-10). Ernest Vogt, a Jesuit scholar, concludes that "the Qumran texts do more than lend decisive support to this reading [εὐδοκίας]. They also indicate that 'God's good pleasure' here refers more naturally to the will of God to confer grace on those he has chosen, than to God's delighting in and approving of the

---

[13] See F. F. Bruce, *Second Thoughts on the Dead Sea Scrollls,* rev. ed. (Grand Rapids: Eerdmans, 1961), 62. This work remains useful to the general reader.

[14] Ronald S. Hendel, "When the Sons of God cavorted with the Daughters of Men," in *Understanding the Dead Sea Scrolls: A Reader from the Biblical Archaeological Review,* ed. Hershel Shanks (New York: Random House, 1992), 167–77 and photograph (no. 27) of the fragment.

goodness in men's lives. Thus neither 'good will toward men' nor 'peace among men with whom he is pleased' is an accurate translation, but rather 'peace among people of God's good pleasure,' i.e., God's chosen ones."[15]

In essay 15, *Understanding the Dead Sea Scrolls,* Hershel Shanks refers to 4Q246, suggesting it as a parallel to Luke 1:32-35, which contains the phrase "Son of God" (pp. 203–4).[16]

The lure of seeming parallels between the scrolls and the New Testament writings can, on the other hand, prove beguiling. Some restraint therefore must be exercised lest one be led to unwarranted identification of possibly divergent thought patterns. The temptation to classify, for example, the "Many" in the Qumran community with the πλῆθος in Acts 6:2, 5; 15:12, under a common technical term in the sense of "ruling assembly"[17] should be compared with Burrows's more cautious discussion.[18] Perhaps more important than the light they may throw on a particular point of interpretation is the larger view these writings give us of the religious and cultural milieu of the New Testament. Sustained reading in them will continue to complement and supplement understanding of the New Testament. They will augment our understanding of the complex history of the transmission of the biblical text, they display some of the diversity in Judaism, and they suggest a setting in which some of the aspects of early Christianity become more meaningful. Coming from insiders they form a more objective base for consideration of variations found among outsiders.

The Dead Sea Scrolls will increasingly share scholarly and popular attention with new discoveries. But much more labor must still be devoted to the Qumran documents, now that the previously unpublished fragments have become available and can be scrutinized by a larger circle of scholars. The task of theological correlation, comparison, and contrast has begun anew, and many a jerry-built structure must still topple at the impact of a fact.

---

[15] *The Scrolls and the New Testament,* ed. Krister Stendahl (New York: Harper, 1957; reprint, with a new introduction by James H. Charlesworth, New York: Crossroad, 1992), 117. Claus-Hunno Hunzinger, "Neues Licht auf Lc 2₁₄ ἄνθρωποι εὐδοκία," *ZNW* 44 (1952/53): 85–90, underlies Vogt's essay. For subsequent evidence, see Hunzinger, "Ein weiterer Beleg zu Lc 2₁₄ ἄνθρωποι εὐδοκία," *ZNW* 49 (1958): 129–30.

[16] *Understanding the Dead Sea Scrolls,* 203–4.

[17] Cross, *The Ancient Library of Qumran,* 231.

[18] *More Light on the Dead Sea Scolls* (New York: Viking, 1958), 114, 359–62. See also Johann Maier, *Die Texte vom Toten Meer* (Munich: E. Reinhardt, 1960), 11, 26–27. The first volume of Maier's work provides in German translation the texts from cave 1 and in an appendix fragments from cave 4. The second volume offers commentary, twenty-five pages of bibliography, a subject index, an index to biblical and intertestamental citations, and a chronological table. Although caution is always to be exercised in evaluation of data, one can also evade responsibility for decision, a charge to which Burrows has fallen heir.

CHAPTER FIFTEEN

Commentaries and Their Uses

E DWARD JOSEPH YOUNG once complained about "how commentators shun each dark passage and hold their farthing candle to the sun." The sentiment has been echoed in some form or other by all who have opened a commentary with high hopes of letting some oracle's light stream in and instead have gazed into a mirror reflecting their own previous understanding (or murky misunderstanding) of the passage. But despite their limitations commentaries can be profitable aids, and in the privacy of the study any serious student of the Bible should be able to reach beyond despair for at least one good commentary on each book of the Bible.

The quality, not the condition, of the dog-eared expositions on pastors' shelves is a fairly good indication of the spiritual diet they serve the people. Yet it is not always easy for the minister or for the seminary student who is beginning to build a theological library to make a judicious selection. In a blizzard of pretentious advertisements, some of which threaten one with expository bankruptcy if this or that allegedly immortal publication is not immediately purchased (at a carefully calculated "discount" for a limited time only), one cannot always see real value clearly. Also, some unscrupulous publishers do not always inform their prospective purchasers of the original date of publication of some of their reprinted items. This chapter therefore intends to provide some guidance in identifying important Bible commentaries and to assist students in determining the comparative functions of each.[1]

MODERN COMMENTARIES

ONE-VOLUME COMMENTARIES

We are reluctant to mention one-volume commentaries on the entire Bible because they are necessarily limited in the treatment of individual passages.

---

[1] For bibliography, see the appendix to this chapter.

No careful student of Scripture will come to rely on them solely and habitually, but the encyclopedic information they offer on most general and some specific introductory matters prompts purchase of at least one good commentary of this sort. Because it gathered up the principal philological and theological contributions of eminent scholars in Great Britain and North America, the revised *Peake's Commentary on the Bible,* ed. Matthew Black and Harold H. Rowley (London: Nelson, 1962), continues to attract inquirers.[2] Inclusion of the "General Articles" from *The Interpreter's Bible* (see below) adds depth to *The Interpreter's One-Volume Commentary on the Bible,* ed. Charles M. Laymon (Nashville: Abingdon, 1971), which includes commentary on the Apocrypha. But developments in a variety of approaches to biblical texts command respect especially for *The New Jerome Biblical Commentary,* ed. Raymond E. Brown, Joseph A. Fitzmyer, and Roland E. Murphy (Englewood Cliffs, N.J.: Prentice Hall, 1990), whose title does not exaggerate the aggregate of new information and refurbishing of its predecessor, *Jerome Biblical Commentary* (1968), by the same editors. Indeed, a comparison of the editions reveals how the passage of a mere two decades can make some of the scholarly production of yesteryear an object of curiosity akin to the hairstyles of the heroes and heroines of earlier flicks.

A marvelous compendium of insight dealing with matters often overlooked in the history of biblical exposition is provided in *The Women's Bible Commentary,* ed. Carol A. Newsom and Sharon H. Ringe (London: SPCK; Louisville, Ky.: Westminster/John Knox, 1992).

All other one-volume commentaries bid less successfully for the attention of students, but a few of them may be mentioned for the benefit of those who feel at home in more familiar expository surroundings. Some who considered *A Catholic Commentary on Holy Scripture,* ed. Bernard Orchard with Edmund F. Sutcliffe, Reginald C. Fuller, and Ralph Russell (London: Nelson, 1953), a bit too traditionalist welcomed the revised edition, *A New Catholic Commentary on Holy Scripture,* ed. R. C. Fuller, E. F. Sutcliffe, and C. Kearns (London: Nelson, 1969). This latter work is in many respects a notable reflection of Roman Catholic advances in biblical studies at the time and contains an extraordinary amount of detailed comment for a work of this type, but those who use the more influential *Jerome* (1990), will feel that history closed down early in the 1969 publication. Of *The New Layman's Bible Commentary in One Volume* (Grand Rapids: Zondervan, 1979), based on the RSV, the editors, G. C. D. Howley, F. F. Bruce, and H. L. Ellison express the hope that despite "conservative" bent, "it will not appear to be obscurantist." Readers

---

[2] Arthur S. Peake published the first edition of this work, *Commentary on the Bible* (1919). Alexander J. Grieve's *Supplement to Peake's Commentary* (London: Nelson, 1936) maintained Peake's legacy. *Peake's* in its new form gained ascendancy over *A New Commentary on Holy Scripture Including the Apocrypha,* ed. Charles Gore, Henry Goudge, and Alfred Guillaume (1928).

with roots in opposition to historical-critical inquiry find congenial the *Concordia Self Study Commentary: An Authoritative In-Home Resource for Students of the Bible* (St. Louis: Concordia, 1979); Walter R. Roehrs did the notes on the Old Testament, and Martin H. Franzmann on the New Testament.

When you are contemplating investment in a one-volume commentary, approach the transaction as you would the purchase of a fine set of golf clubs. The product ought to serve you long and well without regular replacement of parts. In general, to gauge worth it is better to scan the roster of contributors than to heed the publisher's advertising claims. The longer and more ecumenically representative the list, the higher you may expect to find the quality of the commentary as a whole.

COMMENTARY SERIES IN ENGLISH AND FRENCH

From the one-volume commentary we turn now to the commentary series. Series on the whole Bible are usually introduced with an elaborate publisher's pitch calculated to relieve the prospective buyer of more than sales resistance. Previews of the work for which the world waits often impress with long, uniform appearance suggesting thoroughgoing resolutions of a wide range of dilemmas. Spines aglitter with swash letters in gold leaf lead one to expect leaves imprinted with equally precious material. The efficiency of a single bill of lading (with goods billed at a "discount" off an already inflated price pitched for the library trade and accompanied by a special prepublication offer) gives the decisive individual impetuous with busyness little time for further debate. Who can afford to ponder the investment and by the delay of indecision forfeit so much exegetical learning?

One who warily waits, when the sirens of sales pitch their song, wisely hesitates. The easiest way to save your dollars and keep your shelves clear of ephemeral clutter is to gather your senses, act the eclectic, and select individual volumes from various sets according to the recognition they have received from representative scholars. Sagacious teachers and recent books on introduction will offer some assistance in choosing volumes on the subject and level of your major interest. Also delay purchase of current publications long enough to consult objective and critical reviews in journals devoted to biblical research. It is wise also to remember that some of the best commentaries do not appear in sets.

Series on the Entire Bible

At the head of the list of commentaries in English, albeit with heavy dependence on European tradition, stands Hermeneia: A Critical and Historical Commentary on the Bible, a major effort of Fortress Press (Minneapolis), begun in 1971 with the publication of Eduard Lohse's *Colossians and Philemon,* trans. William R. Poehlmann and Robert J. Karris; ed. Helmut Koester. A translation of Hans Walter Wolff's commentary on Hosea initiated the Old Testament section. The methodologies exhibited in these impressive volumes range from traditional historical-criticism to contemporary literary analysis. In the foreword to the first volume, Frank Moore Cross and Helmut Koester, the first editors of the series, stated:

> The series is designed to be a critical and historical commentary to the Bible without arbitrary limits in size or scope. It will utilize the full range of philological and historical tools including textual criticism (often ignored in modern commentaries), the methods of the history of tradition (including genre and prosodic analysis), and the history of religion.

To ease the burden for students who are weak in Greek and Latin and Semitic languages, the commentary provides translations of all citations from ancient sources. With eyes focused beyond limited denominational boundaries, the various editors and translators have brought exceptional midwifery skill to the task of also bringing commentaries on apocryphal and pseudepigraphic works to birth. Especially welcome in the category of commentaries on non-canonical works is William R. Schoedel, *Ignatius of Antioch* (1985). Unfortunately, the series suffers from the malady that befalls almost all commentary series: disproportionate allocation of space. For instance: the Epistle of James occupies less than 10 pages in the Nestle text, yet commands 284 pages in Hermeneia. But Acts, with 89 pages in Nestle that bristle with problems and excite one with their veritable smorgasbord of tempting philological delights, many of them ignored even by such a respected interpreter as Ernst Haenchen, merits from Hans Conzelmann only two pages more than the volume on James. At the outset, the editors of the series promised that "published volumes of the series" would "be revised continually," and that "eventually new commentaries" would "be assigned to replace older works in order that the series can be open ended." Certainly not guilty of low aim, the editors must assuredly think about maintaining established patterns of performance in the face of relentless reality in an age that casually invents ingenious ways to devour scholars' time. Given the rapid rate of movement in scholarly fashions, what methodological resemblance will the most recent volume bear to earlier ones? One thing is certain, to relieve the burden of critical response, the publishers have wedded wealth of thought to beauty of the printer's art. But the future will determine whether the managers of commerce will encourage such embellishment of thought in the decades to come, especially if ministers, who would certainly consider themselves "serious" students of the Bible, are to use these weighty instruments as a necessary base for informed proclamation.

Endeavoring to vie with the best is Word Biblical Commentary (WBC), whose pilot volume on Colossians and Philemon appeared in 1982. The general editors, David A. Hubbard and Glenn W. Barker, did not cast their "wide net" in vain, and speed of delivery by enmeshed scholars from around the world, representing "a rich diversity of denominational allegiance," has been achieved, but not always without detriment to the quality of the work. "The broad stance of our contributors," states Hubbard, "can rightly be called evangelical, and this term is to be understood in its positive, historic sense of a commitment to Scripture as divine revelation, and to the truth and power of the Christian gospel." Unlike Hermeneia this series contains no commentaries originally published in another language and is therefore at some points more up-to-date. As in many of the newer commentaries, the authors offer their own translations of the biblical texts. Hebrew and Greek are sprinkled freely in these commentaries, but only the Hebrew is offered also in transliterated form. Each unit of text is presented in four stages: translation, notes (especially text-critical), form/structure/setting, and comment. A substantial bibliography precedes each unit. Used in connection with especially Hermeneia (which contains much more contextual "color") and some of the meatier treatments in series yet to be mentioned, the commentaries in the Word series will aid preachers in developing a philological base for messages that are full with meaning and that signify much, without mouthing of antique lore. Perhaps such homiletical improvement may even slow down some furious backdoor exiting from mainline churches.

For several generations The International Critical Commentary on the Holy Scriptures of the Old and New Testaments (ICC), begun under the editorship of Charles Augustus Briggs, Samuel Rolles Driver, and Alfred Plummer and first published jointly by T. & T. Clark of Edinburgh and Charles Scribner's Sons of New York, held a large share of the market. This series was initiated in 1895 with Driver's volume on Deuteronomy and was designed to match the best that Germany had to offer. British and American scholars cooperated in the production of a critical and comprehensive commentary that was to be abreast of what was then modern biblical scholarship and in a measure to set the pace for commentary production. The authors of the individual volumes were to discuss in detail archaeological, historical, hermeneutical, and specifically theological questions without expatiating on practical or homiletical concerns and were to arrange their material in such a way that it would be serviceable also to those not having the gift of the Greek and particularly the Hebrew tongue. The series remained incomplete and in limbo after the publication of the volume on Kings by James A. Montgomery and Henry Gehman (1951).

Recognizing the fact that methodologies are of optimum value at the time in which they meet consumers' needs, the publishers of ICC climbed aboard the now-crowded vehicle of producers of "new" this and that, and in 1975 published Charles E. B. Cranfield's first of two volumes on Romans. In keeping with the trend of the times, it was twice as long as the one by William Sanday and Arthur C. Headlam (1895) in the older series. In a preface the general editors, Cranfield and J. A. Emerton, expressed their awareness of "new linguistic, textual, historical, and archeological evidence," and of "changes and developments in methods of study." They also promised to commission commentaries for the biblical books that had not been treated and to replace some of the older volumes. Yet, even though the demands of the present dare not be denied, one must grant that the earlier volumes of the ICC have held up well, and the later volumes through 1951 display remarkable stability amid the many shifts of scholarly opinion and approach.[3] Among the better volumes in the Old Testament are those on Genesis (John Skinner), Numbers (George B. Gray), Judges (George Foot Moore), Proverbs (Crawford H. Toy), Ecclesiastes (George A. Barton); in the New Testament, Matthew (William Allen), Romans (William Sanday and Arthur C. Headlam), 1 Corinthians (Archibald T. R. Robertson and Alfred Plummer), 2 Corinthians (Plummer and Francis Brown), Galatians (Ernest De Witt Burton), 1 and 2 Thessalonians (James E. Frame), Pastorals (Walter Lock), and Revelation (Robert H. Charles). With discriminating awareness students may profitably use their comments in conjunction with those in newer works and thus find in the new and the old stepping stones to a solid philological foundation.

Gabalda of Paris long held the enviable reputation of publishing Études Bibliques (EB), a series for earnest students of the original texts of both Testaments. The series was begun in 1903 under the leadership of Marie-Joseph Lagrange, whose comments on the Synoptics set standards that stimulated such richly laden expositions as E. B. Allo on 1 Corinthians (1934), 2 Corinthians (1936), and Revelation (1921; 3d ed. 1933); Béda Rigaux on 1 and 2 Thessalonians (1956); and Ceslaus Spicq on Hebrews (1947) and the Pastorals (1947). Dominicans of the École Biblique de Jerusalem ensured continuation of the painstaking philological standards set by Lagrange. The contrast between volumes in this series and some of those in AB (see below) in the matter of approaches to ecclesiastically entrenched lines of exposition will be apparent even to the most casual user.

La Sainte Bible, in 43 installments (Paris, 1948–54), prepared under the direction of the École Biblique de Jerusalem, includes a scholarly French translation

---

[3] Demonstrative of the degree to which the writers of the ICC achieved their goal of competing successfully with German scholarship, and representative of the high regard in which even German exegetes held their work, is this remark of Ethelbert Stauffer: "Am stolzesten gedeiht das International Critical Commentary, das heute in Exegeticis die wohlverdiente Führung hat" ("The ICC can be most proud of the fact that it enjoys at the present time a well-earned leadership role in the exegetical field"). See "Der Stand der neutestamentlichen Forschung," *Theologie und Liturgie: Eine Gesamtschau der gegenwärtigen Forschung in Einzeldarstellungen,* ed. Liemar Hennig (Kassel, 1952), 77.

and instructive notes on the text. An abridged one-volume edition was first published in Paris in 1956.

Because of the loss of Hebrew and Greek in many schools, series designed with the "general" reader in mind have proliferated, but frequently with hybrid progeny, of which the most distinguished is the Anchor Bible (AB), begun in 1964 under the direction of William Foxwell Albright and David Noel Freedman. Designed "to make available all the significant historical and linguistic knowledge which bears on the interpretation of the biblical record," this series has the "general reader with no special formal training" as its client, yet with maintenance of the "most exacting standards of scholarship, reflecting the highest technical accomplishment." The remarkable expectation is that one must presumably read this statement with a straight face while looking at advertisements of more than 1,600 pages of text for only one half of St. Luke's literary output. One must also evaluate the editorial claim in the light of the varying degrees of health exhibited in the series, from Bo Reicke's allergy to social change exhibited in his composition on the epistles of James, Peter, and Jude, to Ephraim A. Speiser's scholarly zest at work on the lead volume on Genesis. Unfortunately, the publishers did not at the beginning allot contributors sufficient time for maturation during assignment, and some volumes that appeared in the first decade of publication, though in cases offering fresh and spirited translation, failed to probe the structural depths of such exciting literature as Genesis, Job, Jeremiah, and the Petrines. Later contributions to the series, notably works by Joseph A. Fitzmyer (2 vols. on Luke) and Raymond Brown (2 vols. on John), helped restore some of the project's tarnished image. In any case, the jury is still out on estimates of the numbers and competence of "general" readers who, after reading the fine translations, may find themselves adrift in a sea of alien terminology even in the area of "Comment" (a running interpretation), where they may be rammed by such driftwood as *pace, vaticinium ex eventu,* or directions to see a certain scholar's *Sonderquelle.* Also, where is the "general" reader who will be able to endure Dahood's bewildering Ugaritic bombardment? New editions of earlier volumes will of course remedy some of the deficiencies. On the other hand, sophisticated readers without Greek or Hebrew, but aware of scholars' need to sift conflicting views, will welcome the transliterations or paraphrases that are offered for most terms from the original texts even in the "Notes," which treat more technical matters.

A number of other series designed to gain the attention of a wider reading public also deserve mention, with the understanding that for the most part they do not present as much technical comment as is found in some of the volumes in AB.

Dominated by homiletical interest, a feature designedly absent in the two series cited above, is *The Interpreter's Bible: The Holy Scriptures in the King James and Revised Standard Versions with General Articles and Introduction, Exegesis, Exposition for Each Book of the Bible* (IB). Prepared and published under the general editorship of George Arthur Buttrick and with the assistance of Walter Russell Bowie, Paul Scherer, John Knox, Samuel Terrien, and Nolan B. Harmon (New York and Nashville: Abingdon, 1952–57), this hefty 12-volume series was designed to bring the student and especially the preacher up-to-date on current discussions and trends among biblical scholars and to aid the expositor in bridging the gap between critical philology and practical application. To achieve these objectives it presents a double commentary. The first outlines an exegesis of the passage; the second suggests applications of the text to contemporary problems and situations. Both the KJV and the RSV are printed in parallel columns throughout the series.

In general the Old Testament section of *IB* is superior to the New Testament treatment. Among the more helpful expositions are G. Ernest Wright on Deuteronomy; Samuel Terrien on Job; William Taylor and W. Stewart McCullough on Psalms; Robert B. Y. Scott on Isaiah; and Herbert G. May on Ezekiel. The sketchiness of some of the notes, which often belabor the obvious, accents the need for more exhaustive treatment, as in Hermeneia and ICC. The publisher could have cut the price in half by eliminating much of the irrelevant, often sentimental, "exposition." The introductory and supplementary articles, including especially those in volumes 1 and 7, are among the strongest and most valuable parts. The *New Interpreter's Bible,* whose first volume is scheduled for 1994, will probably remedy some of these defects.

One of the older publications that ought not be lost to memory is The Cambridge Bible for Schools and Colleges (CB), a series begun in Cambridge in 1877 under John J. S. Perowne (1823–1904), who was succeeded by Alexander Francis Kirkpatrick as editor of this series. The appearance of the volumes belies the value of the resources contained in them, and many of them have gone through numerous reprintings or editions. The series is not designed for specialists, but some knowledge of Hebrew is presumed in the exposition of the Old Testament, and a little Greek is expected of users of the New Testament section. Although the comment is somewhat less lengthy than in corresponding volumes of WC (see below), frequent revisions and completeness give CB a distinct advantage over the Westminster series. Publication of the *New English Bible* encouraged CB to move in new directions. Aubrey Argyle issued the pilot volume for Cambridge Bible Commentary on the NEB (CBCNT) in 1963. In the Old Testament portion (CBCOT), which began with the publication of Peter R. Ackroyd's commentary on 1 Samuel and covers also the Apocrypha, Norman Habel captures the titanic conflict of a man in grief with his commentary on Job (1975).

Confusing are the following general serial titles: The Century Bible: New Edition Based on the Revised Standard Version, gen. eds. Harold H. Rowley and Matthew Black, published by Nelson (London) beginning in the 1960s; alternately, The Century Bible: New Series Based on the Revised Standard Version; and New Century Bible, gen. eds. Ronald E. Clements and Matthew

Black, for Old and New Testament respectively, published by Oliphants (London). This last series also goes under the title New Century Bible Commentary (Grand Rapids). Most of the works in these series will be found on any "best commentary" list, for they are composed by masters of the exegetical craft and present mid-twentieth-century exegetical developments in semipopular form.

Assisting teachers and pastors in their educational and homiletical work is an ongoing series, based on the RSV, from John Knox Press titled Interpretation: A Bible Commentary for Teaching and Preaching, gen. ed. James L. Mays, with Patrick D. Miller in charge of the Old Testament and Paul J. Achtemeier heading production on the New Testament. The editors claim that the series presents "the integrated result of historical and theological work with the biblical text." Proclaimers will require other commentaries to test the validity of the editorial boast in connection with specific texts. Political correctness is a hazard in commentaries of this kind, but the type of exposition given, for example, by Gerard Sloyan on the Gospel of John (Atlanta, 1988), will urge them to think more seriously about their pastoral responsibilities.

Special denominational interests continue to be met by publishing houses. *The Broadman Bible Commentary* (Nashville, 1969–72) embodies the RSV in expositions that reflect modern exegetical developments. The spirit of John Wesley and Adam Clarke moves freely in *The Wesleyan Bible Commentary,* 6 vols., but not in chronological sequence (Grand Rapids: Eerdmans, 1964–69). Given awareness of the Adventists' special belief system (e.g., in view of warnings in Scripture about abuse of alcohol, it is unlikely, the writer claims, that John 2 describes anything but grape juice), one can use with profit *The Seventh-day Adventist Bible Commentary,* ed. Francis D. Nichol with assistance by Julia Neuffen, 7 vols. (Washington: Review and Herald Publishing Association, 1953–57); Ellen G. White's comments are listed separately, but with cross-reference.

Still useful, despite its age, is the series Westminster Commentaries (WC), ed. Walter Lock (1846–1933) and David Capell Simpson (London, 1899–), both Old and New Testament, but never completed. It includes such notable works as Samuel R. Driver on Genesis, William O. E. Oesterley on Proverbs, Sydney L. Brown on Hosea, and J. Wand on 2 Peter and Jude. The superior scholarship embedded here is aimed at combining critical principles and concern for clear and cogent articulation of the catholic faith. Each commentary in the series includes an introduction and notes on the text of the Revised Version. Reference to Hebrew and Greek words has been held to a minimum.

Series on the Old Testament

With the aid of imports from Germany, the Old Testament Library (OTL) endeavored to meet the need for a stronger theological accent, akin to the thinking that motivated G. E. Wright for the doing of "biblical archaeology." Initiated under the editorship of George Ernest Wright, John Bright, James Barr, and Peter Runham Ackroyd (London: SCM Press; Philadelphia: Westminster, 1961–), this series has translations of the ATD commentary (see below) as well as new treatments, including John Gray on 1 and 2 Kings (1971) and Brevard S. Childs, who subordinates the prehistory of the text to interpretation of its canonical form, in Exodus (1974). Other new presentations embrace various themes, such as David Syme Russell, *The Method and Message of Jewish Apocalyptic, 200 B.C.–A.D. 100* (1964), whose work should be supplemented with Harold H. Rowley, *The Relevance of Apocalyptic: A Study of Jewish and Christian Apocalypses from Daniel to the Revelation,* new, rev. ed. (London, 1963). In general the comment in OTL interprets the text as structured literary argument with thematic ("theological") content, while AB accents philological detail, with various levels of interest in literary appreciation.

Somewhat similar to OTL are the Old Testament volumes in the Continental Commentary Series, produced variously by Augsburg and Fortress Press. It includes translations of commentaries by Hans-Joachim Kraus (Psalms, 2 vols., 1988–89), Hans Walter Wolff (Obadiah and Jonah, 1986; Haggai, 1988; Micah, 1990), a 3-vol. set on Isaiah, by Hans Wildberger (1991–), and Claus Westermann, 3 vols. on Genesis (1984–1986)

Series on the New Testament

For many years, *The Expositor's Greek Testament* (*EGT*), ed. William Robertson Nicoll, 5 vols. (London, New York, Toronto: Hodder and Stoughton, 1897–1910), was the favorite of ministers and seminarians. This series was designed to supersede Henry Alford, *The Greek Testament,* 4 vols. (London, 1849–60) and contains some time-defeating expositions, such as R. Knowling's on Acts and H. Kennedy's on Philippians. Since reprints of both works are frequently advertised without indication of their antiquity, it is necessary to emphasize that they are too outmoded for professional use, despite the fact that Alford's work contained much valuable material that was not caught up in its successor.[4] Yet, even specialists are advised to consult these and other works before sending out a cockcrow for new discovery or prematurely fixing the date of origin for alleged "fresh" interpretation. It is, moreover, certain

---

[4] Both *The Expositor's Greek Testament,* 5 vols., and *The Expositor's Bible,* 6 vols., have been reprinted in new editions (Grand Rapids: Eerdmans, 1956). In 1958 Moody Press of Chicago revived Alford's work in two double volumes with a few revisions and additions by Everett F. Harrison, using the 7th ed. for vols. 1 and 2, the 5th ed. for vols. 3 and 4. In his "Introduction," 1:v–xiv, Harrison recounts how the sharp criticisms that greeted Alford's importation of the critical views of German exegetes have come to be blended with expressions of warm appreciation and genuine praise.

that some of the commentaries most highly recommended in the present work will likewise appear quaint and inadequate a few decades hence.

The Cambridge Greek Testament for Schools and Colleges (CGT), seemingly initiated with Arthur Carr's comments on Matthew (Cambridge: Cambridge University Press, 1881), reached nineteen volumes in 1919. It was projected as a series parallel to the New Testament section of CB to assist in gaining an understanding of the Greek underlying the English New Testament. The diminutive volumes do not clear up all exegetical difficulties, but they have come to be well known for their succinct and pithy comment and for their clarification of linguistic phenomena. John J. S. Perowne, Joseph Armitage Robinson, Frederick Henry Chase, Reginald St. John Parry, and Alexander Nairne served notably as successive editors of the series.

In 1957, CGT began to appear in a new format as the Cambridge Greek Testament Commentary (CGTC). General editor Charles Francis Digby Moule's own *The Epistles of Paul the Apostle to the Colossians and to Philemon: An Introduction and Commentary* (Cambridge and New York) initiated the new series. The quality of exposition presented in the pilot volume stimulated eager anticipation for the remainder of the series, which gives special attention to setting the theological and religious contents of the New Testament in the context of the life and worship of Christian communities. Elimination of a printing of the full Greek text and citation of textual evidence only when the issue is important have made room for more detailed philological treatment.

With his commentary on the Gospel of Luke (Grand Rapids: Eerdmans, 1978) I. Howard Marshall, Senior Lecturer in New Testament Exegesis at the University of Aberdeen, Scotland, initiated The New International Greek Testament Commentary, whose editorial responsibilities he shares with W. Ward Gasque. This sturdy series, based on the 1973 UBS Greek New Testament, also includes expositions by F. F. Bruce (Galatians), Charles A. Wanamaker (1 and 2 Thessalonians), and Peter Davids (James).

Several series of a more popular nature are intended as supplements to the New Testament bill of fare. We do not recommend them as a sole or even as a primary source of exegetical information, but their broader appeal prompts some comment here. Using the *NEB* as its base is the New Clarendon Bible, which began in 1963, under the general editorship of H. F. D. Sparks, with the publication of C. K. Barrett's commentary on the Pastorals, thereby terminating the Clarendon Bible, which was based on the RV. Well known is The Moffatt New Testament Commentary (MNTC), 17 vols. (London, New York, Toronto: Hodder and Stoughton, 1926–1950), a series that has enjoyed reprinting of many of its volumes. According to editor James Moffatt (1870–1944), on whose Bible version the series is based, the intent of the writers was to "bring out the religious meaning and message of the New Testament writings." Historical and literary concerns pace a running commentary intended to reproduce the meaning of the text for the reader who knows no Greek. Frederick John Foakes Jackson, Acts (1931); George Simpson Duncan, Galatians (1934); Charles Harold Dodd, Johannine Letters (1946); and Martin Kiddle, assisted by M. K. Ross, Revelation (1940) offer some of the better MNTC expositions, all designed for pastors and other educated readers.

Charles Kingsley Barrett, *A Commentary on the Epistle to the Romans,* was the forerunner of several notable contributions that helped build both the British Black's New Testament Commentaries (London: Adam & Charles Black, 1957–), later made available in low-priced paperback, and the American Harper's New Testament Commentaries (HNTC), ed. Henry Chadwick (New York, 1957–). The commentaries published in these parallel series tread a middle course between detailed philology and popular interpretation while sweeping across a broad range of critical opinion. Capable and original translations precede the treatment of the text.

Publication of The New International Commentary on the New Testament (NIC), ed. Ned B. Stonehouse and written by South African, Dutch, British, and American scholars, began with Norval Geldenhuys, *Commentary on the Gospel of Luke* (London and Grand Rapids: Eerdmans, 1951), the first volume in a series projected to articulate Reformed theology with no uncertain sound. The editors seek "to provide earnest students of the New Testament with an exposition that is thorough and abreast of modern scholarship and at the same time loyal to the Scriptures as the infallible Word of God," Stonehouse explains in his general foreword. In each volume the introduction and major exposition are written exclusively in English, though they are based on a careful study of the original. Footnotes, special notes, and appendixes absorb discussions of more technical matters, including detailed studies of choice Greek words, phrases, and idiomatic expressions. Revisions of works in this series have appeared. The comment is more detailed than in HNTC.

In the series The Tyndale New Testament Commentaries (TNTC), ed. Randolph Vincent Greenwood Tasker, 20 vols. (Grand Rapids: Eerdmans, 1957–1974), commentators follow the traditional verse-by-verse exposition, but through transliteration of all Greek citations bar no one from the expository feast. As in many series, editorial policy has given the edge in space to the Epistles. There are revisions of various volumes, under the general editorship of Leon Morris.

With its Continental Commentary Series (see above on Old Testament) Augsburg began publication of translations of important European New Testament commentaries with Ulrich Luz on the first seven chapters of Matthew (Minneapolis, 1989).

Designed to meet the needs of "laypeople, students, and pastors," the Augsburg Commentary on the New Testament, begun in 1980 with Roy A. Harrisville on Romans, contains some important discussions that also challenge scholars to take a second look at cherished conclusions. All of the works in this series are of fine quality.

Although subtitled "New Testament Witnesses for Preaching," many of the books in the Fortress series Proclamation Commentaries, published by the producers of Hermeneia, with Gerhard Krodel as general editor, will also serve well as textbooks for advanced courses in biblical study. The brief commentaries in this series are designed as introductions to more detailed study of the biblical text. Some of them offer original contributions for advancement of exegetical understanding. Ministers can use them with great profit, and the general reader will relish their modest sophistication. Because of the generally high quality of the volumes in this series, it is not necessary to select any for special mention. New editions are constantly being added.

In almost all these commentary series on the New Testament, the regular user soon discovers that the four Gospels are shortchanged. The comment on the Epistles is usually two to four times more concentrated and thorough. It is worth observing that the rich and complex account in Luke 1 and 2 is equivalent in length to a quarter of Romans. Some newer series have reversed the trend.

COMMENTARY SERIES IN GERMAN AND FRENCH

Series on the Old Testament

The student who is able to profit from German exegesis will find commentaries of high quality to meet almost any condition of purse and hermeneutical requirement. Many of the series are at various stages of publication, some have been discontinued, and others revive interminably with ever new editions.

High on the list of generally recognized commentaries on the Old Testament is Biblischer Kommentar: Altes Testament (BKAT), ed. Martin Noth and a number of associates, with S. Herrmann and H. W. Wolff as successors. This moderately critical German series, launched with the first *Lieferung* of Walther Zimmerli, *Ezechiel,* BKAT 13 (Neukirchen-Vluyn: Neukirchener Verlag, 1955), and projected to include twenty-three volumes in all, aims at providing pastor and student with a commentary combining scientific philology and practical theological concerns. Contributors must demonstrate the contemporary significance of the ancient documents according to a systematic and effective outline of development. Text units are treated in six successive steps indicated by marginal headings. After the pertinent *Literatur* (bibliography) has been cited, there follows a translation of the particular chapter or section of *Text* to be discussed. Superior letters interspersed in the translation signal text-critical notes; at a glance the reader may identify the portions to be treated technically in the lengthy paragraph following the passage in

German. After this lower criticism comes a study of the literary *Form*. Then in a section with the marginal heading *Ort* (setting), the commentator strokes in the historical situation (*Sitz im Leben*) out of which the passage speaks. The rubric *Wort* (interpretation) signals a verse-by-verse commentary, and finally under *Ziel* (aim) we find a discussion of the "Word in the Word," that is, a summary presentation of the line of thought or theological content. The completion of this series is certainly an exegetical event that no serious scholar of Scripture anticipates with apathy. To gauge its importance one has only to note that Hermeneia includes in translation, and with fidelity to BKAT's format, the two-volume work of Walther Zimmerli on Ezekiel (BKAT 13/1 and 2, 1969); Hans Walter Wolff on Hosea (BKAT 14/1, 1965), and Wolff on Joel and Amos (BKAT 14/2, 2d rev. ed., 1975).

German scholars have long been known as the primary producers of technical series on the Old Testament. Of older works, the Göttinger Handkommentar zum Alten Testament (HKAT), ed. Wilhelm Gustav Hermann Nowack (Göttingen: Vandenhoeck & Ruprecht, 1892–) still commands respect. Hermann Gunkel, *Genesis übersetzt und erklärt*, HKAT 1/1 (1901; 3d ed., 1910), and *Einleitung in die Psalmen: Die Gattungen der religiösen Lyrik Israels,* completed and ed. Joachim Begrich, vol. 2, supplementary vol. (1933), are both included in this series, as well as Carl Steuernagel's comments on Deuteronomy (1898) and Joshua (1899), bound together with a third contribution under the title *Übersetzung und Erklärung der Bücher Deuteronomium und Josua und allgemeine Einleitung in den Hexateuch* HKAT 1/3 (1900).

Kommentar zum Alten Testament (KAT), ed. Ernst Friedrich Max Sellin, et al. (Leipzig and Erlangen: A Deichertsche Verlagsbuchhandlung, 1913–39), boasted among its contributors such scholars as Otto Procksch, *Die Genesis übersetzt und erklärt,* KAT 1 (1913); Rudolf Kittel, *Die Psalmen übersetzt und erklärt,* KAT 13 (1914; 3d and 4th ed., 1922); and Paul Volz, *Der Prophet Jeremia übersetzt und erklärt,* KAT 10 (1922). In 1962 the series took a fresh start under the editorship of Wilhelm Rudolph, Karl Elliger, and Franz Hesse with the publication of Rudolph's *Das Buch Ruth, Das Hohe Lied, Die Klagelieder,* KAT 17/1–3 (Gütersloh: Gerd Mohn, 1962).

Standing out in the category of the less technical series is Handbuch zum Alten Testament (HAT), ed. Otto Hermann Wilhelm Leonhard Eissfeldt (Tübingen: J. C. B. Mohr [Siebeck], 1934–). Among the more notable volumes incorporated in HAT are Kurt Galling's *Biblisches Reallexikon* (BRL), HAT 1/1 (1937); Martin Noth's erudite *Das Buch Josua,* HAT 1/7 (1938; 2d ed., 1953); and Wilhelm Rudolph's *Jeremia,* HAT 1/12 (1947; 2d ed. rev., 1958), one of the finest appreciations of that dramatic seer made more of oak than willow, his undeserved reputation for lamentations notwithstanding. Designed for a similar clientele is Die Heilige Schrift des Alten Testamentes (="Die Bonnerbibel"), prepared by Roman Catholic scholars under the general editorship of Franz Feldmann, Heinrich Herkenne, and Friedrich Nötscher (Bonn, 1912). Nor do those who labored to produce Kurzer Hand-Commentar zum Alten Testament (KHC) merit oblivion as reward for their rich legacy merely because they bore their burden at the turn of the nineteenth century, when Karl Marti served as editor, with the assistance of Immanuel Gustav Adolf Benzinger, Alfred Bertholet, Karl Ferdinand Reinhard Budde, Bernhard Leward Duhm, Heinrich Holzinger, and Gerrit Wildeboer (21 vols.; Tübingen, Leipzig, and Freiburg im Breisgau, 1897–1906).

For the general reader, Germany offers Das Alte Testament Deutsch: Neues Göttinger Bibelwerk (ATD), ed. Volkmar Herntrich and Artur Weiser, volumes of which began to appear in Göttingen (Vandenhoeck & Ruprecht) in 1949. This work appears to be designed to aid pastors in moving their constituencies off spiritual dead center. In effect, this series, replete with discernment expressed in some of the most lean and thoughtful prose one can find in commentaries, helped break ground for stronger emphasis on the thought content of the Scriptures as distinguished from stress on philological minutiae and historical trivia. As such it is one of the forerunners of the emphasis on literary appreciation of biblical documents in the last decades of the twentieth century. It resembles WC, but with profounder appreciation of the thought content in the biblical documents. Gerhard von Rad's three-volume commentary on Genesis, ATD 2 (1949), ATD 3 (1952), ATD 4 (1953; 5th ed. in one vol., 1958), and Artur Weiser's interpretations of Job, ATD 13 (1951; 2d ed., 1956), and Psalms ATD 14 and 15 (1950; 5th ed., 1959), lend distinction to the series, which has exported some volumes to OTL.

Series on the New Testament

German scholars have long been recognized as the primary producers of technical series on the New Testament. The standard New Testament series for decades has been Kritisch-exegetischer Kommentar über das Neue Testament (KEK, or Meyer Series), begun by Heinrich Wilhelm Meyer (1800–73), who is also remembered for his Latin edition of the Lutheran confessional writings (Göttingen: Vandenhoeck & Ruprecht, 1830). The individual books of this Göttingen publication have gone through a varying number of editions since the first two volumes, the text of the New Testament with a translation, appeared in 1829. Over the years contributors to the various *Abteilungen* have pitched their thoroughly pondered, often ponderous and philologically exacting, presentations at nearly every level of undulating criticism. To name the various contributors would be to call a large part of the roll of New Testament scholars in Germany.[5] Much of KEK has been translated into English.

---

[5] Post-1950 editions include Ernst Lohmeyer, *Das Evangelium des Matthäus: Nachgelassene Ausarbeitungen und Entwürfe zur Übersetzung und Erklärung,* supplementary vol. prepared for

For example, Hermeneia includes Hans Conzelmann on 1 Corinthians; Eduard Lohse on Colossians and Philemon; Martin Dibelius/Heinrich Greeven on James; and Rudolf Bultmann on the Johannine Epistles. At the same time, what was said above about reprints of older works applies to this series: some of the advertised English translations of "Meyer" are based on very antiquated German editions. A further word of caution prompted by the fortunes of KEK is in order. Although awareness of the most recent information available on a particular book of the Bible is commendable, eager buyers of latest editions should investigate before hastily reordering each time they read about the issuing of a newer edition. Many of these "new editions" may be no more than photomechanically reproduced, corrected reprints of frequently the first or second reworking of the material at the hand of the current editor. In this connection the reader should also note the very commendable German practice of issuing supplements, although these may be a bit inconvenient to use. The function of the supplements is to bring the work up to date, chart the genesis and evolution of the particular commentary, save publishing costs in meeting the demand at a profit, and stave off every hint of planned obsolescence. The owner of an earlier edition can usually renovate his reference volume simply by picking up a copy of the latest *Ergänzungsheft.*

Also held in high respect is Handbuch zum Neuen Testament (HNT), the predecessor of its counterpart HAT (see below). It was founded by Hans Lietzmann (1875–1942) and continued by Martin Dibelius, but without the publication of additional volumes. After the latter's death in 1947, the series was serviced by Günther Bornkamm. Except for Ernst Käsemann's commentary on Romans, in which Käsemann's theological perspective makes an indelible impact—it is interesting to compare Käsemann and Cranfield on Romans—this series is less ponderous than "Meyer." Published by J. C. B. Mohr (Paul Siebeck) of Tübingen (1906–), it competes effectively by spanning a shorter period of time in production and by including information not found in any edition of the "Meyer" series. Included in it are such additional helps as Ludwig Radermacher, *Neutestamentliche Grammatik: Das Griechisch des Neuen Testaments im Zusammenhang mit der Volkssprache,* HNT 1/1 (1912; 2d ed. enlarged, 1925); Wilhelm Bousset, *Die Religion des Judentums im späthelle-*

publication and edited by Werner Schmauch (1956; 3d ed., 1962); Lohmeyer, *Das Evangelium des Markus,* KEK 1/2, 16th ed. (1963); Rudolf Bultmann, *Das Evangelium des Johannes,* 18th ed. (1964); Ernst Haenchen, *Die Apostelgeschichte,* KEK 3, 13th ed. (1962); Otto Michel, *Der Brief an die Römer,* KEK 4, 12th ed. (1963); Hans Conzelmann, *Der Erste Brief an die Korinther* (1969); Heinrich Schlier, *Der Brief an die Galater,* KEK 7, 12th ed. (1962); Lohmeyer, *Der Brief an die Philipper,* KEK 9/1, 13th ed. (1964); Lohmeyer, *Die Briefe an die Kolosser und an Philemon,* KEK 9/2, 13th ed. (1964); Eduard Lohse, *Die Briefe an die Kolosser und an Philemon,* 1st ed. (1968); Michel, *Der Brief an die Hebräer,* KEK 13, 12th ed. (1966); Martin Dibelius, *Der Brief des Jakobus,* KEK 15, 11th ed. edited by Heinrich Greeven (1964); Rudolf Bultmann, *Die drei Johannesbriefe,* 2d ed. (1967).

nistischen Zeitalter, HNT 21, 3d ed. rev. Hugo Gressmann (1926; reprinted with rev. bibliography by E. Lohse, 1966);[6] and four commentaries on the apostolic fathers.[7] Contributions by Hans Conzelmann to HNT (Acts, 2d ed. 1972) and Martin Dibelius (Pastorals, 1955; 4th rev. ed., 1966, Hans Conzelmann) have enriched Hermeneia. Decades were to pass before the emphasis on history-of-religion material in this commentary would become standard fare in the exegetical craft.

Herders Theologischer Kommentar zum Neuen Testament (HThK), edited initially (1953) by Alfred Wikenhauser and since his death (1960) by Anton Vögtle and Rudolf Schnackenburg, has made a strong bid for ecumenical scholarly attention with the latter's superb lead volume, *Die Johannesbriefe,* HThK 13/3 (Freiburg im Breisgau, 1953). The projected 14-volume series, with numerous volumes appearing in multiple format, is being translated, beginning with Schnackenburg's *The Gospel According to St. John,* vol. 1: *Introduction and Commentary on Chapters 1–4,* trans. Kevin Smyth (New York, 1968; German ed., 1965). Josephine Massyngberde Ford collaborates with Smyth in editing the English-language series.

Not to note the exegetical work exhibited in the various editions of Kommentar zum Neuen Testament (KzNT), ed. Theodor Zahn (Leipzig and Erlangen: A. Deichertsche Verlagsbuchhandlung, 1903–), would be deserving of rebuke for failure to take account of profound learning, even though one must grant that too tight a rein has been held to critical expression.[8]

Theologischer Handkommentar zum Neuen Testament mit Text und Paraphrase (Leipzig and Berlin, 1928–), abbreviated THKNT, is intended primarily for pastors and students. The original series (Leipzig: A. Deichertsche Verlagsbuchhandlung), which came to include Friedrich Hauck's comments on the Gospels of Mark and Luke and Friedrich Büchsel's interpretation of the Epistles

---

[6] The first edition of Bousset's work appeared separately under the title *Die Religion des Judentums im neutestamentlichen Zeitalter* (Berlin: Reuther & Reichard, 1903).

[7] Rudolf Knopf, *Die apostolischen Väter: 1. Die Lehre der zwölf Apostel. Die zwei Clemensbriefe* (1920); Walter Bauer, *Die apostolischen Väter: 2. Die Briefe des Ignatius von Antiochia und der Polykarpbrief* (1920); Hans Windisch, *Die apostolischen Väter: 3. Der Barnabasbrief* (1920); and Martin Dibelius, *Die apostolischen Väter: 4. Der Hirt des Hermas* (1923). All are bound separately as parts of a single supplementary volume. For the disciplined preacher who conscientiously follows the church year, the series also includes two volumes on the pericopes by Leonhard Fendt, *Die alten Perikopen: Für die theologische Praxis erläutert,* HNT 22 (1931), and *Die neuen Perikopen (der Eisenacher Kirchenkonferenz von 1896): Für die theologische Praxis erläutert,* HNT 23 (1941).

[8] For further appreciation of this widely recognized scholar of the New Testament and patristic writings, whose works consistently give evidence of his vast erudition and equally enviable thoroughness, see the autobiography "Theodor Zahn: Mein Werdegang und meine Lebensarbeit," in *Die Religionswissenschaft der Gegenwart in Selbstdarstellungen,* ed. Erich Stange (Leipzig: F. Meiner, 1925), 1:221–48. See also his *Ein Winter in Tübingen* (Stuttgart, 1896).

of John,[9] was never completed and was superseded by a new series edited by Erich Fascher (Berlin: Evangelische Verlagsanstalt). The new series itself has undergone constant revision and incorporation of new works, including Walter Grundmann's Matthew (1968); a revised edition of Mark by Grundmann (1984); and a new work on Luke by Wolfgang Weifel (1988). A commentary first published in the earlier series, Albrecht Oepke's *Der Brief des Paulus an die Galater,* THKNT 9 (Leipzig, 1937), was reissued in a revision (Berlin, 1957) as the pilot volume for the new series and was subsequently revised by Joachim Rohde in a 5th ed. (1984).

Corresponding to ATD is Das Neue Testament Deutsch: Neues Göttinger Bibelwerk (NTD), whose twelve polished parts, published by Vandenhoeck & Ruprecht, matured through numerous editions, especially under the careful guidance of Paul Althaus and Gerhard Friedrich. A genuine theological concern gives vigor to these highly respected volumes designed for ministers and an educated public. The Roman Catholic counterpart, but with an ecclesiastical flavor not found in ATD, is Die Heilige Schrift des Neuen Testamentes, ed. Fritz Tillmann, 10 vols. (Bonn, 1931–), also known as the Bonner Bibelwerk. Its two supplementary volumes present Max Meinertz's *Theologie des Neuen Testamentes* (1950), considered the first major work on biblical theology to come from Roman Catholic quarters in many years.

Very similar in thrust to NTD is Die Neue Echter Bibel: Kommentar zum Alten Testament mit der Einheitsübersetzung, begun in 1980 with Norbert Lohfink's *Kohelet* and published by the Echter Verlag (Würzburg). This series also includes, among many others, helpful commentaries by Josef Scharbert on Genesis, 2 vols. (1983–86) and Exodus (1989); Heinrich Gross on Tobit and Judith (1987); and Werner Dommershausen on 1 and 2 Maccabees (1985). The Einheitsübersetzung is the product of a joint translation effort supported by Roman Catholic episcopal authority in several European countries and the leadership of the Evangelical Church in Germany.

A series in two sections, Commentaire de l'ancien testament (CAT) and Commentaire du nouveau testament (CNT), by Martin Dibelius began production under the auspices of the Protestant theological faculty of the Université de Strasbourg, with Robert Martin-Achard as head of the editorial board for the Old Testament series, which was piloted by Samuel Terrien on Job (Neuchatel: Delachaux & Niestlé, 1963). The New Testament series began in 1949, under the editorship of Pierre Bonnard and associates, with Jean Héring's enlightening interpretation of 1 Corinthians.

German ecumenicity has led to the production of Evangelisch-katholischer Kommentar zum Neuen Testament (Einsiedeln and Neukirchen-Vluyn (1969–),

---

[9] Hauck, *Das Evangelium des Markus (Synoptiker I)*, THKNT 2 (1931), and *Das Evangelium des Lukas (Synoptiker II)*, THKNT 3 (1934), and Büchsel, *Die Johannesbriefe*, THKNT 17 (1933).

whose producers do not lose sight of contemporary concerns while solving philological problems.

OLDER COMMENTARIES

Up to this point we have confined our evaluations almost exclusively to exegetical works published since 1890. A superficial examination of almost any of the more detailed modern commentaries will expose the great debt owed to the past. There is much more that is silently absorbed and seldom acknowledged, not because it is too minute to mention but because it has come to be claimed as common property.

In the years to come patristic exegesis is certain to move into the forefront. Two major schools of interpretation, the Alexandrine and the Antiochene, thrived in the early centuries. So imaginatively and generously did the Alexandrines extend Philo's allegorical method that they often obliterated the original intent of the writers with a maze of fanciful exegesis both astounding and depressing to behold. Pantaenus, Clement and Dionysius of Alexandria, Cyril, and Origen are among the more notable representatives of this school. At Antioch, Diodorus, who emphasized the literal or historical sense, came to be immortalized by two preeminent pupils, Theodore of Mopsuestia and John Chrysostom. Thomas Aquinas held Chrysostom in such high regard that he is said to have declared he would rather possess the homilies on Matthew's Gospel written by that eloquent doctor of the church than be master of all Paris. Ephraem Syrus, who was given to the trying habit of nesting his voluminous writing in pillows of verse, thick with repetitions and accumulated metaphors, belongs to the same school. Theodoret, Basil, Gregory of Nazianzus, Gregory of Nyssa, Hilary of Poitiers, "Ambrosiaster," Augustine, Jerome, and others assumed a mediating position.

Much patristic exegesis lies preserved in the work of the medieval catenists, who strung together as in a chain excerpts from esteemed ecclesiastical writers. The best-known Eastern exegetes are Theophylact (eleventh century) and Euthymius Zigabenus (early twelfth century). Theophylact, archbishop of Achrida and metropolitan of Bulgaria, is noted for his lucid expositions of various books of the Old Testament and of most of the New Testament. For the Psalms and Minor Prophets Theodoret of Cyrus seems to be his primary source; in the New Testament works Chrysostom seems to have been both authoritative and unknowingly generous. Theophylact was fond of allegory, especially in his interpretation of the parables, but many a genuine pearl of penetrating perception will reward the patient reader. Emperor Alexios Komnenos considered the second, Euthymius Zigabenus, twelfth-century Byzantine theologian, so competent that he particularly encouraged him to write vigorously in defense of orthodoxy. In addition to his *Panoplia*

Dogmatike, Euthymius wrote on the Psalms, the four Gospels, and the Pauline Epistles. His sane course between allegorical and historical exposition reveals at many points a very willing leaning on Basil, Gregory of Nazianzus, and Chrysostom for guidance.[10] Anselm, Thomas Aquinas, and the Venerable Bede are among the better-known catenists of Western Christendom.

The spirit of the Antiochenes flared in the more creative work of such Victorine pioneers as Hugo (ca. 1096–1141), precursor of thirteenth-century scholasticism, and his pupil Andrew (d. 1175), an ardent Hebraist. In her carefully documented *The Study of the Bible in the Middle Ages,* 2d ed. (Oxford, 1952), 112–95, Beryl Smalley has done much to rescue from comparative oblivion that instinctive rationalist Andrew, "who, being merely a scholar, is unknown to text-books and almost unknown to modern works of reference" (p. 111). To a remarkable degree he anticipated modern historical-critical approaches to the Bible, as he grew methodically from burrowing in both Jewish and Christian sources for the collection of scraps of information to discriminating, soberly serene expositions that enhance the literal sense of Scripture. Among the exegetical conclusions fused by this interpreter, so refreshingly audacious amid so much that tended toward sterility, is a view widely held today that in the suffering servant of Isaiah 53 the prophet "refers collectively to the Jews of the captivity, who expiate by their sufferings the sins of their whole race" (p. 163). In many scholarly circles during the later scholastic period, Scripture was unfortunately retired to the background in the interest of dogmatic theology; only one commentary of note, Nicholas of Lyra (ca. 1270 to 1349), *Postillae perpetuae in universam sacram scripturam,* perpetuated exegesis, with major emphasis on philology, as a separate discipline. So highly did Luther esteem this universally influential work that his opponents are said to have quipped:

> Si Lyra non lyrasset,
> Lutherus non saltasset.[11]

The Reformation, with its firm emphasis on the meaning of the Scriptures, evoked renewed interest in biblical exegesis. The work on the four Gospels

---

[10] See Karl Krumbacher, "21. Euthymios Zigabenos (Εὐθύμιος Ζιγαβηνός, auch Ζιγαδηνός)," 82–85, and "52. Theophylaktos (Θεοφύλακτος)," 133–35, in *Geschichte der byzantinischen Literatur von Justinian bis zum Ende des oströmischen Reiches (527–1453),* 2d ed. with the assistance of A. Ehrhard and H. Gelzer, Handbuch der klassischen Altertumswissenschaft in systematischer Darstellung 9/1, ed. Iwan von Müller (Munich, 1897).

[11] "No lyre for Lyra, no frolic for Luther." For the various forms in which this *proverbium inter theologos* may be found and for its later fortunes see Hartmann Grisar, *Luther,* trans. E. M. Lamond from the German; ed. Luigi Cappadelta (St. Louis and London, 1916), 5:535, esp. n. 2; Frederic W. Farrar, *History of Interpretation: Eight Lectures Preached Before the University of Oxford in the Year MDCCCLXXXV* (London, 1886), 277; and Smalley, *The Study of the Bible,* xvi.

by Juan Maldonado (1533–83), also known as Johannes Maldonatus, is a noteworthy collation of patristic opinion with emphasis on the literal sense of Scripture. Unfortunately, the author was somewhat deficient in hermeneutical initiative. For originality and vigor we must go on to Martin Luther, whose interpretations continue to provoke astonishment because of his extraordinary gift for extracting the meaning from the wording. Of that dazzling monument to a master exegete's memory from pupils' pens the tinker's son John Bunyan wrote: "I do prefer this book of Martin Luther upon the Galatians, excepting the Holy Bible, before all the books that ever I have seen, as most fit for a wounded conscience."[12] In addition to Luther's work on Galatians, consult his studies of Genesis, Deuteronomy, and Psalms in connection with the recommended commentaries cited below.

Less of the heart and more of the humanist's mind moved John Calvin to masterful expositions on almost every book of the Bible. His scrupulous concern for the sense of the sacred words makes his approach congenial to many a modern exegete. For example, he would have been among the last to deny the doctrine of the Trinity, but he refused to construe the plural form of the name of God in Genesis 1 as another shred of evidence.[13] Like his master, Calvin's successor Theodore Beza was adept in tracing and trailing arguments.

---

[12] *Grace Abounding to the Chief of Sinners,* in *A Treasury of Christian Books,* ed. Hugh Martin (London, 1955), parg. 130, p. 64. The standard critical text of Luther's commentary on Galatians (1535) is D. *Martin Luthers Werke: Kritische Gesamtausgabe* 40/1 and 2 (Weimar: Hermann Böhlhau, 1883–), 1–184. This edition of Luther's lectures delivered in 1531 is not to be confused with his earlier, more brief comments (1516–17 and 1519). Of the more than thirty English editions, the best in the judgment of many is *A Commentary on St. Paul's Epistle to the Galatians: Based on Lectures Delivered by Martin Luther at the University of Wittenberg in the Year 1531 and First Published in 1535,* ed. Philip S. Watson (London and Westwood, N.J., 1953). For much of Luther's other exegetical work, see the translations in *Luther's Works,* American Edition, 55 vols. (Saint Louis: Concordia; Philadelphia: Fortress Press, 1955–1986), under the general editorship of Jaroslav Jan Pelikan and Helmut T. Lehmann. See also Pelikan's companion volume, *Luther the Expositor: Introduction to the Reformer's Exegetical Writings* (Saint Louis: Concordia, 1959). A few decades after Luther's comments on Galatians, a Puritan named William Perkins displayed a similar lively appreciation in a commentary on the same epistle in 1604. A facsimile of his 1617 edition was published by Pilgrim Press, *A Commentary on Galatians* (Cleveland, 1989). A comment on Galatians 6 indicates what is in store for the reader: "If regeneration bee *a new creation,* it must needes follow, that before our conversion we were not onely dead, but even flat nothing, in godliness and grace" (p. 564).

[13] "Commentariorum in quinque libros Mosis. Pars I," *Ioannis Calvini opera exegetica et homiletica,* I, ed. Eduard Cunitz, Eduard Reuss, Paul Lobstein, *Ioannis Calvini opera quae supersunt omnia,* 23; ed. Johann Wilhelm Baum, Eduard Cunitz, Eduard Reuss, Corpus Reformatorum 51 (Brunswick, 1882), col. 15; *Commentaries on the First Book of Moses Called Genesis,* trans. John King from original Latin and compared with French edition, I (Grand Rapids, 1948), 70–72. It was the special concern of Calvin that one not slip into Sabellianism while refuting Arianism. No sponsor of limited interest, Calvin shares with Melanchthon and other colleagues of philological mastery in his era the honor of having produced a commentary, itself a classic, on Seneca's *De clementia.*

Hugo Grotius breathes less spirituality than either Calvin or Beza, but his writings spring from the depths of great learning and sound judgment. Among his best that might well be remembered as supplements to modern works are commentaries on Genesis, Joshua (his last), Psalms (many consider it his best), Isaiah, Daniel, and Romans.

The seventeenth-century commentaries are notable chiefly for their prolixity and for their curioso-like display of what Spurgeon called "intellectual crockery." This was the period during which John Collinges could devote 909 pages to the first chapter of Canticles, only to content himself with a mere 530 pages for the second chapter. Time that one may be inclined to spend on the works of these men who wrote *currente calamo* will be more wisely invested in the study of the patristic commentators who supplied much of the bulk for those tiresome tomes. Far less verbose, despite the fact that opinions from more than a hundred biblical critics compose the five volumes, is Matthew Poole, *Synopsis criticorum aliorumque Sacrae Scripturae interpretum et commentatorum* (London, 1669–76).

A gust of fresh air enters with Matthew Henry (1662–1714), who is remembered for his frequently reprinted *Exposition of the Old and New Testament*, 5 vols. (London, 1708–10; new ed., New York, 1896). This humble Christian combines quaintness with felicitous expression, and a balanced judgment with extraordinary insight into the meaning of Scripture in a work not intended to be of critical value. It is not generally known that Matthew Henry left his work beyond Acts in manuscript for completion by his nonconformist colleagues.

A collection of historical materials is to be had in Antoine Augustin Calmet, a learned Benedictine (1672–1757), *Commentaire littéral sur tous les livres de l'Ancien et du Nouveau Testament*, 23 vols. (Paris, 1707–16; 3d ed., 8 vols. in 9, Paris, 1724–26). Johann Jakob Wetstein's two-volume edition of the New Testament has been systematically ransacked for over two hundred years without being robbed of its unparalleled collection of rabbinic and classical quotations.[14] Nonetheless, the wreath is reserved for Johann Albrecht Bengel (1687–1752), whose *Gnomon Novi Testamenti* (Tübingen, 1742) anticipates

---

[14] *Novum Testamentum graecum editionis receptae cum lectionibus variantibus codicum mss., editionum aliarum, versionum et patrum nec non commentario pleniore ex scriptoribus veteribus hebraeis, graecis et latinis historiam et vim verborum illustrante opera et studio Joannis Jacobi Wetstenii* (Amsterdam, 1751–52). The careful student will not appropriate Wetstein's collection of quotations without checking them in context in some critical edition. The ease with which Wetstein rationalized his way through the maze of material has not escaped cunning criticism: "While some parts are useful, others are such as only excite surprise at their appearance on the same page as the text of the New Testament," Samuel Prideaux Tregelles, *Account of the Printed Text of the New Testament* (London, 1854), quoted by Carl Bertheau, "Wettstein (Wetstenius, Wetstein), Johann Jakob," *The New Schaff-Herzog Encyclopedia of Religious Knowledge*, ed. Samuel Macauley Jackson (Grand Rapids, 1950), 12:334.

and influences considerably both German and English scholarship of the next century and combines perspicuity with brevity in a most remarkable manner. In a single line of Bengel's comment there is frequently more meaningful freight than his garrulous predecessors and contemporaries packed into a page. *Gnomon* is the Latin term, now adopted into English, for the pin, or style, of a sundial. Bengel's comments are just that: his style points the student directly to the timely meaning of the text and is not simply the dress of thought, tailored to fit some fixed fashion.

The nineteenth century is studded with the names of scholars eminent in the history of interpretation. The new critical approach fostered during the Enlightenment is reflected in chastened form in Wilhelm Martin Leberecht de Wette's (d. 1849) commentaries on the New Testament. Although his exegetical work appeared in another century, the student can usually dip into it without fear of coming up with dust or empty-handed. A contemporary, Heinrich Friedrich Wilhelm Gesenius (d. 1842), proved in a commentary on Isaiah that devotion to grammar and lexicography are not inimical to the grasp of a prophetic vision. Not outdone in perception is Heinrich Georg August Ewald, who sensed the lively throbbing of Old Testament poetical and prophetic books and captured the the breadth of expression in the Gospels and Paul's Epistles.

The writings of Ernst Wilhelm Hengstenberg (d. 1869) mark a reaction in the direction of more traditional views. His commentary on Ecclesiastes, *Der Prediger Salomo* (Berlin, 1859), trans. D. W. Simon (Philadelphia, 1860), is one of his best works. Johann Keil carried much of the spirit of Hengstenberg into the series, which he produced jointly with Franz Delitzsch. The latter's interpretations of Genesis (Leipzig, 1852) and Psalms (Leipzig, 1859–60) still find appreciative readers, but in a later edition of his Genesis (Leipzig, 1887), Delitzsch, to the regret of some, shifted sharply toward Wellhausian views. The mediating influence of Schleiermacher tempers many of Friedrich Tholuck's labors, which include commentaries on Psalms (Halle, 1843), John's Gospel (Hamburg, 1827), Romans (Berlin, 1824), Hebrews (Hamburg, 1836), and the Sermon on the Mount (1833; 2d ed., Hamburg, 1835). Spiritual sensitivity rather than precise philology characterizes Tholuck's exegetical work.

In England the names of three bishops stand out above all others. Charles John Ellicott (1819–1905) cultivated a discriminating linguistic sense that was well adapted to trimming and inspecting analytically the meatier parts of the Pauline corpus. Joseph Barber Lightfoot (1828–89) demonstrates greater breadth of learning, a more comprehensive perspective, and conscious independence of treatment in his commentaries on Galatians (London, 1865), Philippians (London, 1868), and Colossians and Philemon (London, 1875). His endeavors are matched only by those of his friend and successor Brooke Foss Westcott, whose commentaries on the Johannine writings and Hebrews are among the foremost. The many reprintings that these episcopal editions have enjoyed are sufficient witness to their lasting value.

On the mainland, the name of the Swiss theologian Frédéric Godet is remembered for his fine work on John's Gospel, as well as on Romans and Corinthians.

There are others who have toiled tediously and fruitfully, but in the names and the works mentioned above students will know that they have made the acquaintance of at least a few scholars on whose creased brows eternity stands written.[15]

THE USE OF COMMENTARIES

It cannot have escaped the notice of the reader that this chapter on commentaries takes last place in a long line of interpreter's aids. Nor should it be inferred that the last shall be first. Commentaries are valuable aids, if properly used, but they are not meant to relieve the interpreter of the task of making his own commentary on the sacred text.

A brief acquaintance with commentaries will soon reveal that commentators are very seldom in agreement on any but the plainest passages — those that require no comment in the first place. Even crystalline clauses often fall unsuspecting victims to a species of interpreter who, as Spurgeon said, delights "to fish up some hitherto undiscovered tadpole of interpretation, and cry it round the town as a rare dainty." A cordial suspicion of commentators is therefore the first rule in approaching them for exegetical assistance. Question the structure of their proof. Determine how well they construct the case for their own interpretations and how fairly they dispose of the interpretations of others.

Bristle when a critic says "unconvincing," without demonstrating why the adverse decision is made. You may be exposed to a cheap shot. Check commentators' parallel passages in context. Does the concordance reflect a discriminating use of all the linguistic data? How do the theological and philosophical presuppositions of the commentator affect the exposition? Sorry to say, commentators are fallible, and the earlier this is recognized the better it will be not only for the exegetical craft in general, but especially for ministers and their congregations. On the other hand, expositors who think they can work independently of commentators display not only consummate arrogance but also ignorance of the conditions that obtain in biblical studies. The many areas of specialty require great leisure for properly assessing and evaluating the many discoveries, investigations, and modes of inquiry that may lead to light on a

---

[15] See the excellent counsel on selection and use of commentaries given by Edgar Krentz and other scholars in *Interpretation* 36/4 (1982), an issue devoted to the subject.

dark portion of the Bible. Such leisure few can lavish. Moreover, Scripture does not always reveal its secrets in the same measure to each generation, much less to every expositor. Interpretive sensitivity is required; people like Chrysostom, Luther, Calvin, Bengel, Westcott, Lightfoot, and others had it. To deprive oneself of an encounter with such princely blood is to impoverish oneself.

It is wise, then, after you have made your own thorough interpretations of the text with liberal use of tools mentioned in the preceding chapters, to check your interpretations against those of others, to reevaluate if necessary, and to supplement if possible. In all there must be an impelling passion to hear out the full-throated accents of the sacred text as it sounded in the hour of its birth.

Spurgeon once told his students of a church he saw in Verona, where the ancient frescoes had been plastered over and obscured by other designs. "I fear," he said, "many do this with Scripture, daubing the text with their own glosses, and laying on their own conceits." He then went on to cite William Cowper's lines:

> A critic on the sacred book should be
> Candid and learn'd, dispassionate and free:
> Free from the wayward bias bigots feel,
> From fancy's influence and intemperate zeal;
> (For) of all arts sagacious dupes invent
> To cheat themnselves and gain the world's assent,
> The worst is—Scripture warp'd from its intent.[16]

APPENDIX

For the benefit of researchers who sometimes forget that what appears to be a discovery may have undergone exposure long ago, we here note some directories of sites of antique expository lore, as well as guides to more modern comment.

On commentaries of various periods in general, see John M'Clintock and James Strong, "Commentary," *Cyclopaedia of Biblical, Theological, and Ecclesiastical Literature* (New York, 1894), 2:427–34; Cornelius Aherne, "Commentaries on the Bible," *The Catholic Encyclopedia* (New York, 1908), 4:157–63; F. J. Marcolongo, "Biblical Commentaries," *New Catholic Encyclopedia* (1967), 2:536–37 (see also T. A. Collins, "Bible, VI [Exegesis])," ibid., 2:496–507; James Orr, rev. F. Danker, "Commentaries," *ISBE* (Grand Rapids, 1979), 1:737–43. For an all-points guide to older biblical commentators and

---

[16] For these rearranged lines, see "The Progress of Error," *The Poetical Works of William Cowper,* ed. H. F. Cary (New York, n.d.), 1:58, 57.

commentaries on each book of the Bible, consult the index of authors under "Werbeck, Wilfrid" in *RGG*[3], "Registerband," col. 261; Werbeck invested an incredible amount of labor to invite latter-day commentators to subdue an unwarranted eureka. On Jewish commentaries, see R. A. Stewart, "Commentaries, Hebrew," *ISBE* (1979), 1: 743–47. On patristic commentaries on the Pauline writings, see Cuthbert H. Turner, "Greek Patristic Commentaries on the Pauline Epistles," *HDB,* extra vol. (New York, 1923), 484–531. Charles Haddon Spurgeon, *Commenting and Commentaries: Two Lectures Addressed to the Students of the Pastor's College, Metropolitan Tabernacle, Together with a Catalog of Biblical Commentaries and Expositions* (London, 1876), 35–200, lists 1,437 entries, most of which are mercifully drowned in obscurity. Just after the turn of the century, British librarian Henry Bond conducted a poll of recognized British theologians to establish which commentaries in English on individual books of the Bible were generally preferred. For a compilation of some sixty replies, see Bond, "The Best Bible Commentaries," *The Expository Times* 14 (1903): 151–55, 203–5. Editor James Hastings added his comments in "Notes on 'The Best Bible Commentaries,'" ibid. 14 (1903): 270–71, 385–86. For brief modern compilations on each book of the Old Testament: Brevard S. Childs, *Old Testament Books for Pastor and Teacher* (Philadelphia: Westminster Press, 1977) and Tremper Longman, III, *Old Testament Commentary Survey* (Grand Rapids: Baker, 1991). Of the two, Childs displays a more comprehensive appreciation of scholars' contributions. For the New Testament: David M. Scholer, *A Basic Bibliographic Guide for New Testament Exegesis,* 2d ed. (Grand Rapids, 1973), 74–85; Erasmus Hort, *The Bible Book: Resources for Reading the New Testament* (New York: Crossroad, 1983), 116–71. Longman, Scholer, and Hort limit themselves to selections in English. Erich Kiehl, *Building Your Biblical Studies Library: A Survey of Current Resources* (St. Louis: Concordia, 1988), covers both Testaments, and with emphasis on traditional theological perspectives. John H. Hayes and Carl R. Holladay combine some bibliographic information and exegetical guidance in *Biblical Exegesis: A Beginner's Handbook* (Atlanta: John Knox Press, 1982). For a listing of modern commentary sets, as well as numerous works in a variety of categories that are of interest to professional interpreters, see Joseph A. Fitzmyer, *An Introductory Bibliography for the Study of Scripture,* Subsidia biblica 3, 3d ed. (Rome, 1990), 115–26. Ralph P. Martin, *New Testament Books for Pastor and Teacher* (Philadelphia: Westminster Press) is pitched to a more popular level. For condensed learning by ounstanding scholars on a variety of topics relating to biblical exposition see two Centennial Publications of the Society of Biblical Literature: Douglas A. Knight and Gene M. Tucker, eds., *The Hebrew Bible and Its Modern Interpreters* (Philadelphia: Fortress Press; Chico, Calif.: Scholars Press, 1985), and Eldon Jay Epp and George W. MacRae, eds., *The New Testament and Its Modern Interpreters* (Philadelphia: Fortress Press; Atlanta: Scholars Press, 1989).

INDEX OF SUBJECTS

Index of Names

BS 511.2 .D355 1993
Danker, Frederick W.
Multipurpose tools for Bible study

DATE DUE

FEB 21 '94			

CONCORDIA COLLEGE LIBRARY
2811 NE Holman St.
Portland, OR 97211